ALSO BY

JUSTICE HUGO L. BLACK

A CONSTITUTIONAL FAITH

(1968)

ALSO BY

IRVING DILLIARD

(EDITOR)

THE SPIRIT OF LIBERTY

Papers and Addresses of Learned Hand

(1952, 1953, 1960)

These are a BORZOI BOOKS, *published in New York by*
ALFRED A. KNOPF

PHOTO: ACKAD

Hugo LaFayette Black

One Man's Stand for Freedom

ONE MAN'S STAND FOR FREEDOM

Mr. JUSTICE BLACK
and the Bill of Rights

===

A COLLECTION OF
HIS SUPREME COURT OPINIONS

SELECTED AND EDITED,

WITH AN INTRODUCTION AND NOTES,

by Irving Dilliard

===

Alfred·A·Knopf  *New York, 1971*

L.C. *catalog card number: 62–8691*

THIS IS A BORZOI BOOK,
PUBLISHED BY ALFRED A. KNOPF, INC.

PUBLISHED APRIL 15, 1963
SECOND PRINTING, SEPTEMBER 1971

DEDICATED TO

THE BELIEF THAT CURRENT EROSIONS

OF THE BILL OF RIGHTS WILL BE HALTED

AND THAT HISTORIC AMERICAN FREEDOMS

AND PROTECTIONS OF THE INDIVIDUAL CITIZEN

WILL BE RESTORED

"TO THE HIGH PREFERRED PLACE

WHERE THEY BELONG IN A

FREE SOCIETY"

The First Ten Amendments to the United States Constitution, Popularly Known as the Bill of Rights

Proposed by the First Congress
September 25, 1789

Declared Ratified by the States
December 15, 1791

Article I

(Religious Establishment Prohibited. Freedom of Speech, the Press, and Right to Petition.)

Congress shall make no law respecting an establishment of religion, or prohibiting the free exercise thereof; or abridging the freedom of speech or of the press; or the right of the people peaceably to assemble and to petition the Government for a redress of grievances.

Article II

(Right to Keep and Bear Arms.)

A well-regulated militia being necessary to the security of a free State, the right of the people to keep and bear arms shall not be infringed.

Article III

(Conditions for Quarters for Soldiers.)

No soldier shall in time of peace be quartered in any house without the consent of the owner, nor in time of war but in a manner to be prescribed by law.

Article IV

(Right of Search and Seizure Regulated.)

The right of the people to be secure in their persons, houses, papers, and effects, against unreasonable searches and seizures, shall not be violated, and no warrants shall issue but upon probable cause, supported by oath or affirmation, and particularly describing the place to be searched, and the persons or things to be seized.

Article V

(Provisions Concerning Prosecution, Trial and Punishment—Private Property Not to Be Taken for Public Use Without Compensation.)

No person shall be held to answer for a capital or other infamous crime unless on a presentment or indictment of a Grand Jury, except in cases arising in the land or naval forces, or in the militia, when in actual service, in time of war or public danger; nor shall any person be subject for the same offense to be twice put in jeopardy of life or limb; nor shall be compelled in any criminal case to be a witness against himself, nor be deprived of life, liberty, or property, without due process of law; nor shall private property be taken for public use without just compensation.

Article VI

(Right to Speedy Trial, Witnesses, Assistance of Counsel.)

In all criminal prosecutions, the accused shall enjoy the right to a speedy and public trial, by an impartial jury of the State and district wherein the crime shall have been committed, which districts shall have been previously ascertained by law, and to be informed of the nature and cause of the accusation; to be confronted with the witnesses against him; to have compulsory process for obtaining witnesses in his favor, and to have the assistance of counsel for his defense.

Article VII

(Right of Trial by Jury.)

In suits at common law, where the value in controversy shall exceed twenty dollars, the right of trial by jury shall be preserved, and no fact tried by a jury shall be otherwise re-examined in any court of the United States than according to the rules of the common law.

Article VIII

(*Excessive Bail or Fines and Cruel Punishments Prohibited.*)

Excessive bail shall not be required, nor excessive fines imposed, nor cruel and unusual punishments inflicted.

Article IX

(*Rule of Construction of Constitution.*)

The enumeration in the Constitution of certain rights shall not be construed to deny or disparage others retained by the people.

Article X

(*Rights of States Under Constitution.*)

The powers not delegated to the United States by the Constitution, nor prohibited by it to the States, are reserved to the States respectively, or to the people.

Editor's Preface

THIS BOOK is about and by a man who possesses the quality of courage to a degree rarely found today in the United States of America. As this man, Hugo L. Black, is a Justice of our people's Supreme Court, it is a book for lay men and women as much as for lawyers, both men and women, wherever they are in this country. But it is also very much a book for the younger people of our day for the simple reason that the younger Americans are, the greater is their individual stake in what we are now doing to our long-cherished liberties.

The materials in this book are not dry-as-dust legalisms. On the contrary, they are the very substance of everyday life for the many millions of Americans. These materials arise from the deeds and misdeeds, the foibles and failures, the strengths and weaknesses, the aspirations and achievements, the convictions and ideals of our people.

The participants are men and women and children with an infinite variety of interests and activities. They are breadwinners and housewives, teachers and students, farm hands and truck drivers, sharecroppers and stock brokers, labor leaders and business men, editors and agitators, soldiers and pacifists, scholars and zealots, booksellers and government officials, religious leaders and gamblers, missionaries and dope peddlers, policemen and criminals, members of the legal profession and members of the medical profession. They are believers and nonbelievers, native born and foreign born, citizens and aliens, radicals and reactionaries. They are the guilty and they are the innocent. They are red and brown and black and yellow and white.

Because this book is for non-members as well as members of the bar, case citations and footnotes have been omitted from the text to facilitate reading. The one exception is in *Barenblatt* v. *United States*, where citations and footnotes are retained in their proper places so that the reader may see how carefully Justice Black documents statement after statement and supports his beliefs and conclusions with constitutional provisions, statutory law, judicial precedents, interpretations, and historical experience. The reader may know from the *Barenblatt* documentation that Justice Black makes it a rule to knit legal authority and social practice into his opinions. Omissions of parts of opinions are marked by ellipses.

The editor is deeply indebted to students and writers about the Supreme Court and Justice Black's contribution to it. Some indication of this indebtedness is given in the bibliography and the references at the end of this volume. The editor's sketch of Justice Black's career and his personal appreciation of Justice Black's work on the Supreme Court has been intentionally restricted in length. It is far more desirable that the reader have at hand a half dozen additional opinions by Justice Black than a lengthy introductory essay.

The brief summaries in the Contents will give the reader a clue to Justice Black's opinion in each case. Some confusion over the dates of the cases and the terms they are listed under in the Contents may be avoided by noting that a term of the Supreme Court opens in October and runs usually into June. Thus, *Dennis* v. *United States*, 341 U.S. 494, which was decided June 4, 1951, belongs to the 1950 term of the Court.

Certiorari, a Latin word that is used frequently in the cases, may need some explanation. It comes from *certiorari volumus*, which means "we wish to be certified." After a complaint from a litigant that he has not received justice, a writ of *certiorari* may be issued by a higher court to call for the record of a proceeding in a lower court so that the case may be reviewed.

A question: Why is it that the selection of opinions is taken only from cases arising in Bill of Rights controversies, when Justice Black has written many important opinions concerning, for example, regulation of the economy? Because, although issues of federal-state relationships and of business and industry are important, they are far less significant than Bill of Rights issues in a time when totalitarian concepts threaten individual freedom, not only throughout most of the world but also, too often and in too many places, here in the United States.

One more question: Why are the opinions presented in chronological order rather than grouped by categories—freedom of speech opinions, freedom of religion opinions, due process opinions, fair trial opinions, and so on? Because these cases came to the Supreme Court over the years, first one and then another, and not in neatly arranged related groups. The great work of Justice Black for a quarter century will be better understood and appreciated if this book makes clear that the Bill of Rights tests have arisen again and again, term after term, that some have been won and then lost, and that others have been lost and then won, and that Hugo Black has dealt with all directly and resolutely and with a courage that is, to repeat, too rare in our times.

IRVING DILLIARD

Constitution Day, 1962
Collinsville, Illinois

Supreme Court succession from 1933 through 1962:
the presidential tenures, the chief justiceships, and
the associate justiceships during Justice Black's long service

Years: 1933–1962

Presidents: ROOSEVELT — TRUMAN (April 12, 1945) — EISENHOWER (Jan. 20, 1953) — KENNEDY (Jan. 20, 1961)

CHIEF JUSTICES:
- HUGHES (June 1 / Oct. 4, 1937; June 2, 1941)
- STONE (Oct. 6, 1941; April 22, 1946)
- VINSON (Oct. 7, 1946; Sept. 8, 1953)
- WARREN (Oct. 5, 1953 – 1962)

ASSOCIATE JUSTICES:

- VAN DEVANTER — BLACK (Aug. 18 / Jan. 31, 1937)
- SUTHERLAND (Jan. 18 / July 9, 1938) — REED — WHITTAKER (Feb. 25, 1957; Mar. 25, 1958) — WHITE (April 1 / April 16, 1962)
- CARDOZO (July 9 / Jan. 30, 1939) — FRANKFURTER — GOLDBERG (Aug. 28 / Oct. 1, 1962)
- BRANDEIS (Feb. 13 / April 17, 1939) — DOUGLAS
- BUTLER (Nov. 16 / Feb. 5, 1940) — MURPHY (July 9 / Oct. 12, 1949) — CLARK (Oct. 15 / Oct. 16, 1954)
- McREYNOLDS (Feb. 1, 1941) — BYRNES (Oct. 6, 1941 / Oct. 5, 1942) — RUTLEDGE (Feb. 15, 1943; Sept. 10 / Oct. 3, 1949) — MINTON (Oct. 12, 1949; Oct. 15 / Oct. 16, 1956) — BRENNAN
- STONE (Oct. 6, 1941) — JACKSON (Mar. 28, 1955) — HARLAN (Oct. 9, 1954)
- ROBERTS (July 31, 1945) — BURTON (Oct. 1, 1945; Oct. 13 / Oct. 14, 1958) — STEWART

Contents

I

Mr. Justice Black

A Personal Appreciation

BY IRVING DILLIARD

THERE WAS a newly elected County Solicitor in Jefferson County, Alabama, in the summer of 1915. He was young as well as new, for he was still in his late twenties. Barely six months earlier, he had taken up his prosecuting duties, but that was long enough for him to see that something was out of joint in the way defendants, especially those who happened to be Negroes, were handled by the police department in the suburban town of Bessemer.

What the young prosecutor, Hugo LaFayette Black, noticed first was that a very large percentage of accused persons in Bessemer, a steel and coal community, pleaded guilty to police charges. The proportion of confessions ran much higher than anywhere else in Jefferson County, including the city of Birmingham. Quietly and on his own, 29-year-old Solicitor Black began to look into law and order, Bessemer style.

The inquiring official soon found that the walls of Bessemer's police department hid a torture chamber in which helpless prisoners were beaten mercilessly, often "until red with their own blood," to use a description from the subsequent grand jury report. When many of those arrested and held incommunicado could no longer bear the pain of beatings given in relays, they signed confessions without regard to whether they were guilty or not. So shameless was the brutality and so long had it been a practice in Bessemer that one could hardly have found a more horrifying reliance on the third degree anywhere else in the United States.

What should be done about it? Hugo Black was a fledgling county official. The brutal offenses were taking place in an incorporated municipality, and were, therefore, the responsibility of Bessemer's elected authorities. But these Bessemer officials had done nothing to correct the wrongs, and there was no reason to believe that they would institute corrective measures unless forced to do so.

After making up his mind with care and deliberation, the young Solicitor took his problem to a grand jury of representative citizens, who were decent and substantial. He presented the facts he had uncovered, with the result that a report was prepared for the county's Criminal Court. After approval by the grand jury, the report was made public, September 18, 1915. It shook a community not easily shaken. The report said:

> We find that, according to their own statements, Officers ———— and ———— have repeatedly been guilty of the practice of the "third degree" in a manner so cruel that it would bring discredit and shame upon the most uncivilized and barbarous community. We find that a uniform practice has been made of taking helpless prisoners, in the late hours of the night, into a secluded room in the presence of these two officers, and others whose names we have not yet been able to obtain, and there beat them until they were red with their own blood, in an effort to obtain confessions. We find that this cowardly practice, in which four big officers with pistols safely strapped on their bodies, would thus take advantage of ignorance and helplessness, has been continuously in operation for a number of years. A leather strap with a buckle on one end, and a big flap on the other was invented for the purpose of assisting the officers in this heinous practice, contrary to the letter and spirit of the Constitution of the United States, the Constitution of Alabama, the universal sympathy of the human heart. . . .

The daring prosecutor not only charged the police with being cowardly brutes, but also reported that on certain occasions several of them were drunken and disorderly. As for the argument that those who had been beaten were guilty of crimes and due to be punished anyway, Hugo Black was quick to set the constitutional issues straight. Accused persons, he said, might be guilty, as some of the Bessemer prisoners indeed were; then, of course, they might be innocent. But innocent or guilty, no one gave up his "right to be treated as a human being by reason of the fact that he is charged with—or any officer suspects that—he is guilty of a crime."

Solicitor Black, beginner though he was, knew exactly what the role of the police should be, and he did not hesitate to define it. The report continued:

> Instead of being ready and waiting to strike a prisoner in his custody, an officer should protect him . . . such practices are dishonorable, tyrannical, and despotic, and such rights must not long be surrendered to any officer or set of officers, so long as human life is held sacred and human liberty and human safety of para-mount importance.

The publication of the report created a sensation, all the more so because the initiator of it was a new, little-known county official not yet thirty years old. Black soundly declined to trust his facts to the aldermanic police committee for evaluation and action, since the aldermen were a part of the scandalous situation. At length it was agreed that the inquiry would be undertaken in public hearings by a committee of three disinterested citizens, one chosen by the aldermen, one by Solicitor Black, and the third by the two others.

Through September and into October, the three citizens investigated the charges before crowds at the county courthouse. Among the many instances of brutality related was one in which four policemen tied a seventy-year-old Negro against a door and beat him to the point of death. The inhumanity of the Bessemer police officials was made starkly plain when one witness testified that Negro prisoners were sometimes beaten with "three or four of us on a prisoner at once," that they used "fist, stick, chair—anything we could get hold of," and that these beatings occurred wherever it was convenient, "no particular place; sometimes in the warden's office."

The citizen's committee published its findings October 19. The conclusions severely criticized the Mayor, called on two aldermen to resign, and proposed the ouster of four policemen. Opinion in Jefferson County divided. Although Black had many supporters, he also had many opponents, who did not like the fact that the ugly truth had been made embarrassingly public. The area's leading newspaper, the Birmingham *Age-Herald*, passed off the disclosures as "conditions such as are prevalent in every other city."

Hugo Black was not in the least dissuaded by indifference or opposition. Pressing for and obtaining indictments, he held firmly to the belief that the people of Jefferson County were primarily responsible for conditions in Jefferson County, and that it was their duty to correct their own evils, insofar as this was possible.

Behind the young Solicitor's stanch belief in individual responsibility lay his family upbringing, his sound education, and his rich experience with people. All of these proved a substantial background for a Justice of the Supreme Court.

Hugo L. Black was born February 27, 1886, the youngest of eight sons and daughters of William LaFayette Black, a Clay County, Alabama, farmer and storekeeper who was Scotch-Irish by descent, and his wife, the former Martha Ardellah Toland. Hugo Black's birthplace was the clapboard-covered, enlarged log cabin on the farmstead adjacent to his father's combined store and post office, of which his mother was postmistress. Outgoing mail bore the mark of Harlan, Alabama, but William Black's home and store and a couple of tenant-farmer's cabins made up the whole of the place.

Everyone had work to do, for even garments were fashioned from cloth woven in the home, but there was time for play and reading, and educational pursuits were particularly encouraged. The youngest born's name reflected an older sister's interest in the novels of Victor Hugo. When the boy was three, William Black set up storekeeping in nearby Ashland, a pleasant, friendly county seat of 350 people with their tree-shaded homes and gardens. The change was made primarily so the Black children might enjoy the advantages of a private secondary school known locally as Ashland College.

A bright, energetic boy and a fast reader, Hugo picked cotton and set type in the weekly newspaper's print shop. More often he folded papers, or hauled supplies from the nearest point on the railroad. Only a few of Ashland's residents were Negroes, but the fatal shooting of a Negro lad by a white youth who was acquitted although guilty made a deep impression on the Black family. Particularly did the tragedy impress Hugo, who had played with the victim.

One of the main concerns of the Black family was politics, which Clay County, with numerous Republican and Populist adherents as well as Democrats, took seriously. Hugo was ten in

1896, the year of the first McKinley-Bryan race. His father was relatively well-to-do and, although a Democrat, was so opposed to Bryan that he supported Palmer, the independent Democratic candidate. But young Hugo attended any and all political meetings and heard the early appeals for improving the lot of the tenant farmer and the lower levels of society generally, through a new tax on incomes, better regulation of the economy, and fairer distribution geographically of the nation's financial resources. Waiting for the local returns on election night was a boyhood thrill. Akin to his interest in politics was his fascination with the courts and trials in Ashland. He looked ahead to cases conducted by visiting lawyers and spent hours listening to arguments, examinations, and verdicts.

Hugo Black's outlook was shaped and enlarged by purposeful reading, by law school, by practice at the bar, by his years in the Senate, but to a large extent his attitudes were set early in life. Above the sound and fury of the economic battles in Washington in the 1930's echoed the political war cries he listened to as a youth in rural Alabama in the 1890's.

Influenced by a physician brother, Hugo went at seventeen to the Birmingham Medical College. But after a school year there and a summer of apprenticeship in his brother's office, he turned from medicine in 1904 to follow a far better-defined interest, the law, at the University of Alabama. Two years later at the age of twenty, he completed the exacting law course and hung out his shingle in Ashland, where the legal pickings were slim. In 1907 a fire destroyed his office, and with it all his law books. Taking the loss as a sign to make a fresh start, at the age of twenty-one he left his family and moved to Birmingham, rented a desk in an older lawyer's office, and promptly affiliated with church, fraternal, civic, and other groups that would help him become acquainted in the big city.

There he continued the investigative work he had begun in Ashland for an Atlanta company that made private reports for large insurance companies. At the rate of fifty cents a report, he did this work in Birmingham for several years and also collected bills for a modest fee. His first important case was put on his desk by the older lawyer in the office. It was a damage suit for fifteen days' pay for work done by a Negro convict who had been leased to a steel mill and had been kept overtime on the job. Opposing counsel was one of the luminaries of the Birmingham bar, William I.

Grubb, later United States District Judge at Birmingham. But that did not awe Hugo Black, who overcame every motion for dismissal and in the end received a verdict of $150 for his lowly client.

The Circuit Judge in the case, A. O. Lane, was impressed by the young counsel for the Negro convict-laborer, and in 1911 was instrumental, as City Commissioner, in having Black appointed Police Court Judge for Birmingham. It was typical police court grist—the undesirable, the unfortunate, the underprivileged of an industrial city with a hinterland of rural slums. The new judge was quick to temper justice with understanding. A sample of his work on Birmingham's lowest bench was his dismissal of 22 Negroes hailed up on charges of "disorderly conduct" at a dance which the police had stopped. The local press reported that Black "told the arresting officer he had no more right to break up that dance than any other."

Alabama was a dry state and Judge Black, who himself was strongly opposed to alcoholic excesses, enforced its prohibition statutes in his jurisdiction. Yet, when he wrote his first formal opinion in a case, he held that the Birmingham Excise Commission could not, under the law, revoke the license of wholesalers who sold to illegal handlers of liquor.

Black stayed on the police bench only until October 1912, but that was long enough for him to become one of Birmingham's best-known municipal officers, to make a mark on the administration of justice locally, and to earn a highly gratifying compliment from a visitor who was studying the administration of police courts in the United States. According to the Birmingham *News*, the visiting observer said: "Judge Black has one of the most analytical minds of which I have ever known and he comes more nearly dealing out real justice than any police court judge I have ever seen." Hugo Black was then twenty-five.

The police court had left time for private practice, and the more legal work Black did, the more he liked it. He particularly relished trying cases and especially examining witnesses, for which he prepared himself with utmost care. His work, which was beginning to pay well, was mostly for individuals and small-sized businesses.

Two years after he left the police bench, Black ran for the county solicitorship and was elected from a field of four. He promised, in his campaign, to bring the criminal docket up to date and he set out to make his pledge good. With 3,238 cases pending, he and his two assistants tried twelve and won eleven capital cases in the first week. He immediately hit at a vicious fee system by dismissing charges against many scores of Negro dice players whose continued incarceration provided extra revenue for the sheriff and the jailkeepers. After showing what could be done, he persuaded the Legislature and Governor to provide additional help on the bench as well as in the prosecutor's office. With this assistance, he cleared the docket.

His prosecution of the Bessemer police department was not Black's only campaign against wrong done by those who should have been setting the community's standards. For example, coal companies found out that there was a law against short weight and, even more notably, a County Solicitor who would enforce it. He conducted many murder trials, including the prosecution of a leading Birmingham businessman.

This period in Hugo Black's life closed with his enlistment in the Army. He was against the involvement of the United States in the war that broke out in Europe in 1914, but after his country became a participant, he was eager to make his contribution. Unmarried, he entered the Officers Training Corps at Fort Oglethorpe, Georgia, August 3, 1917. He served in the 81st Field Artillery and as adjutant of the 19th Artillery Brigade. Rising to captain, he served on three posts within the United States. After his discharge following the Armistice, he returned to Birmingham and again took up private practice.

The first postwar landmark in the life of Hugo Black was his marriage to Josephine Foster, who was at Sweetbriar College when the war led her to the Yeomanettes, in whose uniform Black first saw her. He was almost thirty-five when they were married in February 1921. A minister's daughter, Josephine Foster Black was a happy-natured woman of talent. She was a great help to her husband and an excellent mother to their two sons and daughter until she died in 1951. Six years later it was the lonely widower's good fortune to marry Elizabeth Seay DeMeritte, who similarly has brightened the Black home since. She was the daughter of Dr. James E. Seay of Birmingham, a close friend of Hugo Black, as were other members of the Seay family.

After practicing alone, Attorney Black went into a series of partnerships and over the next five years did very well for both his clients and himself. One of the companies he represented was the Zurich Insurance Company of Switzerland, which did a lot of

business in Birmingham. He became the regularly retained lawyer
for the carpenters' and the railroad trainmen's unions and also
represented the United Mine Workers of America as a special
attorney. As counsel for working people, he handled many personal injury cases with large awards of damages. By the time he
was forty, he was widely known in legal circles as a union-labor
lawyer, regularly successful in winning over juries through persuasive presentation of his side, coupled with unerring demonstration
of any weaknesses in the opposition.

Though personally out of politics, Black campaigned as a
Democrat for John W. Davis, the Wall Street lawyer, in the 1924
campaign against Calvin Coolidge. Philosophically, however, he
was far closer to the third-party nominee, Progressive "Fighting
Bob" La Follette of Wisconsin. But Black could be wholly sincere
in condemning Harry M. Daugherty, Harding's malodorous
Attorney General, which he did in speech after speech. When
Harlan Fiske Stone became Attorney General, the Department of
Justice, lacking a competent Alabama Republican, drafted Black to
prosecute several prominent violators of the federal prohibition
law in Mobile. It was Black's first connection with the United
States Government, aside from his military service, and oddly
enough it came through a New England Coolidge Republican.

Meantime, his entry into an organization during this period
was to bring him much hostility some fifteen years later. On
September 11, 1923, he became a member of the Birmingham Ku
Klux Klan. At the time, the Klan, with more than 2,000,000
members in the South, was politically potent there as well as in
some Northern states, and was considered by many in it to be
primarily a fraternal organization. Most, if not all, the Protestant
clergy in Birmingham were on its rolls. So were many hundreds of
workingmen as well as prominent business and professional men,
and in both groups were many close friends of Black. To countless
Alabamans in politics and out, the Klan of the middle 1920's was
pro-Protestant rather than anti-Catholic, anti-Jewish, or anti-
Negro. The acts of violence and crime were not justified by these
members, but were accounted for as the work of extremists who
were not representative of a generally tolerant and humane rank
and file.

Black's membership was designed to increase his circle of
acquaintances who might be able to assist him in his practice or in
politics. It was that and nothing more. His record of help to

Negroes, for example, was too plain and too long to allow for the slightest misunderstanding on that score. Moreover, his Klan membership was of short duration. On June 10, 1925, he announced that he would be a candidate for the Democratic nomination for the Senate seat held by economic conservative Oscar W. Underwood, a critic of the Klan and an opponent of prohibition. Since Black shared the common belief in Alabama that a Klan member ought not to run for public office, he submitted his resignation on a friendly basis, after less than two years of membership.

The campaign was long and hard, even though Underwood withdrew soon after Black's announcement. That left a field of five including a former Governor, a reputable judge, an established businessman, and a representative of the celebrated Bankhead family. Although he was the youngest in the race and not well known outside Birmingham, Black called himself the candidate of the ordinary people. He crisscrossed Alabama in a model T Ford, met his own bills, greeted voters in every county, and, without organization support, received 40 percent of the first-place votes and enough second-place votes to give him the nomination at the August 1926 primary, and, in effect, automatically the subsequent election.

The Birmingham Klan met to honor the nominees and Black was presented with a "Grand Passport," a kind of honorary life membership. He responded in a complimentary vein but also said that he would rather resign his office in the Senate than pander "to the things that are wrong and contrary to American tradition and instincts." He also declared his devotion to those "principles of liberty which were written in the Constitution of this country and in the great historical documents."

The Senate that Hugo Black entered in 1927 contained outstanding figures. Among the Democrats were Ashurst, Caraway, Glass, Harrison, Reed, Robinson, Wagner, Wheeler, and the Walshes. On the Republican side were Borah, Cutting, Johnson, McNary, Moses, Norris, Smoot, and Wadsworth. With colleagues so notable, the freshman from Alabama said very little for a long time and instead devoted himself largely to studying legislative procedure and the growing domestic and international issues about which he felt he knew almost nothing.

To fill in big gaps in his education, he began by reading *The Wealth of Nations* by Adam Smith and went on to major biographies and historical works on the origins and development of English and American society, philosophy, literature, law, and courts. He read not only Charles Warren's admiring history of the United States Supreme Court but also the sharply critical volume by Gustavus Myers. Since there was much ancient and European history that he did not know, he read translations of the Greek and Latin classics and modern European masters such as Rousseau, Locke, Mill, and Marx. If he reflected with Thoreau at Walden Pond and steamboated on the Mississippi with Mark Twain, he also pondered with the Beards the change from an agricultural economy to one of mills and factories, cities and slums, and dissected the new society with Veblen. Probably no other Senator of those years was doing the kind of reading that the junior colleague to J. Thomas Heflin so eagerly pursued.

A relatively new issue in the Senate at the time was that of excessive expenditures in political campaigns. The year of Black's election, 1926, was marred by the "golden primaries" in Illinois and Pennsylvania, and the Senate, although controlled by Republicans, held off on seating the Republican Senators nominated and presumably elected in those states that year, respectively Frank L. Smith and William S. Vare.

The first major legislation during his tenure was the Muscle Shoals public power bill, a subject on which Black had spoken in his campaign. Believing that a private chemical corporation would manufacture low-cost fertilizer for Southern farmers, the new Senator from Alabama declared himself in favor of the company's bid for the great natural water-power site. Here he collided head on with Senator George W. Norris of Nebraska, whose basic position was that Muscle Shoals was needed for public power and the proposal to manufacture fertilizer was a mask for private power interests.

This clash between Black and Norris was substantial at first, but each learned from the other, and Black later became a far better-informed ally of public power. His first investigative work as a Senator was in handling the Muscle Shoals phase of the Caraway inquiry into lobbying. What he uncovered opened his eyes to the lengths to which a large corporation would go to influence the course of government for private financial gain. When the Muscle Shoals bill passed Congress in 1928, thanks to the Black-Norris interchange the Alabaman's concern for legitimate production of fertilizer was taken into account and the bill's public power clauses were stronger than originally. Coolidge suffocated the measure with a pocket veto and Hoover also vetoed the 1931 bill when it came to him. Enactment had to wait for the election of Franklin D. Roosevelt and the coming of the New Deal in 1933.

Gradually Black penetrated deeply into state and national politics. Two years after his own election, he supported Gov. Alfred E. Smith of New York in his 1928 presidential race against Hoover. Smith was far from the ideal Democratic standard bearer in Alabama, but Black believed he should be upheld for the sake of party loyalty. This stand led to an open break with his demagogic senior colleague, Heflin, who jumped the Democratic traces and campaigned for Hoover. The loyalists won out in Alabama, which went narrowly to Smith. All this led Heflin to intensify his Catholic baiting and that in turn became a factor in the decision of Black to oppose Heflin's re-election in 1930. With the Klan arrayed strongly for Heflin, who ran as an independent, Black campaigned hard for the regular Democratic choice, John H. Bankhead, one of Black's 1926 primary opponents. Bankhead won and the national political scene was well rid of the noxious Heflin.

Black followed a cautious program as his first term ran its six-year course. He offered a bill to suspend immigration. It did not pass. He also took a preliminary look into the fiscal affairs of the United States Shipping Board, but further investigation was blocked by the Republican majority. In a defense of anti-trust laws, he called on the Department of Justice not to weaken the consent decree standing against packers. With the coming of the Great Depression after the 1929 crash, he began a study of wages and hours as a means of mitigating economic declines and distress among jobless workers. He distrusted pump-priming as a method of trickling buying power down to the unemployed, favoring instead direct relief payments that assured the purchase of necessities at the grass roots. But he wanted local administration of relief, and helped defeat the La Follette-Costigan bill because it did not provide for state control.

Even more important in Black's first term than the twice-vetoed Muscle Shoals bill was the Hawley-Smoot tariff of 1929, which Hoover supported and signed. In the main Black was against that most protective of protective tariffs, and even opposed higher duties for such major Alabama industrial products as iron and cement, but he did unsuccessfully propose an exception for his native Clay County's graphite. What showed his basic attitude toward the tariff was his call for consumer representation by expert counsel at all tariff hearings.

Out of the Hawley-Smoot debate arose an indication of things to come. The tariff bill, as approved by the Senate Finance Committee, allowed customs officials to decide whether books from other countries should be barred as immoral or revolutionary. Republican Senator Bronson Cutting of New Mexico believed that this determination of obscenity or subversiveness should not be left to minor government employees at ports of entry. He introduced an amendment restricting port authority in such matters and establishing the procedure by which any ruling by these functionaries could be appealed. Breaking from Heflin, Black wholeheartedly backed the Cutting amendment. In one of his most significant statements as Senator, he pointed out that what one reader found objectionable might not be in the least objectionable to the next reader. He said that it was the responsibility of the home, the church, and the school to teach good taste in reading and that the Government should leave the adult citizen to be "persuaded in no way except by logic." Acknowledging his indebtedness to the philosophical writings of Thomas Jefferson, he declared: "I have an inherent, well-grounded opposition against investing in the hands of an individual judicial powers on matters of supreme importance with reference to the dissemination of human knowledge."

Black was fortunate in having committee assignments that put him in the Senate's main stream. On the always important Foreign Relations Committee, he favored independence for the Philippines and objected to secrecy at the London Naval Conference. On the Judiciary, he began to study the federal court system as well as the machinery and handiwork of the Supreme Court and its effect on the lives of millions of Americans. He followed Borah and Norris in their opposition to Hoover's appointment of Charles Evans Hughes and John J. Parker to the highest tribunal.

In 1932 Black came up for re-election and so ran on the same ticket as Franklin D. Roosevelt in the New Deal President's first national campaign. Again the Alabama primary field included five senatorial candidates. Black's opponents in Birmingham spread about broadly a reproduction of the "Grand Passport" which the Klan had given him in 1926. The intention was to hurt him two ways—with Klan members who were reminded of Black's break with the Klan in the Heflin campaign, and also with opponents of the Klan. But by now Black was reasonably well established as something new in the South—an informed, genuinely liberal Senator who viewed issues from the standpoint of the rank and file and who, in appreciation, received the strong backing of small farmers and workers and union leaders. He polled 49 percent of the vote in the primary proper and some 60 percent in the runoff, even though he had stayed close to his duties in Washington and engaged in almost the minimum of campaigning in his home state. But it is only fair to say that what he did in Washington often brought him favorable attention in the Alabama press.

As a member of the new Democratic majority, overwhelmingly returned on his own record, Alabama's now senior Senator entered in 1933 the busiest as well as the most rewarding period of his life up to that time. He had ready for the opening week of the first New Deal session a bill to limit the work week to 30 hours. His purpose was not to regulate individual lives, but to reduce the stalking menace of unemployment and also to stabilize production; by this he hoped to help lift the economy out of its slough. He documented his case with a wealth of statistical information and was persuasive enough to win the support of President Roosevelt, whose commendatory call to Senate Leader Joseph T. Robinson led to a favorable vote of 53 to 40 in the upper chamber. An undesirable House amendment turned both Roosevelt and Black against the measure, with the result that the President supported instead the bill for a National Industrial Recovery Administration, which Black promptly opposed.

His opposition to NIRA, because it gave too much price-fixing power to business, marked one of the few major times when Black broke with the Roosevelt leadership. He also was for overriding the bonus veto and he strongly defended an amendment to write the principle of the prevailing wage into relief-work legislation. But these divergences only underscored the fact that on the whole Black was an exceedingly able, largely dependable New Dealer in the Senate.

Hugo Black's investigative talent, which had dug into the hidden brutality in the Bessemer jail, now went to work in earnest. Previously it had been blocked by the Republican majority when Black wanted to investigate inefficiency and suspected corruption in the United States Shipping Board. Now he sponsored a resolution to study ocean mail contracts, and was made chairman of a special committee of inquiry. From his disclosures of maladministration and even worse practices in the handling of mail carried on ships, he turned to contracts with airlines for transporting mail. The ensuing revelations inevitably produced big headlines. Black brought into the open the ugly facts about fantastic profits made overnight by airline manipulators into whose hands generous government subsidies had been entrusted. He showed, for example, how one executive of a subsidized airline turned an investment of $259.14 into a fortune of $5,332,284, how another with an investment of $207 reaped $7,796,293. Black spoke to Roosevelt about the Chief Executive's authority to rescind contracts tainted by fraud, and the President soon afterward canceled all pertinent contracts, effective February 19, 1934. When a public controversy arose over the fatal crashes of Army planes that flew the mails temporarily, Black delivered an emphatic radio address which lamented the casualties but held to the central point, namely, the excesses and illegalities of the airline operations under the subsidized contracts.

However, it was Black's investigation of the outrageously dishonest lobbying against the public utility holding company bill in 1935 that made him a truly national figure. A major weapon in the New Deal arsenal against financial manipulation and trickery in utility management was the Wheeler-Rayburn "death sentence" clause designed to break up the utility holding company systems. That these pyramided financial monstrosities milked local utility companies at the expense of consumers was not open to question. Yet the companies fought the remedial measure tooth and nail, and in doing so they grossly overplayed their hand.

An inquiry into the lobbying, with Black as committee chairman, brought out the fact that thousands of telegrams were sent to members of Congress by utility agents and signed with names taken without permission from city and telephone directories. One holding company executive said under oath that he had directed the expenditure of around $900,000, much of which went to influence the press. Black said that if the total spent against the measure could be known it would come close to $5,000,000.

Angry publishers and editors, whose newspapers were shown to be under obligation to the utility largess, yearned for an occasion to hit back at Black. They found it when the investigating committee, unable to obtain the originals of thousands of telegrams destroyed in the utility offices, subpoenaed copies from the Western Union Company files. Black was censured for invading private correspondence and for other high crimes. The calm chairman's temperate answer was to show that he was following a procedure previously used by some of his loudest congressional critics. And he made it plain that no honest citizen had anything to fear from an inquiry designed to protect the interests of poorly defended consumers against exploitation by public utility holding companies. Friends and foes alike now saw that Hugo L. Black like Montana's Walsh was a skilled, effective user of the congressional investigation as a necessary, legitimate part of the legislative process.

Meantime, as Congress and the President labored together to restore the country's economy in the middle 1930's—and Senator Black was among the hardest workers day after day and night on night—the Supreme Court was undoing a major part of the legislative-executive achievement. In a series of crucial decisions, key recovery laws were struck down as unconstitutional by a supreme bench that had gone on unchanged following the retirement of Holmes in 1932. The far advanced average age of the Justices caused them to be widely and disrespectfully called "the Nine Old Men." When they split, 5 to 4, as they not infrequently did, the division was usually into the same groups. In the invalidating majority were Justices Willis Van Devanter, James Clark Mc-Reynolds, George Sutherland, Pierce Butler, and Owen J. Roberts. The sustaining minority consisted of Chief Justice Hughes and Justices Louis D. Brandeis, Harlan F. Stone, and Benjamin N. Cardozo. There were other alignments of the Justices, but this one occurred so often that it disturbed many observers of the Supreme Court and its work.

The consequence was that an unprecedentedly popular President and a series of co-operating Congresses were being frustrated by adverse Supreme Court decisions. Making the situation even more difficult to accept was a strange circumstance. Although vacancies had occurred at the rate of one every 18 months on the average between 1902 and 1932, and notwithstanding the high age of the members, no opportunity to appoint a Supreme Court Justice had come to Roosevelt in his entire first term. When, by this same one-judge margin, the Court invalidated the New York state minimum-wage law in 1936, it created a no man's land in which the worker could be exploited, without protection from either federal or state regulation. Making the Supreme Court position even more vulnerable was a newspaper editorial writer's discovery that, in a span of just twenty years, 10 of the 17 Justices who had participated in major minimum wage cases had found the wage laws, both state and federal, constitutional. Yet the Court's holdings went against the new laws. That anomaly was possible because the Justices who found the laws unconstitutional held onto their seats longer than their brethren who supported the constitutionality of minimum wage legislation.

This condition had to be coped with somehow, and Roosevelt made it first order of business after his overwhelming re-election in 1936. Without realizing that several appointments soon would come to him in natural course, the President sponsored a bill in February 1937, to encourage retirement of elderly Justices and to appoint up to six new Justices if these elderly members did not avail themselves of retirement provisions. Tagged at once "Roosevelt's court-packing scheme," the proposal stirred up one of the hottest controversies in American history. Newspapers with but few exceptions denounced the bill, and so did bar and other professional leaders. Chief Justice Hughes and Justices Van Devanter and Brandeis appeared before the Senate Judiciary Committee to show by statistical tables that the Supreme Court was handling its business competently and did not need additional members. Many congressional Democrats joined the enraged Republicans, but Black, who had followed the course of Supreme Court decisions and their impact on the national life more carefully than most of his colleagues on Capitol Hill, stood by Roosevelt through the battle.

Both defeat and victory were in the making. The bill was rejected, but before it was, the Supreme Court, taking judicious notice, upheld the National Labor Relations and Social Security Acts and in effect reversed itself on the state minimum wage issue. Then Justice Van Devanter retired in June 1937, and Roosevelt, after five long years, could at last make an appointment to the Supreme Court. Had Senator Joseph T. Robinson of Arkansas lived, the seat unquestionably would have gone to him, for he had carried the heavy burden of the court bill in the Senate; but Robinson died in the midst of the fight, and the President and his staff drew up a long list of possible appointees. After deliberating over the pros and cons, the White House chose the Senator from Alabama, who as a boy had gone to the Clay County courthouse to hear the lawyers argue their cases and watch the litigants and the witnesses and the judges.

Now there were new outcries of anger—and also shouts of

delight. Black was denounced as "unfit" and lacking in even "the slightest qualification." He was also praised as "one of the most learned members of the Senate," respected for convictions that came to him "by a reasoned, intellectual process." In short, the reactionaries were outraged and the liberals overjoyed. Each group's reaction was inspired by Black's progressive record in the Senate and the knowledge that he would take his outlook with him to the Supreme Court.

Norris spoke not only for many fellow Senators but also for millions of little people over the country when he wrote, from a sickbed at home, to Chairman Ashurst of the Judiciary Committee:

> I feel greatly grieved at the bitter, unreasonable and sometimes malicious attacks which are being made upon him. His work in the Senate must convince everyone that he possesses a superior ability and undaunted courage which are seldom equalled or surpassed. His nomination to that great tribunal expresses the wish and hope of the struggling citizen asking only for justice for all alike. . . . He is a worthy representative of the common people. He understands their hopes and ambitions, and their liberties in his hands will be safe.

It was a moving testimonial not unlike that which Woodrow Wilson sent to the same committee twenty-one years earlier when a similar attack was being made against the confirmation of Louis D. Brandeis for the same high tribunal. But not everyone cared to remember.

The nomination went to the Senate August 12, and was referred to the Judiciary Committee, which considered it promptly and reported favorably. The Senate debated the question of confirmation for two days and then approved, 63 to 16. Only ten Republicans and six Democrats voted No. Undoubtedly the rule of senatorial courtesy, under which the Senate almost automatically approves one of its members for federal appointment, was a factor in the heavy vote to confirm. Yet there were many Senators who answered Aye not because of Black the member of the Senate, but because of Black the man. After he took the oath as Associate Justice, he and Mrs. Black sailed to England, where they visited people like Harold J. Laski and places like Toynbee Hall.

With the new Justice out of the country, Ray Sprigle of the violently anti-New Deal *Pittsburgh Post-Gazette* went to Alabama, and prepared a series of six articles rehashing the Klan connections, largely from the front pages of the *Montgomery Advertiser*. There was almost nothing new in this Pulitzer-prize-to-be series which started September 13. It was, however, reprinted under large headlines in other papers, and the furor started up all over again. There were demands that Black resign, demands that he be impeached. Newspapers which had condemned the appointment in the first place keyed their voices to a still higher pitch. On his side, Black, as before, had his strong defenders in government, in labor circles, and elsewhere, including even a few in the press such as Heywood Broun and William T. Evjue. Norris, the senior fighter for Muscle Shoals, again shot straight to the mark: "Actually Justice Black is being subjected to all this criticism because he is a liberal, because he wants to bring the Supreme Court closer to the people—not because he is a Klansman."

In the face of requests for a statement, Black kept his counsel in London. On October 1, the day after his return, he addressed the American people over the radio. Though he spoke briefly, he said all there was to say. His message in part was:

> An effort is being made to convince the people of America that I am intolerant and that I am prejudiced against people of the Jewish and Catholic faiths, and against members of the Negro race. . . . I believe that my record as a Senator refutes every implication of racial or religious intolerance. It shows that I was of that group of liberal Senators who have consistently fought for the civil, economic and religious rights of all Americans, without regard to race or creed. . . . The insinuations of racial and religious intolerance made concerning me are based on the fact that I joined the Ku Klux Klan about fifteen years ago. I did join the Klan. I later resigned. I never rejoined. I never have considered and do not now consider the unsolicited card given me shortly after my nomination to the Senate as a membership of any kind in the Ku Klux Klan. I never used it. I did not even keep it. Before becoming a Senator I dropped the Klan. I have had nothing to do with it since that time. . . . I have no sympathy with any group which, anywhere or at any time, arrogates to itself the un-American power to interfere in the slightest with complete religious freedom.

Nevertheless, the irreconcilables among his critics continued to clamor for Black's resignation and some even professed that his radio talk had made a bad matter worse; but the controversy began to quiet down and a test of public opinion showed that many people were reassured by words so frank and honest. For the new Justice it was a closed chapter on October 4, when he took his seat on the bench of Marshall, Story, and Taney, of Harlan, Holmes, and Brandeis.

By the end of his first term, less than nine months later, it was evident to the perceptive that Black was already making his mark as a Justice. His position on cases was that of the people, and from this point of view he went readily to the heart of the issue, and wrote his opinions so clearly that laymen could understand them. He spoke for a unanimous Court in a case in which the defendant company attempted to excuse its intentional dishonesty with the argument that its advertising was so manifestly untrue that no one would be foolish enough to believe it. Black demolished this brazen contention in sentences that are models of clarity. "Laws," he said, "are made to protect the trusting as well as the suspicious. . . . There is no duty resting upon the citizen to suspect the honesty of those with whom he does business. . . . The rule of *caveat emptor* should not be relied upon to reward fraud and deception."

Aware that he wore only his own collar, he began within a few weeks to dissent from majority opinions when his intelligence told him to speak out for himself, as he did, for example, in the *Indianapolis Water Company Case* in which he was the lone dissenter. This willingness to dissent disturbed some of his colleagues, who apparently felt that there should have been a period of relative silence and going along on Black's part. Questions as to his "competence" and "craftsmanship" began to appear in print, even in so thoughtful a magazine as *Harper's*. In *The New Republic*, however, the farseeing, vigilant Walton H. Hamilton, writing on "Mr. Justice Black's First Year," applauded the new member's "integrity and independence" and described him as bringing "a new breath of fresh air into a rather musty court-room." About the same time, Washington correspondent Paul Y. Anderson wrote in *The Nation:*

> Time may prove that the most brilliant single stroke of the Roosevelt Administration was the appointment of Hugo L. Black to the Supreme Court. Laymen as well as lawyers are beginning to realize that Black's solitary dissents, instead of revealing a perverse temperament and a lack of "legal craftsmanship," may well guide the Court out of the metaphysical wilderness into which it has wandered. . . . Black is opposed to any compromise. He believes that the way to resume constitutional government is to resume.

Soon other appointments to the Court were coming to Roosevelt. Sutherland left early in 1938 and was replaced by Stanley F. Reed. Cardozo died that same year and Felix Frankfurter was named to the vacancy. Then Brandeis retired in 1939 and William O. Douglas was called to his seat. Butler was succeeded by Frank Murphy in 1940 and McReynolds by James F. Byrnes in 1941. When Hughes stepped down as Chief Justice in 1941, Stone was moved up and Robert H. Jackson came on. Thus, by 1941, when Black had been on the Court hardly more than four years, he was outranked in seniority among the Associate Justices only by Roberts. After Stone's death in 1946, he became the senior member of the entire bench, and that in only nine years.

In Black's quarter-century, Justices Reed, Murphy, Byrnes, and Jackson plus Chief Justice Fred M. Vinson and Justices Wiley B. Rutledge, Harold H. Burton, Sherman Minton, Charles Evans Whittaker, and Felix Frankfurter have served tenures ending in retirement or death. In more recent years, other brethren of the Court have been Chief Justice Earl Warren and Justices Tom C. Clark, John Marshall Harlan, William J. Brennan, Jr., Potter Stewart, Byron R. White, and Arthur J. Goldberg. Black has served with four Chief Justices and as many Presidents. After Stone's death and before confirmation of Vinson, he presided as senior Justice.

A particularly unhappy episode came in June 1946, after the appointment of Vinson as Chief Justice. Justice Jackson, then on loan to the International Military Tribunal as United States prosecutor, made a bitter, intemperate, ill-informed attack on Black in an emotionally charged statement released at Nürnberg. The gist of this verbal assault was that Black had failed to disqualify himself in the *Jewell Ridge* portal-to-portal pay case, in which Black's long-ago law partner was counsel, and had thereby sullied his record as a Justice. The Jackson blast was utterly without merit. Moreover, it completely mystified the international press corps at Nürnberg, which had been summoned to a special conference presumably concerned with the war crimes trial. Inevitably an explanation was sought in Jackson's disappointment in not being elevated to the chief justiceship, for Jackson seemed to have the mistaken notion that Black had opposed him for successor to Stone. As any reply would have added to the damage already done, Black said nothing. That angry eruption had hurt the good name of the Court, and Black correctly saw that the only way to repair it was by hard and thoughtful work on the part of the Court itself.

As the terms have come and gone and the mountains of cases have been handled, Black has done his share and more. He has been with the majority most of the time, has spoken for it frequently, and he has written his separate concurrences when an individual expression on the side of the decision seemed in order. But time and again he has dissented, often with three colleagues, sometimes with one or two, or even alone. In one period he and Douglas, Murphy, and Rutledge were frequently together, and, when joined by Stone or one other Justice, constituted a narrow majority. In recent terms, he and Chief Justice Warren and Justices Douglas and Brennan have made up another phalanx of four, which has required the Court, under its procedure, at least to hear cases that otherwise would not even have been taken for review.

With the intensification of the Cold War in the late 1940's, and the 1950's, the Black who had become known for his straightforward views on federal and state powers and the regulation of the economy through law in the public interest found himself increasingly concerned with the liberties of individual citizens in cases arising under the Constitution's historic Bill of Rights. This concern has continued in the 1960's, and, although tests of the First Amendment freedoms have evoked memorable opinions from him down through the years, his dissents in a series of free speech cases in the 1960–1 term constitute the high point of his judicial career.

Even though Supreme Court decisions generally are important, it is those that deal with the civil liberties of the citizen that are transcendently so in a world that knows only too well the meaning of such terms as Iron Curtain, police state, fascism, repression and oppression, totalitarianism, and dictatorship. The decision in a Bill of Rights case may determine whether a man will go to prison for life or die in the electric chair or climb the gallows' steps to the hangman's noose. It may determine whether he will stay behind bars even though he is prepared to show that his trial rights were ignored in the court that sentenced him. It may speak the final order in an issue of free speech, free press, free religion, free assembly, of the security of the citizen in his own home against official invasion. To many people these rights are as precious as life itself and to their eternal credit there are Americans today who will give up months and years of liberty rather than contribute to the weakening of the freedoms that distinguish the United States of America from so much of the rest of the world.

Senator Norris has been quoted and Walton Hamilton. Two students in the Harvard University Law School could see the shape of the service of Hugo Black on the Supreme Court as far back as 1939. Milton I. Goldstein and Leo L. Laskoff wrote in a joint thesis: "He is a good pathfinder . . . he blazes a trail as he goes. As the extremist on what appears to be a revolutionary Court, Mr. Justice Black will probably sit in judgment on the corpses of many cherished doctrines. More substantial ones will probably replace them."

Now, before the Justice speaks for himself, a few extracts from appraisals of Hugo Black.

John P. Frank (1949):

He is a representative of that movement in American history which we have variously called the Grange, the Populists, the New Freedom, and the New Deal. He is one of the tiny handful of representatives of that movement ever to reach the Supreme Court of the United States. His significance as a Justice is that he knows what to do with the power thus given him.

Charles A. Beard (1949):

Personally familiar with the straitened circumstances of men and women who labor with their hands for a living, he has a vivid sense of the perplexities confronting them when they become involved in the toils of the law, unprotected by the wit and learning of counsel. In all the annals of the Court it would be difficult, if not impossible, to find another Justice so intimately acquainted with the disadvantages they encounter in the struggle for existence, and the meaning of judicial decisions in terms of life and equity for them.

Charlotte Williams (1950):

History has now gone far enough to allow no doubt of Justice Black's learning and ability. No one ever doubted his intellectual energy. By dint of these qualities directed in behalf of the common man and grounded upon a faith in the possibility of just and efficient democratic government, he has earned a unique distinction among those who have held membership upon the Supreme Court.

William O. Douglas (1956):

Justice Black has an ear finely tuned to facts and quite deaf to dogma and generalities. . . . When the critical account is written, none will be rated higher than Justice Black for consistency in construing the laws and the Constitution so as to protect the civil rights of citizens and aliens, whatever the form of repression may be.

Edmond Cahn (1956):

In Justice Black's hands, the Bill of Rights is directed toward the values that lie beyond. He reads it as a people's charter of edification, and postulates the kind of national community whose practices would do daily honor to the First Amendment. It would be an American community not unworthy of Madison's and Jefferson's best aspirations.

Eugene V. Rostow (1956):

The possibility of arbitrary and uncontrolled actions by officers of the state, often based on secret information, and governed by meaninglessly vague criteria of judgment is now a threatening force in millions of lives. This totalitarian practice must not, and will not endure. Twenty years from now, and perhaps sooner, Justice Black will appear as one of the key figures in the process through which the standards of the Constitution came to prevail over principles and practices of tyranny.

Charles A. Madison (1961):

Justice Black looks upon the world with the vision of the philosopher—being moved neither by personal ambition nor by transient events. He works long hours to assure thorough attention to the duties of his office. An insatiable reader, he keeps abreast of world affairs and national trends and observes the follies and foibles of men with an anxious wistfulness. Withal he remains a passionate libertarian, the forthright defender of Jeffersonian democracy, the perspicacious and incisive man of law—in truth one of our most distinguished living Americans.

Daniel M. Berman (1961):

Serving at a time when many a liberal balanced the public's interest in security against the individual's interest in free expression and came up with something just this side of fascism, Black clung obstinately to his faith that there is no conflict between the public and the private interest—that both demand the full freedom of expression for the individual.

Clifford J. Durr (1961):

Black has never stood forth as the champion of the Negro or of any other specific racial or religious group, as such. His concern is not with the defense of the constitutional rights of members of specific groups, but rather with the defense of the rights of people as people. He is aware that our legal and constitutional safeguards are not selective; they must protect everybody—regardless of race, creed, or political belief—or they will not long protect anybody.

Marquis W. Childs (1961):

This writer was one of those who at the time (1937) helped give widespread currency to these doubts [as to legal competence and craftsmanship]. That was a disservice to Justice Black, coming as it did on top of the fierce attack that followed the Klan disclosure —that attack, incidentally being aimed almost as much at Roosevelt as at the new Justice. The way in which Black mastered the techniques of the Court quickly refuted the doubters. Both among his admirers and his critics, there is no one who would today dream of questioning his ability.

Fred Rodell (1961):

This man is meant for the ages. No future Supreme Court Justice, a hundred years hence or a thousand, will ignore with inner impunity the myriad brilliant insights, learned analyses, yes, and fervent faiths that mark, in majority or dissent, his judicial record. The pity is only that Hugo LaFayette Black in person—he of the warm wisdom and the quiet courage and gentle strength—cannot, as will his opinions, live forever.

Earl Warren (1962):

Of the 97 Justices who have been appointed to this Court, only 16 have served as long as Mr. Justice Black and none with greater fidelity or singleness of purpose. His unflagging devotion has been to the Constitution of the United States.

And finally, what does the layman who has read and re-read the opinions of Hugo Black in civil liberties cases, who has sorted them out from the hundreds written by the Justice over a quarter century, who has tried to see them in their setting and to estimate their implications for the future—how does this one citizen see the public services of the straight-thinking, soft-spoken, tennis-playing, garden-tending jurist from among the cotton fields and steel mills of Alabama?

The question can be readily answered in part at least. Beginning with the very foundations of the Republic, no one else has stood up so resolutely over so long a period in times so trying for the sacred freedoms of the individual American under the Bill of Rights.

Mr. Justice Black and his good works should be cause for daily thanksgiving by an understanding and grateful people.

I I

———

The Bill of Rights

James Madison Lecture

BY HUGO L. BLACK

II

The Bill of Rights

JAMES MADISON LECTURE

THE *New York University School of Law inaugurated its annual James Madison Lecture Series on February 17, 1960. Since James Madison was the "Father of the Constitution of the United States" and a major influence in the formulation and adoption of the Bill of Rights, the selection of Justice Black to give the first lecture in the series was particularly appropriate. He called it simply "The Bill of Rights." Here is the text of what he said, as it appeared in the* New York University Law Review, *April 1960.*

I am honored to be the first speaker in your new annual series of James Madison lectures. The title of the series suggested the title of my talk: The Bill of Rights. Madison lived in the stirring times between 1750 and 1836, during which the Colonies declared, fought for, and won their independence from England. They then set up a new national government dedicated to Liberty and Justice. Madison's role in creating that government was such a major one that he has since been generally referred to as the Father of our Constitution. He was a most influential member of the Philadelphia Convention that submitted the Constitution to the people of the states; he alone kept a comprehensive report of the daily proceedings of the Convention; he was an active member of the Virginia Convention that adopted the Constitution after a bitter fight; finally, as a member of the First Congress, he offered and sponsored through that body proposals that became the First Ten Amendments, generally thought of as our Bill of Rights. For these and many other reasons, Madison's words are an authentic source to help us understand the Constitution and its Bill of Rights. In the course of my discussion I shall have occasion to refer to some of the many things Madison said about the meaning of the Constitution and the First Ten Amendments. In doing so, I shall refer to statements made by him during the Bill of Rights debates as reported in the Annals of Congress. There has been doubt cast upon the accuracy of some of the reports of congressional debates and transactions in the Annals. I am assured by Mr. Irving Brant, the eminent biographer of Madison, that Madison's discussions of the Bill of Rights as reported in the Annals are shown to be correct by Madison's own manuscripts on file in the Library of Congress.

What is a bill of rights? In the popular sense it is any document setting forth the liberties of the people. I prefer to think of our Bill of Rights as including all provisions of the original Constitution and Amendments that protect individual liberty by barring government from acting in a particular area or from acting except under certain prescribed procedures. I have in mind such clauses in the body of the Constitution itself as those which safeguard the right of *habeas corpus*, forbid bills of attainder and *ex post facto* laws, guarantee trial by jury, and strictly define treason and limit the way it can be tried and punished. I would certainly add to this list the last constitutional prohibition in Article Six that "no religious Test shall ever be required as a Qualification to any Office or public Trust under the United States."

I shall speak to you about the Bill of Rights only as it bears on powers of the Federal Government. Originally, the First Ten Amendments were not intended to apply to the States but, as the Supreme Court held in 1833 in *Barron* v. *Baltimore,* were adopted to quiet fears extensively entertained that the powers of the big new national government "might be exercised in a manner dangerous to liberty." I believe that by virtue of the Fourteenth Amendment, the First Ten Amendments are now applicable to the States, a view I stated in *Adamson* v. *California.* I adhere to that view. In this talk, however, I want to discuss only the extent to which the Bill of Rights limits the Federal Government.

In applying the Bill of Rights to the Federal Government there is today a sharp difference of views as to how far its provisions should be held to limit the law-making power of Congress. How this difference is finally resolved will, in my judgment, have far-reaching consequences upon our liberties. I shall first summarize what those different views are.

Some people regard the prohibitions of the Constitution, even its most unequivocal commands, as mere admonitions which Congress need not always observe. This viewpoint finds many different verbal expressions. For example, it is sometimes said that Congress may abridge a constitutional right if there is a clear and present danger that the free exercise of the right will bring about a substantive evil that Congress has authority to prevent. Or it is said that a right may be abridged where its exercise would cause so much injury to the public that this injury would outweigh the injury to the individual who is deprived of the right. Again, it is sometimes said that the Bill of Rights' guarantees must "compete" for survival against general powers expressly granted to Congress, and that the individual's right must, if outweighed by the public interest, be subordinated to the Government's competing interest in denying the right. All of these formulations, and more with which you are doubtless familiar, rest, at least in part, on the premise that there are no "absolute" prohibitions in the Constitution, and that all constitutional problems are questions of reasonableness, proximity, and degree. This view comes close to the English doctrine of legislative omnipotence, qualified only by the possibility of a judicial veto if the Supreme Court finds that a congressional choice between "competing" policies has no reasonable basis.

I cannot accept this approach to the Bill of Rights. It is my belief that there *are* "absolutes" in our Bill of Rights, and that they were put there on purpose by men who knew what words meant, and meant their prohibitions to be "absolutes." The whole history and background of the Constitution and Bill of Rights, as I understand it, belies the assumption or conclusion that our ultimate constitutional freedoms are no more than our English ancestors had when they came to this new land to get new freedoms. The historical and practical purposes of a Bill of Rights, the very use of a written constitution, indigenous to America, the language the Framers used, the kind of three-department government they took pains to set up, all point to the creation of a government which was denied all power to do some things under any and all circumstances, and all power to do other things except precisely in the manner prescribed. In this talk I will state some of the reasons why I hold this view. In doing so, however, I shall not attempt to discuss the wholly different and complex problem of the marginal scope of

each individual amendment as applied to the particular facts of
particular cases. For example, there is a question as to whether the
First Amendment was intended to protect speech that courts find
"obscene." I shall not stress this or similar differences of construction, nor shall I add anything to the views I expressed in the
recent case of *Smith* v. *California.* I am primarily discussing here
whether liberties *admittedly* covered by the Bill of Rights can
nevertheless be abridged on the ground that a superior public interest justifies the abridgment. I think the Bill of Rights made its
safeguards superior.

Today most Americans seem to have forgotten the ancient
evils which forced their ancestors to flee to this new country and
to form a government stripped of old powers used to oppress them.
But the Americans who supported the Revolution and the adoption
of our Constitution knew firsthand the dangers of tyrannical governments. They were familiar with the long existing practice of
English persecutions of people wholly because of their religious or
political beliefs. They knew that many accused of such offenses
had stood, helpless to defend themselves, before biased legislators
and judges.

John Lilburne, a Puritan dissenter, is a conspicuous example.
He found out the hard way that a citizen of England could not get
a court and jury trial under English law if Parliament wanted to
try and punish him in some kind of summary and unfair method of
its own. Time and time again, when his religious or political activities resulted in criminal charges against him, he had demanded jury
trials, under the "law of the land," but had been refused. Due to
"trials" either by Parliament, its legislative committees, or courts
subservient to the King or to Parliament, against all of which he
vigorously protested as contrary to "due process," or "the law of
the land," Lilburne had been whipped, put in the pillory, sent to
prison, heavily fined and banished from England, all its islands and
dominions, under penalty of death should he return. This last sentence was imposed by a simple Act of Parliament, without any
semblance of a trial. Upon his defiant return he was arrested and
subjected to an unfair trial for his life. His chief defense was that
the Parliamentary conviction was a nullity, as a denial of "due process of law," which he claimed was guaranteed under Magna Carta,
the 1628 Petition of Right, and statutes passed to carry them out.
He also challenged the power of Parliament to enact bills of attainder on the same grounds—due process of law. Lilburne repeatedly

and vehemently contended that he was entitled to notice, an indictment, and court trial by jury under the known laws of England; that he had a right to be represented by counsel; that he had a right to have witnesses summoned in his behalf and be confronted by the witnesses against him; that he could not be compelled to testify against himself. When Lilburne finally secured a jury it courageously acquitted him, after which the jury itself was severely punished by the Court.

Prompted largely by the desire to save Englishmen from such legislative mockeries of fair trials, Lilburne and others strongly advocated adoption of an "Agreement of the People" which contained most of the provisions of our present Bill of Rights. That Agreement would have done away with Parliamentary omnipotence. Lilburne pointed out that the basic defect of Magna Carta and statutes complementing it was that they were not binding on Parliament since "that which is done by one Parliament, as a Parliament, may be undone by the next Parliament; but an Agreement of the People begun and ended amongst the people can never come justly within the Parliament's cognizance to destroy." The proposed "Agreement of the People," Lilburne argued, could be changed only by the people and would bind Parliament as the supreme "law of the land." This same idea was picked up before the adoption of our Federal Constitution by Massachusetts and New Hampshire, which adopted their constitutions only after popular referendums. Our Federal Constitution is largely attributable to the same current of thinking.

Unfortunately, our own Colonial history also provided ample reasons for people to be afraid to vest too much power in the national government. There had been bills of attainder here; women had been convicted and sentenced to death as "witches"; Quakers, Baptists, and various Protestant sects had been persecuted from time to time. Roger Williams left Massachusetts to breathe the free air of new Rhode Island. Catholics were barred from holding office in many places. Test oaths were required in some of the Colonies to bar any but Christians from holding office. In New England Quakers suffered death for their faith. Baptists went to jail in Virginia for preaching, which caused Madison, while a very young man, to deplore what he called that "diabolical hell-conceived principle of persecution."

In the light of history, therefore, it is not surprising that, when our Constitution was adopted without specific provisions to safeguard cherished individual rights from invasion by the Legislative, as well as the Executive and Judicial Departments of the national government, a loud and irresistible clamor went up throughout the country. These protests were so strong that the Constitution was ratified by the very narrowest of votes in some of the States. It has been said, and I think correctly, that had there been no general agreement that a supplementary Bill of Rights would be adopted as soon as possible after Congress met, the Constitution would not have been ratified. It seems clear that this widespread demand for a Bill of Rights was due to a common fear of political and religious persecution should the national legislative power be left unrestrained as it was in England.

The form of government which was ordained and established in 1789 contains certain unique features which reflected the Framers' fear of arbitrary government and which clearly indicate an intention absolutely to limit what Congress could do. The first of these features is that our Constitution is written in a single document. Such constitutions are familiar today and it is not always remembered that our country was the first to have one. Certainly one purpose of a written constitution is to define and therefore more specifically limit government powers. An all-powerful government that can act as it pleases wants no such constitution—unless to fool the people. England had no written constitution and this once proved a source of tyranny, as our ancestors well knew. Jefferson said about this departure from the English type of Government: "Our peculiar security is in the possession of a written Constitution. Let us not make it a blank paper by construction."

A second unique feature of our Government is a Constitution supreme over the Legislature. In England, statutes, Magna Carta, and later declarations of rights had for centuries limited the power of the King, but they did not limit the power of Parliament. Although commonly referred to as a constitution, they were never the "supreme law of the land" in the way in which our Constitution is, much to the regret of statesmen like Pitt the elder. Parliament could change this English "Constitution"; Congress cannot change ours. Ours can only be changed by amendments ratified by three-fourths of the States. It was one of the great achievements of our Constitution that it ended legislative omnipotence here and placed all departments and agencies of government under one supreme law.

A third feature of our Government, expressly designed to

limit its powers, was the division of authority into three co-ordinate branches, none of which was to have supremacy over the others. This separation of powers with the checks and balances which each branch was given over the others was designed to prevent any branch, including the legislative, from infringing individual liberties safeguarded by the Constitution.

Finally, our Constitution was the first to provide a really independent judiciary. Moreover, as the Supreme Court held in *Marbury* v. *Madison*, correctly, I believe, this judiciary has the power to hold legislative enactments void that are repugnant to the Constitution and the Bill of Rights. In this country the judiciary was made independent because it has, I believe, the primary responsibility and duty of giving force and effect to constitutional liberties and limitations upon the executive and legislative branches. Judges in England were not always independent and they could not hold parliamentary acts void. Consequently, English courts could not be counted on to protect the liberties of the people against invasion by the Parliament, as many unfortunate Englishmen found out, such as Sir Walter Raleigh, who was executed as the result of an unfair trial, and a lawyer named William Prynne, whose ears were first cut off by court order and who subsequently, by another court order, had his remaining ear stumps gouged out while he was on a pillory. Prynne's offenses were writing books and pamphlets.

All of the unique features of our Constitution show an underlying purpose to create a new kind of limited government. Central to all of the Framers of the Bill of Rights was the idea that since government, particularly the national government newly created, is a powerful institution, its officials—all of them—must be compelled to exercise their powers within strictly defined boundaries. As Madison told Congress, the Bill of Rights' limitations point "sometimes against the abuse of the Executive power, sometimes against the Legislative, and in some cases against the community itself; or, in other words, against the majority in favor of the minority." Madison also explained that his proposed amendments were intended "to limit and qualify the powers of Government, by excepting out of the grant of power those cases in which the Government ought not to act, or to act only in a particular mode." In the light of this purpose, let us now turn to the language of the First Ten Amendments to consider whether their provisions were written as mere admonitions to Congress or as absolute commands, proceeding for convenience from the last to the first.

The last two Amendments, the Ninth and Tenth, are general in character, but both emphasize the limited nature of the Federal Government. Number Ten restricts federal power to what the Constitution delegates to the central government, reserving all other powers to the States or to the people. Number Nine attempts to make certain that enumeration of some rights must "not be construed to deny or disparage others retained by the people." The use of the words, "the people," in both these Amendments strongly emphasizes the desire of the Framers to protect individual liberty.

The Seventh Amendment states that "In suits at common law, where the value in controversy shall exceed twenty-dollars, the right of trial by jury shall be preserved . . ." This language clearly requires that jury trials must be afforded in the type of cases the Amendment describes. The Amendment goes on in equally unequivocal words to command that "no fact tried by a jury, shall be otherwise re-examined in any Court of the United States, than according to the rules of the common law."

Amendments Five, Six, and Eight relate chiefly to the procedures that government must follow when bringing its powers to bear against any person with a view to depriving him of his life, liberty, or property.

The Eighth Amendment forbids "excessive bail," "excessive fines," or the infliction of "cruel or unusual punishments." This is one of the less precise provisions. The courts are required to determine the meaning of such general terms as "excessive" and "unusual." But surely that does not mean that admittedly "excessive bail," "excessive fines," or "cruel punishments" could be justified on the ground of a "competing" public interest in carrying out some generally granted power like that given Congress to regulate commerce.

Amendment Six provides that in a criminal prosecution an accused shall have a "speedy and public trial, by an impartial jury of the State and district wherein the crime shall have been committed, which district shall have been previously ascertained by law, and to be informed of the nature and cause of the accusation; to be confronted with the witnesses against him; to have compulsory process for obtaining witnesses in his favor, and have the Assistance of Counsel for his defense." All of these requirements are cast in terms both definite and absolute. Trial by jury was also guaranteed in the original constitution. The additions here, doubtless prompted by English trials of Americans away from their homes, are that a trial must be "speedy and public," "by an impartial jury," and in a district which "shall have been previously ascertained by law." If there is any one thing that is certain, it is that the Framers intended both in the original Constitution and in the Sixth Amendment that persons charged with crime by the Federal Government have a right to be tried by jury. Suppose juries began acquitting people Congress thought should be convicted. Could Congress then provide some other form of trial, say by an administrative agency, or the military, where convictions could be more readily and certainly obtained, if it thought the safety of the nation so required? How about secret trials? By *partial* juries? Can it be that these are not absolute prohibitions?

The Sixth Amendment requires notice of the cause of an accusation, confrontation by witnesses, compulsory process, and assistance of counsel. The experience of centuries has demonstrated the value of these procedures to one on trial for crime. And this Amendment purports to guarantee them by clear language. But if there are no absolutes in the Bill of Rights, these guarantees too can be taken away by Congress on findings that a competing public interest requires that defendants be tried without notice, without witnesses, without confrontation, and without counsel.

The Fifth Amendment provides:

No person shall be held to answer for a capital, or otherwise infamous crime, unless on a presentment or indictment of a Grand Jury, except in cases arising in the land or naval forces, or in the Militia, when in actual service in time of War or public danger; nor shall any person be subject for the same offence to be twice put in jeopardy of life or limb; nor shall be compelled in any criminal case to be a witness against himself, nor be deprived of life, liberty, or property, without due process of law; nor shall private property be taken for public use, without just compensation.

Most of these Fifth Amendment prohibitions are both definite and unequivocal. There has been much controversy about the meaning of "due process of law." Whatever its meaning, however, there can be no doubt that it must be granted. Moreover, few doubt that it has an historical meaning which denies Government the right to take away life, liberty, or property without trials properly conducted according to the Constitution and laws validly made in accordance with it. This, at least, was the meaning of "due process of law" when used in Magna Carta and other old English Statutes where it was referred to as "the law of the land."

The Fourth Amendment provides:

> The right of the people to be secure in their persons, houses, papers, and effects, against unreasonable searches and seizures, shall not be violated, and no Warrants shall issue, but upon probable cause, supported by Oath or affirmation, and particularly describing the place to be searched, and the persons or things to be seized.

The use of the word "unreasonable" in this Amendment means, of course, that not *all* searches and seizures are prohibited. Only those which are unreasonable are unlawful. There may be much difference of opinion about whether a particular search or seizure is unreasonable and therefore forbidden by this Amendment. But if it *is* unreasonable, it is absolutely prohibited.

Likewise, the provision which forbids warrants for arrest, search, or seizure without "probable cause" is itself an absolute prohibition.

The Third Amendment provides that:

> No Soldier shall in time of peace be quartered in any house, without the consent of the owner, nor in time of war, but in a manner to be prescribed by law.

Americans had recently suffered from the quartering of British troops in their homes, and so this Amendment is written in language that apparently no one has ever thought could be violated on the basis of an overweighing public interest.

Amendment Two provides that:

> A well regulated militia, being necessary to the security of a free State, the right of the people to keep and bear Arms, shall not be infringed.

Although the Supreme Court has held this Amendment to include only arms necessary to a well-regulated militia, as so construed, its prohibition is absolute.

This brings us to the First Amendment. It reads:

> Congress shall make no law respecting an establishment of religion, or prohibiting the free exercise thereof; or abridging the freedom of speech, or of the press; or the right of the people peaceably to assemble, and to petition the Government for a redress of grievances.

The phrase, "Congress shall make no law" is composed of plain words, easily understood. The Framers knew this. The language used by Madison in his proposal was different, but no less emphatic and unequivocal. That proposal is worth reading:

> The civil rights of none shall be abridged on account of religious belief or worship, nor shall any national religion be established, nor shall the full and equal rights of conscience be in any manner, or on any pretext, infringed.
>
> The people shall not be deprived or abridged of their right to speak, to write, or to publish their sentiments; and the freedom of the press, as one of the great bulwarks of liberty, shall be inviolable.
>
> The people shall not be restrained from peaceably assembling and consulting for their common good; nor from applying to the Legislature by petitions, or remonstrances, for redress of their grievances.

Neither as offered nor as adopted is the language of this Amendment anything less than absolute. Madison was emphatic about this. He told the Congress that under it, "The right of freedom of speech is secured; the liberty of the press is expressly declared to be *beyond the reach of this Government* . . ." (Emphasis supplied in all quotations.) Some years later Madison wrote that "it would seem scarcely possible to doubt that *no power whatever* over the press was supposed to be delegated by the Constitution, as it originally stood, and that the amendment was intended as a *positive and absolute reservation of it*." With reference to the positive nature of the First Amendment's command against infringement of religious liberty, Madison later said that "there is not a shadow of right in the general government to intermeddle with religion," and that "this subject is, for the honor of America, perfectly free and unshackled. The *government has no jurisdiction over it*."

To my way of thinking, at least, the history and language of the Constitution and the Bill of Rights, which I have discussed with you, make it plain that one of the primary purposes of the Constitution with its amendments was to withdraw from the Government all power to act in certain areas—whatever the scope of those areas may be. If I am right in this, then there is, at least in those areas, no justification whatever for "balancing" a particular right against some expressly granted power of Congress. If the Constitution withdraws from Government all power over subject matter in an area, such as religion, speech, press, assembly, and petition, there is nothing over which authority may be exerted.

The Framers were well aware that the individual rights they sought to protect might be easily nullified if subordinated to the general powers granted to Congress. One of the reasons for adoption of the Bill of Rights was to prevent just that. Specifically the people feared that the Necessary and Proper Clause could be used to project the generally granted congressional powers into the protected areas of individual rights. One need only read the debates in the various States to find out that this is true. But if these debates leave any doubt, Mr. Madison's words to Congress should remove it. In speaking of the Necessary and Proper Clause and its possible effect on freedom of religion, he said, as reported in the Annals of Congress:

> Whether the words are necessary or not, he did not mean to say, but they had been required by some of the State Conventions, who seemed to entertain an opinion that under the clause of the Constitution, which gave power to Congress to make all laws *necessary and proper* to carry into execution the Constitution, and the laws made under it, enabled them to make laws of such a nature as might infringe the rights of conscience, and establish a national religion; to prevent these effects he presumed the amendment was intended, and he thought it as well expressed as the nature of the language would admit.

It seems obvious to me that Congress, in exercising its general powers, is expressly forbidden to use means prohibited by the Bill of Rights. Whatever else the phrase "necessary and proper" may mean, it must be that Congress may only adopt such means to carry out its powers as are "proper," that is, not specifically prohibited.

It has also been argued that since freedom of speech, press, and religion in England were narrow freedoms at best, and since there were many English laws infringing those freedoms, our First Amendment should not be thought to bar similar infringements by Congress. Again one needs only to look to the debates in Congress over the First Amendment to find that the First Amendment cannot be treated as a mere codification of English law. Mr. Madison made a clear explanation to Congress that it was the purpose of the First Amendment to grant greater protection than England afforded its citizens. He said:

> In the declaration of rights which that country has established, the truth is, they have gone no farther than to raise a barrier against

the power of the Crown; the power of the Legislature is left altogether indefinite. Although I know whenever the great rights, the trial by jury, freedom of the press, or liberty of conscience, came in question in that body, invasion of them is resisted by able advocates, yet their Magna Carta does not contain any one provision for the security of those rights, respecting which the people of America are most alarmed. The freedom of the press and rights of conscience, those choicest privileges of the people, are unguarded in the British Constitution.

But although the case may be widely different, and it may not be thought necessary to provide limits for the legislative power in that country, yet a different opinion prevails in the United States.

It was the desire to give the people of America greater protection against the powerful Federal Government than the English had had against their government that caused the Framers to put these freedoms of expression, again in the words of Madison, "beyond the reach of this Government."

When closely analyzed, the idea that there can be no "absolute" constitutional guarantees in the Bill of Rights is frightening to contemplate even as to individual safeguards in the original Constitution. Take, for instance, the last clause in Article Six that "no religious Test shall ever be required" for a person to hold office in the United States. Suppose Congress should find that some religious sect was dangerous because of its foreign affiliations. Such was the belief on which English test oaths rested for a long time and some of the States had test oaths on that assumption at the time, and after, our Constitution was adopted in 1789. Could Congress, or the Supreme Court, or both, put this precious privilege to be free from test oaths on scales, find it outweighed by some other public interest, and therefore make United States officials and employees swear they did not and never had belonged to or associated with a particular religious group suspected of disloyalty? Can Congress, in the name of over-balancing necessity, suspend *habeas corpus* in peacetime? Are there circumstances under which Congress could, after nothing more than a legislative bill of attainder, take away a man's life, liberty, or property? Hostility of the Framers toward bills of attainder was so great that they took the unusual step of barring such legislative punishments by the States as well as the Federal Government. They wanted to remove any possibility of such proceedings anywhere in this country. This is not strange in view of

the fact that they were much closer than we are to the great Act of
Attainder by the Irish Parliament, in 1688, which condemned between two and three thousand men, women, and children to exile
or death without anything that even resembled a trial.

Perhaps I can show you the consequences of the balancing
approach to the Bill of Rights liberties by a practical demonstration
of how it might work. The last clause of the Fifth Amendment is:
"nor shall private property be taken for public use, without just
compensation." On its face this command looks absolute, but if one
believes that it should be weighed against the powers granted to
Congress, there might be some circumstances in which this right
would have to give way, just as there are some circumstances in
which it is said the right of freedom of religion, speech, press, assembly, and petition can be balanced away. Let us see how the
balancing concept would apply to the just compensation provision
of the Bill of Rights in the following wholly imaginary judicial
opinion of Judge X:

> This case presents an important question of constitutional law.
> The United States is engaged in a stupendous national defense un-
> dertaking which requires the acquisition of much valuable land
> throughout the country. The plaintiff here owns 500 acres of land.
> The location of the land gives it a peculiarly strategic value for
> carrying out the defense program. Due to the great national
> emergency that exists, Congress concluded that the United States
> could not afford at this time to pay compensation for the lands
> which it needed to acquire. For this reason an Act was passed au-
> thorizing seizure without compensation of all the lands required
> for the defense establishment.
>
> In reaching a judgment on this case, I cannot shut my eyes to
> the fact that the United States is in a desperate condition at this
> time. Nor can I, under established canons of constitutional con-
> struction, invalidate a Congressional enactment if there are any
> rational grounds upon which Congress could have passed it. I
> think there are such grounds here. Highly important among the
> powers granted Congress by the Constitution are the powers to
> declare war, maintain a navy, and raise and support armies. This,
> of course, means the power to conduct war successfully. To make
> sure that Congress is not unduly restricted in the exercise of these
> constitutional powers, the Constitution also gives Congress power
> to make all laws "necessary and proper to carry into execution
> the foregoing powers . . ." This necessary and proper clause ap-
> plies to the powers to make war and support armies as it does to
> all the other granted powers.

Plaintiff contends, however, that the Fifth Amendment's provision about compensation is so absolute a command that Congress is wholly without authority to violate it, however great this nation's emergency and peril may be. I must reject this contention. We must never forget that it is a constitution we are expounding. And a constitution, unlike ordinary statutes, must endure for ages; it must be adapted to changing conditions and the needs of changing communities. Without such capacity for change, our Constitution would soon be outmoded and become a dead letter. Therefore its words must never be read as rigid absolutes. The Bill of Rights' commands, no more than any others, can stay the hands of Congress from doing that which the general welfare imperatively demands. When two great constitutional provisions like these conflict—as here the power to make war conflicts with the requirements for just compensation—it becomes the duty of courts to weigh the constitutional right of an individual to compensation against the power of Congress to wage a successful war.

While the question is not without doubt, I have no hesitation in finding the challenged Congressional Act valid. Driven by the absolute necessity to protect the nation from foreign aggression, the national debt has risen to billions of dollars. The Government's credit is such that interest rates have soared. Under these circumstances, Congress was rationally entitled to find that if it paid for all the lands it needs it might bankrupt the nation and render it helpless in its hour of greatest need. Weighing as I must the loss the individual will suffer because he has to surrender his land to the nation without compensation against the great public interest in conducting war, I hold the Act valid. A decree will be entered accordingly.

Of course, I would not decide this case this way nor do I think any other judge would so decide it today. My reason for refusing this approach would be that I think the Fifth Amendment's command is absolute and not to be overcome without constitutional amendment even in times of grave emergency. But I think this wholly fictitious opinion fairly illustrates the possibilities of the balancing approach, not only as to the Just Compensation Clause, but as to other provisions of the Bill of Rights as well. The great danger of the judiciary balancing process is that in times of emergency and stress it gives Government the power to do what it thinks necessary to protect itself, regardless of the rights of individuals. If the need is great, the right of Government can always be said to outweigh the rights of the individual. If "balancing" is accepted as the test, it would be hard for any conscientious judge to hold otherwise in times of dire need. And laws adopted in times of dire need are often very hasty and oppressive laws, especially when, as often happens, they are carried over and accepted as normal. Furthermore, the balancing approach to basic individual liberties assumes to legislators and judges more power than either the Framers or I myself believe should be entrusted, without limitation, to any man or any group of men.

It seems to me that the "balancing" approach also disregards all of the unique features of our Constitution which I described earlier. In reality this approach returns us to the state of legislative supremacy which existed in England and which the Framers were so determined to change once and for all. On the one hand, it denies the judiciary its constitutional power to measure acts of Congress by the standards set down in the Bill of Rights. On the other hand, though apparently reducing judicial powers by saying that acts of Congress may be held unconstitutional only when they are found to have no rational legislative basis, this approach really gives the Court, along with Congress, a greater power, that of overriding the plain commands of the Bill of Rights on a finding of weighty public interest. In effect, it changes the direction of our form of government from a government of limited powers to a government in which Congress may do anything that Courts believe to be "reasonable."

Of course, the decision to provide a constitutional safeguard for a particular right, such as the fair trial requirements of the Fifth and Sixth Amendments and the right of free speech protection of the First, involves a balancing of conflicting interests. Strict procedures may release guilty men; protecting speech and press may involve dangers to a particular government. I believe, however, that the Framers themselves did this balancing when they wrote the Constitution and the Bill of Rights. They appreciated the risks involved and they decided that certain rights should be guaranteed regardless of these risks. Courts have neither the right nor the power to review this original decision of the Framers and to attempt to make a different evaluation of the importance of the rights granted in the Constitution. Where conflicting values exist in the field of individual liberties protected by the Constitution, that document settles the conflict, and its policy should not be changed without constitutional amendments by the people in the manner provided by the people.

Misuse of government power, particularly in times of stress, has brought suffering to humanity in all ages about which we have authentic history. Some of the world's noblest and finest men have suffered ignominy and death for no crime—unless unorthodoxy is a crime. Even enlightened Athens had its victims such as Socrates. Because of the same kind of bigotry, Jesus, the great Dissenter, was put to death on a wooden cross. The flames of inquisitions all over the world have warned that men endowed with unlimited government power, even earnest men, consecrated to a cause, are dangerous.

For my own part, I believe that our Constitution, with its absolute guarantees of individual rights, is the best hope for the aspirations of freedom which men share everywhere. I cannot agree with those who think of the Bill of Rights as an Eighteenth Century strait jacket, unsuited for this age. It is old but not all old things are bad. The evils it guards against are not only old, they are with us now, they exist today. Almost any morning you open your daily paper you can see where some person somewhere in the world is on trial or has just been convicted of supposed disloyalty to a new group controlling the government which has set out to purge its suspected enemies and all those who had dared to be against its successful march to power. Nearly always you see that these political heretics are being tried by military tribunals or some other summary and sure method for disposition of the accused. Now and then we even see the convicted victims as they march to their execution.

Experience all over the world has demonstrated, I fear, that the distance between stable, orderly government and one that has been taken over by force is not so great as we have assumed. Our own free system to live and progress has to have intelligent citizens, citizens who cannot only think and speak and write to influence people, but citizens who are free to do that without fear of governmental censorship or reprisal.

The provisions of the Bill of Rights that safeguard fair legal procedures came about largely to protect the weak and the oppressed from punishment by the strong and the powerful who wanted to stifle the voices of discontent raised in protest against oppression and injustice in public affairs. Nothing that I have read in the congressional debates on the Bill of Rights indicates that there was any belief that the First Amendment contained any qualifications. The only arguments that tended to look in this direction at all were those that said "that all paper barriers against the power of the Community are too weak to be worthy of attention." Suggestions were also made in and out of Congress that a Bill of Rights would be a futile gesture since there would be no way to enforce the safeguards for freedom it provided. Mr. Madison answered this argument in these words:

> If they [the Bill of Rights Amendments] are incorporated into the Constitution, independent tribunals of justice will consider themselves in a peculiar manner the guardians of those rights; they will be an impenetrable bulwark against any assumption of power in the Legislative or Executive; they will be naturally led to resist every encroachment upon rights expressly stipulated for in the Constitution by the declaration of rights.

I fail to see how courts can escape this sacred trust.

Since the earliest days, philosophers have dreamed of a country where the mind and spirit of man would be free; where there would be no limits to inquiry; where men would be free to explore the unknown and to challenge the most deeply rooted beliefs and principles. Our First Amendment was a bold effort to adopt this principle—to establish a country with no legal restrictions of any kind upon the subjects people could investigate, discuss, and deny. The Framers knew, better perhaps than we do today, the risks they were taking. They knew that free speech might be the friend of change and revolution. But they also knew that it is always the deadliest enemy of tyranny. With this knowledge they still believed that the ultimate happiness and security of a nation lies in its ability to explore, to change, to grow and ceaselessly to adapt itself to new knowledge born of inquiry free from any kind of governmental control over the mind and spirit of man. Loyalty comes from love of good government, not fear of a bad one.

The First Amendment is truly the heart of the Bill of Rights. The Framers balanced its freedoms of religion, speech, press, assembly, and petition against the needs of a powerful central government, and decided that in those freedoms lies this nation's only true security. They were not afraid for men to be free. We should not be. We should be as confident as Jefferson was when he said in his First Inaugural Address:

> . . . If there be any among us who would wish to dissolve this Union or to change its republican form, let them stand undisturbed as monuments of the safety with which error of opinion may be tolerated where reason is left free to combat it. . . .

III

Mr. Justice Black
and the Bill of Rights

A Selection from His Opinions

Johnson v. Zerbst

304 U.S. 458

Decided May 23, 1938

For a new member of the Supreme Court, Justice Black was extremely busy in his first term from October 1937 to June 1938. The Court was shorthanded during much of the term owing to Justice Cardozo's illness and Justice Reed's appointment in January, after many cases had been argued. Justice Black wrote fifteen majority opinions, three concurring opinions, and nine dissenting opinions, for a total of twenty-seven, nearly one opinion a week. Several of them were outstanding pieces of work for a newcomer to the bench, as, for example, the one-man dissent to the per curiam *decision in* McCart et al. v. Indianapolis Water Co. *In this opinion, Justice Black boldly and painstakingly defended the right of the State of Indiana to regulate the price of water in Indianapolis "free from interference by federal courts."*

Justice Black's first notable opinion in the field of the Bill of Rights was John A. Johnson v. Fred G. Zerbst, Warden, *which was handed down near the end of this term. Speaking for himself and four other members of the Supreme Court—Chief Justice Hughes and Justices Brandeis, Stone, and Roberts—the junior Justice came to the aid of two men who had little education, no funds, and were without friends in Charleston, South Carolina, where they were arrested and charged with the federal crime of counterfeiting. The record of their prosecution showed the scantest respect for the Sixth Amendment's guarantee of the right to assistance of counsel, and an outright denial by the District Court of their right to writs of* habeas corpus *after being convicted and imprisoned without the safeguard of defense counsel to protect their rights as defendants. The latter was the immediate issue.*

The Black opinion reversed the Federal Court of Appeals and sent the case back to this District Court for a clear-cut determination as to habeas corpus *on the basis of the facts involved. Justice Reed concurred in the reversal; Justices McReynolds and Butler supported the judgment of the court below; and Justice Cardozo did not take part. This majority opinion by Justice Black strongly suggested how he would thereafter direct himself in civil liberties tests arising from the Bill of Rights.*

MR. JUSTICE BLACK *delivered the opinion of the Court*

Petitioner, while imprisoned in a federal penitentiary, was denied *habeas corpus* by the District Court. . . . It appears from the opinion of the District Judge denying *habeas corpus* that he believed petitioner was deprived, in the trial court, of his constitutional right under the provision of the Sixth Amendment that "In all criminal prosecutions, the accused shall enjoy the right . . . to have the Assistance of Counsel for his defence." However, he held that proceedings depriving petitioner of his constitutional right to assistance of counsel were not sufficient "to make the trial void and justify its annulment in a *habeas corpus* proceeding, but that they constituted trial errors or irregularities which could only be corrected on appeal." . . .

The record discloses that:

Petitioner and one Bridwell were arrested in Charleston, South Carolina, November 21, 1934, charged with feloniously uttering and passing four counterfeit twenty-dollar Federal Reserve notes and possessing twenty-one such notes. Both were then enlisted men in the United States Marine Corps, on leave. They were bound over to await action of the United States Grand Jury, but were kept in jail due to inability to give bail. January 21, 1935, they were indicted; January 23, 1935, they were taken to court and there first given notice of the indictment; immediately were arraigned, tried, convicted, and sentenced that day to four and one-half years in the penitentiary; and January 25, were transported to the Federal Penitentiary in Atlanta. While counsel had represented them in the preliminary hearings before the commissioner in which they—some two months before their trial—were bound over to the Grand Jury, the accused were unable to employ counsel for their trial. Upon arraignment, both pleaded not guilty, said that they had no lawyer, and—in response to an inquiry of the court—stated that they were ready for trial. They were then tried, convicted, and sentenced, without assistance of counsel. . . .

Reviewing the evidence on the petition for *habeas corpus*, the District Court said that, after trial, petitioner and Johnson [Bridwell?] ". . . were remanded to jail, where they asked the jailer to call a lawyer for them, but were not permitted to contact one. They did not however, undertake to get any message to the judge. . . ."

. . . Omitted from the Constitution as originally adopted, provisions of this [Sixth Amendment] and other Amendments were submitted by the first Congress convened under that Constitution as essential barriers against arbitrary or unjust deprivation of human rights. The Sixth Amendment stands as a constant admonition that if the constitutional safeguards it provides be lost, justice will not "still be done." It embodies a realistic recognition of the obvious truth that the average defendant does not have the professional skill to protect himself when brought before a tribunal with power to take his life or liberty, wherein the prosecution is presented by experienced and learned counsel. That which is simple, orderly, and necessary to the lawyer—to the untrained layman—may appear intricate, complex, and mysterious. . . .

The purpose of the constitutional guaranty of a right to counsel is to protect an accused from conviction resulting from his own ignorance of his legal and constitutional rights, and the guaranty would be nullified by a determination that an accused's ignorant failure to claim his rights removes the protection of the Constitution. . . .

Petitioner, convicted and sentenced without the assistance of counsel, contends that he was ignorant of his right to counsel, and incapable of preserving his legal and constitutional rights during trial. Urging that—after conviction—he was unable to obtain a lawyer; was ignorant of the proceedings to obtain new trial or appeal and the time limits governing both; and that he did not possess the requisite skill or knowledge properly to conduct an appeal, he says that it was—as a practical matter—impossible for him to obtain relief by appeal. If these contentions be true in fact, it necessarily follows that no legal procedural remedy is available to grant relief for a violation of constitutional rights, unless the courts

protect petitioner's rights by *habeas corpus*. Of the contention that
the law provides no effective remedy for such a deprivation of
rights affecting life and liberty, it may well be said—as in *Mooney*
v. *Holohan*—that it "falls with the premise." To deprive a citizen
of his only effective remedy would not only be contrary to the
"rudimentary demands of justice" but destructive of a constitutional guaranty specifically designed to prevent injustice.

Since the Sixth Amendment constitutionally entitles one
charged with crime to the assistance of counsel, compliance with
this constitutional mandate is an essential jurisdictional prerequisite
to a Federal court's authority to deprive an accused of his life or
liberty. When this right is properly waived, the assistance of
counsel is no longer a necessary element of the court's jurisdiction to
proceed to conviction and sentence. If the accused, however, is not
represented by counsel and has not competently and intelligently
waived his constitutional right, the Sixth Amendment stands as a
jurisdictional bar to a valid conviction and sentence depriving him
of his life or his liberty. A court's jurisdiction at the beginning of
trial may be lost "in the course of the proceedings" due to failure to
complete the court—as the Sixth Amendment requires—by providing counsel for an accused who is unable to obtain counsel, who
has not intelligently waived this constitutional guaranty, and whose
life or liberty is at stake. If this requirement of the Sixth Amendment
is not complied with, the court no longer has jurisdiction to proceed. The judgment of conviction pronounced by a court without
jurisdiction is void, and one imprisoned thereunder may obtain release by *habeas corpus*. . . .

. . . Where a defendant, without counsel, acquiesces in a trial
resulting in his conviction and later seeks release by the extraordinary remedy of *habeas corpus*, the burden of proof rests upon him
to establish that he did not competently and intelligently waive his
constitutional right to assistance of counsel. If in a *habeas corpus*
hearing, he does meet this burden and convinces the court by a
preponderance of evidence that he neither had counsel nor properly
waived his constitutional right to counsel, it is the duty of the court
to grant the writ. . . .

. . . In this state of the record we deem it necessary to remand the cause. If—on remand—the District Court finds from all
of the evidence that petitioner has sustained the burden of proof
resting upon him and that he did not competently and intelligently
waive his right to counsel, it will follow that the trial court did not

have jurisdiction to proceed to judgment and conviction of petitioner, and he will therefore be entitled to have his petition granted. If petitioner fails to sustain this burden, he is not entitled to the writ.

The cause is reversed and remanded to the District Court for action in harmony with this opinion.

Reversed.

Pierre v. Louisiana

306 U.S. 354

Decided February 27, 1939

From almost the outset of his career on the Supreme Court, Justice Black became a stalwart protector of the trial rights of citizens who suffer handicaps in criminal proceedings because of the color of their skin. In the case of Hugh Pierre v. *State of Louisiana, Justice Black gave the unanimous opinion that reversed a murder conviction, because Negroes had been systematically excluded from jury service. With his colleagues—now Chief Justice Hughes and Justices McReynolds, Butler, Stone, Roberts, Reed, and Frankfurter —Justice Black found that the Louisana courts had acted unconstitutionally in approving a local practice of selecting only white persons to serve on juries. The opinion shows the care Justice Black took in demonstrating the unfairness to a defendant, accused of a grave crime, of a jury system that applied racial discrimination.*

MR. JUSTICE BLACK delivered the opinion of the Court

Indicted for murder, petitioner, a member of the Negro race, was convicted and sentenced to death in a State court of the Parish of St. John the Baptist, Louisiana. The Louisiana Supreme Court affirmed. His petition for *certiorari* to review the Louisiana Supreme Court's judgment rested upon the grave claim—earnestly, but unsuccessfully urged in both State courts—that because of his race he had not been accorded the equal protection of the laws guaranteed to all races in all the States by the Fourteenth Amendment to the Federal Constitution. For this reason, we granted *certiorari*.

The indictment against petitioner was returned January 18, 1937. He made timely motion to quash the indictment and the general *venire* from which had been drawn both the grand jury that returned the indictment and the petit jury for the week of his trial. His motion also prayed that the grand jury panel and the petit jury panel be quashed. This sworn motion alleged that petitioner was a Negro and had been indicted for murder of a white man; that at least one third of the population of the Parish from which the grand and petit juries were drawn were members of the Negro race, but the general *venire* had contained no names of Negroes when the grand jury that indicted petitioner was drawn; that the State officers charged by law with the duty of providing names for the general *venire* had "deliberately excluded therefrom the names of any Negroes qualified to serve as Grand or Petit Jurors . . ." and had "systematically, unlawfully and unconstitutionally excluded Negroes from the Grand or Petit Jury in said Parish" for at least twenty years "solely and only because of their race and color"; and that petitioner had thus been denied the equal protection of the laws guaranteed him by the Constitution of Louisiana and the Fourteenth Amendment to the Constitution of the United States.

No pleadings denying these allegations appear in the record, and the State offered no witnesses on the motion. Petitioner offered twelve witnesses who were questioned by his counsel, the State's Assistant District Attorney, and the court. On the basis of this evidence, the trial judge sustained the motion to quash the petit jury panel and *venire* and subsequently ordered the box containing the general *venire* (from which both grand and petit juries had been drawn) emptied, purged, and refilled. This was done; a new petit jury panel composed of both whites and Negroes was subsequently drawn from the refilled jury box and from this panel a petit jury was selected which tried and convicted petitioner. Although the grand jury that indicted petitioner and the quashed petit jury panel had been selected from the same original general *venire* the trial judge overruled that part of petitioner's motion seeking to quash the grand jury panel and the indictment. . . .

. . . Petitioner does not here contend that Louisiana laws required an unconstitutional exclusion of Negroes from the grand jury which indicted him. His evidence was offered to show that

Louisiana—acting through its administrative officers—had deliberately and systematically excluded Negroes from jury service because of race, in violation of the laws and Constitutions of Louisiana and the United States.

If petitioner's evidence of such systematic exclusion of Negroes from the general *venire* was sufficient to support the trial court's action in quashing the petit jury drawn from that general *venire*, it necessarily follows that the indictment returned by a grand jury, selected from the same general *venire*, should also have been quashed.

But the State insists, and the Louisiana Supreme Court held (the Chief Justice dissenting), that this evidence failed to establish that members of the Negro race were excluded from the grand jury *venire* on account of race, and that the trial court's finding of discrimination was erroneous. Our decision and judgment must therefore turn upon these disputed questions of fact.

In our consideration of the facts the conclusions reached by the Supreme Court of Louisiana are entitled to great respect. Yet, when a claim is properly asserted—as in this case—that a citizen whose life is at stake has been denied the equal protection of his country's laws on account of his race, it becomes our solemn duty to make independent inquiry and determination of the disputed facts—for equal protection to all is the basic principle upon which justice under law rests. Indictment by grand jury and trial by jury cease to harmonize with our traditional concepts of justice at the very moment particular groups, classes, or races—otherwise qualified to serve as jurors in a community—are excluded as such from jury service. The Fourteenth Amendment intrusts those who because of race are denied equal protection of the laws in a State first "to the revisory power of the higher courts of the State, and ultimately to the review of this court."

Petitioner's witnesses on the motion were the clerk of the court—ex-officio a member of the Jury Commission; the sheriff of the Parish; the superintendent of schools, who had served the Parish for eleven years; and other residents of the Parish, both white and colored. The testimony of petitioner's witnesses (the State offered no witnesses) showed that from 1896 to 1936 no Negro had served on the grand or petit juries in the Parish; that a *venire* of three hundred in December 1936, contained the names of three Negroes, one of whom was then dead, one of whom (D. N. Din-

baut) was listed on the *venire* as F. N. Dinfant; the third—called
for petit jury service in January 1937—was the only Negro who
had ever been called for jury service within the memory of the
clerk of the court, the sheriff, or any other witnesses who testified;
and that there were many Negro citizens of the Parish qualified
under the laws of Louisiana to serve as grand or petit jurors. According to the testimony, Negroes constituted 25 to 50 percent of
a total Parish population of twelve to fifteen thousand. The report
of the United States Department of Commerce, Bureau of the
Census, for 1930, shows that the total Parish population was fourteen thousand and seventy-eight, 49.7 percent native white, and
49.3 percent Negro. In a total Negro population (ten years old
and over) of five thousand two hundred and ninety, 29.9 percent
were classified by the census as illiterate.

The Louisiana Supreme Court found—contrary to the trial
judge—that Negroes had not been excluded from jury service on
account of race, but that their exclusion was the result of a *bona
fide* compliance by the Jury Commission with State laws prescribing jury qualifications. With this conclusion we cannot agree.
Louisiana law requires the commissioners to select names for the
general *venire* from persons qualified to serve without distinction
as to race or color. In order to be qualified a person must be:

(a) A citizen of the State, over twenty-one years of age with
two years' residence in the Parish,

(b) Able to read and write the English language,

(c) Not charged with any offense or convicted of a felony,

(d) Of well known good character and standing in the community.

The fact that approximately one-half of the Parish's population were Negroes demonstrates that there could have been no lack
of colored residents over twenty-one years of age.

It appears from the 1930 census that 70 percent of the Negro
population of the Parish was literate, and the county superintendent
of schools testified that fully two thousand five hundred (83 percent) of the Parish's Negro population, estimated by him at only
three thousand, were able to read and write. Petitioner's evidence
established beyond question that the majority of the Negro population could read and write, and, in this respect, were eligible under
the statute for selection as jurymen.

There is no evidence on which even an inference can be based that any appreciable number of the otherwise qualified Negroes in the Parish were disqualified for selection because of bad character or criminal records.

We conclude that the exclusion of Negroes from jury service was not due to their failure to possess the statutory qualifications.

The general *venire* box for the Parish in which petitioner was tried was required—under Louisiana law—to contain a list of three hundred names selected by Jury Commissioners appointed by the District Judge, and this list had to be supplemented from time to time so as to maintain the required three hundred names. Although petit jurors are drawn from the general *venire* box after the names have been well mixed, the law provides that "the commission shall *select* . . . [from the general *venire* list] the names of twenty citizens, possessing the qualifications of grand jurors . . ." (Italics supplied.) The twenty names out of which the challenged Grand Jury of twelve was drawn, actually were the first twenty names on a new list of fifty names supplied—on the day the grand jury list was selected—by the Jury Commission as a "supplement" to the general *venire* of three hundred. Thus, if colored citizens had been named on the general *venire*, they apparently were not considered, because the commission went no further than the first twenty names on the supplemental list which itself contained no names of Negroes. Furthermore, the uncontradicted evidence on the motion to quash showed that no Negro had ever been *selected* for grand jury service in the Parish within the memory of any of the witnesses who testified on that point.

The testimony introduced by petitioner on his motion to quash created a strong *prima facie* showing that Negroes had been systematically excluded—because of race—from the grand jury and the *venire* from which it was selected. Such an exclusion is a denial of equal protection of the laws, contrary to the Federal Constitution—the supreme law of the land. "The fact that the testimony . . . was not challenged by evidence appropriately direct, cannot be brushed aside." Had there been evidence obtainable to contradict and disprove the testimony offered by petitioner, it cannot be assumed that the State would have refrained from introducing it. The Jury Commissioners, appointed by the District Judge, were not produced as witnesses by the State. The trial judge, who had appointed the Commission, listening to the evidence and aided by a familiarity with conditions in the Parish of many years' standing, as judge, prosecutor, and practicing attorney, concluded that Negroes had been excluded from jury service because of their race, and ordered the *venire* quashed and the box purged and refilled. Our examination of the evidence convinces us that the bill of exceptions which he signed correctly stated that petitioner "did prove at the trial of said motion to Quash that Negroes as persons of color had been purposely excluded from the Grand Jury Venire and Panel which returned said indictment against . . . [petitioner] on account of their color and race . . ."

Principles which forbid discrimination in the selection of petit juries also govern the selection of grand juries. "It is a right to which every colored man is entitled, that, in the selection of Jurors to pass upon his life, liberty, or property, there shall be no exclusion of his race, and no discrimination against them because of their color." This record requires the holding that the court below was in error both in affirming the conviction of petitioner and in failing to hold that the indictment against him should have been quashed. The cause is reversed and remanded to the Supreme Court of Louisiana.

Reversed.

Chambers v. Florida

309 U.S. 227

Decided February 12, 1940

Any appraisal of the work of Justice Black must accord a very high place to his year-in and year-out efforts to lift up the level of justice in criminal proceedings. As we have seen, when he was a young prosecutor in Alabama, he took a determined stand against use of the third degree in obtaining confessions. He was already revolted by beatings and other forms of torture devised to cause accused persons, or suspects, whether guilty or innocent, to "break down" under continuous pressure and make a confession to escape further bodily harm.

In his third term on the Supreme Court, there arrived a particularly flagrant case—Isiah (Izell) Chambers, Jack Williamson, Charlie Davis, and Walter Woodward (Woodard) v. State of Florida. Following an outrageous murder in Florida, the accused men—young Negro tenant farmers—were held in closest confinement without access to friends or counsel for five days. During this time they were subjected to almost continuous questioning, in a highly hostile atmosphere, by officials who treated them abusively.

Justice Black's opinion, handed down in the chief justiceship of Charles Evans Hughes without dissent (Justice Murphy, newcomer to the bench, did not participate), has been described as the best of his opinions. Certainly it is one of his best, its worth having been recognized by President Roosevelt at the time of its delivery.

In essence the Justice's position is that law enforcement is necessary, but that enforcement by lawless means is prohibited by the

Constitution regardless of the end sought. The Supreme Court, he said, has "no more solemn responsibility" than that of "maintaining this constitutional shield [due process] . . . for every human being subject to our Constitution—of whatever race, creed or persuasion." The influence of one Chambers opinion is incalculable.

MR. JUSTICE BLACK *delivered the opinion of the Court*

The grave question presented by the petition for *certiorari*, granted in *forma pauperis*, is whether proceedings in which confessions were utilized, and which culminated in sentences of death upon four young Negro men in the State of Florida, failed to afford the safeguard of that due process of law guaranteed by the Fourteenth Amendment.

First. The State of Florida challenges our jurisdiction to look behind the judgments below, claiming that the issues of fact upon which petitioners base their claim that due process was denied them have been finally determined because passed upon by a jury. However, use by a state of an improperly obtained confession may constitute a denial of due process of law as guaranteed in the Fourteenth Amendment. Since petitioners have seasonably asserted the right under the Federal Constitution to have their guilt or innocence of a capital crime determined without reliance upon confessions obtained by means proscribed by the Due Process Clause of the Fourteenth Amendment, we must determine independently whether petitioners' confessions were so obtained, by review of the facts upon which that issue necessarily turns.

Second. The record shows:

About nine o'clock on the night of Saturday, May 13, 1933, Robert Darcy, an elderly white man, was robbed and murdered in Pompano, Florida, a small town in Broward County about twelve miles from Fort Lauderdale, the County seat. The opinion of the Supreme Court of Florida affirming petitioners' conviction for this crime stated that "It was one of those crimes that induced an enraged community . . ." And, as the dissenting judge pointed out, "The murder and robbery of the elderly Mr. Darcy . . . was a most dastardly and atrocious crime. It naturally aroused great and well justified public indignation."

Between 9:30 and 10 o'clock after the murder, petitioner Charlie Davis was arrested, and within the next twenty-four hours from twenty-five to forty Negroes living in the community, including petitioners Williamson, Chambers, and Woodward, were arrested without warrants and confined in the Broward County jail, at Fort Lauderdale. On the night of the crime, attempts to trail the murderers by bloodhounds brought J. T. Williams, a convict guard, into the proceedings. From then until confessions were obtained and petitioners were sentenced, he took a prominent part. About 11 p.m. on the following Monday, May 15, the sheriff and Williams took several of the imprisoned Negroes, including Williamson and Chambers, to the Dade County jail at Miami. The sheriff testified that they were taken there because he felt a possibility of mob violence and "wanted to give protection to every prisoner . . . in jail." Evidence of petitioners was that on the way to Miami a motorcycle patrolman drew up to the car in which the men were riding and the sheriff "told the cop that he had some Negroes that he [was] . . . taking down to Miami to escape a mob." This statement was not denied by the sheriff in his testimony and Williams did not testify at all; Williams apparently has now disappeared. Upon order of Williams, petitioner Williamson was kept in the death cell of the Dade County jail. The prisoners thus spirited to Miami were returned to the Fort Lauderdale jail the next day, Tuesday.

It is clear from the evidence of both the State and petitioners that from Sunday, May 14, to Saturday, May 20, the thirty to forty Negro suspects were subjected to questioning and cross questioning (with the exception that several of the suspects were in Dade County jail over one night). From the afternoon of Saturday, May 20, until sunrise of the 21st, petitioners and possibly one or two others underwent persistent and repeated questioning. The Supreme Court of Florida said the questioning "was in progress several days and all night before the confessions were secured" and referred to the last night as an "all night vigil." The sheriff who supervised the procedure of continued interrogation testified that he questioned the prisoners "in the day time all the week," but did not question them during any night before the all-night vigil of Saturday, May 20, because after having "questioned them all day . . . [he] was tired." Other evidence of the State was "that the officers of Broward County were in that jail almost continually during the whole week questioning these boys, and other boys, in connection with this" case.

The process of repeated questioning took place in the jailer's quarters on the fourth floor of the jail. During the week following their arrests and until their confessions were finally acceptable to the State's attorney in the early dawn of Sunday, May 21st, petitioners and their fellow prisoners were led one at a time from their cells to the questioning room, quizzed, and returned to their cells to await another turn. So far as appears, the prisoners at no time during the week were permitted to see or confer with counsel or a single friend or relative. When carried singly from his cell and subjected to questioning, each found himself, a single prisoner, surrounded in a fourth-floor jail room by four to ten men, the county sheriff, his deputies, a convict guard, and other white officers and citizens of the community.

The testimony is in conflict as to whether all four petitioners were continually threatened and physically maltreated until they finally, in hopeless desperation and fear of their lives, agreed to confess on Sunday morning just after daylight. Be that as it may, it is certain that by Saturday, May 20th, five days of continued questioning had elicited no confession. Admittedly, a concentration of effort—directed against a small number of prisoners including petitioners—on the part of the questioners, principally the sheriff and Williams, the convict guard, began about 3:30 that Saturday afternoon. From that hour on, with only short intervals for food and rest for the questioners—"They all stayed up all night." "They bring one of them at a time backwards and forwards . . . until they confessed." And Williams was present and participating that night, during the whole of which the jail cook served coffee and sandwiches to the men who "grilled" the prisoners.

Sometime in the early hours of Sunday, the 21st, probably about 2:30 a.m., Woodward apparently "broke"—as one of the State's witnesses put it—after a fifteen or twenty minute period of questioning by Williams, the sheriff and the constable "one right after the other." The State's attorney was awakened at his home, and called to the jail. He came, but was dissatisfied with the confession of Woodward which he took down in writing at that time, and said something like "tear this paper up, that isn't what I want, when you get something worthwhile call me." This same State's attorney conducted the State's case in the circuit court below and also made himself a witness, but did not testify as to why Woodward's first alleged confession was unsatisfactory to him. The sheriff did, however:

A. No, it wasn't false, part of it was true and part of it wasn't; Mr. Maire (the State's attorney) said there wasn't enough. It wasn't clear enough.

Q. . . . Was that voluntarily made at that time?

A. Yes, sir.

Q. It was voluntarily made that time?

A. Yes, sir.

Q. You didn't consider it sufficient?

A. Mr. Maire.

Q. Mr. Maire told you that it wasn't sufficient, so you kept on questioning him until the time you got him to make a free and voluntary confession of other matters that he hadn't included in the first?

A. No sir, we questioned him there and we caught him in lies.

Q. Caught all of them telling lies?

A. Caught every one of them lying to us that night, yes, sir.

Q. Did you tell them they were lying?

A. Yes, sir.

Q. Just how would you tell them that?

A. Just like I am talking to you.

Q. You said, "Jack, you told me a lie"?

A. Yes, sir.

After one week's constant denial of all guilt, petitioners "broke."

Just before sunrise, the State officials got something "worthwhile" from petitioners which the State's attorney would "want"; again he was called; he came; in the presence of those who had carried on and witnessed the all night questioning, he caused his questions and petitioners' answers to be stenographically reported. These are the confessions utilized by the State to obtain the judgments upon which petitioners were sentenced to death. No formal charges had been brought before the confessions. Two days thereafter, petitioners were indicted, were arraigned, and Williamson and Woodward pleaded guilty; Chambers and Davis pleaded not guilty. Later the sheriff, accompanied by Williams, informed an attorney who presumably had been appointed to defend Davis that Davis wanted his plea of not guilty withdrawn. This was done, and Davis then pleaded guilty. When Chambers was tried, his conviction rested upon his confession and testimony of the other three confessors. The convict guard and the sheriff "were in the Court room sitting down in a seat." And from arrest until sentenced to death, petitioners were never—either in jail or in court—wholly removed from the constant observation, influence, custody, and control of those whose persistent pressure brought about the sunrise confessions.

Third. The scope and operation of the Fourteenth Amendment have been fruitful sources of controversy in our constitutional history. However, in view of its historical setting and the wrongs which called it into being, the due process provision of the Fourteenth Amendment—just as that in the Fifth—has led few to doubt that it was intended to guarantee procedural standards adequate and appropriate, then and thereafter, to protect, at all times, people charged with or suspected of crime by those holding positions of power and authority. Tyrannical governments had immemorially utilized dictatorial criminal procedure and punishment to make scapegoats of the weak, or of helpless political, religious, or racial minorities and those who differed, who would not conform, and who resisted tyranny. The instruments of such governments were in the main two. Conduct, innocent when engaged in, was subsequently made by fiat criminally punishable without legislation. And a liberty loving people won the principle that criminal punishments could not be inflicted save for that which proper legislative action had already by "the law of the land" forbidden when done. But even more was needed. From the popular hatred and abhorrence of illegal confinement, torture, and extortion of confessions of violations of the "law of the land" evolved the fundamental idea that no man's life, liberty, or property be forfeited as criminal punishment for violation of that law until there had been a charge fairly made and fairly tried in a public tribunal free of prejudice, passion, excitement, and tyrannical power. Thus, as assurance against ancient evils, our country, in order to preserve "the blessings of liberty," wrote into its basic law the requirement, among others, that the forfeiture of the lives, liberties, or property of people accused of crime can only follow if procedural safeguards of due process have been obeyed.

The determination to preserve an accused's right to procedural due process sprang in large part from knowledge of historical truth that the rights and liberties of people accused of crime could not be safely entrusted to secret inquisitorial processes. The testimony of centuries, in governments of varying kinds over populations of different races and beliefs, stood as proof that physical and mental torture and coercion had brought about the tragically unjust sacrifices of some who were the noblest and most useful of their generations. The rack, the thumbscrew, the wheel, solitary confinement, protracted questioning and cross questioning, and other ingenious forms of entrapment of the helpless or unpopular had left their wake of mutilated bodies and shattered minds along the way to the cross, the guillotine, the stake, and the hangman's noose. And they who have suffered most from secret and dictatorial proceedings have almost always been the poor, the ignorant, the numerically weak, the friendless, and the powerless.

This requirement—of conforming to fundamental standards of procedure in criminal trials—was made operative against the States by the Fourteenth Amendment. Where one of several accused had limped into the trial court as a result of admitted physical mistreatment inflicted to obtain confessions upon which a jury had returned a verdict of guilty of murder, this Court recently declared, *Brown* v. *Mississippi*, that "it would be difficult to conceive of methods more revolting to the sense of justice than those taken to procure the confessions of these petitioners, and the use of the confessions thus obtained as the basis for conviction and sentence was a clear denial of due process."

Here, the record develops a sharp conflict upon the issue of physical violence and mistreatment, but shows, without conflict, the dragnet methods of arrest on suspicion without warrant, and the protracted questioning and cross questioning of these ignorant young colored tenant farmers by State officers and other white citizens, in a fourth-floor jail room, where as prisoners they were without friends, advisers, or counselors, and under circumstances calculated to break the strongest nerves and the stoutest resistance. Just as our decision in *Brown* v. *Mississippi* was based upon the fact that the confessions were the result of compulsion, so in the present case, the admitted practices were such as to justify the statement that "The undisputed facts showed that compulsion was applied."

For five days petitioners were subjected to interrogations culminating in Saturday's (May 20th) all-night examination. Over a period of five days they steadily refused to confess and disclaimed any guilt. The very circumstances surrounding their confinement and their questioning without any formal charges having been brought, were such as to fill petitioners with terror and frightful misgivings. Some were practical strangers in the community; three were arrested in a one-room farm tenant house which was their home; the haunting fear of mob violence was around them in an atmosphere charged with excitement and public indignation. From virtually the moment of their arrest until their eventual confessions, they never knew when just any one would be called back to the fourth-floor room, and there, surrounded by his accusers and others, interrogated by men who held their very lives—so far as these ignorant petitioners could know—in the balance. The rejection of petitioner Woodward's first "confession," given in the early hours of Sunday morning, because it was found wanting, demonstrates the relentless tenacity which "broke" petitioners' will and rendered them helpless to resist their accusers further. To permit human lives to be forfeited upon confessions thus obtained would make of the constitutional requirement of due process of law a meaningless symbol.

We are not impressed by the argument that law enforcement methods such as those under review are necessary to uphold our laws. The Constitution proscribes such lawless means irrespective of the end. And this argument flouts the basic principle that all people must stand on an equality before the bar of justice in every American court. Today, as in ages past, we are not without tragic proof that the exalted power of some governments to punish manufactured crime dictatorially is the handmaid of tyranny. Under our constitutional system, courts stand against any winds that blow as havens of refuge for those who might otherwise suffer because they are helpless, weak, outnumbered, or because they are nonconforming victims of prejudice and public excitement. Due process of law, preserved for all by our Constitution, commands that no such practice as that disclosed by this record shall send any accused to his death. No higher duty, no more solemn responsibility, rests upon this Court, than that of translating into living law and maintaining this constitutional shield deliberately planned and inscribed for the benefit of every human being subject to our Constitution—of whatever race, creed, or persuasion.

The Supreme Court of Florida was in error and its judgment is reversed.

Reversed.

Smith v. Texas

311 U.S. 128

Decided November 25, 1940

The constitutional principle of equal protection of the laws in the selection of jurors for trials involving Negro defendants, applied in Pierre v. Louisiana *(page 56), was asserted soon again by Justice Black. The later case was* Edgar Smith v. *State of Texas, and the unanimous opinion exposed thoroughly a pattern of racial discrimination in jury service, which the jury commissioners and courts of Texas had approved. The facts in the case and Justice Black's opinion made it crystal clear that if there were no Supreme Court there would be no appeal from such local practices, however discriminatory. Joining the Black opinion were Chief Justice Hughes and Justices McReynolds, Stone, Roberts, Reed, Frankfurter, Douglas, and Murphy.*

MR. JUSTICE BLACK *delivered the opinion of the Court*

In Harris County, Texas, where petitioner, a Negro, was indicted and convicted of rape, Negroes constitute over 20 percent of the population, and almost 10 percent of the poll-tax payers; a minimum of from three to six thousand of them measure up to the qualifications prescribed by Texas statutes for grand jury service. The court clerk, called as a state witness and testifying from court records covering the years 1931 through 1938, showed that only 5 of the 384 grand jurors who served during that period were Negroes; that of 512 persons summoned for grand jury duty, only 18 were Negroes; that of these 18, the names of 13 appeared as the last name on the 16-man jury list, the custom being to select the 12-man grand jury in the order that the names appeared on the list; that of the 5 Negroes summoned for grand jury service who were not given the number 16, 4 were given numbers between 13 and 16, and 1 was number 6; that the result of this numbering was that of the 18 Negroes summoned, only 5 ever served, whereas 379 of the 494 white men summoned actually served; that of 32 grand juries empanelled, only 5 had Negro members, while 27 had none; that of these 5, the same individual served 3 times, so that only 3 individual Negroes served at all; that there had been no Negroes on any of the grand juries in 1938, the year petitioner was indicted; that there had been none on any of the grand juries in 1937; that the service of Negroes by years had been: 1931, 1; 1932, 2; 1933, 1; 1934, 1; 1935, none; 1936, 1; 1937, none; 1938, none.

It is petitioner's contention that his conviction was based on an indictment obtained in violation of the provision of the Fourteenth Amendment that "No state shall . . . deny to any person within its jurisdiction the equal protection of the laws." And the contention that equal protection was denied him rests on a charge that Negroes were in 1938 and long prior thereto intentionally and systematically excluded from grand jury service solely on account of their race and color. That a conviction based upon an indictment returned by a jury so selected is a denial of equal protection is well settled, and is not challenged by the State. But both the trial court and the Texas Court of Criminal Appeals were of opinion that the evidence failed to support the charge of racial discrimination. For that reason the Appellate Court approved the trial court's action in denying petitioner's timely motion to quash the indictment. But the question decided rested upon a charge of denial of equal protection, a basic right protected by the Federal Constitution. And it is therefore our responsibility to appraise the evidence as it relates to this constitutional right.

It is part of the established tradition in the use of juries as instruments of public justice that the jury be a body truly representative of the community. For racial discrimination to result in the exclusion from jury service of otherwise qualified groups not only violates our Constitution and the laws enacted under it but is at war with our basic concepts of a democratic society and a representative government. We must consider this record in the light of these important principles. The fact that the written words of a state's laws hold out a promise that no such discrimination will be practiced is not enough. The Fourteenth Amendment requires that equal protection to all must be given—not merely promised.

Here, the Texas statutory scheme is not in itself unfair; it is capable of being carried out with no racial discrimination whatsoever. But by reason of the wide discretion permissible in the various steps of the plan, it is equally capable of being applied in such a manner as practically to proscribe any group thought by the law's administrators to be undesirable. And from the record before us, the conclusion is inescapable that it is the latter application that has prevailed in Harris County. Chance and accident alone could hardly have brought about the listing for grand jury service of so few Negroes from among the thousands shown by the undisputed evidence to possess the legal qualifications for jury service. Nor could chance and accident have been responsible for the combination of circumstances under which a Negro's name, when listed at all, almost invariably appeared as number 16, and under which number 16 was never called for service unless it proved impossible to obtain the required jurors from the first 15 names on the list.

The State argues that the testimony of the commissioners themselves shows that there was no arbitrary or systematic exclusion. And it is true that two of the three commissioners who drew the September 1938 panel testified to that effect. Both of them admitted that they did not select any Negroes, although the subject was discussed, but both categorically denied that they intentionally, arbitrarily or systematically discriminated against Negro jurors as such. One said that their failure to select Negroes was because they did not know the names of any who were qualified and the other said that he was not personally acquainted with any member of the Negro race. This is, at best, the testimony of two individuals who participated in drawing 1 out of the 32 jury panels discussed in the record. But even if their testimony were given the greatest possible effect, and their situation considered typical of that of the 94 commissioners who did not testify, we would still feel compelled to reverse the decision below. What the Fourteenth Amendment prohibits is racial discrimination in the selection of grand juries. Where jury commissioners limit those from whom grand juries are selected to their own personal acquaintance, discrimination can arise from commissioners who know no Negroes as well as from commissioners who know but eliminate them. If there has been discrimination, whether accomplished ingeniously or ingenuously, the conviction cannot stand.

Reversed.

Milk Wagon Drivers Union
v. Meadowmoor Dairies

312 U.S. 287

Decided February 10, 1941

Few Supreme Court decisions in the first half of the twentieth century were so notable in the Bill of Rights field as the unanimous ruling made in 1940 in Thornhill v. Alabama. *That decision, which found Justice Black joining the opinion by Justice Murphy, held picketing to be a form of speech or expression and therefore entitled to the constitutional safeguards of the First Amendment.*

The next year Justice Black applied the Thornhill *Decision in a case that grew out of a strike of Chicago milk wagon drivers. In the Chicago case, however,* Milk Wagon Drivers Union of Chicago, Local 753 et al. v. Meadowmoor Dairies, Inc., *Justice Black was one of three dissenters, the others being Justice Douglas who joined his opinion, and Justice Reed who dissented separately. Upholding the rulings in the Illinois courts, Justice Frankfurter, who wrote the majority opinion, said that the enjoining of peaceful picketing was permissible under state authority when peaceful picketing was "enmeshed" in violence. The Frankfurter opinion was joined by Chief Justice Hughes and Justices McReynolds, Stone, Roberts, and Murphy.*

In his dissent Justice Black differentiated carefully between lawful and proper enjoining of violence in labor controversies and the prohibition of picketing when it is conducted peaceably as a

means of expressing an opinion. This dissent was Justice Black's
first break in an important Bill of Rights case from the stand taken
by a Supreme Court majority. It presaged much that was to come.

MR. JUSTICE BLACK, *dissenting*

In my belief the opinion just announced gives approval to an injunction which seriously infringes upon the constitutional rights of freedom of speech and the press. To such a result I cannot agree.

Before detailing the reasons for my disagreement, some pre-liminary observations will doubtless aid in clarifying the subsidiary issues. The right of the Illinois courts to enjoin violence is not de-nied in this case. And I agree that nothing in the Federal Constitu-tion deprives them of that right. But it is claimed that Illinois—through its courts—has here sanctioned an injunction so sweeping in its terms as to deny to petitioners and others their constitutional rights freely to express their views on matters of public concern. And this is the single federal question we must decide. In their brief, petitioners state that they "have never and do not at the present time in any way condone or justify any violence by any member of the defendant union. Petitioners did not object to the issuance of an injunction restraining acts of violence. There is no contention made that the act of the Chancellor in granting such an injunction was erroneous." "Ethically, morally and legally," the petitioning union disclaims and condemns the acts of violence. And the master who conducted the hearings in the case specifically found that the union officials had instructed their pickets to refrain from violence. The record shows that the officials gave these instructions (which were obeyed), not only because they realized that resort to force and violence would be reprehensible and indefensible, but also be-cause they recognized that such lawless conduct injures a labor un-ion far more than it helps it. Aside from this, it cannot be doubted that attempts to persuade others by the application of physical force and violence as a substitute for persuasion by reason and peaceable argument is contrary to the first principles of our government. Nor can it be questioned that it is a prime function of courts to provide law enforcement means intended both to punish such illegal con-duct and to protect against it. But this great responsibility is en-trusted to courts not merely to determine the guilt or innocence of defendants, but to do so in such manner that those brought before them may enjoy a trial in which all their constitutional rights are safeguarded—including the constitutional guarantees of freedom of speech and the press.

In determining whether the injunction does deprive petitioners of their constitutional liberties, we cannot and should not lose sight of the nature and importance of the particular liberties that are at stake. And in reaching my conclusion, I view the guarantees of the First Amendment as the foundation upon which our governmental structure rests and without which it could not continue to endure as conceived and planned. Freedom to speak and write about public questions is as important to the life of our government as is the heart to the human body. In fact, this privilege is the heart of our government. If that heart be weakened, the result is debilitation; if it be stilled, the result is death.

In addition, I deem it essential to our federal system that the States should be left wholly free to govern within the ambit of their powers. Their deliberate governmental actions should not lightly be declared beyond their powers. For us to shear them of power not denied to them by the Federal Constitution would amount to judicial usurpation. But this Court has long since—and I think properly—committed itself to the doctrine that a State cannot, through any agency, either wholly remove, or partially whittle away, the vital individual freedoms guaranteed by the First Amendment. And in solemnly adjudicating the validity of state action touching these cherished privileges we cannot look merely at the surface of things, for were we to do so, these constitutional guarantees would become barren and sterile. We must look beneath the surface, and must carefully examine each step in proceedings which lead a court to enjoin peaceful discussion. In this case, in order to determine whether or not the State has overstepped constitutional boundaries, I find it necessary to give consideration to a number of factors, including the nature of the proceedings; the definiteness, indefiniteness, and constitutional validity of the basic law upon which the injunction is said to rest; the findings and the evidence; the definiteness, indefiniteness and scope of the language of the injunction itself; and the alleged imminence of the threatened dangers said to justify the admitted abridgment of free speech. My conclusion that the injunction as directed by the Supreme Court of Illinois invades the constitutional guarantees of freedom of speech and the press rests on my belief that these propositions are correct: (1) the subjects banned from public discussion by the injunction are matters of public concern, touching which the

Constitution guarantees the right of freedom of expression; (2) the law of Illinois, as declared by its Supreme Court, makes illegal the exercise of constitutionally guaranteed privileges, and that is an inadequate basis upon which to defend this abridgment of free speech; (3) the rule upon which the injunction is supported here and which this Court now declares to be the Illinois law is not the rule upon which the Illinois Supreme Court relied; (4) the rule announced here as supporting the right of the state to abridge freedom of expression is so general and sweeping in its implications that it opens up broad possibilities for invasion of these constitutional rights; (5) in any event, the injunction here approved is too broad and sweeping in its terms to find justification under the rule announced by the Illinois court, and even though under other circumstances such an injunction would be permissible under the rule now announced by this Court, still in this case such an injunction is supported neither by the findings nor the evidence. . . .

. . . In my opinion the sweeping injunction here approved is justified by neither of the rules, and is not supported by the record.

For our purposes, in order to reach a proper conclusion as to just what is the sweep of the injunction, we must necessarily turn to the complaint, the answer, the evidence, the findings, and the decision and judgment of the Illinois courts. And whether the injunction will restrain the exercise of constitutional rights depends upon the effect it will have upon the minds of those whose freedom of expression might be abridged by its mandate. This effect in turn depends upon the language appearing upon the face of the injunction. By that language we must judge it. For this injunction does not run merely against lawyers who might give it a legalistic interpretation, but against laymen as well. Our question then becomes: To what extent will the layman who might wish to write about or discuss the prohibited subjects feel that he cannot do so without subjecting himself to the possibility of a jail sentence under a summary punishment for contempt? This injunction, like a criminal statute, prohibits conduct under fear of punishment. There is every reason why we should look at the injunction as we would a statute, and if upon its face it abridges the constitutional guarantees of freedom of expression, it should be stricken down. This is especially true because we must deal only with the federal question presented, which is whether petitioners have been denied their rights under the First Amendment. The injunction, like a statute, stands as an overhanging threat of future punishment. The law of

Illinois has been declared by its highest court in such manner as to infringe upon constitutional guarantees. And by this injunction that law as actually applied abridges freedom of expression. Looking at the injunction, we find that under pain of future punishment by a trial judge all of the members of the petitioning union (about six thousand) are prohibited "From interfering, hindering or otherwise discouraging or diverting, or attempting to interfere with, hinder, discourage or divert persons desirous of or contemplating purchasing milk or cream or other products aforesaid, including the use of said signs, banners or placards, and walking up and down in front of said stores as aforesaid, and further preventing the deliveries to said stores of other articles which said stores sell through retail; [or] From threatening in any manner to do the foregoing acts. . . ." It surely cannot be doubted that an Act of the Illinois Legislature, couched in this sweeping language, would be held invalid on its face. For this language is capable of being construed to mean that none of those enjoined can, without subjecting themselves to summary punishment, speak, write, or publish anything anywhere or at any time which the Illinois court—acting without a jury in the exercise of its broad power to punish for contempt—might conclude would result in discouraging people from buying milk products of the complaining dairy. And more than that—if the language is so construed, those enjoined can be sent to jail if they even threaten to write, speak, or publish in such way as to discourage prospective milk purchasers. I find not even slight justification for an interpretation of this injunction so as to confine its prohibitions to conduct near stores dealing in respondent's milk. Neither the language of the injunction nor that of the complaint which sought the injunction indicates such a limitation. Mr. Justice Cardozo approved no such injunction as this in *Nann* v. *Raimist*. In fact, he ordered expunged from the injunction those prohibitions which impaired "defendant's indubitable right to win converts over to its fold by recourse to peaceable persuasion, and to induce them by like methods to renounce allegiance to its rival."

But the injunction approved here does not stop at closing the mouths of the members of the petitioning union. It brings within its all-embracing sweep the spoken or written words of any other person "who may . . . now . . . or hereafter . . . agree or arrange with them. . . ." So, if a newspaper should "agree or arrange" with all or some of those here enjoined to publish their side of the controversy, thereby necessarily tending to "discourage" the sale of cut-rate milk, the publishers might likewise be subject to punishment for contempt. Ordinarily the scope of the decree is co-extensive with the allegations of the bill, its supporting affidavits or findings of fact. In other words, the acts enjoined are the acts alleged in the bill as the basis for complaint. And the complaint on which the injunction here rests specifically charged that the union had caused "announcement to be made by the public press of the City of Chicago, for the purpose of intimidating the said storekeepers and causing them to cease purchasing the milk sold by said plaintiffs through fear and terror of the renewal of said conspiracy. . . ." Specific reference was made to these newspaper stories as appearing in the *Chicago Tribune* and the *Chicago Evening American*. Proof was made of these publications. And the injunction of the trial judge, set aside by the Supreme Court of Illinois, specifically saved to petitioners—as in effect did Justice Cardozo in the New York case—their right to publicize their cause by means of "advertisement or communication." But the injunction sustained here is to be issued as prayed for in the bill of complaint. And since the acts enjoined are the acts alleged in the bill as the basis for complaint, newspaper publications of the type referred to in the complaint are literally enjoined. Since the literal language of the injunction, read in the light of the complaint, the supporting evidence, and the language of the trial judge's saving clause—stricken down by action sustained here—thus unconstitutionally abridges the rights of freedom of speech and press, we cannot escape our responsibility by the simple expedient of declaring that those who might be sent to jail for violating the plain language of the injunction might eventually obtain relief by appeal to this Court. To sanction vague and undefined terminologies in dragnet clauses directly and exclusively aimed at restricting freedom of discussion upon the theory that we might later acquit those convicted for violation of such terminology amounts in my judgment to a prior censorship of views. No matter how the decree might eventually be construed, its language, viewed in the light of the whole proceedings, stands like an abstract statute with an overhanging and undefined threat to freedom of speech and the press. All this, of course, is true only as to those who argue on the side of the opponents of cut-rate distribution. No such undefined threat hangs over those who "agree or arrange" with the advocates of the cut-rate system to encourage their method of distribution. . . .

A careful study of the entire record in this case convinces me that neither the findings nor the evidence, even viewed in the light most favorable to respondent, showed such imminent, clear, and present danger as to justify an abridgment of the rights of freedom of speech and the press. The picketing, which did not begin until September 1934, has at all times been peaceful. Usually one picket, and never more than two, walked along the street bearing a sign. These pickets never impeded traffic either on the sidewalks or in the street, nor did they disturb any passersby or customers. In fact, it is stipulated in the record that pickets "made no threats against any of these storekeepers, but peacefully picketed these stores. They made no attempt to stop any customers or to stop delivery except insofar as their situation and the signs they bore had that tendency." There was no evidence to connect them with any kind or type of violence at any time or place. As was found by the master, this was in accordance with the instruction which was given to them by the union officials. There is no evidence and no finding that dissemination or information by pickets stimulated anyone else to commit any act of violence.

There was evidence that violence occurred—some committed by identified persons and some by unidentified persons. A strike of farmers supplying most of Chicago's milk took place in the early part of January 1934. This strike practically stopped the inflow of milk into the city. As a result, the union drivers were ordered not to report for work on January 8 and 9, at the height of the strike. It was during this period that the larger part of the major acts of violence occurred. According to the complaint and the evidence, seven trucks were seized or damaged on the 8th and 9th of January 1934, and one on the 6th. These are the only trucks that were ever seized or damaged, according to both the complaint and the evidence, and it was in connection with these seizures that the injuries to truck drivers, the shootings, and the threats referred to in this Court's opinion took place. Undoubtedly, some of the members of the union participated in this violence, as is shown by the fact that several were arrested, criminal prosecutions were instituted, and the cases later settled with the approval of the trial judge. It was eight months after this before any picketing occurred; four years afterward before the trial judge granted an injunction, limited to violence alone; five years before the Supreme Court of Illinois directed a more stringent injunction against peaceful persuasion; and seven years before this Court sustained the injunction.

During the period of the farmers' strike in 1934, and in the immediately succeeding months, five stores were either bombed or burned. Three union members were tried, convicted and sentenced to the penitentiary for arson in connection with one of these burnings. All of this violence took place many months before any of the picketing occurred. In addition to these 1934 acts of violence, the evidence showed that one stench bomb was thrown into a store in 1935, one in 1936, and two in 1937. The identity of the persons throwing these stench bombs was not shown.

The only other violence alleged or testified to was the breaking of windows in cut-rate stores. Most of the testimony as to these acts of violence was given by respondent's vendors, and was extremely indefinite. The master made no findings as to specific acts of violence, nor as to the dates of their occurrence. . . .

It is on the basis of my study of the entire record that I rest my conclusion that the forfeiture of the right to free speech effected by the injunction is not warranted. In reaching this conclusion, I fully recognize that the union members guilty of violence were subject to punishment in accordance with the principles of due process of law. And some of them have in fact been prosecuted and convicted. Punishment of lawless conduct is in accord with the necessities of government and is essential to the peace and tranquillity of society. But it is going a long way to say that because of the acts of these few men, six thousand other members of their union can be denied the right to express their opinion to the extent accomplished by the sweeping injunction here sustained. Even those convicted of crime are not in this country punished by having their freedom of expression curtailed except under prison rules and regulations, and then only for the duration of their sentence.

No one doubts that Illinois can protect its storekeepers from being coerced by fear of damage to their property from window-smashing, or burnings, or bombings. And to that end Illinois is free to use all its vast resources and powers, nor should this Court stand in the way so long as Illinois does not take away from its people rights guaranteed to them by the Constitution of the United States. When clear and present danger of riot, disorder, interference with traffic upon the public streets, or other immediate threat to public safety, peace, or order appears, the power of the Illinois courts to prevent or punish is obvious. Furthermore, this is true because a state has the power to adopt laws of general application to provide that the streets shall be used for the purpose for which they primarily exist, and because the preservation of peace and order is one of the first duties of government. But in a series of cases we have held that local laws ostensibly passed pursuant to this admittedly possessed general power could not be enforced in such a way as to amount to a prior censorship on freedom of expression, or to abridge that freedom as to those rightfully and lawfully on the streets. Illinois, like all the other states of the Union, is part of a national democratic system, the continued existence of which depends upon the right of free discussion of public affairs—a right whose denial to some leads in the direction of its eventual denial to all. I am of opinion that the court's injunction strikes directly at the heart of our government, and that deprivation of these essential liberties cannot be reconciled with the rights guaranteed to the people of this Nation by their Constitution.

Bridges v. *California*

314 U.S. 252

Decided December 8, 1941

*By strange coincidence two contrasting contempt of court con-
troversies arose in California in the late 1930's. One involved a
widely known labor union leader, the other a prominent and conservative newspaper that was highly critical of many labor union
personalities and practices. These two proceedings were joined in
the Supreme Court, which they reached on appeal, in a single
sharply contested 5-to-4 decision. The issue in each case concerned
the extent to which a court might be criticized while a legal proceeding was pending. The cases were* Harry Bridges v. State of
California *and* The Times-Mirror Company and L. D. Hotchkiss
v. Superior Court of California.

The matter cited as contemptuous in the Bridges Case *was a
telegram sent by the longshoremen's leader, Harry Bridges, to the
Secretary of Labor following a decision by Judge Reuben Schmidt
in a case growing out of a dispute between unions. A subsequent
and related proceeding was pending when Bridges wired the Cabinet official as follows: "Attempted enforcement of Schmidt decision will tie up port of Los Angeles and involve entire Pacific
coast." Bridges's publication, or acquiescence in the publication,
of the telegram was held by the California courts to be in contempt and he was fined $125.*

The Los Angeles Times Case *arose from an editorial, "Probation for Gorillas?" which was published May 5, 1938. The editorial*

took notice of the conviction of two men who were reported to have assaulted non-union truck drivers and warned the judge that he would "make a serious mistake if he grants probation." What the community needed, so the editorial continued, was "the example of their assignment to the jute mill." Since the criminal case against the convicted men was still pending, the newspaper was fined $300 for contempt.

These cases, which weighed heavily on the Supreme Court, were first argued in October 1940. As there was no decision by the end of the term, they were restored to the docket and rearguments were held just a year after the first arguments. Finally, some fifteen months after the Supreme Court first heard them, the cases were decided. Notwithstanding this long period of consideration, there was nothing approaching unanimity in the result. Justice Black, speaking for the narrowest of majorities, reversed both of the contempt orders. He was joined by Justices Reed, Douglas, Murphy, and Jackson. Justice Frankfurter wrote the dissent, which was supported by Chief Justice Stone and Justices Roberts and Byrnes.

This decision was the first in which Justice Black spoke for the Supreme Court in a major test of the First Amendment's protection of freedom of expression. Partly because of its closeness, with Roosevelt-appointed Justices ranged against each other, the result attracted more public attention to Justice Black than any opinion he had written in his four years on the Supreme Court. He had taken a stand for freedom of the press, from which he was not to swerve over many years.

Mr. Justice Black *delivered the opinion of the Court*

These two cases, while growing out of different circumstances and concerning different parties, both relate to the scope of our national constitutional policy safeguarding free speech and a free press. All of the petitioners were adjudged guilty and fined for contempt of court by the Superior Court of Los Angeles County. Their conviction rested upon comments pertaining to pending litigation which were published in newspapers. In the Superior Court and later in the California Supreme Court, petitioners challenged the State's action as an abridgment, prohibited by the Federal Constitution, of freedom of speech and of the press, but the Superior Court overruled this contention, and the [State] Supreme Court affirmed. The importance of the constitutional question prompted us to grant *certiorari*.

In brief, the State courts asserted and exercised a power to punish petitioners for publishing their views concerning cases not in all respects finally determined, upon the following chain of reasoning: California is invested with the power and duty to provide an adequate administration of justice; by virtue of this power and duty, it can take appropriate measures for providing fair judicial trials free from coercion or intimidation; included among such appropriate measures is the common law procedure of punishing certain interferences and obstructions through contempt proceedings; this particular measure, devolving upon the courts of California by reason of their creation as courts, includes the power to punish for publications made outside the court room if they tend to interfere with the fair and orderly administration of justice in a pending case; the trial court having found that the publications had such a tendency, and there being substantial evidence to support the finding, the punishments here imposed were an appropriate exercise of the State's power; insofar as these punishments constitute a restriction on liberty of expression, the public interest in that liberty was properly subordinated to the public interest in judicial impartiality and decorum.

If the inference of conflict raised by the last clause be correct, the issue before us is of the very gravest moment. For free speech and fair trials are two of the most cherished policies of our civilization, and it would be a trying task to choose between them. But even if such a conflict is not actually raised by the question before us, we are still confronted with the delicate problems entailed in passing upon the deliberations of the highest court of a state. This is not, however, solely an issue between State and Nation, as it would be if we were called upon to mediate in one of those troublous situations where each claims to be the repository of a particular sovereign power. To be sure, the exercise of power here in question was by a state judge. But in deciding whether or not the sweeping constitutional mandate against any law "abridging the freedom of speech or of the press" forbids it, we are necessarily measuring a power of all American courts, both state and federal, including this one.

I

It is to be noted at once that we have no direction by the legislature of California that publications outside the court room which comment upon a pending case in a specified manner should be punishable. As we said in *Cantwell* v. *Connecticut,* such a "declaration of the State's policy would weigh heavily in any challenge of the law as infringing constitutional limitations." But as we also said there, the problem is different where "the judgment is based on a common law concept of the most general and undefined nature." For here the legislature of California has not appraised a particular kind of situation and found a specific danger sufficiently imminent to justify a restriction on a particular kind of utterance. The judgments below, therefore, do not come to us encased in the armor wrought by prior legislative deliberation. Under such circumstances, this Court has said that "it must necessarily be found, as an original question" that the specified publications involved created "such likelihood of bringing about the substantive evil as to deprive (them) of the constitutional protection.". . .

Moreover, the likelihood, however great, that a substantive evil will result cannot alone justify a restriction upon freedom of speech or the press. The evil itself must be "substantial"; it must be "serious." And even the expression of "legislative preferences or beliefs" cannot transform minor matters of public inconvenience or annoyance into substantive evils of sufficient weight to warrant the curtailment of liberty of expression.

What finally emerges from the "clear and present danger" cases is a working principle that the substantive evil must be extremely serious and the degree of imminence extremely high before utterances can be punished. Those cases do not purport to mark the furthermost constitutional boundaries of protected expression, nor do we here. They do no more than recognize a minimum compulsion of the Bill of Rights. For the First Amendment does not speak equivocally. It prohibits any law "abridging the freedom of speech or of the press." It must be taken as a command of the broadest scope that explicit language, read in the context of a liberty-loving society, will allow.

I I

Before analyzing the punished utterances and the circumstances surrounding their publication, we must consider an argument which, if valid, would destroy the relevance of the foregoing discussion to this case. In brief, this argument is that the publications here in question belong to a special category marked off by history, a category to which the criteria of constitutional immunity from punishment used where other types of utterances are concerned are not applicable. For, the argument runs, the power of judges to punish by contempt out-of-court publications tending to obstruct the orderly and fair administration of justice in a pending case was deeply rooted in English common law at the time the Constitution was adopted. That this historical contention is dubious has been persuasively argued elsewhere. In any event it need not detain us, for to assume that English common law in this field became ours is to deny the generally accepted historical belief that "one of the objects of the Revolution was to get rid of the English common law on liberty of speech and of the press."

More specifically, it is to forget the environment in which the First Amendment was ratified. In presenting the proposals which were later embodied in the Bill of Rights, James Madison, the leader in the preparation of the First Amendment, said: "Although I know whenever the great rights, the trial by jury, freedom of the press, or liberty of conscience, come in question in that body (Parliament), the invasion of them is resisted by able advocates, yet their Magna Charta does not contain any one provision for the security of those rights, respecting which the people of America are most alarmed. The freedom of the press and rights of conscience, those choicest privileges of the people, are unguarded in the British Constitution." And Madison elsewhere wrote that "the state of the press . . . under the common law, cannot . . . be the standard of its freedom in the United States."

There are no contrary implications in any part of the history of the period in which the First Amendment was framed and adopted. No purpose in ratifying the Bill of Rights was clearer than that of securing for the people of the United States much greater freedom of religion, expression, assembly, and petition than the people of Great Britain had ever enjoyed. It cannot be denied, for example, that the religious test oath or the restrictions upon assembly then prevalent in England would have been regarded as measures which the Constitution prohibited the American Congress from passing. And since the same unequivocal language is used with respect to freedom of the press, it signifies a similar enlargement of that concept as well. Ratified as it was while the memory of many oppressive English restrictions in the enumerated liberties was still fresh, the First Amendment cannot reasonably be taken as approving prevalent English practices. On the contrary, the only conclusion supported by history is that the unqualified prohibitions laid down by the framers were intended to give to liberty of the press, as to the other liberties, the broadest scope that could be countenanced in an orderly society. . . .

I I I

We may appropriately begin our discussion of the judgments below by considering how much, as a practical matter, they would affect liberty of expression. It must be recognized that public interest is much more likely to be kindled by a controversial event of the day than by a generalization, however penetrating, of the historian or scientist. Since they punish utterances made during the pendency of a case, the judgments below therefore produce their restrictive results at the precise time when public interest in the matters discussed would naturally be at its height. Moreover, the ban is likely to fall not only at a crucial time but upon the most important topics of discussion. Here, for example, labor controversies were the topics of some of the publications. Experience shows that the more acute labor controversies are, the more likely it is that in some aspect they will get into court. It is therefore the controversies that command most interest that the decisions below would remove from the arena of public discussion.

No suggestion can be found in the Constitution that the freedom there guaranteed for speech and the press bears an inverse ratio to the timeliness and importance of the ideas seeking expression. Yet, it would follow as a practical result of the decisions below that anyone who might wish to give public expression to his views on a pending case involving no matter what problem of public interest, just at the time his audience would be most receptive, would be as effectively discouraged as if a deliberate statutory scheme of censorship had been adopted. Indeed, perhaps more so, because under a legislative specification of the particular kinds of expressions prohibited and the circumstances under which the prohibitions are to operate, the speaker or publisher might at least have an authoritative guide to the permissible scope of comment, instead of being compelled to act at the peril that judges might find in the utterance a "reasonable tendency" to obstruct justice in a pending case.

This unfocused threat is, to be sure, limited in time, terminating as it does upon final disposition of the case. But this does not change its censorial quality. An endless series of moratoria on public discussion, even if each were very short, could hardly be dismissed as an insignificant abridgment of freedom of expression. And to assume that each would be short is to overlook the fact that the "pendency" of a case is frequently a matter of months or even years rather than days or weeks.

For these reasons we are convinced that the judgments below result in a curtailment of expression that cannot be dismissed as insignificant. If they can be justified at all, it must be in terms of some serious substantive evil which they are designed to avert. The substantive evil here sought to be averted has been variously described below. It appears to be double: disrespect for the judiciary; and disorderly and unfair administration of justice. The assumption that respect for the judiciary can be won by shielding judges from published criticism wrongly appraises the character of American public opinion. For it is a prized American privilege to speak one's mind, although not always with perfect good taste, on all public institutions. And an enforced silence, however limited, solely in the name of preserving the dignity of the bench, would probably engender resentment, suspicion, and contempt much more than it would enhance respect.

The other evil feared, disorderly and unfair administration of justice, is more plausibly associated with restricting publications which touch upon pending litigation. The very word "trial" connotes decisions on the evidence and arguments properly advanced in open court. Legal trials are not like elections, to be won through the use of the meeting-hall, the radio, and the newspaper. But we cannot start with the assumption that publications of the kind here involved actually do threaten to change the nature of legal trials, and that to preserve judicial impartiality, it is necessary for judges to have a contempt power by which they can close all channels of public expression to all matters which touch upon pending cases. We must therefore turn to the particular utterances here in question and the circumstances of their publication to determine to what extent the substantive evil of unfair administration of justice was a likely consequence, and whether the degree of likelihood was sufficient to justify summary punishment.

The Los Angeles Times Editorials. The Times-Mirror Company, publisher of the Los Angeles *Times,* and L. D. Hotchkiss, its managing editor, were cited for contempt for the publication of three editorials. Both found by the trial court to be responsible for one of the editorials, the company and Hotchkiss were each fined

$100. The company alone was held responsible for the other two, and was fined $100 more on account of one, and $300 more on account of the other.

The $300 fine presumably marks the most serious offense. The editorial thus distinguished was entitled "Probation for Gorillas?" After vigorously denouncing two members of a labor union who had previously been found guilty of assaulting non-union truck drivers, it closes with the observation: "Judge A. A. Scott will make a serious mistake if he grants probation to Matthew Shannon and Kennan Holmes. This community needs the example of their assignment to the jute mill." Judge Scott had previously set a day (about a month after the publication) for passing upon the application of Shannon and Holmes for probation and for pronouncing sentence.

The basis for punishing the publication as contempt was by the trial court said to be its "inherent tendency" and by the Supreme Court its "reasonable tendency" to interfere with the orderly administration of justice in an action then before a court for consideration. In accordance with what we have said on the "clear and present danger" cases, neither "inherent tendency" nor "reasonable tendency" is enough to justify a restriction of free expression. But even if they were appropriate measures, we should find exaggeration in the use of those phrases to describe the facts here.

From the indications in the record of the position taken by the Los Angeles *Times* on labor controversies in the past, there could have been little doubt of its attitude toward the probation of Shannon and Holmes. In view of the paper's long-continued militancy in this field, it is inconceivable that any judge in Los Angeles would expect anything but adverse criticism from it in the event probation were granted. Yet such criticism after final disposition of the proceedings would clearly have been privileged. Hence, this editorial, given the most intimidating construction it will bear, did no more than threaten future adverse criticism which was reasonably to be expected anyway in the event of a lenient disposition of the pending case. To regard it, therefore, as in itself of substantial influence upon the course of justice would be to impute to judges a lack of firmness, wisdom, or honor, which we cannot accept as a major premise. . . .

The Bridges Telegram. While a motion for a new trial was pending in a case involving a dispute between an A.F. of L. union and a C.I.O. union of which Bridges was an officer, he either caused to be published or acquiesced in the publication of a telegram which he had sent to the Secretary of Labor. The telegram referred to the judge's decision as "outrageous"; said that attempted enforcement of it would tie up the port of Los Angeles and involve the entire Pacific Coast; and concluded with the announcement that the C.I.O. union, representing some twelve thousand members, did "not intend to allow state courts to override the majority vote of members in choosing its officers and representatives and to override the National Labor Relations Board."

Apparently Bridges's conviction is not rested at all upon his use of the word "outrageous." The remainder of the telegram fairly construed appears to be a statement that if the court's decree should be enforced there would be a strike. It is not claimed that such a strike would have been in violation of the terms of the decree, nor that in any other way it would have run afoul of the law of California. On no construction, therefore, can the telegram be taken as a threat either by Bridges or the union to follow an illegal course of action.

Moreover, this statement of Bridges was made to the Secretary of Labor, who is charged with official duties in connection with the prevention of strikes. Whatever the cause might be, if a strike was threatened or possible the Secretary was entitled to receive all available information. Indeed, the Supreme Court of California recognized that, publication in the newspapers aside, in sending the message to the Secretary, Bridges was exercising the right of petition to a duly accredited representative of the United States Government, a right protected by the First Amendment.

It must be recognized that Bridges was a prominent labor leader speaking at a time when public interest in the particular labor controversy was at its height. The observations we have previously made here upon the timeliness and importance of utterances as emphasizing rather than diminishing the value of constitutional protection, and upon the breadth and seriousness of the censorial effects of punishing publications in the manner followed below are certainly no less applicable to a leading spokesman for labor than to a powerful newspaper taking another point of view.

In looking at the reason advanced in support of the judgment of contempt, we find that here, too, the possibility of causing unfair disposition of a pending case is the major justification asserted. And here again the gist of the offense, according to the court below, is intimidation.

Let us assume that the telegram could be construed as an announcement of Bridges's intention to call a strike, something which, it is admitted, neither the general law of California nor the court's decree prohibited. With an eye on the realities of the situation, we cannot assume that Judge Schmidt was unaware of the possibility of a strike as a consequence of his decision. If he was not intimidated by the facts themselves, we do not believe that the most explicit statement of them could have sidetracked the course of justice. Again, we find exaggeration in the conclusion that the utterance even "tended" to interfere with justice. If there was electricity in the atmosphere, it was generated by the facts; the charge added by the Bridges telegram can be dismissed as negligible. The words of Mr. Justice Holmes, spoken in reference to very different facts, seem entirely applicable here: "I confess that I cannot find in all this or in the evidence in the case anything that would have affected a mind of reasonable fortitude, and still less can I find there anything that obstructed the administration of justice in any sense that I possibly can give to those words."

Reversed.

Betts v. Brady

316 U.S. 455

Decided June 1, 1942

There is at least one area in which the Supreme Court has sanctioned a double standard of justice. That is in criminal trials in which the defendants, who may be innocent, are too poor to hire legal counsel to protect their rights and interests.

If the case involves an Act of Congress and hence is in Federal Court, the accused is entitled to a lawyer and the judge, if necessary, sees to it that defense counsel is appointed. Justice Black's opinion in Johnson v. Zerbst *(page 51) has helped to make this a regularly applied rule. If, however, the defendant is accused of violating a State law and hence is brought to trial in a state court, he may go to prison without the assistance of counsel at any stage of the proceedings, the Sixth Amendment notwithstanding.*

The record of state right-to-counsel cases in the Supreme Court is one that twists and turns, and generalization is not easy, except to say that too often the Court's decision has approved a criminal trial or proceeding in which the accused, because of poverty, could not hire counsel and none was appointed. This means that criminal justice may vary not only between the federal and the state cases but also between cases of various states since some states are alert to see that counsel is assigned to indigent defendants, while other states are less concerned.

The Maryland case of Smith Betts v. Patrick J. Brady, Warden *still stirs many who read it. Denied counsel even though he asked for legal assistance, the poorly educated, poverty-stricken, jobless farm hand attempted to defend himself against professional prose-cution, and, as might have been expected, was found guilty. After being imprisoned he sought release on the ground that a funda-mental trial right had been denied him. Justice Roberts rejected the plea and was supported by Chief Justice Stone and Justices Reed, Frankfurter, Jackson, and Byrnes. Justice Black's dissent spoke as well for Justices Douglas and Murphy. To his opinion Justice Black appended a detailed report on practices with respect to right-to-counsel in the States of the Union—an area of injustice that touched Justice Black deeply.*

MR. JUSTICE BLACK, *dissenting, with whom* MR. JUSTICE DOUG-LAS *and* MR. JUSTICE MURPHY *concur*

To hold that the petitioner had a constitutional right to coun-sel in this case does not require us to say that "no trial for any of-fense, or in any court, can be fairly conducted and justice accorded a defendant who is not represented by counsel." This case can be determined by a resolution of a narrower question: whether in view of the nature of the offense and the circumstances of his trial and conviction, this petitioner was denied the procedural protection which is his right under the Federal Constitution. I think he was.

The petitioner, a farm hand, out of a job and on relief, was in-dicted in a Maryland state court on a charge of robbery. He was too poor to hire a lawyer. He so informed the court and requested that counsel be appointed to defend him. His request was denied. Put to trial without a lawyer, he conducted his own defense, was found guilty, and was sentenced to eight years' imprisonment. The court below found that the petitioner had "at least an ordinary amount of intelligence." It is clear from his examination of wit-nesses that he was a man of little education.

If this case had come to us from a federal court, it is clear that we should have to reverse it, because the Sixth Amendment makes the right to counsel in criminal cases inviolable by the Federal Gov-ernment. I believe that the Fourteenth Amendment made the Sixth applicable to the States. But this view, although often urged in dis-sents, has never been accepted by a majority of this Court and is not accepted today. A statement of the grounds supporting it is, therefore, unnecessary at this time. I believe, however, that, under the prevailing view of due process, as reflected in the opinion just announced, a view which gives this Court such vast supervisory powers that I am not prepared to accept it without grave doubts, the judgment below should be reversed.

This Court has just declared that due process of law is denied if a trial is conducted in such manner that it is "shocking to the universal sense of justice" or "offensive to the common and fundamental ideas of fairness and right." On another occasion, this Court has recognized that whatever is "implicit in the concept of ordered liberty" and "essential to the substance of a hearing" is within the procedural protection afforded by the constitutional guaranty of due process.

The right to counsel in a criminal proceeding is "fundamental." It is guarded from invasion by the Sixth Amendment, adopted to raise an effective barrier against arbitrary or unjust deprivation of liberty by the Federal Government.

An historical evaluation of the right to a full hearing in criminal cases, and the dangers of denying it, were set out in the *Powell Case*, where this Court said:

> What . . . does a hearing include? Historically and in practice, in our own country at least, it has always included the right to the aid of counsel when desired and provided by the person asserting the right. . . . Even the intelligent and educated layman . . . lacks both the skill and knowledge adequately to prepare his defense, even though he have a perfect one. He requires the guiding hand of counsel in every step in the proceedings against him. Without it, though he be not guilty, he faces the danger of conviction because he does not know how to establish his innocence.

A practice cannot be reconciled with "common and fundamental ideas of fairness and right," which subjects innocent men to increased dangers of conviction merely because of their poverty. Whether a man is innocent cannot be determined from a trial in which, as here, denial of counsel has made it impossible to conclude, with any satisfactory degree of certainty, that the defendant's case was adequately presented. No one questions that due process requires a hearing before conviction and sentence for the serious crime of robbery. As the Supreme Court of Wisconsin said, in 1859, ". . . would it not be a little like mockery to secure to a pauper these solemn constitutional guaranties for a fair and full trial of the matters with which he was charged, and yet say to him when on trial, that he must employ his own counsel, who could alone render these guaranties of any real permanent value to him. . . . Why this great solicitude to secure him a fair trial if he cannot have the benefit of counsel?"

Denial to the poor of the request for counsel in proceedings based on charges of serious crime has long been regarded as shocking to the "universal sense of justice" throughout this country. In 1854, for example, the Supreme Court of Indiana said: "It is not to be thought of, in a civilized community, for a moment, that any citizen put in jeopardy of life or liberty should be debarred of counsel because he was too poor to employ such aid. No Court could be respected, or respect itself, to sit and hear such a trial. The defense of the poor, in such cases, is a duty resting somewhere, which will be at once conceded as essential to the accused, to the Court, and to the public." And most of the other states have shown their agreement by constitutional provisions, statutes, or established practice judicially approved, which assure that no man shall be deprived of counsel merely because of his poverty. Any other practice seems to me to defeat the promise of our democratic society to provide equal justice under the law.

Jones v. Opelika

316 U.S. 584

Decided June 8, 1942

One of the most remarkable opinions in the entire history of the
Supreme Court—and one probably unique—is the single paragraph
at the end of Jones v. Opelika. It is so remarkable because Justices
Black, Douglas, and Murphy disavowed their earlier support of
Justice Frankfurter's 8-to-1 majority opinion in the First Flag
Salute Case.

In that case, Minersville School District v. Gobitis, decided
June 3, 1940, the Supreme Court, with only Justice Stone dissenting, upheld the authority of a public-school board in Pennsylvania to require all children to participate in flag-salute exercises
as a condition of school attendance. Lillian Gobitis, aged twelve,
and her brother, William, aged ten, adherents of the Jehovah's
Witnesses, refused to salute the flag in the belief that the act would
violate the Biblical commandment not to bow down before a
graven image. When the children were expelled from school, the
parents challenged the compulsory flag salute as an interference
with the Constitution's guarantee of freedom of religion.

The Supreme Court had previously refused to decide flag-
salute controversies, giving as the reason its belief that they raised
no federal question. But 1940 brought the conquest of the Low
Countries by the Nazi armored divisions and also Dunkirk's heroic
evacuation under fire. When the flag-salute issue came up anew

*from Minersville, Pennsylvania, the Supreme Court agreed to
hear it.*

*Justice Frankfurter, a native of Vienna and deeply committed
emotionally in the European tragedy, was assigned by Chief Justice
Hughes to write the Court's opinion. In assessing the values involved, Justice Frankfurter gave heavy weight to the fact that the
public school provides "the binding tie of cohesive sentiment"
which, he said, is "the ultimate foundation of a free society." Supporting Justice Frankfurter in his emphasis on the flag as a national symbol were Chief Justice Hughes and Justices Roberts,
Black, Reed, Douglas, and Murphy, with Justice McReynolds concurring. Dissenter Stone spoke out strongly for the widest freedom
in the exercise of religious beliefs, however unorthodox, and for
the view that the Supreme Court is duty-bound to provide protection for minority religious groups whose principles run counter to
prevailing opinion.*

The Gobitis *Decision, for all its overwhelming majority, was
short-lived. The first step, and an amazing one, toward reversal
came in the combined cases of* Rosco Jones v. City of Opelika,
Alabama; Lois Bowden and Zada Sanders v. City of Fort Smith,
Arkansas; *and* Charles Jobin v. State of Arizona (Casa Grande).
In the Opelika Case *Justice Reed delivered a 5-to-4 majority opinion sustaining the constitutionality of municipal ordinances under
which members of the Jehovah's Witnesses were convicted for not
paying license taxes on the sale of their tracts and other religious
publications. By this time, Justices Black, Douglas, and Murphy,
after growing increasingly uneasy in their support of the* Gobitis
*Decision, were ready to repudiate it. They did so in the notable but
brief opinion given here, which appeared in addition to Chief Justice Stone's dissent for the four. Justice Reed could muster only
Justices Roberts, Frankfurter, Byrnes, and Jackson to join in holding the line.*

*Nevertheless, outright reversal was well on the way. Liber-
tarian Justice Rutledge would soon take the seat resigned by Justice
Byrnes, and the flag-salute issue would come up again in* West
Virginia State Board of Education v. Barnette, *decided 6 to 3, on
June 14, 1943. Of the eight who made up the majority in the*
Gobitis *Case, only Justices Roberts, Reed, and Frankfurter voted
to allow the compulsory flag-salute in the* West Virginia Case.
Justice Black's concurring opinion in the Second Flag Salute Case
is on page 104. Here following is the transitional step made in the
Jones v. Opelika *Decision, an honest confession of a judicial mis-
take.*

MR. JUSTICE BLACK, MR. JUSTICE DOUGLAS,
MR. JUSTICE MURPHY

The opinion of the Court sanctions a device which in our opinion suppresses or tends to suppress the free exercise of a religion practiced by a minority group. This is but another step in the direction which *Minersville School District* v. *Gobitis* took against the same religious minority and is a logical extension of the principles upon which that decision rested. Since we joined in the opinion in the *Gobitis Case*, we think this is an appropriate occasion to state that we now believe that it was also wrongly decided. Certainly our democratic form of government functioning under the historic Bill of Rights has a high responsibility to accommodate itself to the religious views of minorities however unpopular and unorthodox those views may be. The First Amendment does not put the right freely to exercise religion in a subordinate position. We fear, however, that the opinions in these and in the *Gobitis Case* do exactly that.

Ex parte Kawato

317 U.S. 69

Decided November 9, 1942

Fully appreciative of the contribution of immigrants to American life, Justice Black has been consistently vigilant in the protection of the rights of aliens. In Ex parte Kumezo Kawato, *he spoke for a unanimous Court in holding that a state of war between Japan and the United States did not suspend the right of a resident alien to sue for wages due him and for damages sustained in his work as a fisherman. The opinion was one that showed the direction of Justice Black's thought in a field that too often tends to be slighted. The major portion of the* Kawato Decision *is presented here. The omitted part contains a review of the pertinent federal laws and finds that no Act of Congress stood in the way of Kumezo Kawato's suit.*

MR. JUSTICE BLACK *delivered the opinion of the Court*

The petitioner, born in Japan, became a resident of the United States in 1905. April 15, 1941, he filed a libel in admiralty against the vessel *Rally* in the District Court for the Southern District of California. He claimed wages were due him for services as a seaman and fisherman on the *Rally*, and sought an allowance for maintenance and cure on allegations that he had sustained severe injuries while engaged in the performance of his duties. Claimants of the vessel appeared and filed an answer on grounds not here material, but later, on January 20, 1942, moved to abate the action on the ground that petitioner, by reason of the state of war then existing between Japan and the United States, had become an enemy alien and therefore had no "right to prosecute any action in any court of the United States during the pendency of said war." The District Judge granted the motion. Petitioner sought *mandamus* in the Circuit Court of Appeals for the Ninth Circuit to compel the District Court to vacate its judgment and proceed to trial of his action, but his motion for leave to file was denied without opinion. . . .

"Alien enemy" as applied to petitioner is at present but the legal definition of his status because he was born in Japan with which we are at war. Nothing in this record indicates, and we cannot assume, that he came to America for any purpose different from that which prompted millions of others to seek our shores— a chance to make his home and work in a free country, governed by just laws, which promise equal protection to all who abide by them. His suit invokes the protection of those laws through our courts both to obtain payment of wages alleged to have been promised him by American citizens for lawful work and reimbursement on account of damages suffered while working for those citizens. . . .

There doubtless was a time when the common law of England would have supported dismissal of petitioner's action, but that time has long since passed. A number of early English decisions, based on a group concept which made little difference between friends and enemies barred all aliens from the courts. This rule was gradually relaxed as to friendly aliens until finally in *Wells* v. *Williams*, the court put the necessities of trade ahead of whatever advantages had been imagined to exist in the old rule, and held that enemy aliens in England under license from the Crown might proceed in the courts. As applied ever since, alien enemies residing in England have been permitted to maintain actions, while those in the land of the enemy were not; and this modern, humane principle has been applied even when the alien was interned as is petitioner here.

The original English common law rule, long ago abandoned there, was, from the beginning, objectionable here. The policy of severity toward alien enemies was clearly impossible for a country whose life blood came from an immigrant stream. In the war of 1812, for example, many persons born in England fought on the American side. Harshness toward immigrants was inconsistent with that national knowledge, present then as now, of the contributions made in peace and war by the millions of immigrants who have learned to love the country of their adoption more than the country of their birth. Hence, in 1813 Chief Justice Kent, in *Clarke* v. *Morey*, set the legal pattern which, with sporadic exceptions, has since been followed. The core of that decision he put in these words: "A lawful residence implies protection, and a capacity to sue and be sued. A contrary doctrine would be repugnant to sound policy, no less than to justice and humanity." Thus the courts aligned their policy with that enjoined upon the President by Congress in 1812 when it directed him to administer the laws controlling aliens in a manner that would be "consistent with the public safety, and according to the dictates of humanity and national hospitality."

In asking that the rights of resident aliens be abrogated in their behalf, private litigants in effect seek to stand in the position of government. But only the Government, and not the private individual, is vested with the power to protect all the people, including loyal aliens, from possible injury from disloyal aliens. If the public welfare demands that this alien shall not receive compensation for his work or payment for his injuries received in the course of his employment, the Government can make the decision without allowing a windfall to these claimants. Even if petitioner were a non-resident enemy alien, it might be more appropriate to release the amount of his claim to the Alien Property Custodian rather than to the claimants; and this is precisely what was done in *Birge-Forbes Co.* v. *Heye*, in which this Court said that the sole objection to giving judgment for an alien enemy "goes only so far as it would give aid and comfort to the other side." The ancient rule against suits by resident alien enemies has survived only so far as necessary to prevent use of the courts to accomplish a purpose which might hamper our own war efforts or give aid to the enemy. This may be taken as the sound principle of the common law today. . . .

Not only has the President not seen fit to use the authority possessed by him under the Trading With the Enemy Act to exclude resident aliens from the courts, but his administration has adopted precisely the opposite program. The Attorney General is primarily responsible for the administration of alien affairs. He has construed the existing statutes and proclamations as not barring this petitioner from our courts, and this stand is emphasized by the Government's appearance in behalf of petitioner in this case.

The consequence of this legislative and administrative policy is a clear authorization to resident enemy aliens to proceed in all courts until administrative or legislative action is taken to exclude them. Were this not true, contractual promises made to them by individuals, as well as promises held out to them under our laws, would become no more than teasing illusions. The doors of our courts have not been shut to peaceable law-abiding aliens seeking to enforce rights growing out of legal occupations. Let the writ issue.

West Virginia State Board of Education v. Barnette

319 U.S. 624

Decided June 14, 1943

The history of the controversy over compulsory saluting of the flag, as reflected in Supreme Court cases, is summarized in the statement of facts concerning the 1942 opinion of Justices Black, Douglas, and Murphy in Jones v. Opelika, *given on page 97. After supporting Justice Frankfurter's 8-to-1 majority opinion in the* First Flag Salute Case, Minersville School District v. Gobitis *(1940), Justices Black, Douglas, and Murphy had long, hard thoughts about the decision, which convinced them that they had made a serious mistake in the Pennsylvania case. In* Jones v. Opelika, *which concerned the distribution of religious tracts by the same sect, the Jehovah's Witnesses, the three Justices joined Chief Justice Stone, the lone dissenter in* Gobitis, *to make a new division of 5 to 4.*

When the flag-salute issue arose again in a case from West Virginia, change in the Court's membership had its effect on the result. The new Justices, Jackson and Rutledge, joined the group led by Chief Justice Stone, and it was Justice Jackson to whom the 6-to-3 majority opinion was assigned. This decision, in West Virginia State Board of Education v. Walter Barnette, Paul Sull and Lucy McClure, *expressly overruled the Court's approval of the Minersville, Pennsylvania, school district's requirement of accept-*

ance of the flag salute as a condition to staying in school. Justice Frankfurter, now on the losing side, wrote a strong dissent. Justices Roberts and Reed adhered to the Court's views in the Gobitis Decision. *Justices Black and Douglas joined a concurring opinion that supported Justice Jackson's majority opinion, and Justice Murphy concurred separately.*

MR. JUSTICE BLACK *and* MR. JUSTICE DOUGLAS, *concurring*

We are substantially in agreement with the opinion just read, but since we originally joined with the Court in the *Gobitis Case,* it is appropriate that we make a brief statement of reasons for our change of view.

Reluctance to make the Federal Constitution a rigid bar against state regulation of conduct thought inimical to the public welfare was the controlling influence which moved us to consent to the *Gobitis Decision.* Long reflection convinced us that although the principle is sound, its application in the particular case was wrong. We believe that the statute before us fails to accord full scope to the freedom of religion secured to the appellees by the First and Fourteenth Amendments.

The statute requires the appellees to participate in a ceremony aimed at inculcating respect for the flag and for this country. The Jehovah's Witnesses, without any desire to show disrespect for either the flag or the country, interpret the Bible as commanding, at the risk of God's displeasure, that they not go through the form of a pledge of allegiance to any flag. The devoutness of their belief is evidenced by their willingness to suffer persecution and punishment, rather than make the pledge.

No well-ordered society can leave to the individuals an absolute right to make final decisions, unassailable by the State, as to everything they will or will not do. The First Amendment does not go so far. Religious faiths, honestly held, do not free individuals from responsibility to conduct themselves obediently to laws which are either imperatively necessary to protect society as a whole from grave and pressingly imminent dangers or which, without any general prohibition, merely regulate time, place, or manner of religious activity. Decision as to the constitutionality of particular laws which strike at the substance of religious tenets and practices must be made by this Court. The duty is a solemn one, and in meeting it we cannot say that a failure, because of religious scruples, to assume a particular physical position and to repeat the words of a patriotic formula creates a grave danger to the nation. Such a statutory exaction is a form of test oath, and the test oath has always been abhorrent in the United States.

Words uttered under coercion are proof of loyalty to nothing but self-interest. Love of country must spring from willing hearts and free minds, inspired by a fair administration of wise laws enacted by the people's elected representatives within the bounds of express constitutional prohibitions. These laws must, to be consistent with the First Amendment, permit the widest toleration of conflicting viewpoints consistent with a society of free men.

Neither our domestic tranquillity in peace nor our martial effort in war depend on compelling little children to participate in a ceremony which ends in nothing for them but a fear of spiritual condemnation. If, as we think, their fears are groundless, time and reason are the proper antidotes for their errors. The ceremonial, when enforced against conscientious objectors, more likely to defeat than to serve its high purpose, is a handy implement for disguised religious persecution. As such, it is inconsistent with our Constitution's plan and purpose.

Ashcraft v. *Tennessee*

322 U.S. 143

Decided May 1, 1944

In his unanimous opinion in the memorable 1940 Chambers v.
Florida Case, *Justice Black declared himself as being unreservedly
opposed to coerced confessions in criminal proceedings (page
62). In 1941, he was just as ready to speak out in a strong minority
protest written for a similar case. Dissenting only with Justice
Douglas, he called on the Supreme Court to apply the principles of
the* Chambers *Decision in the case of* Major Raymond Lisenba v.
People of the State of California.

Three years later in E. E. Ashcraft and John Ware v. State of
Tennessee, *Justice Black was with the majority and speaking for
it in a strong opinion that voided a forced confession. The facts are
described in detail in his 6-to-3 opinion, which was supported by
Chief Justice Stone and Justices Reed, Douglas, Murphy, and
Rutledge. A dissenting opinion by Justice Jackson was joined by
Justices Roberts and Frankfurter.*

MR. JUSTICE BLACK *delivered the opinion of the Court*

About three o'clock on the morning of Thursday, June 5,
1941, Mrs. Zelma Ida Ashcraft got in her automobile at her home
in Memphis, Tennessee, and set out on a trip to visit her mother's
home in Kentucky. Late in the afternoon of the same day, her car
was observed a few miles out of Memphis, standing on the wrong

side of a road which she would likely have taken on her journey. Just off the road, in a slough, her lifeless body was found. On her head were cut places inflicted by blows sufficient to have caused her death. Petitioner Ware, age 20, a Negro, was indicted in a state court and found guilty of her murder. Petitioner Ashcraft, age 45, a white man, husband of the deceased, charged with having hired Ware to commit the murder, was tried jointly with Ware and convicted as an accessory before the fact. Both were sentenced to ninety-nine years in the state penitentiary. The Supreme Court of Tennessee affirmed the convictions. . . .

This treatment of the confessions by the two state courts, the manner of the confessions' submission to the jury, and the emphasis upon the great weight to be given confessions make all the more important the kind of "independent examination" of petitioners' claims which, in any event, we are bound to make. Our duty to make that examination could not have been "foreclosed by the finding of a court, or the verdict of a jury, or both." We proceed therefore to consider the evidence relating to the circumstances out of which the alleged confessions came.

First, as to Ashcraft. Ashcraft was born on an Arkansas farm. At the age of eleven he left the farm and became a farm hand working for others. Years later he gravitated into construction work, finally becoming a skilled dragline and steam-shovel operator. Uncontradicted evidence in the record was that he had acquired for himself "an excellent reputation." In 1929 he married the deceased Zelma Ida Ashcraft. Childless, they accumulated, apparently through Ashcraft's earnings, a very modest amount of jointly held property including bank accounts and an equity in the home in which they lived. The Supreme Court of Tennessee found "nothing to show but what the home life of Ashcraft and the deceased was pleasant and happy." Several of Mrs. Ashcraft's friends who were guests at the Ashcraft home on the night before her tragic death testified that both husband and wife appeared to be in a happy frame of mind.

The officers first talked to Ashcraft about 6 p.m. on the day of his wife's murder as he was returning home from work. Informed by them of the tragedy, he was taken to an undertaking establishment to identify her body which previously had been identified only by a driver's license. From there he was taken to the county jail where he conferred with the officers until about 2 a.m. No clues of ultimate value came from this conference, though it did result in the officers' holding and interrogating the Ashcraft's maid and several of her friends. During the following week the officers made extensive investigations in Ashcraft's neighborhood and elsewhere and further conferred with Ashcraft himself on several occasions, but none of these activities produced tangible evidence pointing to the identity of the murderer.

Then, early in the evening of Saturday, June 14, the officers came to Ashcraft's home and "took him into custody." In the words of the Tennessee Supreme Court,

> They took him to an office or room on the northwest corner of the fifth floor of the Shelby County jail. This office is equipped with all sorts of crime and detective devices such as a fingerprint outfit, cameras, high-powered lights, and such other devices as might be found in a homicide investigating office. . . . It appears that the officers placed Ashcraft at a table in this room on the fifth floor of the county jail with a light over his head and began to quiz him. They questioned him in relays until the following Monday morning, June 16, 1941, around nine-thirty or ten o'clock. It appears that Ashcraft from Saturday evening at seven o'clock until Monday morning at approximately nine-thirty never left this homicide room on the fifth floor.

Testimony of the officers shows that the reason they questioned Ashcraft "in relays" was that they became so tired they were compelled to rest. But from 7:00 Saturday evening until 9:30 Monday morning Ashcraft had no rest. One officer did say that he gave the suspect a single five minutes' respite, but except for this five minutes the procedure consisted of one continuous stream of questions.

As to what happened in the fifth-floor jail room during this thirty-six hour secret examination, the testimony follows the usual pattern and is in hopeless conflict. Ashcraft swears that the first thing said to him when he was taken into custody was, "Why in hell did you kill your wife?"; that during the course of the examination he was threatened and abused in various ways; and that as the hours passed his eyes became blinded by a powerful electric light, his body became weary, and the strain on his nerves became unbearable. The officers, on the other hand, swear that throughout the questioning they were kind and considerate. They say that they did not accuse Ashcraft of the murder until four hours after he was brought to the jail building, though they freely admit that from that time on their barrage of questions was constantly directed at him on the assumption that he was the murderer. Together with other persons whom they brought in on Monday morning to witness the culmination of the thirty-six hour ordeal the officers declare that at that time Ashcraft was "cool," "calm," "collected," "normal"; that his vision was unimpaired and his eyes not bloodshot; and that he showed no outward signs of being tired or sleepy.

As to whether Ashcraft actually confessed, there is a similar conflict of testimony. Ashcraft maintains that although the officers incessantly attempted by various tactics of intimidation to entrap him into a confession, not once did he admit knowledge concerning or participation in the crime. And he specifically denies the officers' statements that he accused Ware of the crime, insisting that in response to their questions he merely gave them the name of Ware as one of several men who occasionally had ridden with him to work. The officers' version of what happened, however, is that about 11 p.m. on Sunday night, after twenty-eight hours' constant questioning, Ashcraft made a statement that Ware had overpowered him at his home and abducted the deceased, and was probably the killer. About midnight the officers found Ware and took him into custody, and, according to their testimony, Ware made a self-incriminating statement as of early Monday morning, and at 5:40 a.m. signed by mark a written confession in which appeared the statement that Ashcraft had hired him to commit the murder. This alleged confession of Ware was read to Ashcraft about six o'clock Monday morning, whereupon Ashcraft is said substantially to have admitted its truth in a detailed statement taken down by a reporter. About 9:30 Monday morning a transcript of Ashcraft's purported statement was read to him. The State's position is that he affirmed its truth but refused to sign the transcript, saying that he first wanted to consult his lawyer. As to this latter 9:30 episode the officers' testimony is reinforced by testimony of the several persons whom they brought in to witness the end of the examination.

In reaching our conclusion as to the validity of Ashcraft's confession we do not resolve any of the disputed questions of fact relating to the details of what transpired within the confession chamber of the jail or whether Ashcraft actually did confess. Such disputes, we may say, are an inescapable consequence of secret inquisitorial practices. And always evidence concerning the inner details of secret inquisitions is weighted against an accused, particularly where, as here, he is charged with a brutal crime, or where, as in many other cases, his supposed offense bears relation to an unpopular economic, political, or religious cause.

Our conclusion is that, if Ashcraft made a confession, it was not voluntary but compelled. We reach this conclusion from facts which are not in dispute at all. Ashcraft, a citizen of excellent reputation, was taken into custody by police officers. Ten days' examination of the Ashcrafts's maid, and of several others, in jail where they were held, had revealed nothing whatever against Ashcraft. Inquiries among his neighbors and business associates likewise had failed to unearth one single tangible clue pointing to his guilt. For thirty-six hours after Ashcraft's seizure, during which period he was held incommunicado, without sleep or rest, relays of officers, experienced investigators, and highly trained lawyers questioned him without respite. From the beginning of the questioning at 7 o'clock on Saturday evening until 6 o'clock on Monday morning, Ashcraft denied that he had anything to do with the murder of his wife. And at a hearing before a magistrate about 8:30 Monday morning Ashcraft pleaded not guilty to the charge of murder which the officers had sought to make him confess during the previous thirty-six hours.

We think a situation such as that here shown by uncontradicted evidence is so inherently coercive that its very existence is irreconcilable with the possession of mental freedom by a lone suspect against whom its full coercive force is brought to bear. It is inconceivable that any court of justice in the land, conducted as our courts are, open to the public, would permit prosecutors serving in relays to keep a defendant witness under continuous cross-examination for thirty-six hours without rest or sleep in an effort to extract a "voluntary" confession. Nor can we, consistently with constitutional due process of law, hold voluntary a confession where prosecutors do the same thing away from the restraining influences of a public trial in an open court room.

The Constitution of the United States stands as a bar against the conviction of any individual in an American court by means of a coerced confession. There have been, and are now, certain foreign nations with governments dedicated to an opposite policy: governments which convict individuals with testimony obtained by police organizations possessed of an unrestrained power to seize persons suspected of crimes against the State, hold them in secret custody, and wring from them confessions by physical or mental torture. So long as the Constitution remains the basic law of our republic, America will not have that kind of government. . . .

Reversed.

Korematsu v. United States

323 U.S. 214

Decided December 18, 1944

There is one time when Justice Black will support action by the Federal Government that normally he would rule out as unconstitutional. That is when the Nation is engaged in war for survival. One of his most widely discussed—and criticized—majority opinions was that in the unprecedented case of Fred Toyosaburo Korematsu v. United States of America. *It upheld the authority of the Federal Government in World War II to assemble all persons, including many native-born American citizens, of Japanese ancestry on the West Coast and to remove them to "relocation centers" as a national defense measure.*

Justice Black's opinion, which Chief Justice Stone and Justices Reed, Douglas, and Rutledge joined, expressly declared that an exclusion order based on racial discrimination would not be allowable. The opinion found no constitutional basis for objection to the order issued by General DeWitt, but instead held it to be a reasonable and valid military precaution in time of grave peril. The date of the exclusion order was five months after the Japanese air attack on Pearl Harbor. As Justice Frankfurter concurred in a separate opinion, there were six Justices on the side of the validity of the commanding general's order.

Notwithstanding the national emergency with which the Korematsu Case dealt, three Justices dissented. Senior among them was Justice Roberts, who said that he thought "the indisputable facts" exhibited "a clear violation of constitutional rights." Justice

Murphy took the position that, in the absence of martial law, the exclusion went over "the brink of constitutional power" and fell "into the ugly abyss of racism." Justice Jackson based his dissent upon his belief that civil courts should not "be asked to execute a military expedient that has no place in law under the Constitution."

Justice Black's majority opinion in Korematsu *needs to be compared with his opinion written for the Court in the unanimous decision in* Ex parte Kawato *(page 100).*

Mr. Justice Black *delivered the opinion of the Court*

The petitioner, an American citizen of Japanese descent, was convicted in a Federal District Court for remaining in San Leandro, California, a "Military Area," contrary to Civilian Exclusion Order No. 34 of the Commanding General of the Western Command, U.S. Army, which directed that after May 9, 1942, all persons of Japanese ancestry should be excluded from that area. No question was raised as to petitioner's loyalty to the United States. The Circuit Court of Appeals affirmed, and the importance of the constitutional question involved caused us to grant *certiorari*.

It should be noted, to begin with, that all legal restrictions which curtail the civil rights of a single racial group are immediately suspect. That is not to say that all such restrictions are unconstitutional. It is to say that courts must subject them to the most rigid scrutiny. Pressing public necessity may sometimes justify the existence of such restrictions; racial antagonism never can.

In the instant case, prosecution of the petitioner was begun by information charging violation of an Act of Congress, of March 21, 1942, which provides that ". . . whoever shall enter, remain in, leave, or commit any act in any military area or military zone prescribed, under the authority of an Executive order of the President, by the Secretary of War, or by any military commander designated by the Secretary of War contrary to the restrictions applicable to any such area or zone or contrary to the order of the Secretary of War or any such military commander, shall, if it appears that he knew or should have known of the existence and extent of the restrictions or order and that his act was in violation thereof, be guilty of a misdemeanor and upon conviction shall be liable to a fine of not to exceed $5,000 or to imprisonment for not more than one year, or both, for each offense."

Exclusion Order No. 34, which the petitioner knowingly and

admittedly violated, was one of a number of military orders and proclamations, all of which were substantially based upon Executive Order No. 9066, 7 Fed. Reg. 1407. That order, issued after we were at war with Japan, declared that "the successful prosecution of the war requires every possible protection against espionage and against sabotage to national-defense material, national-defense premises, and national-defense utilities. . . ."

One of the series of orders and proclamations, a curfew order, which like the exclusion order here was promulgated pursuant to Executive Order 9066, subjected all persons of Japanese ancestry in prescribed West Coast military areas to remain in their residences from 8 p.m. to 6 a.m. As is the case with the exclusion order here, that prior curfew order was designed as a "protection against espionage and against sabotage." In *Hirabayashi* v. *United States*, we sustained a conviction obtained for violation of the curfew order. The Hirabayashi conviction and this one thus rest on the same 1942 Congressional Act and the same basic executive and military orders, all of which orders were aimed at the twin dangers of espionage and sabotage.

The 1942 Act was attacked in the *Hirabayashi Case* as an unconstitutional delegation of power; it was contended that the curfew order and other orders on which it rested were beyond the war powers of the Congress, the military authorities and of the President, as Commander in Chief of the Army; and finally that to apply the curfew order against none but citizens of Japanese ancestry amounted to a constitutionally prohibited discrimination solely on account of race. To these questions, we gave the serious consideration which their importance justified. We upheld the curfew order as an exercise of the power of the Government to take steps necessary to prevent espionage and sabotage in an area threatened by Japanese attack.

In the light of the principles we announced in the *Hirabayashi Case*, we are unable to conclude that it was beyond the war power of Congress and the Executive to exclude those of Japanese ancestry from the West Coast war area at the time they did. True, exclusion from the area in which one's home is located is a far greater deprivation than constant confinement to the home from 8 p.m. to 6 a.m. Nothing short of apprehension by the proper military authorities of the gravest imminent danger to the public safety can constitutionally justify either. But exclusion from a threatened area, no less than curfew, has a definite and close relationship to the prevention of espionage and sabotage. The military authorities, charged with the primary responsibility of defending our shores, concluded that curfew provided inadequate protection and ordered exclusion. They did so, as pointed out in our *Hirabayashi* opinion, in accordance with congressional authority to the military to say who should, and who should not, remain in the threatened areas.

In this case, the petitioner challenges the assumptions upon which we rested our conclusions in the *Hirabayashi Case*. He also urges that by May 1942, when Order No. 34 was promulgated, all danger of Japanese invasion of the West Coast had disappeared. After careful consideration of these contentions, we are compelled to reject them.

Here, as in the *Hirabayashi Case*, "we cannot reject as unfounded the judgment of the military authorities and of Congress that there were disloyal members of that population, whose number and strength could not be precisely and quickly ascertained. We cannot say that the war-making branches of the Government did not have ground for believing that in a critical hour such persons could not readily be isolated and separately dealt with, and constituted a menace to the national defense and safety, which demanded that prompt and adequate measures be taken to guard against it."

Like curfew, exclusion of those of Japanese origin was deemed necessary because of the presence of an unascertained number of disloyal members of the group, most of whom we have no doubt were loyal to this country. It was because we could not reject the finding of the military authorities, that it was impossible to bring about an immediate segregation of the disloyal from the loyal, that we sustained the validity of the curfew order as applying to the whole group. In the instant case, temporary exclusion of the entire group was rested by the military on the same ground. The judgment that exclusion of the whole group was for the same reason a military imperative answers the contention that the exclusion was in the nature of group punishment based on antagonism to those of Japanese origin. That there were members of the group who retained loyalties to Japan has been confirmed by investigations made subsequent to the exclusion. Approximately five thousand American citizens of Japanese ancestry refused to swear unqualified allegiance to the United States and to renounce allegiance to the Japanese Emperor, and several thousand evacuees requested repatriation to Japan.

We uphold the exclusion order as of the time it was made and when the petitioner violated it. In doing so, we are not unmindful of the hardships imposed by it upon a large group of American citizens. But hardships are part of war, and war is an aggregation of hardships. All citizens alike, both in and out of uniform, feel the impact of war in greater or lesser measure. Citizenship has its responsibilities as well as its privileges, and in time of war the burden is always heavier. Compulsory exclusion of large groups of citizens from their homes, except under circumstances of direst emergency and peril, is inconsistent with our basic governmental institutions. But when under conditions of modern warfare our shores are threatened by hostile forces, the power to protect must be commensurate with the threatened danger.

It is argued that on May 30, 1942, the date the petitioner was charged with remaining in the prohibited area, there were conflicting orders outstanding, forbidding him both to leave the area and to remain there. Of course, a person cannot be convicted for doing the very thing which it is a crime to fail to do. But the outstanding orders here contained no such contradictory commands.

There was an order issued March 27, 1942, which prohibited petitioner and others of Japanese ancestry from leaving the area, but its effect was specifically limited in time "until and to the extent that a future proclamation or order should so permit or direct.". . .

It does appear, however, that on May 9, the effective date of the exclusion order, the military authorities had already determined that the evacuation should be effected by assembling together and placing under guard all those of Japanese ancestry, at central points, designated as "assembly centers," in order "to insure the orderly evacuation and resettlement of Japanese voluntarily migrating from military area No. 1 to restrict and regulate such migration." And on May 19, 1942, eleven days before the time petitioner was charged with unlawfully remaining in the area, Civilian Restrictive Order No. 1, provided for detention of those of Japanese ancestry in assembly or relocation centers. It is now argued that the validity of the exclusion order cannot be considered apart from the orders requiring him, after departure from the area, to report and to remain in an assembly or relocation center. The contention is that we must treat these separate orders as one and inseparable; that, for this reason, if detention in the assembly or relocation center would have illegally deprived the petitioner of his liberty, the exclusion order and his conviction under it cannot stand.

We are thus being asked to pass at this time upon the whole

subsequent detention program in both assembly and relocation centers, although the only issues framed at the trial related to petitioner's remaining in the prohibited area in violation of the exclusion order. Had petitioner here left the prohibited area and gone to an assembly center we cannot say either as a matter of fact or law, that his presence in that center would have resulted in his detention in a relocation center. Some who did report to the assembly center were not sent to relocation centers, but were released upon condition that they remain outside the prohibited zone until the military orders were modified or lifted. This illustrates that they pose different problems and may be governed by different principles. The lawfulness of one does not necessarily determine the lawfulness of the others. This is made clear when we analyze the requirements of the separate provisions of the separate orders. These separate requirements were that those of Japanese ancestry (1) depart from the area; (2) report to and temporarily remain in an assembly center; (3) go under military control to a relocation center there to remain for an indeterminate period until released conditionally or unconditionally by the military authorities. Each of these requirements, it will be noted, imposed distinct duties in connection with the separate steps in a complete evacuation program. Had Congress directly incorporated into one Act the language of these separate orders, and provided sanctions for their violations, disobedience of any one would have constituted a separate offense. There is no reason why violations of these orders, insofar as they were promulgated pursuant to congressional enactment, should not be treated as separate offenses.

The *Endo Case*, decided today, graphically illustrates the difference between the validity of an order to exclude and the validity of a detention order after exclusion has been effected.

Since the petitioner has not been convicted of failing to report or to remain in an assembly or relocation center, we cannot in this case determine the validity of those separate provisions of the order. It is sufficient here for us to pass upon the order which petitioner violated. To do more would be to go beyond the issues raised, and to decide momentous questions not contained within the framework of the pleadings or the evidence in this case. It will be time enough to decide the serious constitutional issues which petitioner seeks to raise when an assembly or relocation order is applied or is certain to be applied to him, and we have its terms before us.

Some of the members of the Court are of the view that

evacuation and detention in an Assembly Center were inseparable. After May 3, 1942, the date of Exclusion Order No. 34, Korematsu was under compulsion to leave the area not as he would choose but via an Assembly Center. The Assembly Center was conceived as a part of the machinery for group evacuation. The power to exclude includes the power to do it by force if necessary. And any forcible measure must necessarily entail some degree of detention or restraint whatever method of removal is selected. But whichever view is taken, it results in holding that the order under which petitioner was convicted was valid.

It is said that we are dealing here with the case of imprisonment of a citizen in a concentration camp solely because of his ancestry, without evidence or inquiry concerning his loyalty and good disposition toward the United States. Our task would be simple, our duty clear, were this a case involving the imprisonment of a loyal citizen in a concentration camp because of racial prejudice. Regardless of the true nature of the assembly and relocation centers—and we deem it unjustifiable to call them concentration camps with all the ugly connotations that term implies—we are dealing specifically with nothing but an exclusion order. To cast this case into outlines of racial prejudice, without reference to the real military dangers which were presented, merely confuses the issue. Korematsu was not excluded from the Military Area because of hostility to him or to his race. He was excluded because we are at war with the Japanese Empire, because the properly constituted military authorities feared an invasion of our West Coast and felt constrained to take proper security measures, because they decided that the military urgency of the situation demanded that all citizens of Japanese ancestry be segregated from the West Coast temporarily, and finally, because Congress, reposing its confidence in this time of war in our military leaders—as inevitably it must—determined that they should have the power to do just this. There was evidence of disloyalty on the part of some, the military authorities considered that the need for action was great, and time was short. We cannot—by availing ourselves of the calm perspective of hindsight—now say that at that time these actions were unjustified.

Affirmed.

In re Summers

325 U.S. 561

―――――

Decided June 11, 1945

How far can the individual citizen go in the exercise of freedom of religion under the Constitution? In his often quoted dissent to the 6-to-3 decision in United States v. Schwimmer *(1928), Justice Oliver Wendell Holmes, who bore the wounds of three separate battles of the Civil War, defended the application of Rosika Schwimmer, a Hungarian-born pacifist, to become a naturalized citizen notwithstanding her refusal to bear arms. By 1931, the division was narrowed to 5 to 4 in the similar cases of* United States v. Macintosh *and* United States v. Bland. *These decisions all were expressly overruled in* Girouard v. United States *(1946), and Justice Black joined Justice Douglas's 5-to-3 majority opinion, which declared the* Schwimmer, Bland *and* Macintosh *Cases "wrongly decided."*

Meantime, In re Clyde Wilson Summers *presented the issue of pacifism and oath-taking in another area, namely, admission to practice law. Dividing 5 to 4, the Supreme Court upheld the courts of Illinois in excluding an applicant whose religious scruples prevented him from agreeing to kill other human beings in time of war. Justice Reed prepared the majority opinion, which Chief Justice Stone and Justices Roberts, Frankfurter, and Jackson joined. Justice Black's dissent was supported by Justices Douglas, Murphy, and Rutledge. From this clear, strong opinion it is plain that in tests between sincerely held religious convictions and as-*

*serted requirements of the Government, Justice Black favors the
fullest possible exercise of freedom of religion.*

*Although he was excluded in Illinois, Clyde Summers had no
difficulty, after a full presentation of the Illinois facts, in being
admitted to the New York bar in 1951. Five years later, he became
a professor in the Yale University Law School. As a member of
the bar, Summers has served on New York and Connecticut state
agencies concerned with labor management practices, unemployment insurance, and civil rights and also with the Labor Relations
Law Section of the American Bar Association, as secretary.*

Notwithstanding this repudiation of its handling of the Summers Case, *Illinois produced still another major bar admission case
involving the First Amendment, in which Justice Black wrote, in
1961, an even stronger protest. The second case was* In re Anastaplo *(see page 408). Here is Justice Black's* Summers *dissent.*

Mr. Justice Black, *dissenting*

The State of Illinois has denied the petitioner the right to
practice his profession and to earn his living as a lawyer. It has
denied him a license on the ground that his present religious beliefs
disqualify him for membership in the legal profession. The question
is, therefore, whether a state which requires a license as a prerequisite to practicing law can deny an applicant a license solely because of his deeply rooted religious convictions. The fact that
petitioner measures up to every other requirement for admission to
the bar set by the State demonstrates beyond doubt that the only
reason for his rejection was his religious beliefs.

The State does not deny that petitioner possesses the following
qualifications:

He is honest, moral, and intelligent, has had a college and a
law school education. He has been a law professor and fully
measures up to the high standards of legal knowledge Illinois has
set as a prerequisite to admission to practice law in that state. He
has never been convicted for, or charged with, a violation of law.
That he would serve his clients faithfully and efficiently if admitted
to practice is not denied. His ideals of what a lawyer should be
indicate that his activities would not reflect discredit upon the bar,
that he would strive to make the legal system a more effective
instrument of justice. Because he thinks that "Lawsuits do not
bring love and brotherliness, they just create antagonisms," he
would, as a lawyer, exert himself to adjust controversies out of

court, but would vigorously press his client's cause in court if efforts to adjust failed. Explaining to his examiners some of the reasons why he wanted to be a lawyer, he told them: "I think there is a lot of work to be done in the law. . . . I think the law has a place to see to it that every man has a chance to eat and a chance to live equally. I think the law has a place where people can go and get justice done for themselves without paying too much, for the bulk of people that are too poor." No one contends that such a vision of the law in action is either illegal or reprehensible.

The petitioner's disqualifying religious beliefs stem chiefly from a study of the New Testament and a literal acceptance of the teachings of Christ as he understands them. Those beliefs are these:

He is opposed to the use of force for either offensive or defensive purposes. The taking of human life under any circumstances he believes to be against the Law of God and contrary to the best interests of man. He would if he could, he told his examiners, obey to the letter these precepts of Christ: "Love your Enemies; Do good to those that hate you; Even though your enemy strikes you on your right cheek, turn to him your left cheek also." The record of his evidence before us bears convincing marks of the deep sincerity of his convictions, and counsel for Illinois with commendable candor does not question the genuineness of his professions.

I cannot believe that a state statute would be consistent with our constitutional guarantee of freedom of religion if it specifically denied the right to practice law to all members of one of our great religious groups, Protestant, Catholic, or Jewish. Yet the Quakers have had a long and honorable part in the growth of our nation, and an *amicus curiae* brief filed in their behalf informs us that under the test applied to this petitioner, not one of them, if true to the tenets of their faith, could qualify for the bar in Illinois. And it is obvious that the same disqualification would exist as to every conscientious objector to the use of force. . . . For a lawyer is no more subject to call for military duty than a plumber, a highway worker, a Secretary of State, or a prison chaplain.

It may be, as many people think, that Christ's gospel of love and submission is not suited to a world in which men still fight and kill one another. But I am not ready to say that a mere profession of belief in that gospel is a sufficient reason to keep otherwise well-qualified men out of the legal profession, or to drive law-abiding lawyers of that belief out of the profession, which would be the next logical development.

Nor am I willing to say that such a belief can be penalized through the circuitous method of prescribing an oath, and then barring an applicant on the ground that his present belief might later prompt him to do or refrain from doing something that might violate that oath. Test oaths, designed to impose civil disabilities upon men for their beliefs rather than for unlawful conduct, were an abomination to the founders of this nation. This feeling was made manifest in Article Six of the Constitution which provides that "no religious test shall ever be required as a Qualification to any Office or public Trust under the United States."

The State's denial of petitioner's application to practice law resolves itself into a holding that it is lawfully required that all lawyers take an oath to support the state constitution and that petitioner's religious convictions against the use of force make it impossible for him to observe that oath. The petitioner denies this and is willing to take the oath. The particular constitutional provision involved authorizes the legislature to draft Illinois citizens from 18 to 45 years of age for militia service. It can be assumed that the State of Illinois has the constitutional power to draft conscientious objectors for war duty and to punish them for a refusal to serve as soldiers—powers which this Court held the United States possesses. But that is not to say that Illinois could constitutionally use the test oath it did in this case. In the *Schwimmer* and *Macintosh Cases,* aliens were barred from naturalization because their then religious beliefs would bar them from bearing arms to defend the country. Dissents in both cases rested in part on the premise that religious tests are incompatible with our constitutional guarantee of freedom of thought and religion. In the *Schwimmer Case* dissent, Mr. Justice Holmes said that "if there is any principle of the Constitution that more imperatively calls for attachment than any other it is the principle of free thought—not free thought for those who agree with us but freedom for the thought that we hate. I think that we should adhere to that principle with regard to admission into, as well as to life within this country." In the *Macintosh Case* dissent, Mr. Chief Justice Hughes said, "To conclude that the general oath of office is to be interpreted as disregarding the religious scruples of these citizens and as disqualifying them for office because they could not take the oath with such an interpretation would, I believe, be generally regarded as contrary not only to the specific intent of the Congress but as repugnant to the fundamental principle of representative government."

I agree with the constitutional philosophy underlying the dissents of Mr. Justice Holmes and Mr. Chief Justice Hughes.

The Illinois Constitution itself prohibits the draft of conscientious objectors except in time of war and also excepts for militia duty persons who are "exempted by the laws of the United States." It has not drafted men into the militia since 1864, and if it ever should again, no one can say that it will not, as has the Congress of the United States, exempt men who honestly entertain the views that this petitioner does. Thus the probability that Illinois would ever call the petitioner to serve in a war has little more reality than an imaginary quantity in mathematics.

I cannot agree that a state can lawfully bar from a semi-public position, a well-qualified man of good character solely because he entertains a religious belief which might prompt him at some time in the future to violate a law which has not yet been and may never be enacted. Under our Constitution men are punished for what they do or fail to do and not for what they think and believe. Freedom to think, to believe, and to worship, has too exalted a position in our country to be penalized on such an illusory basis.

I would reverse the decision of the State Supreme Court.

Mr. Justice Douglas, Mr. Justice Murphy, *and* Mr. Justice Rutledge *concur in this opinion*

Marsh v. Alabama

326 U.S. 501

—

Decided January 7, 1946

One of the most controversial among the many Supreme Court decisions involving the energetic missionary sect known as the Jehovah's Witnesses was handed down by Justice Black in the sharply disputed 5-to-3 case of Grace Marsh v. State of Alabama. *In it a distributor of denominational literature appeared on the street of a company town, Chickasaw, Alabama, owned by the Gulf Shipbuilding Corporation, after she had been instructed by the company not to use the street for religious purposes.*

Linking freedom of speech, freedom of religion, and freedom of the press, Justice Black wrote the Court's opinion, which held that a company town was no different from any other community in the observance of these fundamental liberties. He was joined by Justices Douglas, Murphy, and Rutledge. Justice Frankfurter concurred in a separate opinion. Justice Reed wrote a vigorous dissent, which Chief Justice Stone and Justice Burton joined. Justice Jackson did not participate. The Black opinion illustrates its author's skill at presenting his position with quiet persuasion.

MR. JUSTICE BLACK *delivered the opinion of the Court*

In this case we are asked to decide whether a state, consistently with the First and Fourteenth Amendments, can impose criminal punishment on a person who undertakes to distribute religious literature on the premises of a company-owned town contrary to the wishes of the town's management. The town, a suburb of

Mobile, Alabama, known as Chickasaw, is owned by the Gulf Shipbuilding Corporation. Except for that, it has all the characteristics of any other American town. The property consists of residential buildings, streets, a system of sewers, a sewage disposal plant, and a "business block" on which business places are situated. A deputy of the Mobile County Sheriff, paid by the company, serves as the town's policeman. Merchants and service establishments have rented the stores and business places on the business block and the United States uses one of the places as a post office from which six carriers deliver mail to the people of Chickasaw and the adjacent area. The town and the surrounding neighborhood, which cannot be distinguished from the Gulf property by anyone not familiar with the property lines, are thickly settled, and according to all indications the residents use the business block as their regular shopping center. To do so, they now, as they have for many years, make use of a company-owned paved street and sidewalk located alongside the store fronts in order to enter and leave the stores and post office. Intersecting company-owned roads at each end of the business block lead into a four-lane public highway which runs parallel to the business block at a distance of thirty feet. There is nothing to stop highway traffic from coming onto the business block, and upon arrival a traveler may make free use of the facilities available there. In short, the town and its shopping district are accessible to and freely used by the public in general and there is nothing to distinguish them from any other town and shopping center except the fact that the title to the property belongs to a private corporation. . . .

Had the title to Chickasaw belonged not to a private but to a municipal corporation and had appellant been arrested for violating a municipal ordinance rather than a ruling by those appointed by the corporation to manage a company town it would have been clear that appellant's conviction must be reversed. Under our decision in *Lovell* v. *Griffin* and others which have followed that case, neither a state nor a municipality can completely bar the distribution of literature containing religious or political ideas on its streets, sidewalks, and public places or make the right to distribute dependent on a flat license tax or permit to be issued by an official who could deny it at will. We have also held that an ordinance completely prohibiting the dissemination of ideas on the city streets cannot be justified on the ground that the municipality holds legal title to them. And we have recognized that the preservation of a free society is so far dependent upon the right of each individual citizen to receive such literature as he himself might desire that a municipality could not, without jeopardizing that vital individual freedom, prohibit door to door distribution of literature. From these decisions it is clear that had the people of Chickasaw owned all the homes, and all the stores, and all the streets, and all the sidewalks, all those owners together could not have set up a municipal government with sufficient power to pass an ordinance completely barring the distribution of religious literature. Our question then narrows down to this: Can those people who live in or come to Chickasaw be denied freedom of press and religion simply because a single company has legal title to all the town? For it is the State's contention that the mere fact that all the property interests in the town are held by a single company is enough to give that company power, enforceable by a state statute, to abridge these freedoms.

We do not agree that the corporation's property interests settle the question. The State urges in effect that the corporation's right to control the inhabitants of Chickasaw is coextensive with the right of a homeowner to regulate the conduct of his guests. We cannot accept that contention. Ownership does not always mean absolute dominion. The more an owner, for his advantage, opens up his property for use by the public in general, the more do his rights become circumscribed by the statutory and constitutional rights of those who use it. Thus, the owners of privately held bridges, ferries, turnpikes, and railroads may not operate them as freely as a farmer does his farm. Since these facilities are built and operated primarily to benefit the public and since their operation is essentially a public function, it is subject to state regulation. And, though the issue is not directly analogous to the one before us, we do want to point out by way of illustration that such regulation may not result in any operation of these facilities, even by privately owned companies, which unconstitutionally interferes with and discriminates against interstate commerce. Had the corporation here owned the cement of the four-lane highway which runs parallel to the "business block" and operated the same under a State franchise, doubtless no one would have seriously contended that the corporation's property interest in the highway gave it power to obstruct through traffic or to discriminate against interstate commerce. And even had there been no express franchise but mere acquiescence by the State in the corporation's use of its property as a segment of the four-lane highway, operation of all the highway, including the segment owned by the corporation, would still have been performance of a public function and discrimination would certainly have been illegal.

We do not think it makes any significant constitutional difference as to the relationship between the rights of the owner and those of the public that here the State, instead of permitting the corporation to operate a highway, permitted it to use its property as a town, operate a "business block" in the town and a street and sidewalk on that business block. Whether a corporation or a municipality owns or possesses the town, the public in either case has an identical interest in the functioning of the community in such manner that the channels of communication remain free. As we have heretofore stated, the town of Chickasaw does not function differently from any other town. The "business block" serves as the community shopping center and is freely accessible and open to the people in the area and those passing through. The managers appointed by the corporation cannot curtail the liberty of press and religion of these people consistently with the purposes of the constitutional guarantees, and a state statute, as the one here involved, which enforces such action by criminally punishing those who attempt to distribute religious literature clearly violates the First and Fourteenth Amendments to the Constitution.

Many people in the United States live in company-owned towns. These people, just as residents of municipalities, are free citizens of their state and country. Just as all other citizens they must make decisions which affect the welfare of community and nation. To act as good citizens they must be informed. In order to enable them to be properly informed their information must be uncensored. There is no more reason for depriving these people of the liberties guaranteed by the First and Fourteenth Amendments than there is for curtailing these freedoms with respect to any other citizen. . . .

When we balance the constitutional rights of owners of property against those of the people to enjoy freedom of press and religion, as we must here, we remain mindful of the fact that the latter occupy a preferred position. . . . Insofar as the State has attempted to impose criminal punishment on appellant for undertaking to distribute religious literature in a company town, its action cannot stand. The case is reversed and the cause remanded for further proceedings not inconsistent with this opinion.

Reversed and remanded.

Duncan v. Kahanamoku

327 U.S. 304

Decided February 25, 1946

How far can military commissions go under the Constitution in sentencing civilians to prison? Courts and judges have divided on this issue of military tribunals versus civil rights for many years, and they were divided in the joined cases of Lloyd C. Duncan *v.* Duke Paoa Kahanamoku, Sheriff of the City and County of Honolulu *and* Harry E. White *v.* William F. Steer, Colonel, Infantry, United States Army, Provost Marshal, Central Pacific Area.

Both Duncan and White were civilians, the former a shipfitter and the latter a Honolulu stockbroker. Duncan was found guilty of engaging in a brawl with Marine sentries, and White was convicted of embezzlement. They were among hundreds of people who were tried in Hawaii by military commissions in World War II and sentenced while Hawaii was under martial law. This meant that the trials were along military lines and did not provide important constitutional safeguards to which accused civilians are entitled.

In habeas corpus *proceedings, the United States District Court for Hawaii held that the military commissions did not have the power to sentence these civilians to prison, and ordered them released. The Court of Appeals reversed the District Court and ordered the freed men sent back to prison. In a majority opinion written by Justice Black, the Supreme Court reversed the Court of Appeals and directed once again that Duncan and White be set free.*

The Black opinion was joined by Justices Reed, Douglas, Murphy, and Rutledge. Chief Justice Stone wrote a separate concurring opinion and so did Justice Murphy. Justices Frankfurter and Burton dissented. Justice Jackson did not participate.

Justice Black's opinion, like so many of his opinions, illuminated the problem before the Supreme Court with the light of history and experience.

MR. JUSTICE BLACK *delivered the opinion of the Court*

. . . Did the [Hawaiian] Organic Act during the period of martial law give the armed forces power to supplant all civilian laws and to substitute military for judicial trials under the conditions that existed in Hawaii at the time these petitioners were tried? The relevant conditions, for our purposes, were the same when both petitioners were tried. The answer to the question depends on a correct interpretation of the Act. But we need not construe the Act, insofar as the power of the military might be used to meet other and different conditions and situations. The boundaries of the situation with reference to which we do interpret the scope of the Act can be more sharply defined by stating at this point some different conditions which either would or might conceivably have affected to a greater or lesser extent the scope of the authorized military power. We note first that at the time the alleged offenses were committed the dangers apprehended by the military were not sufficiently imminent to cause them to require civilians to evacuate the area or even to evacuate any of the buildings necessary to carry on the business of the courts. In fact, the buildings had long been open and actually in use for certain kinds of trials. Our question does not involve the well-established power of the military to exercise jurisdiction over members of the armed forces, those directly connected with such forces, or enemy belligerents, prisoners of war, or others charged with violating the laws of war. We are not concerned with the recognized power of the military to try civilians in tribunals established as a part of a temporary military government over occupied enemy territory or territory regained from an enemy where civilian government cannot and does not function. For Hawaii since annexation has been held by and loyal to the United States. Nor need we here consider the power of the military simply to arrest and detain civilians interfering with a necessary military function at a time of turbulence and danger from insurrection or war. And finally, there was no specialized effort of the military, here, to enforce orders which related only to military functions, such as, for illustration, curfew rules or blackouts. For these petitioners were tried before tribunals set up under a military program which took over all government and superseded all civil laws and courts. If the Organic Act, properly interpreted, did not give the armed forces this awesome power, both petitioners are entitled to their freedom.

In interpreting the Act we must first look to its language. Section 67 makes it plain that Congress did intend the Governor of Hawaii, with the approval of the President, to invoke military aid under certain circumstances. But Congress did not specifically state to what extent the army could be used or what power it could exercise. It certainly did not explicitly declare that the Governor in conjunction with the military could for days, months or years close all the courts and supplant them with military tribunals. If a power thus to obliterate the judicial system of Hawaii can be found at all in the Organic Act, it must be inferred from Section 67's provision for placing the Territory under "martial law." But the term "martial law" carries no precise meaning. The Constitution does not refer to "martial law" at all and no Act of Congress has defined the term. It has been employed in various ways by different people and at different times. By some it has been identified as "military law" limited to members of, and those connected with, the armed forces. Others have said that the term does not imply a system of established rules but denotes simply some kind of day to day expression of a General's will dictated by what he considers the imperious necessity of the moment. In 1857 the confusion as to the meaning of the phrase was so great that the Attorney General in an official opinion had this to say about it: "The Common Law authorities and commentators afford no clue to what martial law as understood in England really is. . . . In this country it is still worse." What was true in 1857 remains true today. The language of Section 67 thus fails to define adequately the scope of the power given to the military and to show whether the Organic Act provides that courts of law be supplanted by military tribunals. . . .

Since both the language of the Organic Act and its legislative history fail to indicate that the scope of "martial law" in Hawaii includes the supplanting of courts by military tribunals, we must look to other sources in order to interpret that term. We think the answer may be found in the birth, development, and growth of our governmental institutions up to the time Congress passed the Organic Act. Have the principles and practices developed during the birth and growth of our political institutions been such as to persuade us that Congress intended that loyal civilians in loyal territory should have their daily conduct governed by military orders substituted for criminal laws, and that such civilians should be tried and punished by military tribunals? Let us examine what those principles and practices have been, with respect to the position of civilian government and the courts, and compare that with the standing of military tribunals throughout our history.

People of many ages and countries have feared and unflinchingly opposed the kind of subordination of executive, legislative, and judicial authorities to complete military rule, which according to the Government Congress has authorized here. In this country that fear has become part of our cultural and political institutions. The story of that development is well known and we see no need to retell it all. But we might mention a few pertinent incidents. As early as the Seventeenth Century, our British ancestors took political action against aggressive military rule. When James I and Charles I authorized martial law for purposes of speedily punishing all types of crimes committed by civilians, the protest led to the historic Petition of Right, which in uncompromising terms objected to this arbitrary procedure and prayed that it be stopped and never repeated. When later the American Colonies declared their independence, one of the grievances listed by Jefferson was that the King had endeavored to render the military superior to the civil power. The executive and military officials, who later found it necessary to utilize the armed forces to keep order in a young and turbulent nation, did not lose sight of the philosophy embodied in the Petition of Right and the Declaration of Independence, that existing civilian government and especially the courts were not to be interfered with by the exercise of military power. In 1787, the year in which the Constitution was formulated, the Governor of Massachusetts Colony used the militia to cope with Shays's Rebellion. In his instructions to the Commander of the troops, the Governor listed the "great objects" of the mission. The troops were to "protect the judicial courts . . .", "to assist the civil magistrates in executing the laws . . .", and to "aid them in apprehending the disturbers of the public peace. . . ." The Commander was to consider himself "constantly as under the direction of the civil officer, saving where any armed force shall appear and oppose . . . [his] marching to execute these orders." President Washington's instructions to the Commander of the troops sent into Pennsylvania to suppress the Whiskey Rebellion of 1794 were to see to it that the laws were enforced and were to deliver the leaders of armed insurgents to the regular courts for trial. The President admonished the Commanding General "that the judge can not be controlled in his functions." In the many instances of the use of troops to control the activities of civilians that followed, the troops were generally again employed merely to aid and not to supplant the civilian authorities. The last noteworthy incident before the enactment of the Organic Act was the rioting that occurred in the Spring of 1899 at the Coeur-d'Alene mines of Shoshone County, Idaho. The President ordered the regular troops to report to the Governor for instructions and to support the civil authorities in preserving the peace. Later the State Auditor as agent of the Governor, and not the Commanding General, ordered the troops to detain citizens without trial and to aid the Auditor in doing all he thought necessary to stop the riot. Once more, the military authorities did not undertake to supplant the courts and to establish military tribunals to try and punish ordinary civilian offenders.

Courts and their procedural safeguards are indispensable to our system of government. They were set up by our founders to protect the liberties they valued. Our system of government clearly is the antithesis of total military rule, and the founders of this country are not likely to have contemplated complete military dominance within the limits of a Territory made part of this country and not recently taken from an enemy. They were opposed to governments that placed in the hands of one man the power to make, interpret and enforce the laws. Their philosophy has been the people's throughout our history. For that reason we have maintained legislatures chosen by citizens or their representatives and courts and juries to try those who violate legislative enactments. We have always been especially concerned about the potential evils of summary criminal trials and have guarded against them by provisions embodied in the Constitution itself. Legislatures and courts are not merely cherished American institutions; they are indispensable to our government.

Military tribunals have no such standing. For as this Court has said before: ". . . the military should always be kept in subjection to the laws of the country to which it belongs, and that he is no friend to the Republic who advocates the contrary. The established principle of every free people is, that the law shall alone govern; and to it the military must always yield." Congress prior to the time of the enactment of the Organic Act had only once authorized the supplanting of the courts by military tribunals. Legislation to that effect was enacted immediately after the South's unsuccessful attempt to secede from the Union. Insofar as that legislation applied to the Southern States after the war was at an end, it was challenged by a series of Presidential vetoes as vigorous as any in the country's history. And in order to prevent this Court from passing on the constitutionality of this legislation, Congress found it necessary to curtail our appellate jurisdiction. Indeed, prior to the Organic Act, the only time this Court had ever discussed the supplanting of courts by military tribunals in a situation other than that involving the establishment of a military government over recently occupied enemy territory, it had emphatically declared that "civil liberty and this kind of martial law cannot endure together; the antagonism is irreconcilable; and, in the conflict, one or the other must perish."

We believe that when Congress passed the Hawaiian Organic Act and authorized the establishment of "martial law" it had in mind and did not wish to exceed the boundaries between military and civilian power, in which our people have always believed, which responsible military and executive officers had heeded, and which had become part of our political philosophy and institutions prior to the time Congress passed the Organic Act. The phrase "martial law" as employed in that Act, therefore, while intended to authorize the military to act vigorously for the maintenance of an orderly civil government and for the defense of the Islands against actual or threatened rebellion or invasion, was not intended to authorize the supplanting of courts by military tribunals. Yet the government seeks to justify the punishment of both White and Duncan on the ground of such supposed congressional authorization. We hold that both petitioners are now entitled to be released from custody.

Reversed.

United States v. Lovett

328 U.S. 303

Decided June 3, 1946

In the aggregate of its thousands of decisions over the years, the Supreme Court does not often declare an Act of Congress or part of an Act unconstitutional. The 1935–36 term of the Court was most exceptional, for in it thirteen provisions of Congress were held to be invalid. Ordinarily a term will pass without so much as one decision declaring a Congressional enactment in violation of the Constitution. Provocation must be strong. And when the Supreme Court does stay the hand of Congress, it usually is done with asserted reluctance and regret.

Such a situation arose in the three cases of United States v. Robert Morss Lovett, United States v. Goodwin B. Watson, and United States v. William E. Dodd, Jr. In 1943 the three respondents were fully satisfactory employees of their employers, namely, three agencies of the United States Government. The prospect was that the Messrs. Lovett, Watson, and Dodd would have been continued indefinitely in the public employ. All were men of standing in prior professional work. Dr. Lovett, for example, had been a distinguished member of the faculty of the University of Chicago and an esteemed writer before his appointment by President Franklin D. Roosevelt as Government Secretary of the Virgin Islands.

Messrs. Lovett, Watson, and Dodd, however, were among thirty-nine public employees denounced in 1943 by Representative Martin Dies of Texas, first chairman of the House Un-American

Activities Committee, as affiliates of Communist-front organiza-
tions. He said that because of their beliefs and past associations,
they were unfit to "hold a Government position," and he called on
Congress to refuse to appropriate funds for their salaries. In so
doing, Representative Dies sought to use the House Un-American
Activities Committee to establish standards of "American" thought
and conduct with regard to orthodox and heretical views in poli-
tics, and almost equally to enforce these standards on public opin-
ion through hearings which were far less legislative than they were
administrative and judicial.

A major legislative effort of the Committee in this period was
the rider that it persuaded the House to attach to the urgent De-
ficiency Appropriation Act of 1943 for the express purpose of
cutting off the salaries of Messrs. Lovett, Watson, and Dodd.
President Roosevelt signed the bill with the rider because the ap-
propriated funds were imperatively needed at the time to carry on
World War II, but he said frankly that he believed the rider was
unconstitutional. In effect the President invited a Supreme Court
test of the issue raised by the rider, Section 304.

These three Government employees were retained on the
United States payroll after the congressional cutoff date of No-
vember 15, 1943. As a necessary step toward collecting their
salaries, they sued to invalidate the rider on the ground that it
operated as a bill of attainder and therefore was contrary to the
Constitution. They won a lower court judgment that compensa-
tion should be paid to them, and this was affirmed by the Supreme
Court in an opinion by Justice Black, which Justices Douglas,
Murphy, Rutledge, and Burton joined. Justices Reed and Frank-
furter concurred in the result. Justice Jackson took no part in the
cases and the chief justiceship was vacant, for Harlan Fiske Stone
died a short time before the arguments.

This firm judicial disciplining of the House Un-American Ac-
tivities Committee in 1946 becomes especially noteworthy in light
of the Committee's judicial victories a decade and a half later, for
example, in the Wilkinson *and* Braden Cases *(pages 385 and 391).*

MR. JUSTICE BLACK *delivered the opinion of the Court*

. . . In the background of the statute here challenged lies the
House of Representatives' feeling in the late thirties that many
"subversives" were occupying influential positions in the Government and elsewhere and their influence must not remain unchallenged. As part of its program against "subversive" activities, the
House, in May 1938, created a Committee on Un-American

Activities, which became known as the Dies Committee after its Chairman, Congressman Martin Dies. This Committee conducted a series of investigations and made lists of people and organizations it thought "subversive." The creation of the Dies Committee was followed by provisions such as Section 9A of the Hatch Act and 17 (b) of the Emergency Relief Appropriations Act of 1941, which forbade the holding of a federal job by anyone who was a member of a political party or organization that advocated the overthrow of our Constitutional form of Government in the United States. It became the practice to include a similar prohibition in all appropriations acts, together with criminal penalties for its violation. Under these provisions the Federal Bureau of Investigation began wholesale investigations of federal employees, which investigations were financed by special congressional appropriations. Thousands were investigated.

While all this was happening, Mr. Dies on February 1, 1943, in a long speech on the floor of the House attacked thirty-nine named Government employees as "irresponsible, unrepresentative, crackpot, radical bureaucrats" and affiliates of "communist front organizations." Among these named individuals were the three respondents. Congressman Dies told the House that respondents, as well as the other thirty-six individuals he named, were, because of their beliefs and past associations, unfit to "hold a government position" and urged Congress to refuse "to appropriate money for their salaries." In this connection he proposed that the Committee on Appropriations "take immediate and vigorous steps to eliminate these people from public office." Four days later an amendment was offered to the Treasury-Post Office Appropriation Bill which provided that "no part of any appropriation contained in this Act shall be used to pay the compensation of" the thirty-nine individuals Dies had attacked. The *Congressional Record* shows that this amendment precipitated a debate that continued for several days. All of those participating agreed that the "charges" against the thirty-nine individuals were serious. Some wanted to accept Congressman Dies's statements as sufficient proof of "guilt," while others referred to such proposed action as "legislative lynching," smacking "of the procedure in the French Chamber of Deputies, during the Reign of Terror." The Dies charges were referred to as "indictments," and many claimed this made it necessary that the named federal employees be given a hearing and a chance to prove themselves innocent. Congressman Dies then suggested that the

Appropriations Committee "weigh the evidence and . . . take immediate steps to dismiss these people from the federal service." Eventually a resolution was proposed to defer action until the Appropriations Committee could investigate, so that accused federal employees would get a chance to prove themselves "innocent" of communism or disloyalty, and so that each "man would have his day in court," and "There would be no star chamber proceedings." . . .

The Senate Appropriations Committee eliminated Section 304 and its action was sustained by the Senate. After the first conference report, which left the matter still in disagreement, the Senate voted 69 to 0 against the conference report which left Section 304 in the bill. The House however insisted on the amendment and indicated that it would not approve any appropriation bill without Section 304. Finally, after the fifth conference report showed that the House would not yield, the Senate adopted Section 304. When the President signed the bill, he stated: "The Senate yielded, as I have been forced to yield, to avoid delaying our conduct of the war. But I cannot so yield without placing on record my view that this provision is not only unwise and discriminatory, but unconstitutional" . . .

We hold that Section 304 falls precisely within the category of Congressional actions which the Constitution barred by providing that "No Bill of Attainder or Ex Post Facto Law shall be passed." In *Cummings* v. *Missouri*, this Court said, "A bill of attainder is a legislative Act which inflicts punishment without a judicial trial. If the punishment be less than death, the act is termed a bill of pains and penalties. Within the meaning of the Constitution, bills of attainder include bills of pains and penalties." The *Cummings Decision* involved a provision of the Missouri Reconstruction Constitution which required persons to take an Oath of Loyalty as a prerequisite to practicing a profession. Cummings, a Catholic Priest, was convicted for teaching and preaching as a minister without taking the oath. The oath required an applicant to affirm that he had never given aid or comfort to persons engaged in hostility to the United States and had never "been a member of or connected with any order, society, or organization inimical to the government of the United States. . . ." In an illuminating opinion which gave the historical background of the constitutional prohibition against bills of attainder, this Court invalidated the Missouri constitutional provision both because it constituted a bill of attainder and because it had an *ex post facto* operation. On the same day the *Cummings Case* was decided, the Court, in *Ex parte Garland,* also held invalid on the same grounds an Act of Congress which required attorneys practicing before this Court to take a similar oath. Neither of these cases has ever been overruled. They stand for the proposition that legislative acts, no matter what their form, that apply either to named individuals or to easily ascertainable members of a group in such a way as to inflict punishment on them without a judicial trial are bills of attainder prohibited by the Constitution. Adherence to this principle requires invalidation of Section 304. We do adhere to it.

Section 304 was designed to apply to particular individuals. Just as the statute in the two cases mentioned, it "operates as a legislative decree of perpetual exclusion" from a chosen vocation. This permanent proscription from any opportunity to serve the Government is punishment, and of a most severe type. It is a type of punishment which Congress has only invoked for special types of odious and dangerous crimes, such as treason, acceptance of bribes by members of Congress, or by other governmental officials, and interference with elections by Army and Navy officers.

Section 304, thus, clearly accomplishes the punishment of named individuals without a judicial trial. The fact that the punishment is inflicted through the instrumentality of an Act specifically cutting off the pay of certain named individuals found guilty of disloyalty, makes it no less galling or effective than if it had been done by an Act which designated the conduct as criminal. No one would think that Congress could have passed a valid law, stating that after investigation it had found Lovett, Dodd, and Watson "guilty" of the crime of engaging in "subversive activities," defined that term for the first time, and sentenced them to perpetual exclusion from any government employment. Section 304, while it does not use that language, accomplishes that result. The effect was to inflict punishment without the safeguards of a judicial trial and "determined by no previous law or fixed rule." The Constitution declares that that cannot be done either by a state or by the United States.

Those who wrote our Constitution well knew the danger inherent in special legislative acts which take away the life, liberty, or property of particular named persons, because the Legislature thinks them guilty of conduct which deserves punishment. They intended to safeguard the people of this country from punishment without trial by duly constituted courts. And even the courts to which this important function was entrusted were commanded to stay their hands until and unless certain tested safeguards were observed. An accused in court must be tried by an impartial jury, has a right to be represented by counsel, he must be clearly informed of the charge against him, the law which he is charged with violating must have been passed before he committed the act charged, he must be confronted by the witnesses against him, he must not be compelled to incriminate himself, he cannot twice be put in jeopardy for the same offense, and even after conviction no cruel and unusual punishment can be inflicted upon him. When our Constitution and Bill of Rights were written, our ancestors had ample reason to know that legislative trials and punishments were too dangerous to liberty to exist in the nation of free men they envisioned. And so they proscribed bills of attainder. Section 304 is one. Much as we regret to declare that an Act of Congress violates the Constitution, we have no alternative here.

Section 304 therefore does not stand as an obstacle to payment of compensation to Lovett, Watson, and Dodd. The judgment in their favor is affirmed.

Affirmed.

Colegrove v. Green

328 U.S. 549

Decided June 10, 1946

Does the Fourteenth Amendment's Clause guaranteeing equal protection of the laws extend to fair representation in legislative chambers whose seats are apportioned on the basis of population distribution? The Supreme Court has said "No" and it has also said "Yes."

It said "No" in the case of Kenneth W. Colegrove, Peter J. Chamales, and Kenneth C. Sears *v.* Dwight H. Green, *as a Member ex officio of the Primary Certifying Board of the State of Illinois, et al. In this case, a professor of political science at Northwestern University and two associates brought suit as three qualified voters in Illinois Congressional districts that had much larger populations than other Illinois Congressional districts. Since the Illinois Legislature had failed, for some 45 years, to redistrict for seats in the national House of Representatives, the populations of the districts ranged disproportionately from 112,116 to 914,053. The case was dismissed in the Federal District Court in Chicago and the dismissal was upheld in the Supreme Court, 4 to 3.*

Justice Frankfurter announced the judgment in an opinion joined by Justices Reed and Burton which said: "To sustain this action would cut very deep into the very being of Congress. Courts ought not to enter this political thicket." Justice Rutledge concurred in the result. Justice Black dissented with the concurrence of Justices Douglas and Murphy. Justice Jackson did not partici-

*pate. The chief justiceship was vacant as Chief Justice Vinson had
not yet been commissioned following the death of Chief Justice
Stone. As senior member, Justice Black presided.*

The decision in Colegrove *stood for approximately sixteen
years. Then in a 6-to-2 decision, March 26, 1962, the Supreme
Court entered resolutely, if cautiously, into "this political thicket"
against which Justice Frankfurter had so strongly warned. It did
so in the case of* Charles W. Baker, et al. v. Joe C. Carr, et al., *369
U.S. 186, which arose among city residents in Tennessee in protest
against the long-continued failure (since 1901) of the rurally dominated Tennessee Legislature to reapportion seats in its own popula-
tion-based chamber in accordance with the growth of Memphis,
Chattanooga, Knoxville, and other Tennessee cities.*

*Justice Brennan's opinion, joined by Chief Justice Warren and
Justice Black, returned the case to a three-judge Federal District
Court in Nashville, which, in applying the* Colegrove *Decision,
had dismissed the suit on the ground that the District Court had
no jurisdiction. The* Brennan *opinion said that "the district court
will be able to fashion relief if violations of constitutional rights
are found." Justices Douglas, Clark, and Stewart concurred in
separate opinions. Only dissenting Justices Frankfurter and Harlan
held to the* Colegrove *Decision. Justice Whittaker, ill and close to
retirement, did not participate.*

*Thus the Supreme Court, in a decision of far-reaching impli-
cations, opened the way for correction of an evil within the machinery for representative government that was becoming worse
with the years. The major part of Justice Black's prophetic dissent
in the much earlier case of* Colegrove v. Green *follows.*

MR. JUSTICE BLACK, *dissenting*

. . . The 1901 [Illinois] State Apportionment Act in reducing the effectiveness of petitioners' votes abridges their privilege as
citizens to vote for Congressmen and violates Article I of the
Constitution. Article I provides that Congressmen "shall be . . .
chosen . . . by the people of the several States." It thus gives those
qualified a right to vote and a right to have their vote counted. This
Court in order to prevent "an interference with the effective choice
of the voters" has held that this right extends to primaries. While
the Constitution contains no express provision requiring that
Congressional election districts established by the States must
contain approximately equal populations, the constitutionally guaranteed right to vote and the right to have one's vote counted

clearly imply the policy that state election systems, no matter what their form, should be designed to give approximately equal weight to each vote cast. To some extent this implication of Article I is expressly stated by Section 2 of the Fourteenth Amendment which provides that "Representatives shall be apportioned among the several States according to their respective numbers. . . ." The purpose of this requirement is obvious: It is to make the votes of the citizens of the several States equally effective in the selection of members of Congress. It was intended to make illegal a nation-wide "rotten borough" system as between the States. The policy behind it is broader than that. It prohibits as well Congressional "rotten boroughs" within the States, such as the ones here involved. The policy is that which is laid down by all the constitutional provisions regulating the election of members of the House of Representatives, including Article I which guarantees the right to vote and to have that vote effectively counted: All groups, classes, and individuals shall to the extent that it is practically feasible be given equal representation in the House of Representatives, which, in conjunction with the Senate, writes the laws affecting the life, liberty, and property of all the people.

It is true that the States are authorized by Section 2 of Article I of the Constitution to legislate on the subject of Congressional elections to the extent that Congress has not done so. Thus the power granted to the State Legislature on this subject is primarily derived from the Federal and not from the State Constitution. But this federally granted power with respect to elections of Congressmen is not to formulate policy but rather to implement the policy laid down in the Constitution, that, so far as feasible, votes be given equally effective weight. Thus, a state legislature cannot deny eligible voters the right to vote for Congressmen and the right to have their vote counted. It can no more destroy the effectiveness of their vote in part and no more accomplish this in the name of "apportionment" than under any other name. For legislation which must inevitably bring about glaringly unequal representation in the Congress in favor of special classes and groups should be invalidated, "whether accomplished ingeniously or ingenuously."

Had Illinois passed an Act requiring that all of its twenty-six Congressmen be elected by the citizens of one county, it would clearly have amounted to a denial to the citizens of the other counties of their constitutionally guaranteed right to vote. And I cannot imagine that an Act that would have apportioned twenty-five Congressmen to the State's smallest county and one Congressman to all the others, would have been sustained by any court. Such an Act would clearly have violated the constitutional policy of equal representation. The 1901 Apportionment Act here involved violates that policy in the same way. The policy with respect to federal elections laid down by the Constitution, while it does not mean that the courts can or should prescribe the precise methods to be followed by state legislatures and the invalidation of all Acts that do not embody those precise methods, does mean that state legislatures must make real efforts to bring about approximately equal representation of citizens in Congress. Here the Legislature of Illinois has not done so. Whether that was due to negligence or was a willful effort to deprive some citizens of an effective vote, the admitted result is that the constitutional policy of equality of representation has been defeated. Under these circumstances it is the Court's duty to invalidate the State law.

It is contended, however, that a court of equity does not have the power, or even if it has the power, that it should not exercise it in this case. To do so, it is argued, would mean that the Court is entering the area of "political questions." I cannot agree with that argument. There have been cases, such as *Coleman* v. *Miller*, where this Court declined to decide a question because it was political. In the *Miller Case*, however, the question involved was ratification of a constitutional amendment, a matter over which the Court believed Congress had been given final authority. To have decided that question would have amounted to a trespass upon the constitutional power of Congress. Here we have before us a State law which abridges the constitutional rights of citizens to cast votes in such way as to obtain the kind of Congressional representation the Constitution guarantees to them.

It is true that voting is a part of elections and that elections are "political." But as this Court said in *Nixon* v. *Herndon*, it is a mere "play on words" to refer to a controversy such as this as "political" in the sense that courts have nothing to do with protecting and vindicating the right of a voter to cast an effective ballot. The *Classic Case*, among myriads of others, refutes the contention with evasions of all "political" rights. *Wood* v. *Broom*, does not preclude the granting of equitable relief in this case. There this Court simply held that the State Apportionment Act did not violate the Congressional Reapportionment Act of 1929, since that Act did not require election districts of equal population. The Court expressly reserved the question of "the right of the complainant to relief in equity." *Giles* v. *Harris* also did not hold that a Court of Equity could not, or should not, exercise its power in a case like this. As we said with reference to that decision in *Lane* v. *Wilson*, it stands for the principle that courts will not attempt to "supervise" elections. Furthermore, the author of the *Giles* v. *Harris* opinion also wrote the opinion in *Nixon* v. *Herndon*, in which a voter's right to cast a ballot was held to give rise to a justiciable controversy.

In this case, no supervision over elections is asked for. What is asked is that this Court do exactly what it did in *Smiley* v. *Holm*. It is asked to declare a state apportionment bill invalid and to enjoin state officials from enforcing it. The only difference between this case and the *Smiley Case* is that there the case originated in the state courts while here the proceeding originated in the Federal District Court. The only type of case in which this Court has held that a federal district court should in its discretion stay its hand any more than a state court is where the question is one which state courts or administrative agencies have special competence to decide. This is not that type of question. What is involved here is the right to vote guaranteed by the Federal Constitution. It has always been the rule that, where a federally protected right has been invaded, the federal courts will provide the remedy to rectify the wrong done. Federal courts have not hesitated to exercise their equity power in cases involving deprivation of property and liberty. There is no reason why they should do so where the case involves the right to choose representatives that make laws affecting liberty and property.

Nor is there any more difficulty in enforcing a decree in this case than there was in the *Smiley Case*. It is true that declaration of invalidity of the State Act and the enjoining of State officials would result in prohibiting the State from electing Congressmen under the system of the old Congressional districts. But it would leave the State free to elect them from the State at large, which, as we held in the *Smiley Case*, is a manner authorized by the Constitution. It is said that it would be inconvenient for the State to conduct the election in this manner. But it has an element of virtue that the more convenient method does not have—namely, it does not discriminate against some groups to favor others, it gives all the people an equally effective voice in electing their representatives as is essential under a free government, and it is constitutional.

MR. JUSTICE DOUGLAS *and* MR. JUSTICE MURPHY *join in this dissent*

Everson v. Board of Education

330 U.S. 1

Decided February 10, 1947

Within a short period of little more than four years, Justice Black delivered three major opinions concerning the relations between Church and State in connection with the attendance of pupils at public and parochial schools. These are among his most widely discussed opinions and all are reproduced in full—except for citations and footnotes—so each reader may have ready access to all of the Justice's arguments and also see how he related the three cases. In the first case, Arch R. Everson v. Board of Education of the Township of Ewing et al., as well in the second, Illinois ex rel. McCollum v. Board of Education (page 182), Justice Black spoke for the majority. In the third, Zorach v. Clauson (page 250), he dissented. The facts in each case, respectively from New Jersey, Illinois, and New York, are adequately summarized in the Black opinions.

The 5-to-4 division in the Everson Case produced an unusual alignment of the Justices. Justice Black was joined by Chief Justice Vinson and Justices Reed, Douglas, and Murphy. Among the four dissenters, Justice Jackson wrote a strong dissenting opinion joined by Justice Frankfurter, and Justice Rutledge wrote a vigorous dissent joined by Justice Burton. Justice Frankfurter also joined the dissent by Justice Rutledge. Thus the decision took Justice Rutledge away from Justices Black, Douglas, and Murphy, with whom Justice Rutledge frequently stood in non-unanimous cases involving the Bill of Rights.

*In this case Justice Black was just as adamant as the strongest
dissenter in his insistence that no church could be helped by a unit
of government. He wrote in the majority opinion one of the most
complete definitions of the separation of Church and State ever to
appear in a court decision. He simply did not see a breach in the
wall arising from the facts in the New Jersey case. As a consequence, he was criticized from both sides—by those who objected
to paying transportation fares for parochial school pupils with tax-
raised funds and by those clerical leaders and others who favored
state aid for parochial schools. Other students of the problem found
the Black opinion making a fair and reasonable distinction.*

MR. JUSTICE BLACK *delivered the opinion of the Court*

A New Jersey statute authorizes its local school districts to
make rules and contracts for the transportation of children to and
from schools. The appellee, a township board of education, acting
pursuant to this statute authorized reimbursement to parents of
money expended by them for the bus transportation of their
children on regular buses operated by the public transportation
system. Part of this money was for the payment of transportation
of some children in the community to Catholic parochial schools.
These church schools give their students, in addition to secular
education, regular religious instruction conforming to the religious
tenets and modes of worship of the Catholic faith. The superintendent of these schools is a Catholic priest.

The appellant in his capacity as a district taxpayer, filed suit
in a state court challenging the right of the Board to reimburse
parents of parochial school students. He contended that the statute
and the resolution passed pursuant to it violated both the State and
the Federal Constitutions. That court held that the Legislature was
without power to authorize such payment under the State Constitution. The New Jersey Court of Errors and Appeals reversed, holding that neither the statute nor the resolution passed pursuant to it
was in conflict with the State Constitution or the provisions of the
Federal Constitution in issue. The case is here on appeal.

Since there has been no attack on the statute on the ground
that a part of its language excludes children attending private
schools operated for profit from enjoying state payment for
their transportation, we need not consider this exclusionary language; it has no relevancy to any constitutional question here
presented. Furthermore, if the Exclusion Clause had been properly

challenged, we do not know whether New Jersey's highest court would construe its statutes as precluding payment of the school transportation of any group of pupils, even those of a private school run for profit. Consequently, we put to one side the question as to the validity of the statute against the claim that it does not authorize payment for the transportation generally of school children in New Jersey.

The only contention here is that the state statute and the resolution, insofar as they authorized reimbursement to parents of children attending parochial schools, violate the Federal Constitution in these two respects, which to some extent, overlap. *First.* They authorize the State to take by taxation the private property of some and bestow it upon others, to be used for their own private purposes. This, it is alleged, violates the Due Process Clause of the Fourteenth Amendment. *Second.* The statute and the resolution forced inhabitants to pay taxes to help support and maintain schools which are dedicated to, and which regularly teach, the Catholic faith. This is alleged to be a use of state power to support church schools contrary to the prohibition of the First Amendment which the Fourteenth Amendment made applicable to the States.

First. The due process argument that the State law taxes some people to help others carry out their private purposes is framed in two phases. The first phase is that a state cannot tax A to reimburse B for the cost of transporting his children to church schools. This is said to violate the Due Process Clause because the children are sent to these church schools to satisfy the personal desires of their parents, rather than the public's interest in the general education of all children. This argument, if valid, would apply equally to prohibit state payment for the transportation of children to any non-public school, whether operated by a church or another non-government individual or group. But the New Jersey Legislature has decided that a public purpose will be served by using tax-raised funds to pay the bus fares of all school children, including those who attend parochial schools. The New Jersey Court of Errors and Appeals has reached the same conclusion. The fact that a state law, passed to satisfy a public need, coincides with the personal desires of the individuals most directly affected is certainly an inadequate reason for us to say that a legislature has erroneously appraised the public need.

It is true that this Court has, in rare instances, struck down state statutes on the ground that the purpose for which tax-raised funds were to be expended was not a public one. But the Court has also pointed out that this far-reaching authority must be exercised with the most extreme caution. Otherwise, a state's power to legislate for the public welfare might be seriously curtailed, a power which is a primary reason for the existence of States. Changing local conditions create new local problems which may lead a state's people and its local authorities to believe that laws authorizing new types of public services are necessary to promote the general well-being of the people. The Fourteenth Amendment did not strip the States of their power to meet problems previously left for individual solution.

It is much too late to argue that legislation intended to facilitate the opportunity of children to get a secular education serves no public purpose. The same thing is no less true of legislation to reimburse needy parents, or all parents, for payment of the fares of their children so that they can ride in public buses to and from schools rather than run the risk of traffic and other hazards incident to walking or "hitchhiking." Nor does it follow that a law has a private rather than a public purpose because it provides that tax-raised funds will be paid to reimburse individuals on account of money spent by them in a way which furthers a public program. Subsidies and loans to individuals such as farmers and home owners, and to privately owned transportation systems, as well as many other kinds of businesses, have been commonplace practices in our state and national history.

Insofar as the second phase of the due process argument may differ from the first, it is by suggesting that taxation for transportation of children to church schools constitutes support of a religion by the State. But if the law is invalid for this reason, it is because it violates the First Amendment's prohibition against the establishment of religion by law. This is the exact question raised by appellant's second contention, to consideration of which we now turn.

Second. The New Jersey statute is challenged as a "law respecting the establishment of religion." The First Amendment, as made applicable to the States by the Fourteenth, commands that a state "shall make no law respecting an establishment of religion, or prohibiting the free exercises thereof." These words of the First Amendment reflected in the minds of early Americans a vivid mental picture of conditions and practices which they fervently wished to stamp out in order to preserve liberty for themselves and for their posterity. Doubtless their goal has not been entirely reached; but so far has the Nation moved toward it that the expression "law respecting the establishment of religion," probably does not so vividly remind present-day Americans of the evils, fears, and political problems that caused that expression to be written into our Bill of Rights. Whether this New Jersey law is one respecting the "establishment of religion" requires an understanding of the meaning of that language, particularly with respect to the imposition of taxes. Once again, therefore, it is not inappropriate briefly to review the background and environment of the period in which that constitutional language was fashioned and adopted.

A large proportion of the early settlers of this country came here from Europe to escape the bondage of laws which compelled them to support and attend government favored churches. The centuries immediately before and contemporaneous with the colonization of America had been filled with turmoil, civil strife, and persecutions, generated in large part by established sects determined to maintain their absolute political and religious supremacy. With the power of government supporting them, at various times and places, Catholics had persecuted Protestants, Protestants had persecuted Catholics, Protestant sects had persecuted other Protestant sects, Catholics of one shade of belief had persecuted Catholics of another shade of belief, and all of these had from time to time persecuted Jews. In efforts to force loyalty to whatever religious group happened to be on top and in league with the government of a particular time and place, men and women had been fined, cast in jail, cruelly tortured, and killed. Among the offenses for which these punishments had been inflicted were such things as speaking disrespectfully of the views of ministers of government-established churches, non-attendance at those churches, expressions of non-belief in their doctrines, and failure to pay taxes and tithes to support them.

These practices of the old world were transplanted to and began to thrive in the soil of the new America. The very charters granted by the English Crown to the individuals and companies designated to make the laws which would control the destinies of the colonials authorized these individuals and companies to erect religious establishments which all, whether believers or non-believers, would be required to support and attend. An exercise of this authority was accompanied by a repetition of many of the old world practices and persecutions. Catholics found themselves hounded and proscribed because of their faith; Quakers who followed their conscience went to jail; Baptists were peculiarly obnoxious to certain dominant Protestant sects; men and women of varied faiths who happened to be in a minority in a particular locality were persecuted because they steadfastly persisted in worshipping God only as their own consciences dictated. And all of these dissenters were compelled to pay tithes and taxes to support government-sponsored churches whose ministers preached inflammatory sermons designed to strengthen and consolidate the established faith by generating a burning hatred against dissenters.

These practices became so commonplace as to shock the freedom-loving Colonials into a feeling of abhorrence. The imposition of taxes to pay ministers' salaries and to build and maintain churches and church property aroused their indignation. It was these feelings which found expression in the First Amendment. No one locality and no one group throughout the Colonies can rightly be given entire credit for having aroused the sentiment that culminated in adoption of the Bill of Rights provisions embracing religious liberty. But Virginia, where the established church had achieved a dominant influence in political affairs and where many excesses attracted wide public attention, provided a great stimulus and able leadership for the movement. The people there, as elsewhere, reached the conviction that individual religious liberty could be achieved best under a government which was stripped of all power to tax, to support, or otherwise to assist any or all religions, or to interfere with the beliefs of any religious individual or group.

The movement toward this end reached its dramatic climax in Virginia in 1785–86 when the Virginia legislative body was about to renew Virginia's tax levy for the support of the established church. Thomas Jefferson and James Madison led the fight against this tax. Madison wrote his great Memorial and Remonstrance against the law. In it, he eloquently argued that a true religion did not need the support of law; that no person, either believer or nonbeliever, should be taxed to support a religious institution of any kind; that the best interest of a society required that the minds of men always be wholly free; and that cruel persecutions were the inevitable result of government-established religions. Madison's Remonstrance received strong support throughout Virginia, and the Assembly postponed consideration of the proposed tax meas-

ure until its next session. When the proposal came up for consideration at that session, it not only died in committee, but the Assembly
enacted the famous "Virginia Bill for Religious Liberty" originally
written by Thomas Jefferson. The preamble to that bill stated
among other things that

> Almighty God hath created the mind free; that all attempts to in-
> fluence it by temporal punishments, or burthens, or by civil in-
> capacitations, tend only to beget habits of hypocrisy and mean-
> ness, and are a departure from the plan of the Holy author of our
> religion who being Lord both of body and mind, yet chose not to
> propagate it by coercions on either . . . ; that to compel a man
> to furnish contributions of money for the propagation of opinions
> which he disbelieves, is sinful and tyrannical; that even the forcing
> him to support this or that teacher of his own religious persuasion,
> is depriving him of the comfortable liberty of giving his contribu-
> tions to the particular pastor, whose morals he would make his
> pattern. . . .

And the statute itself enacted

> That no man shall be compelled to frequent or support any reli-
> gious worship, place, or ministry whatsoever, nor shall be en-
> forced, restrained, molested, or burthened, in his body or goods,
> nor shall otherwise suffer on account of his religious opinions or
> belief.

This Court has previously recognized that the provisions of
the First Amendment, in the drafting and adoption of which Madison and Jefferson played such leading roles, had the same objective
and were intended to provide the same protection against governmental intrusion on religious liberty as the Virginia statute. Prior to
the adoption of the Fourteenth Amendment, the First Amendment
did not apply as a restraint against the States. Most of them did soon
provide similar constitutional protections for religious liberty. But
some states persisted for about half a century in imposing restraints
upon the free exercise of religion and in discriminating against
particular religious groups. In recent years, so far as the provision
against the establishment of a religion is concerned, the question
has most frequently arisen in connection with proposed state aid to
church schools and efforts to carry on religious teachings in the
public schools in accordance with the tenets of a particular sect.
Some churches have either sought or accepted state financial support for their schools. Here again the efforts to obtain state aid or
acceptance of it have not been limited to any one particular faith.

The state courts, in the main, have remained faithful to the language of their own constitutional provisions designed to protect religious freedom and to separate religions and governments. Their decisions, however, show the difficulty in drawing the line between tax legislation which provides funds for the welfare of the general public and that which is designed to support institutions which teach religion.

The meaning and scope of the First Amendment, preventing establishment of religion or prohibiting the free exercise thereof, in the light of its history and the evils it was designed forever to suppress, have been several times elaborated by the decisions of this Court prior to the application of the First Amendment to the States by the Fourteenth. The broad meaning given the Amendment by these earlier cases has been accepted by this Court in its decisions concerning an individual's religious freedom rendered since the Fourteenth Amendment was interpreted to make the prohibitions of the First applicable to state action abridging religious freedom. There is every reason to give the same application and broad interpretation to the Establishment of Religion Clause. The interrelation of these complementary clauses was well summarized in a statement of the Court of Appeals of South Carolina, quoted with approval by this Court in *Watson* v. *Jones:* "The structure of our Government has, for the preservation of civil liberty, rescued the temporal institutions from religious interference. On the other hand, it has secured religious liberty from the invasion of civil authority."

The Establishment of Religion Clause of the First Amendment means at least this: Neither a state nor the Federal Government can set up a church. Neither can pass laws which aid one religion, aid all religions, or prefer one religion over another. Neither can force nor influence a person to go to or to remain away from church against his will or force him to profess a belief or disbelief in any religion. No person can be punished for entertaining or professing religious beliefs or disbeliefs, for church attendance or non-attendance. No tax in any amount, large or small, can be levied to support any religious activities or institutions, whatever they may be called, or whatever form they may adopt to teach or practice religion. Neither a state nor the Federal Government can, openly or secretly, participate in the affairs of any religious organizations or groups and *vice versa*. In the words of Jefferson, the clause against establishment of religion by law was intended to erect "a wall of separation between Church and State."

We must consider the New Jersey statute in accordance with the foregoing limitations imposed by the First Amendment. But we must not strike that State statute down if it is within the State's constitutional power even though it approaches the verge of that power. New Jersey cannot consistently with the Establishment of Religion Clause of the First Amendment contribute tax-raised funds to the support of an institution which teaches the tenets and faith of any church. On the other hand, other language of the Amendment commands that New Jersey cannot hamper its citizens in the free exercise of their own religion. Consequently, it cannot exclude individual Catholics, Lutherans, Mohammedans, Baptists, Jews, Methodists, Non-believers, Presbyterians, or the members of any other faith, *because of their faith, or lack of it,* from receiving the benefits of public welfare legislation. While we do not mean to intimate that a state could not provide transportation only to children attending public schools, we must be careful, in protecting the citizens of New Jersey against state-established churches, to be sure that we do not inadvertently prohibit New Jersey from extending its general State law benefits to all its citizens without regard to their religious belief.

Measured by these standards, we cannot say that the First Amendment prohibits New Jersey from spending tax-raised funds to pay the bus fares of parochial school pupils as a part of a general program under which it pays the fares of pupils attending public and other schools. It is undoubtedly true that children are helped to get to church schools. There is even a possibility that some of the children might not be sent to the church schools if the parents were compelled to pay their children's bus fares out of their own pockets when transportation to a public school would have been paid for by the State. The same possibility exists where the State requires a local transit company to provide reduced rates to school children including those attending parochial schools, or where a municipally owned transportation system undertakes to carry all school children free of charge. Moreover, state-paid policemen, detailed to protect children going to and from church schools from the very real hazards of traffic, would serve much the same purpose and accomplish much the same result as state provisions intended to guarantee free transportation of a kind which the State deems to be best for the school children's welfare. And parents might refuse to risk their children to the serious danger of traffic accidents going to and from parochial schools, the approaches to which were not protected by policemen. Similarly, parents might be reluctant to permit their children to attend schools which the State had cut off from such general government services, as ordinary police and fire protection, connections for sewage disposal, public highways, and sidewalks. Of course, cutting off church schools from these services, so separate and so indisputably marked off from the religious function, would make it far more difficult for the schools to operate. But such is obviously not the purpose of the First Amendment. That Amendment requires the State to be a neutral in its relations with groups of religious believers and non-believers; it does not require the State to be their adversary. State power is no more to be used so as to handicap religions than it is to favor them.

This Court has said that parents may, in the discharge of their duty under state compulsory education laws, send their children to a religious rather than a public school if the school meets the secular educational requirements which the State has power to impose. It appears that these parochial schools meet New Jersey's requirements. The State contributes no money to the schools. It does not support them. Its legislation, as applied, does no more than provide a general program to help parents get their children, regardless of their religion, safely and expeditiously to and from accredited schools.

The First Amendment has erected a wall between Church and State. That wall must be kept high and impregnable. We could not approve the slightest breach. New Jersey has not breached it here.

Affirmed.

United Public Workers
v. Mitchell

330 U.S. 75

———

Decided February 10, 1947

Among Justice Black's firmest convictions is his belief that every citizen of the United States must be free to contribute his skills and abilities to the successful operation of the Government. He finds it an intolerable hobble on our democracy if legal strictures, however well-meant, shut people away from opportunities to take part in the orderly and necessary processes of nominations, campaigns, elections, and officeholding.

Knowing this about Justice Black, it is not surprising to see him dissenting in United Public Workers of America (C.I.O.) et al. v. Harry B. Mitchell, Frances Perkins, and Arthur S. Flemming, *a case whose decision upheld the constitutionality of the Hatch Act. Passed in 1940, the Hatch Act set strict limits on the freedom of United States Government employees to engage in political activity. The purpose of the Hatch Act was meritorious enough —to create a climate of "clean politics" in the federal establishment by reducing the influence of spoils and patronage.*

The effect of the Federal law, however, was to go beyond the intentions of many of its supporters, and in this test case the Supreme Court was so closely split that three Justices concurred in part and dissented in part. Justice Reed delivered the majority opinion in the 4-to-3 decision. He was supported by Chief Justice

*Vinson and Justices Frankfurter (in part) and Burton. Justice
Black's dissent was supported in substantial part by Justice Rut-
ledge. Justice Douglas dissented in part. Justices Murphy and
Jackson did not participate.*

*The alternative, in the view of Justice Black, is not to leave
the field of political activity wholly unprotected against spoilsmen.
His answer, in this opinion, is to punish those public officials who
engage in unhealthy political practices.*

Mr. Justice Black, *dissenting*

The sentence in Section 9 of the statute, here upheld, makes
it unlawful for any person employed in the executive branch of the
Federal Government, with minor numerical exceptions, to "take
any active part in political management or in political campaigns."
The punishment provided is immediate discharge and a permanent
ban against re-employment in the same position. The number of
federal employees thus barred from political action is approximately three million. Section 12 of the same Act affects the participation in political campaigns of many thousands of state employees.
No one of all these millions of citizens can, without violating this
law, "take any active part" in any campaign for a cause or for a
candidate if the cause or candidate is "specifically identified with
any National or State political party." Since under our common
political practices most causes and candidates are espoused by political parties, the result is that, because they are paid out of the
public treasury, all these citizens who engage in public work can
take no really effective part in campaigns that may bring about
changes in their lives, their fortunes, and their happiness.

We are not left in doubt as to how numerous and varied are
the "activities" prohibited. For Section 15 sweepingly describes
them as "the same activities . . . as the United States Civil Service
Commission has heretofore determined are at the time this section
takes effect prohibited on the part of employees in the classified
civil service of the United States. . . ." Along with the vague and
uncertain prior prohibitions of the Commission, are these things
which the Commission had clearly prohibited: serving as an election
officer; publicly expressing political views at a party caucus or political gathering for or against any candidate or cause identified
with a party; soliciting votes for a party or candidate; participating
in a political parade; writing for publication or publishing any letter
or article, signed or unsigned, in favor of or against any political

party, candidate, or faction; initiating, or canvassing for signatures on, community petitions or petitions to Congress.

In view of these prohibitions, it is little consolation to employees that the Act contradictorily says that they may "express their opinions on all political subjects and candidates." For this permission to "express their opinions," is, the Commission has rightly said, "subject to the prohibition that employees may not take any active part in . . . political campaigns." The hopeless contradiction between this privilege of an employee to talk and the prohibition against his talking stands out in the Commission's further warning to all employees that they can express their opinions publicly, but "Public expression of opinion in such way as to constitute taking an active part in political management or in political campaigns is accordingly prohibited." Thus, whatever opinions employees may dare to express, even secretly, must be at their peril. They cannot know what particular expressions may be reported to the Commission and held by it to be a sufficient political activity to cost them their jobs. Their peril is all the greater because of another warning by the Commission that "Employees are . . . accountable for political activity by persons other than themselves, including wives or husbands, if, in fact, the employees are thus accomplishing by collusion and indirection what they may not lawfully do directly and openly." Thus are the families of public employees stripped of their freedom of political action. The result is that the sum of political privilege left to government and state employees, and their families, to take part in political campaigns seems to be this: They may vote in silence; they may carefully and quietly express a political view at their peril; and they may become "spectators" (this is the Commission's word) at campaign gatherings, though it may be highly dangerous for them to "second a motion" or let it be known that they agree or disagree with a speaker. . . .

Had this measure deprived five million farmers, or a million businessmen of all right to participate in elections, because Congress thought that federal farm or business subsidies might prompt some of them to exercise, or be susceptible to, a corrupting influence on politics or government, I would not sustain such an Act on the ground that it could be interpreted so as to apply only to some of them. Certainly laws which restrict the liberties guaranteed by the First Amendment should be narrowly drawn to meet the evil aimed at and to affect only the minimum number of people imperatively necessary to prevent a grave and imminent danger to the public. Furthermore, what federal employees can or cannot do, consistently with the various civil service regulations, rules, warnings, etc., is a matter of so great uncertainty that no person can even make an intelligent guess. This was demonstrated by the Government's briefs and oral arguments in this case. I would hold that the provision here attacked is too broad, ambiguous, and uncertain in its consequences to be made the basis of removing deserving employees from their jobs.

The rights to vote and privately to express an opinion on political matters, important though they be, are but parts of the broad freedoms which our Constitution has provided as the bulwark of our free political institutions. Popular government, to be effective, must permit and encourage much wider political activity by all the people. Real popular government means "that men may speak as they think on matters vital to them and that falsehoods may be exposed through the processes of education and discussion. . . . Those who won our independence had confidence in the power of free and fearless reasoning and communication of ideas to discover and spread political and economic truth." Legislation which muzzles several million citizens threatens popular government, not only because it injures the individuals muzzled, but also because of its harmful effect on the body politic in depriving it of the political participation and interest of such a large segment of our citizens. Forcing public employees to contribute money and influence can well be proscribed in the interest of "clean politics" and public administration. But I think the Constitution prohibits legislation which prevents millions of citizens from contributing their arguments, complaints, and suggestions to the political debates which are the essence of our democracy; prevents them from engaging in organizational activity to urge others to vote and take an interest in political affairs; bars them from performing the interested citizen's duty of insuring that his and his fellow citizens' votes are counted. Such drastic limitations on the right of all the people to express political opinions and take political action would be inconsistent with the First Amendment's guaranty of freedom of speech, press, assembly, and petition. And it would violate, or come dangerously close to violating, Article I and the Seventeenth Amendment of the Constitution, which protect the right of the people to vote for their Congressmen and their United States Senators and to have their votes counted.

There is nothing about federal and state employees as a class which justifies depriving them or society of the benefits of their participation in public affairs. They, like other citizens, pay taxes and serve their country in peace and in war. The taxes they pay and the wars in which they fight are determined by the elected spokesmen of all the people. They come from the same homes, communities, schools, churches, and colleges as do the other citizens. I think the Constitution guarantees to them the same right that other groups of good citizens have to engage in activities which decide who their elected representatives shall be. . . .

It may also be true, as contended, that if public employees are permitted to exercise a full freedom to express their views in political campaigns, some public officials will discharge some employees and grant promotion to others on a political rather than on a merit basis. For the same reasons other public officials, occupying positions of influence, may use their influence to have their own political supporters appointed or promoted. But here again, if the practice of making discharges, promotions, or recommendations for promotions on a political basis is so great an evil as to require legislation, the law could punish those public officials who engage in the practice. To punish millions of employees and to deprive the nation of their contribution to public affairs, in order to remove temptation from a proportionately small number of public officials, seems at the least to be a novel method of suppressing what is thought to be an evil practice. . . .

The section of the Act here held valid reduces the constitutionally protected liberty of several million citizens to less than a shadow of its substance. It relegates millions of federal, state, and municipal employees to the role of mere spectators of events upon which hinge the safety and welfare of all the people, including public employees. It removes a sizable proportion of our electorate from full participation in affairs destined to mold the fortunes of the Nation. It makes honest participation in essential political activities an offense punishable by proscription from public employment. It endows a governmental board with the awesome power to censor the thoughts, expressions, and activities of law-abiding citizens in the field of free expression from which no person should be barred by a government which boasts that it is a government of, for, and by the people—all the people. Laudable as its purpose may be, it seems to me to hack at the roots of a government by the people themselves; and consequently I cannot agree to sustain its validity.

Adamson v. California

332 U.S. 46

Decided June 23, 1947

In his tenth year on the Supreme Court, Justice Black delivered what many students of his work consider the most important opinion of his first decade. This was his definitive statement of his basic policy in the application of the Bill of Rights to the States through the Fourteenth Amendment, which safeguards the right of all United States citizens to "due process of law" and protects their "privileges or immunities." It came in his dissent in the case of Admiral Dewey Adamson v. People of the State of California.

Adamson was found guilty of murder in California and sentenced to death. At the trial the prosecutor, calling attention to the fact that the defendant had not taken the witness stand in his own defense, claimed that under California law is was permissible for him to argue before the jury that guilt could be inferred from the defendant's failure to deny evidence submitted against him. This led to a challenge of the conviction on the ground that in effect Adamson had been required to testify against himself in violation of the Fifth Amendment.

A 5-to-4 majority of the Supreme Court decided that the Fifth Amendment did not hold in this case and that the State might adhere to its own rule with respect to the prosecutor's comment on self-incrimination. Justice Reed wrote the majority opinion and was supported by Chief Justice Vinson and Justices Frankfurter, Jackson, and Burton. Justice Frankfurter also wrote a separate concurring opinion. To his long and carefully documented dissent,

Justice Black attached a 17-page historical appendix dealing with the origin, submission, and adoption of the Fourteenth Amendment. He presented extensive extracts from the debates in Congress as support for his belief that by ratification of the Fourteenth Amendment, the Bill of Rights, including the protections of the Fifth Amendment, was made binding on the States. Justice Douglas joined the dissent of Justice Black. Justice Murphy also wrote a dissenting opinion and was joined by Justice Rutledge; this dissent agreed substantially with that of Justice Black.

Thus as long ago as 1947, the Supreme Court came within one vote of agreeing with Justice Black that the Fourteenth Amendment extended to the States the freedoms and protections in the Constitution's entire Bill of Rights.

MR. JUSTICE BLACK, *dissenting*

The appellant was tried for murder in a California state court. He did not take the stand as a witness in his own behalf. The prosecuting attorney, under purported authority of a California statute, argued to the jury that an inference of guilt could be drawn because of appellant's failure to deny evidence offered against him. The appellant's contention in the state court and here has been that the statute denies him a right guaranteed by the Federal Constitution. The argument is that (1) permitting comment upon his failure to testify has the effect of compelling him to testify so as to violate that provision of the Bill of Rights contained in the Fifth Amendment that "No person . . . shall be compelled in any criminal case to be a witness against himself"; and (2) although this provision of the Fifth Amendment originally applied only as a restraint upon federal courts, *Barron* v. *Baltimore,* the Fourteenth Amendment was intended to, and did, make the prohibition against compelled testimony applicable to trials in state courts.

The Court refuses to meet and decide the appellant's first contention. But while the Court's opinion, as I read it, strongly implies that the Fifth Amendment does not, of itself, bar comment upon failure to testify in federal courts, the Court nevertheless assumes that it does in order to reach the second constitutional question involved in appellant's case. I must consider the case on the same assumption that the Court does. For the discussion of the second contention turns out to be a decision which reaches far beyond the relatively narrow issues on which this case might have turned.

This decision reasserts a constitutional theory spelled out in *Twining* v. *New Jersey*, that this Court is endowed by the Constitution with boundless power under "natural law" periodically to expand and contract constitutional standards to conform to the Court's conception of what at a particular time constitutes "civilized decency" and "fundamental liberty and justice." Invoking this *Twining* rule, the Court concludes that, although comment upon testimony in a federal court would violate the Fifth Amendment, identical comment in a state court does not violate today's fashion in civilized decency and fundamentals and is therefore not prohibited by the Federal Constitution as amended.

The *Twining Case* was the first, as it is the only, decision of this Court which has squarely held that states were free, notwithstanding the Fifth and Fourteenth Amendments, to extort evidence from one accused of crime. I agree that if *Twining* be reaffirmed, the result reached might appropriately follow. But I would not reaffirm the *Twining Decision*. I think that decision and the "natural law" theory of the Constitution upon which it relies degrade the constitutional safeguards of the Bill of Rights and simultaneously appropriate for this Court a broad power which we are not authorized by the Constitution to exercise. Furthermore, the *Twining Decision* rested on previous cases and broad hypotheses which have been undercut by intervening decisions of this Court. My reasons for believing that the *Twining Decision* should not be revitalized can best be understood by reference to the constitutional, judicial, and general history that preceded and followed the case. That reference must be abbreviated far more than is justified but for the necessary limitations of opinion writing.

The First Ten Amendments were proposed and adopted largely because of fear that Government might unduly interfere with prized individual liberties. The people wanted and demanded a Bill of Rights written into their Constitution. The amendments embodying the Bill of Rights were intended to curb all branches of the Federal Government in the fields touched by the amendments— Legislative, Executive, and Judicial. The Fifth, Sixth, and Eighth Amendments were pointedly aimed at confining exercise of power by courts and judges within precise boundaries, particularly in the procedure used for the trial of criminal cases. Past history provided strong reasons for the apprehensions which brought these procedural amendments into being and attest the wisdom of their adoption. For the fears of arbitrary court action sprang largely from the past use of courts in the imposition of criminal punishments to suppress speech, press, and religion. Hence the constitutional limitations of courts' powers were, in the view of the Founders, essential supplements to the First Amendment, which was itself designed to protect the widest scope for all people to believe and to express the most divergent political, religious, and other views.

But these limitations were not expressly imposed upon state court action. In 1833, *Barron* v. *Baltimore* was decided by this Court. It specifically held inapplicable to the States that provision of the Fifth Amendment which declares: "nor shall private property be taken for public use, without just compensation." In deciding the particular point raised, the Court there said that it could not hold that the first eight Amendments applied to the States. This was the controlling constitutional rule when the Fourteenth Amendment was proposed in 1866.

My study of the historical events that culminated in the Fourteenth Amendment, and the expressions of those who sponsored and favored, as well as those who opposed its submission and passage, persuades me that one of the chief objects that the provisions of the Amendment's first section, separately, and as a whole, were intended to accomplish was to make the Bill of Rights, applicable to the States. With full knowledge of the import of the *Barron Decision*, the framers and backers of the Fourteenth Amendment proclaimed its purpose to be to overturn the constitutional rule that case had announced. This historical purpose has never received full consideration or exposition in any opinion of this Court interpreting the Amendment.

In construing other constitutional provisions, this Court has almost uniformly followed the precept of *Ex parte Bain* that "It is never to be forgotten that, in the construction of the language of the Constitution . . . as indeed in all other instances where construction becomes necessary, we are to place ourselves as nearly as possible in the condition of the men who framed that instrument.". . .

In the *Twining Case* itself, the Court was cited to a then recent book, Guthrie, *Fourteenth Amendment to the Constitution* (1898). A few pages of that work recited some of the legislative background of the Amendment, emphasizing the speech of Senator Howard. But Guthrie did not emphasize the speeches of Congressman Bingham, nor the part he played in the framing and adoption of the first section of the Fourteenth Amendment. Yet Congressman Bingham may, without extravagance, be called the Madison of the first section of the Fourteenth Amendment. In the *Twining* opinion, the Court explicitly declined to give weight to the historical demonstration that the first section of the Amendment was intended to apply to the States the several protections of the Bill of Rights. It held that that question was "no longer open" because of previous decisions of this Court which, however, had not appraised the historical evidence on that subject. The Court admitted that its action had resulted in giving "much less effect to the Fourteenth Amendment than some of the public men active in framing it" had intended it to have. With particular reference to the guarantee against compelled testimony, the Court stated that "Much might be said in favor of the view that the privilege was guaranteed against state impairment as a privilege and immunity of National citizenship, but, as has been shown, the decisions of this court have foreclosed that view." Thus the Court declined, and again today declines, to appraise the relevant historical evidence of the intended scope of the first section of the Amendment. Instead it relied upon previous cases, none of which had analyzed the evidence showing that one purpose of those who framed, advocated, and adopted the Amendment had been to make the Bill of Rights applicable to the States. None of the cases relied upon by the Court today made such an analysis.

For this reason, I am attaching to this dissent an appendix which contains a résumé, by no means complete, of the Amendment's history. In my judgment that history conclusively demonstrates that the language of the first section of the Fourteenth Amendment, taken as a whole, was thought by those responsible for its submission to the people, and by those who opposed its submission, sufficiently explicit to guarantee that thereafter no state could deprive its citizens of the privileges and protections of the Bill of Rights. Whether this Court ever will, or whether it now should, in the light of past decisions, give full effect to what the Amendment was intended to accomplish is not necessarily essential to a decision here. However that may be, our prior decisions, including *Twining,* do not prevent our carrying out that purpose, at least to the extent of making applicable to the States, not a mere part, as the Court has, but the full protection of the Fifth Amendment's provision against compelling evidence from an accused to convict him of crime. And I further contend that the "natural law" formula which the Court uses to reach its conclusion in this case should be abandoned as an incongruous excrescence on our Constitution. I believe that formula to be itself a violation of our Constitution, in that it subtly conveys to courts, at the expense of legislatures, ultimate power over public policies in fields where no specific provision of the Constitution limits legislative power. And my belief seems to be in accord with the views expressed by this Court, at least for the first two decades after the Fourteenth Amendment was adopted.

In 1872, four years after the Amendment was adopted, the *Slaughter-House Cases* came to this Court. The Court was not presented in that case with the evidence which showed that the special sponsors of the Amendment in the House and Senate had expressly explained one of its principal purposes to be to change the Constitution as construed in *Barron* v. *Baltimore,* and make the Bill of Rights applicable to the States. Nor was there reason to do so. For the State law under consideration in the *Slaughter-House Cases* was only challenged as one which authorized a monopoly, and the brief for the challenger properly conceded that there was "no direct constitutional provision against a monopoly." The argument did not invoke any specific provision of the Bill of Rights, but urged that the state monopoly statute violated "the natural right of a person" to do business and engage in his trade or vocation. On this basis, it was contended that "bulwarks that have been erected around the investments of capital are impregnable against State legislation." These natural law arguments, so suggestive of the premises on which the present due process formula rests, were flatly rejected by a majority of the Court in the *Slaughter-House Cases.* What the Court did hold was that the privileges and immunities clause of the Fourteenth Amendment only protected from state invasion such rights as a person has because he is a citizen of the United States. The Court enumerated some, but refused to enumerate all of these national rights. The majority of the Court emphatically declined the invitation of counsel to hold that the Fourteenth Amendment subjected all state regulatory legislation to continuous censorship by this Court in order for it to determine whether it collided with this Court's opinion of "natural" right and justice. In effect, the *Slaughter-House Cases* rejected the very natural justice formula the Court today embraces. The Court did not meet the question of whether the safeguards of the Bill of Rights were protected against state invasion by the Fourteenth Amendment. And it specifically did not say as the Court now does, that particular provisions of the Bill of Rights could be breached by states in part, but not breached in other respects, according to this Court's notions of "civilized standards," "canons of decency," and "fundamental justice.". . .

Thus, up to and for some years after 1873, when *Munn* v. *Illinois*, was decided, this Court steadfastly declined to invalidate states' legislative regulation of property rights or business practices under the Fourteenth Amendment unless there were racial discrimination involved in the State law challenged. The first significant breach in this policy came in 1889, in *Chicago, M. & St. P. R. Co.* v. *Minnesota*. A state's railroad rate regulatory statute was there stricken as violative of the Due Process Clause of the Fourteenth Amendment. This was accomplished by reference to a due process formula which did not necessarily operate so as to protect the Bill of Rights' personal liberty safeguards, but which gave a new and hitherto undiscovered scope for the Court's use of the Due Process Clause to protect property rights under natural law concepts. And in 1896, in *Chicago, B. & Q. R. Co.* v. *Chicago*, this Court, in effect, overruled *Davidson* v. *New Orleans*, by holding, under the new due process-natural law formula, that the Fourteenth Amendment forbade a state from taking private property for public use without payment of just compensation.

Following the pattern of the new doctrine formalized in the foregoing decisions, the Court in 1896 applied the Due Process Clause to strike down a state statute which had forbidden certain types of contracts. In doing so, it substantially adopted the rejected argument of counsel in the *Slaughter-House Cases*, that the Fourteenth Amendment guarantees the liberty of all persons under "natural law" to engage in their chosen business or vocation. In the *Allgeyer* opinion, the Court quoted with approval the concurring opinion of Mr. Justice Bradley in a second *Slaughter-House Case, Butchers' Union Co.* v. *Crescent City Co.*, which closely followed one phase of the argument of his dissent in the original *Slaughter-House Cases*—not that phase which argued that the Bill of Rights was applicable to the States. And in 1905, three years before the *Twining Case, Lochner* v. *New York* followed the argument used in *Allgeyer* to hold that the Due Process Clause was violated by a state statute which limited the employment of bakery workers to sixty hours per week and ten hours per day.

The foregoing constitutional doctrine, judicially created and adopted by expanding the previously accepted meaning of "due process," marked a complete departure from the *Slaughter-House* philosophy of judicial tolerance of state regulation of business activities. Conversely, the new formula contracted the effectiveness of the Fourteenth Amendment as a protection from state infringement of individual liberties enumerated in the Bill of Rights. Thus the Court's second-thought interpretation of the Amendment was an about-face from the *Slaughter-House* interpretation and represented a failure to carry out the avowed purpose of the Amendment's sponsors. This reversal is dramatized by the fact that the *Hurtado Case*, which had rejected the Due Process Clause as an instrument for preserving Bill of Rights liberties and privileges, was cited as authority for expanding the scope of that clause so as to permit this Court to invalidate all state regulatory legislation it believed to be contrary to "fundamental" principles.

The *Twining Decision*, rejecting the Compelled Testimony Clause of the Fifth Amendment, and indeed rejecting all the Bill of Rights, is the end product of one phase of this philosophy. At the same time, that decision consolidated the power of the Court assumed in past cases by laying broader foundations for the Court to invalidate state and even federal regulatory legislation. For the *Twining Decision*, giving separate consideration to "due process" and "privileges or immunities," went all the way to say that the Privileges or Immunities Clause of the Fourteenth Amendment "did not forbid the States to abridge the personal rights enumerated in the first eight Amendments. . . ."

And in order to be certain, so far as possible, to leave this Court wholly free to reject all the Bill of Rights as specific restraints upon state action, the decision declared that even if this Court should decide that the Due Process Clause forbids the States to infringe personal liberties guaranteed by the Bill of Rights, it would do so, not "because those rights are enumerated in the first eight Amendments, but because they are of such a nature that they are included in the conception of due process of law."

At the same time that the *Twining Decision* held that the States need not conform to the specific provisions of the Bill of Rights, it consolidated the power that the Court had assumed under the Due Process Clause by laying even broader foundations for the Court to invalidate state and even federal regulatory legislation. For under the *Twining* formula, which includes non-regard for the first eight Amendments, what are "fundamental rights" and in accord with "canons of decency," as the Court said in *Twining*, and today reaffirms, is to be independently "ascertained from time to time by judicial action . . ."; "what is due process of law depends on circumstances." Thus the power of legislatures became what this Court would declare it to be at a particular time independently of the specific guarantees of the Bill of Rights such as the right to freedom of speech, religion, and assembly, the right to just compensation for property taken for a public purpose, the right to jury trial, or the right to be secure against unreasonable searches and seizures. Neither the contraction of the Bill of Rights safeguards nor the invalidation of regulatory laws by this Court's appraisal of "circumstances" would readily be classified as the most satisfactory contribution of this Court to the Nation. In 1912, four years after the *Twining Case* was decided, a book written by Mr. Charles Wallace Collins [*The Fourteenth Amendment and the States*] gave the history of this Court's interpretation and application of the Fourteenth Amendment up to that time. It is not necessary for one fully to agree with all he said in order to appreciate the sentiment of the following comment concerning the disappointments caused by this Court's interpretation of the Amendment.

> . . . It was aimed at restraining and checking the powers of wealth and privilege. It was to be a charter of liberty for human rights against property rights. The transformation has been rapid and complete. It operates to-day to protect the rights of property to the detriment of the rights of man. It has become the Magna Carta of accumulated and organized capital.

That this feeling was shared, at least in part, by members of this Court is revealed by the vigorous dissents that have been written in almost every case where the *Twining* and *Hurtado* doctrines have been applied to invalidate state regulatory laws.

Later decisions of this Court have completely undermined that phase of the *Twining* doctrine which broadly precluded reliance on the Bill of Rights to determine what is and what is not a "fundamental" right. Later cases have also made the *Hurtado Case* an inadequate support for this phase of the *Twining* formula. For despite *Hurtado* and *Twining*, this Court has now held that the Fourteenth Amendment protects from state invasion the following "fundamental" rights safeguarded by the Bill of Rights; right to counsel in criminal cases; freedom of assembly; at the very least, certain types of cruel and unusual punishment and former jeopardy; the right of an accused in a criminal case to be informed of the charge against him; the right to receive just compensation on account of taking private property for public use. And the Court has now through the Fourteenth Amendment literally and emphatically applied the First Amendment to the States in its very terms.

In *Palko* v. *Connecticut,* a case which involved former jeopardy only, this Court re-examined the path it had traveled in interpreting the Fourteenth Amendment since the *Twining* opinion was written. In *Twining* the Court had declared that none of the rights enumerated in the first eight Amendments were protected against state invasion because they were incorporated in the Bill of Rights. But the Court in *Palko,* answered a contention that all eight applied with the more guarded statement, similar to that the Court had used in *Maxwell* v. *Dow,* that "there is no such general rule." Implicit in this statement, and in the cases decided in the interim between *Twining* and *Palko* and since, is the understanding that some of the eight Amendments do apply by their very terms. Thus the Court said in the *Palko Case* that the Fourteenth Amendment may make it unlawful for a state to abridge by its statutes the "freedom of speech which the First Amendment safeguards against encroachment by the Congress . . . or the like freedom of the press . . . or the free exercise of religion . . . or the right of peaceable assembly . . . or the right of one accused of crime to the benefit of counsel. . . . In these and other situations immunities that are valid as against the federal government by force of the specific pledges of particular amendments have been found to be implicit in the concept of ordered liberty, and thus, through the Fourteenth Amendment, become valid as against the states." The Court went on to describe the Amendments made applicable to the States as "the privileges and immunities that have been taken over from the earlier articles of the federal bill of rights and brought within the Fourteenth Amendment by a process of absorption." In the *Twining Case* fundamental liberties were things apart from the Bill of Rights. Now it appears that at least some of the provisions of the Bill of Rights in their very terms satisfy the Court as sound and meaningful expressions of fundamental liberty. If the Fifth Amendment's protection against self-incrimination be such as an expression of fundamental liberty, I ask, and have not found a satisfactory answer, why the Court today should consider that it should be "absorbed" in part but not in full? Nothing in the *Palko* opinion requires that, when the Court decides that a Bill of Rights provision is to be applied to the States, it is to be applied piecemeal. Nothing in the *Palko* opinion recommends that the Court apply part of an Amendment's established meaning and discard that part which does not suit the current style of fundamentals.

The Court's opinion in *Twining*, and the dissent in that case, made it clear that the Court intended to leave the States wholly free to compel confessions, so far as the Federal Constitution is concerned. Yet in a series of cases since *Twining* this Court has held that the Fourteenth Amendment does bar all American courts, state or federal, from convicting people of crime on coerced confessions. Federal courts cannot do so because of the Fifth Amendment. And state courts cannot do so because the principles of the Fifth Amendment are made applicable to the States through the Fourteenth by one formula or another. And taking note of these cases, the Court is careful to point out in its decision today that coerced confessions violate the Federal Constitution if secured "by fear of hurt, torture or exhaustion." Nor can a state, according to today's decision, constitutionally compel an accused to testify against himself by "any other type of coercion that falls within the scope of due process." Thus the Court itself destroys or at least drastically curtails the very *Twining Decision* it purports to reaffirm. It repudiates the foundation of that opinion, which presented much argument to show that compelling a man to testify against himself does not "violate" a "fundamental" right or privilege.

It seems rather plain to me why the Court today does not attempt to justify all of the broad *Twining* discussion. That opinion carries its own refutation on what may be called the factual issue the Court resolved. The opinion itself shows, without resort to the powerful argument in the dissent of Mr. Justice Harlan, that outside of Star Chamber practices and influences, the "English-speaking" peoples have for centuries abhorred and feared the practice of compelling people to convict themselves of crime. I shall not attempt to narrate the reasons. They are well known and those interested can read them in both the majority and dissenting opinions in the *Twining Case*, in *Boyd* v. *United States*, and in the cases cited in *Ashcraft* v. *Tennessee*. Nor does the history of the practice of compelling testimony in this country, relied on in the *Twining* opinion, support the degraded rank which that opinion gave the Fifth Amendment's privilege against compulsory self-incrimination. I think the history there recited by the Court belies its conclusion.

The Court in *Twining* evidently was forced to resort for its degradation of the privilege to the fact that Governor Winthrop in trying Mrs. Anne Hutchinson in 1627 was evidently "not aware of any privilege against self-incrimination or conscious of any duty to respect it." Of course not. Mrs. Hutchinson was tried, if trial it can be called, for holding unorthodox religious views. People with a consuming belief that their religious convictions must be forced on others rarely ever believe that the unorthodox have any rights which should or can be rightfully respected. As a result of her trial and compelled admissions, Mrs. Hutchinson was found guilty of unorthodoxy and banished from Massachusetts. The lamentable experience of Mrs. Hutchinson and others, contributed to the overwhelming sentiment that demanded adoption of a Constitutional Bill of Rights. The Founders of this Government wanted no more such "trials" and punishments as Mrs. Hutchinson had to undergo. They wanted to erect barriers that would bar legislators from passing laws that encroached on the domain of belief, and that would, among other things, strip courts and all public officers of a power to compel people to testify against themselves.

I cannot consider the Bill of Rights to be an outworn Eighteenth Century "strait jacket" as the *Twining* opinion did. Its provisions may be thought outdated abstractions by some. And it is true that they were designed to meet ancient evils. But they are the same kind of human evils that have emerged from century to century wherever excessive power is sought by the few at the expense of the many. In my judgment the people of no nation can lose their liberty so long as a Bill of Rights like ours survives and its basic purposes are conscientiously interpreted, enforced, and respected so as to afford continuous protection against old, as well as new, devices and practices which might thwart those purposes. I fear to see the consequences of the Court's practice of substituting its own concepts of decency and fundamental justice for the language of the Bill of Rights as its point of departure in interpreting and enforcing that Bill of Rights. If the choice must be between the selective process of the *Palko Decision* applying some of the Bill of Rights to the States, or the *Twining* rule applying none of them, I would choose the *Palko* selective process. But rather than accept either of these choices, I would follow what I believe was the original purpose of the Fourteenth Amendment—to extend to all the people of the Nation the complete protection of the Bill of Rights. To hold that this Court can determine what, if any, provisions of the Bill of Rights will be enforced, and if so to what degree, is to frustrate the great design of a written Constitution.

Conceding the possibility that this Court is now wise enough to improve on the Bill of Rights by substituting natural law concepts for the Bill of Rights, I think the possibility is entirely too speculative to agree to take that course. I would therefore hold in this case that the full protection of the Fifth Amendment's proscription against compelled testimony must be afforded by California. This I would do because of reliance upon the original purpose of the Fourteenth Amendment.

It is an illusory apprehension that literal application of some or all of the provisions of the Bill of Rights to the States would unwisely increase the sum total of the powers of this Court to invalidate state legislation. The Federal Government has not been harmfully burdened by the requirement that enforcement of Federal laws affecting civil liberty conform literally to the Bill of Rights. Who would advocate its repeal? It must be conceded, of course, that the natural-law-due-process formula, which the Court today reaffirms, has been interpreted to limit substantially this Court's power to prevent state violations of the individual civil liberties guaranteed by the Bill of Rights. But this formula also has been used in the past, and can be used in the future, to license this Court, in considering regulatory legislation, to roam at large in the broad expanses of policy and morals and to trespass, all too freely, on the legislative domain of the States as well as the Federal Government.

Since *Marbury* v. *Madison* was decided, the practice has been firmly established, for better or worse, that courts can strike down legislative enactments which violate the Constitution. This process, of course, involves interpretation, and since words can have many meanings, interpretation obviously may result in contraction or extension of the original purpose of a constitutional provision, thereby affecting policy. But to pass upon the constitutionality of statutes by looking to the particular standards enumerated in the Bill of Rights and other parts of the Constitution is one thing; to invalidate statutes because of application of "natural law" deemed to be above and undefined by the Constitution is another. "In the one instance, courts proceeding within clearly marked constitutional boundaries seek to execute policies written into the Constitution; in the other, they roam at will in the limitless area of their own beliefs as to reasonableness and actually select policies, a responsibility which the Constitution entrusts to the legislative representatives of the people."

MR. JUSTICE DOUGLAS *joins in this opinion*

Foster v. Illinois

332 U.S. 134

———

Decided June 23, 1947

Few decisions in his first half-dozen terms on the Supreme Court disturbed Justice Black as much as Betts v. Brady *(page 93). The nine Justices, dividing 6 to 3, rejected the claim of a poverty-stricken Maryland farmhand that his constitutional safeguard of right to counsel had been violated when he was charged with robbery, tried, found guilty, and imprisoned without the benefit of counsel. In his* Betts *dissent, with its impressive appendix of the right-to-counsel rules and practices in the States, Justice Black looked hopefully to the future for reversal. An opportunity to reverse came five years later in the case of* Nelson Foster and George Payne v. People of the State of Illinois.

The petitioners, Foster and Payne, after eleven years in the Illinois Penitentiary on pleas of guilty to an indictment charging them with burglary and larceny, asked the Illinois Supreme Court in 1946 for discharge. They claimed, among other things, that the record failed to show compliance with the Fourteenth Amendment insofar as the Due Process Clause of that Amendment requires an accused to have the benefit of counsel. By 1947 the Betts *dissenters gained one to their ranks—Justice Rutledge, who took the place of Justice Byrnes, one of the majority in the* Betts *Case. Thus the two sides in* Foster v. Illinois *were the majority of Chief Justice Stone and Justices Roberts, Reed, Frankfurter, and Jackson; and the minority of Justices Black, Douglas, Murphy, and Rutledge.*

Near the end of the majority's opinion, its author, Justice

Frankfurter, wrote: "It does not militate against respect for the deeply rooted systems of criminal justice in the States that such an abrupt innovation as recognition of the constitutional claim here made implies, would furnish opportunities hitherto uncontemplated for opening wide the prison doors of the land."

Justice Black's brief comment on this consideration raised by Justice Frankfurter stands out as one of Black's most direct and utterly simple statements in a quarter century of clear and forceful opinion writing. The final sentence of the paragraph beginning, "One thing more," makes the Foster v. Illinois *dissent an opinion that belongs in any collection of Justice Black's judicial handiwork.*

MR. JUSTICE BLACK, *with whom* MR. JUSTICE DOUGLAS, MR. JUSTICE MURPHY, *and* MR. JUSTICE RUTLEDGE *join, dissenting*

In *Adamson* v. *California,* this day decided, the Court waters down the Fourteenth Amendment's application to the States of the Bill of Rights guarantee against self-incrimination so as to make it compatible with the Court's standards of decency and a fair trial. In this case the Court similarly waters down the Bill of Rights guarantee of counsel in criminal cases. In both cases, the Court refuses to strike down convictions obtained in disregard of Bill of Rights guarantees, assuming all the while that identical convictions obtained in federal courts would violate the Bill of Rights. For the Court, in the instant case, concedes that, by virtue of the Sixth Amendment, "counsel must be furnished an indigent defendant in every case whatever the circumstances." This, of course, relates to convictions following both pleas of not guilty and pleas of guilty.

In the *Adamson Case,* I have voiced my objections to dilution of constitutional protections against self-incrimination in state courts. This decision is another example of the consequences which can be produced by substitution of this Court's day-to-day opinion of what kind of trial is fair and decent for the kind of trial which the Bill of Rights guarantees. This time it is the right of counsel. We cannot know what Bill of Rights provision will next be attenuated by the Court. We can at least be sure that there will be more, so long as the Court adheres to the doctrine of this and the *Adamson Case.*

The Court's decision relies heavily on *Betts* v. *Brady.* In that case, a man on relief, too poor to hire a lawyer, and whose request for the appointment of a lawyer was denied, was compelled to act as his own lawyer on a charge of robbery. Conviction followed.

That case is precedent for this one. But it is the kind of precedent that I had hoped this Court would not perpetuate.

One thing more. The Court seems to fear that protecting these defendants' right to counsel to the full extent defined in the Bill of Rights would furnish "opportunities hitherto uncontemplated for opening wide the prison doors of the land," because, presumably, there are many people like Betts, Foster, and Payne behind those doors after trials without having had the benefit of counsel. I do not believe that such a reason is even relevant to a determination that we should decline to enforce the Bill of Rights.

Oyama v. California

332 U.S. 633

Decided January 19, 1948

California enacted an Alien Land Law that had the effect of prohibiting Japanese citizens from owning land within the State. An
asserted purpose was to "discourage" Japanese people from "coming to California." The constitutionality of a prosecution under the
law came up for test in the case of Fred Y. Oyama and Kajiro
Oyama, Individually and as Guardian of Fred Y. Oyama v. State
of California. A Japanese father paid for land transferred to his
son, an American citizen by birth, and the California courts found
in the transfer an intent to evade the Land Law.

Chief Justice Vinson handed down the Supreme Court's majority opinion, which objected to the application of the California
statute as an unconstitutional discrimination against the American
son because of his parents' country of origin. Justices Black, Frankfurter, Douglas, Murphy, and Rutledge either joined or supported
the Vinson opinion. Justice Black, with Justice Douglas agreeing,
said it would have been preferable to overturn the California judgment on the broader grounds that the California Alien Land Law
violated the Fourteenth Amendment's Equal Protection Clause.
Justices Black and Douglas noted other objections including the
conflict between the California law and the United States pledge in
the United Nations to co-operate in the promotion of "fundamental freedoms for all without distinction as to race, sex, language, or religion."

Justice Murphy, with Justice Rutledge joining him, wrote a

separate concurring opinion, which declared the California law to be in conflict on its face with the Fourteenth Amendment. Justice Reed, joined by Justice Burton, dissented, having found no unconstitutional discrimination in the facts of the case. Justice Jackson also dissented on the ground that, since California had the power to forbid certain aliens to own land, the State must also have the power to prevent evasion of the law through prosecution and adjudication.

MR. JUSTICE BLACK, *with whom* MR. JUSTICE DOUGLAS *agrees, concurring*

I concur in the Court's judgment and its opinion. But I should prefer to reverse the judgment on the broader ground that the basic provisions of the California Alien Land Law violate the equal protection clause of the Fourteenth Amendment and conflict with federal laws and treaties governing the immigration of aliens and their rights after arrival in this country. The California law in actual effect singles out aliens of Japanese ancestry, requires the escheat of any real estate they own, and its language is broad enough to make it a criminal offense, punishable by imprisonment up to ten years, for them to acquire, enjoy, use, possess, cultivate, occupy, or transfer real property. It would therefore appear to be a crime for an alien of Japanese ancestry to own a home in California, at least if the land around it is suitable for cultivation. This is true although the statute does not name the Japanese as such, and although its terms also apply to a comparatively small number of aliens from other countries. That the effect and purpose of the law is to discriminate against Japanese because they are Japanese is too plain to call for more than a statement of that well-known fact.

We are told, however, that, despite the sweeping prohibition against Japanese ownership or occupancy, it is no violation of the law for a Japanese to work on land as a hired hand for American citizens or for foreign nationals permitted to own California lands. And a Japanese man or woman may also use or occupy land if acting only in the capacity of a servant. In other words, by this Alien Land Law, California puts all Japanese aliens within its boundaries on the lowest possible economic level. And this Land Law has been followed by another which now bars Japanese from the fishing industry. If there is any one purpose of the Fourteenth Amendment that is wholly outside the realm of doubt, it is that the Amendment was designed to bar States from denying to some groups, on account of their race or color, any rights, privileges, and opportunities accorded to other groups. I would now overrule the previous decisions of this Court that sustained state land laws which discriminate against people of Japanese origin residing in this country.

Congress has provided strict immigration tests and quotas. It has also enacted laws to regulate aliens after admission into the country. Other statutes provide for deportation of aliens. Although Japanese are not permitted to become citizens by the ordinary process of naturalization, still Congress permitted the admission of some Japanese into this country. All of this means that Congress, in the exercise of its exclusive power over immigration, decided that certain Japanese, subject to federal laws, might come to and live in any one of the States of the Union. The Supreme Court of California has said that one purpose of that state's Land Law is to "discourage the coming of Japanese into this State. . . ." California should not be permitted to erect obstacles designed to prevent the immigration of people whom Congress has authorized to come into and remain in the country. There are additional reasons now why that law stands as an obstacle to the free accomplishment of our policy in the international field. One of these reasons is that we have recently pledged ourselves to co-operate with the United Nations to "promote . . . universal respect for, and observance of, human rights and fundamental freedoms for all without distinction as to race, sex, language, or religion." How can this nation be faithful to this international pledge if state laws which bar land ownership and occupancy by aliens on account of race are permitted to be enforced?

Illinois ex rel. McCollum
v. Board of Education

333 U.S. 203

Decided March 8, 1948

Did the widely used system of "released time" for religions instruction in the public schools circumvent the Constitution's wise separation of Church and State? This question was before Justice Black in the second of his three major opinions in this highly controversial field of Church-State relations concerning attendance at public and parochial schools. The second of these cases arrived at the Supreme Court as People of the State of Illinois ex rel. Vashti McCollum v. Board of Education of School District No. 71, Champaign County, Illinois et al. Justice Black's Everson opinion (page 147) and his Zorach opinion (page 250) were the others in the group that arose in little more than four years.

The second case was brought by Mrs. Vashti McCollum, humanist, wife of a University of Illinois horticulturist and mother of three boys, one of whom, James Terry McCollum, came under the "released time" program as a fourth-grader. Because his nonattendance at the religious instruction classes caused him embarrassment, Mrs. McCollum went to the Board of Education to protest against the system as a misuse of school time, school property, and school funds. The School Board rejected her complaint as did the Circuit Court. After losing her case also in the Illinois Supreme Court, she appealed to the United States Supreme Court where she

*was vindicated, 8 to 1. The story of her long, hard, unpleasant bat-
tle, with no little social ostracism, is told in Mrs. McCollum's book,
One Woman's Fight, published in 1951.*

*Speaking for the Supreme Court, Justice Black held that the
Champaign public schools were violating the First Amendment
prohibition against an establishment of religion, made applicable to
the States by the Fourteenth Amendment. Joining Justice Black
were Chief Justice Vinson and Justices Douglas, Murphy, Rutledge, and Burton. Justice Frankfurter wrote a separate concurring
opinion, which Justices Jackson, Rutledge, and Burton joined. The
sole dissenter, Justice Reed, found so little help to religion by the
State that he saw no cause to upset local practices.*

MR. JUSTICE BLACK *delivered the opinion of the Court*

This case relates to the power of a state to utilize its tax-
supported public school system in aid of religious instruction insofar
as that power may be restricted by the First and Fourteenth
Amendments to the Federal Constitution.

The appellant, Vashti McCollum, began this action for *mandamus* against the Champaign Board of Education in the Circuit
Court of Champaign County, Illinois. Her asserted interest was that
of a resident and taxpayer of Champaign and of a parent whose
child was then enrolled in the Champaign public schools. Illinois
has a compulsory education law which, with exceptions, requires
parents to send their children, aged seven to sixteen, to its tax-
supported public schools where the children are to remain in attendance during the hours when the schools are regularly in
session. Parents who violate this law commit a misdemeanor punishable by fine unless the children attend private or parochial
schools which meet educational standards fixed by the State. District boards of education are given general supervisory powers over
the use of the public school buildings within the school districts.

Appellant's petition for *mandamus* alleged that religious teachers, employed by private religious groups, were permitted to come
weekly into the school buildings during the regular hours set apart
for secular teaching, and then and there for a period of thirty minutes substitute their religious teaching for the secular education provided under the compulsory education law. The petitioner charged
that this joint public-school religious-group program violated the
First and Fourteenth Amendments to the United States Constitution. The prayer of her petition was that the Board of Education

be ordered to "adopt and enforce rules and regulations prohibiting all instruction in and teaching of religious education in all public schools in Champaign School District Number 71 . . . and in all public school houses and buildings in said district when occupied by public schools."

The board first moved to dismiss the petition on the ground that under Illinois law appellant had no standing to maintain the action. This motion was denied. An answer was then filed, which admitted that regular weekly religious instruction was given during school hours to those pupils whose parents consented and that those pupils were released temporarily from their regular secular classes for the limited purpose of attending the religious classes. The answer denied that this co-ordinated program of religious instruction violated the State or Federal Constitution. Much evidence was heard, findings of fact were made, after which the petition for *mandamus* was denied on the ground that the school's religious instruction program violated neither the federal nor state constitutional provisions invoked by the appellant. On appeal the State Supreme Court affirmed. Appellant appealed to this Court, and we noted probable jurisdiction on June 2, 1947.

The appellees press a motion to dismiss the appeal on several grounds, the first of which is that the judgment of the State Supreme Court does not draw in question the "validity of a statute of any State" as required by 28 U.S.C.A. Section 344 (a), 8 F.C.A. title 28, Section 344 (a). This contention rests on the admitted fact that the challenged program of religious instruction was not expressly authorized by statute. But the State Supreme Court has sustained the validity of the program on the ground that the Illinois statutes granted the board authority to establish such a program. This holding is sufficient to show that the validity of an Illinois statute was drawn in question within the meaning of 28 U.S.C.A. Section 344 (a), 8 F.C.A. title 28, Section 344 (a). A second ground for the motion to dismiss is that the appellant lacks standing to maintain the action, a ground which is also without merit. A third ground for the motion is that the appellant failed properly to present in the State Supreme Court her challenge that the state program violated the Federal Constitution. But in view of the express rulings of both state courts on this question, the argument cannot be successfully maintained. The motion to dismiss the appeal is denied.

Although there are disputes between the parties as to various inferences that may or may not properly be drawn from the evidence concerning the religious program, the following facts are shown by the record without dispute. In 1940 interested members of the Jewish, Roman Catholic, and a few of the Protestant faiths formed a voluntary association called the Champaign Council on Religious Education. They obtained permission from the Board of Education to offer classes in religious instruction to public school pupils in grades four to nine inclusive. Classes were made up of pupils whose parents signed printed cards requesting that their children be permitted to attend; they were held weekly, thirty minutes for the lower grades, forty-five minutes for the higher. The council employed the religious teachers at no expense to the school authorities, but the instructors were subject to the approval and supervision of the superintendent of schools. The classes were taught in three separate religious groups by Protestant teachers, Catholic priests, and a Jewish rabbi, although for the past several years there have apparently been no classes instructed in the Jewish religion. Classes were conducted in the regular classrooms of the school building. Students who did not choose to take the religious instruction were not released from public school duties; they were required to leave their classrooms and go to some other place in the school building for pursuit of their secular studies. On the other hand, students who were released from secular study for the religious instructions were required to be present at the religious classes. Reports of their presence or absence were to be made to their secular teachers.

The foregoing facts, without reference to others that appear in the record, show the use of tax-supported property for religious instruction and the close cooperation between the school authorities and the religious council in promoting religious education. The operation of the state's compulsory education system thus assists and is integrated with the program of religious instruction carried on by separate religious sects. Pupils compelled by law to go to school for secular education are released in part from their legal duty upon the condition that they attend the religious classes. This is beyond all question a utilization of the tax-established and tax-supported public school system to aid religious groups to spread their faith. And it falls squarely under the ban of the First Amendment (made applicable to the States by the Fourteenth) as we interpreted it in *Everson* v. *Board of Education.* There we said: "Neither a state nor the Federal Government can set up a church.

Neither can pass laws which aid one religion, aid all religions, or prefer one religion over another. Neither can force or influence a person to go to or to remain away from church against his will or force him to profess a belief or disbelief in any religion. No person can be punished for entertaining or professing religious beliefs or disbeliefs, for church attendance or nonattendance. No tax in any amount, large or small, can be levied to support any religious activities or institutions, whatever they may be called, or whatever form they may adopt to teach or practice religion. Neither a state nor the Federal Government can, openly or secretly, participate in the affairs of any religious organizations or groups and vice versa. In the words of Jefferson, the clause against establishment of religion by law was intended to erect 'a wall of separation between Church and State.' " The majority in the *Everson Case*, and the minority as shown by quotations from the dissenting views . . . agreed that the First Amendment's language, properly interpreted, had erected a wall of separation between Church and State. They disagreed as to the facts shown by the record and as to the proper application of the First Amendment's language to those facts.

Recognizing that the Illinois program is barred by the First and Fourteenth Amendments if we adhere to the views expressed both by the majority and the minority in the *Everson Case*, counsel for the respondents challenge those views as dicta and urge that we reconsider and repudiate them. They argue that historically the First Amendment was intended to forbid only government preference of one religion over another, not an impartial governmental assistance of all religions. In addition they ask that we distinguish or overrule our holding in the *Everson Case* that the Fourteenth Amendment made the "establishment of religion" clause of the First Amendment applicable as a prohibition against the States. After giving full consideration to the arguments presented we are unable to accept either of these contentions.

To hold that a state cannot consistently with the First and Fourteenth Amendments utilize its public school system to aid any or all religious faiths or sects in the dissemination of their doctrines and ideals does not, as counsel urge, manifest a governmental hostility to religion or religious teachings. A manifestation of such hostility would be at war with our national tradition as embodied in the First Amendment's guaranty of the free exercise of religion. For the First Amendment rests upon the premise that both religion and government can best work to achieve their lofty aims if each is left free from the other within its respective sphere. Or, as we said in the *Everson Case*, the First Amendment has erected a wall between Church and State which must be kept high and impregnable.

Here not only are the State's tax-supported public school buildings used for the dissemination of religious doctrines. The State also affords sectarian groups an invaluable aid in that it helps to provide pupils for their religious classes through use of the State's compulsory public school machinery. This is not separation of Church and State.

The cause is reversed and remanded to the State Supreme Court for proceedings not inconsistent with this opinion.

Reversed and remanded.

Ludecke v. Watkins

335 U.S. 160

Decided June 21, 1948

When the Supreme Court in a 5-to-4 decision turned the clock back to the hated and repudiated Alien and Sedition Acts of 1798, Justice Black said it was doing just that and he said so in terms that no one could misunderstand. The case was Kurt G. W. Ludecke v. W. Frank Watkins, as District Director of Immigration.

Under the authority of the Attorney General, Ludecke was ordered to be removed from the United States as an enemy alien who was dangerous to the public peace and safety. He petitioned for habeas corpus in the lower courts and that was denied. The Supreme Court upheld the proceedings against Ludecke by finding that they were not subject to judicial review. Joining Justice Frankfurter, who gave the majority opinion, were Chief Justice Vinson and Justices Reed, Jackson, and Burton. Although it was more than three years after the cessation of hostilities between Germany and the United States, the Supreme Court also took the position that the war was not terminated.

Justice Black, in a dissent joined by Justices Douglas, Murphy, and Rutledge, characterized the majority's notion that the United States was still at war with Germany as "nothing but a fiction." In a detailed historical analysis, he showed how the decision was at variance with the experience of World War I, following the cessation of hostilities. His last paragraph contained a dark prophecy that was borne out most unhappily in the next dozen years. Justice Douglas also dissented separately with the concurrence of Justices

Murphy and Rutledge on the ground that an enemy alien is entitled to the same safeguards of due process of law, including reasonable notice and fair hearing, that would be observed in any other deportation proceeding. The dissenters also took the position that Ludecke was entitled to judicial review.

MR. JUSTICE BLACK, *with whom* MR. JUSTICE DOUGLAS, MR. JUSTICE MURPHY, *and* MR. JUSTICE RUTLEDGE *join, dissenting*

The petition for *habeas corpus* in this case alleged that petitioner, a legally admitted resident of the United States, was about to be deported from this country to Germany as a "dangerous" alien enemy, without having been afforded notice and a fair hearing to determine whether he was "dangerous." The Court now holds, as the Government argued, that because of a presidential proclamation, petitioner can be deported by the Attorney General's order without any judicial inquiry whatever into the truth of his allegations. The Court goes further and holds, as I understand its opinion, that the Attorney General can deport him whether he is dangerous or not. The effect of this holding is that any unnaturalized person, good or bad, loyal or disloyal to this country, if he was a citizen of Germany before coming here, can be summarily seized, interned, and deported from the United States by the Attorney General, and that no court of the United States has any power whatever to review, modify, vacate, reverse, or in any manner affect the Attorney General's deportation order. Mr. Justice Douglas has given reasons in his dissenting opinion why he believes that deportation of aliens, without notice and hearing, whether in peace or war, would be a denial of due process of law. I agree with Mr. Justice Douglas for many of the reasons he gives that deportation of petitioner without a fair hearing as determined by judicial review is a denial of due process of law. But I do not reach the question of power to deport aliens of countries with which we are at war while we are at war, because I think the idea that we are still at war with Germany in the sense contemplated by the statute controlling here is a pure fiction. Furthermore, I think there is no Act of Congress which lends the slightest basis to the claim that after hostilities with a foreign country have ended the President or the Attorney General, one or both, can deport aliens without a fair hearing reviewable in the courts. On the contrary, when this very question came before Congress after World War I in the interval between the Armistice and the conclusion of formal peace with Germany, Congress unequivocally required that enemy aliens be given a fair hearing before they could be deported. . . .

German aliens could not now, if they would, aid the German Government in war hostilities against the United States. For as declared by the United States Department of State, June 5, 1945, the German armed forces on land and sea had been completely subjugated and had unconditionally surrendered. "There is no central Government or authority in Germany capable of accepting responsibility for the maintenance of order, the administration of the country and compliance with the requirements of the victorious Powers." And the State Department went on to declare that the United States, Russia, Great Britain, and France had assumed "supreme authority with respect to Germany, including all the powers possessed by the German Government, the High Command, and any state, municipal, or local government or authority." And on March 17, 1948, the President of the United States told the Congress that "Almost three years have passed since the end . . ." of the war with Germany.

Of course, it is nothing but a fiction to say that we are now at war with Germany. Whatever else that fiction might support, I refuse to agree that it affords a basis for today's holding that our laws authorize the peacetime banishment of any person on the judicially unreviewable conclusion of a single individual. The 1798 Act did not grant its extraordinary and dangerous powers to be used during the period of fictional wars. As previously pointed out, even Mr. Otis, with all of his fervent support of anti-French legislation, repudiated the suggestion that the Act would vest the President with such dangerous powers in peacetime. Consequently, the Court today gives the 1798 Act a far broader meaning than it was given by one of the most vociferous champions of the 1798 series of anti-alien and anti-sedition laws.

Furthermore, the holding today represents an entirely new interpretation of the 1798 Act. For nearly 150 years after the 1798 Act there never came to this Court any case in which the Government asked that the Act be interpreted so as to allow the President or any other person to deport alien enemies without allowing them access to the courts. In fact, less than two months after the end of the actual fighting in the First World War, Attorney General Gregory informed the Congress that, although there was power to

continue the internment of alien enemies after the cessation of actual hostilities and until the ratification of a peace treaty, still there
was no statute under which they could then be deported. For this
reason the Attorney General requested Congress to enact new legislation to authorize deportation of enemy aliens at that time. The
bill thereafter introduced was endorsed by both the Attorney
General and the Secretary of Labor in a joint letter in which they
asked that it be given "immediate consideration" in view of the
"gravity of this situation." Several months later Attorney General
Palmer submitted substantially the same statements to the House
and Senate Committees on Immigration.

A bill to carry out the recommendations of the Wilson administration was later passed, but not until it had been amended
on the floor of the House of Representatives to require that all
alien enemies be given a fair hearing before their deportation. That
a fair hearing was the command of Congress is not only shown by
the language of the Act but by the text of the congressional hearings, by the Committee reports and by congressional debates on
the bill. In fact, the House was assured by the ranking member of
the Committee reporting the bill that in hearings to deport alien
enemies under the bill "a man is entitled to have counsel present,
entitled to subpoena witnesses and summon them before him and
have a full hearing, at which the stenographer's minutes must be
taken." Congress therefore, after the fighting war was over, authorized the deportation of interned alien enemies only if they were
"given full hearing, as in all cases of deportation under existing
laws."

This petitioner is in precisely the same status as were the interned alien enemies of the First World War for whom Congress
specifically required a fair hearing with court review as a prerequisite to their deportation. Yet the Court today sanctions a procedure
whereby petitioner is to be deported without any determination of
his charge that he has been denied a fair hearing. The Court can
reach such a result only by rejecting the interpretation of the 1798
Act given by two Attorney Generals, upon which Congress acted
in 1920. It is held that Congress and the two Attorney Generals of
the Wilson administration were wrong in believing that the 1798
Act did not authorize deportation of interned enemy aliens after
hostilities and before a peace treaty. And in making its novel interpretation of the 1798 Act the Court today denies this petitioner and

others the kind of fair hearing that due process of law was intended to guarantee.

The Court's opinion seems to fear that Germans if now left in the United States might somehow have a "potency for mischief" even after the complete subjugation and surrender of Germany, at least so long as the "peace of Peace has not come." This "potency for mischief" can of course have no possible relation to apprehension of any invasion by or war with Germany. The apprehension must therefore be based on fear that Germans now residing in the United States might emit ideas dangerous to the "peace of Peace." But the First Amendment represents this nation's belief that the spread of political ideas must not be suppressed. And the avowed purpose of the Alien Enemy Act was not to stifle the spread of ideas after hostilities had ended. Others in the series of Alien and Sedition Acts did provide for prison punishment of people who had or at least who dared to express political ideas. I cannot now agree to an interpretation of the Alien Enemy Act which gives a new life to the long repudiated anti-free speech and anti-free press philosophy of the 1798 Alien and Sedition Acts. I would not disinter that philosophy which the people have long hoped Thomas Jefferson had permanently buried when he pardoned the last person convicted for violation of the Alien and Sedition Acts.

Finally, I wish to call attention to what was said by Circuit Judge Augustus Hand in this case speaking for himself and Circuit Judges Learned Hand and Swan, before whom petitioner argued his own cause. Believing the deportation order before them was not subject to judicial review, they saw no reason for discussing the ". . . nature or weight of the evidence before the Repatriation Hearing Board, or the finding of the Attorney General. . . ." But they added: "However, on the face of the record it is hard to see why the relator should now be compelled to go back. Of course there may be much not disclosed to justify the step; and it is of doubtful propriety for a court ever to express an opinion on a subject over which it has no power. Therefore we shall, and should, say no more than to suggest that justice may perhaps be better satisfied if a reconsideration be given him in the light of the changed conditions, since the order of removal was made eighteen months ago."

It is not amiss, I think, to suggest my belief that because of today's opinion individual liberty will be less secure tomorrow than it was yesterday. Certainly the security of aliens is lessened, particularly if their ideas happen to be out of harmony with those of the governmental authorities of a period. And there is removed a segment of judicial power to protect individual liberty from arbitrary action, at least until today's judgment is corrected by Congress or by this Court.

Kovacs v. Cooper

336 U.S. 77

Decided *January 31, 1949*

The City of Trenton, New Jersey, enacted an ordinance prohibiting the operation on its streets of sound amplifiers and other instruments that give off "loud and raucous noises." In the case of Charles Kovacs v. Albert Cooper, Jr., Judge of the First District Police Court of Trenton, *the Supreme Court was confronted with a conviction for violation of the ordinance, as upheld by the New Jersey courts.*

A reading of the majority, the concurring, and the dissenting opinions shows that eight members of the Supreme Court, excepting only Justice Murphy, joined in the belief that reasonable regulation of sound amplifiers on streets and in public places is within the authority of municipalities. Justice Reed announced the judgment of the Court upholding the conviction and wrote an opinion that Chief Justice Vinson and Justice Burton joined. In their separate concurrences Justices Frankfurter and Jackson went further and held that the use of sound trucks on streets could be absolutely prohibited without infringing on freedom of speech as protected in the Bill of Rights.

Justice Black, in a dissent joined by Justices Douglas and Rutledge, found that Kovacs was convicted without the slightest evidence that his sound truck was producing "loud and raucous noises." Furthermore, Justice Black saw in the decision "a dangerous and unjustifiable breach in constitutional barriers designed to insure freedom of expression."

Justice Murphy seemingly accepted no part of the Court's judgment, since he dissented without opinion and noted no agreement of any kind.

MR. JUSTICE BLACK, *with whom* MR. JUSTICE DOUGLAS *and* MR. JUSTICE RUTLEDGE *concur, dissenting*

The question in this case is not whether appellant may constitutionally be convicted of operating a sound truck that emits "loud and raucous noises." The appellant was neither charged with nor convicted of operating a sound truck that emitted "loud and raucous noises." The charge against him in the police court was that he violated the city ordinance "in that he did, on South Stockton Street, in said City, play, use and operate a device known as a sound truck." The record reflects not even a shadow of evidence to prove that the noise was either "loud or raucous," unless these words of the ordinance refer to any noise coming from an amplifier, whatever its volume or tone.

After appellant's conviction in the police court, the case was taken to the Supreme Court of New Jersey for review. That court, composed of three judges, stated with reference to the ordinance and charge: "In simple, unambiguous language it prohibits the use upon the public streets of any device known as a sound truck, loud speaker or sound amplifier. This is the only charge made against the defendant in the complaint." That this court construed the ordinance as an absolute prohibition of all amplifiers on any public street at any time and without regard to volume of sound is emphasized by its further statement that "the ordinance leaves untouched the right of the prosecutor to express his views *orally without the aid of an amplifier.*" (Emphasis supplied.) Thus the New Jersey Supreme Court affirmed the conviction on the ground that the appellant was shown guilty of the only offense of which he was charged—speaking through an amplifier on a public street. If, as some members of this Court now assume, he was actually convicted for operating a machine that emitted "loud and raucous noises," then he was convicted on a charge for which he was never tried. "It is as much a violation of due process to send an accused to prison following conviction of a charge on which he was never tried as it would be to convict him upon a charge that was never made."

Furthermore, when the conviction was later affirmed in the

New Jersey Court of Errors and Appeals by an equally divided court, no one of that court's judges who voted to affirm expressed any doubt as to the correctness of the New Jersey Supreme Court's interpretation; indeed those judges wrote no opinion at all. One of the six who voted to reverse did base his judgment on the fact that there was not "a scintilla of evidence that the music or voice was loud or raucous" and that under the wording of the ordinance such proof was essential. In construing the statute as requiring a proof of loud and raucous noises, the dissenting judge made the initial mistake of the majority of this Court, but he conceded that under this construction of the statute there was a fatal absence of proof to convict. The other five judges who were for reversal concluded that the ordinance represented "an attempt by the municipality under the guise of regulation, to prohibit and outlaw, under all circumstances and conditions, the use of sound amplifying systems."

It thus appears that the appellant was charged and convicted by interpreting the ordinance as an absolute prohibition against the use of sound amplifying devices. The New Jersey Supreme Court affirmed only on that interpretation of the ordinance. There is no indication whatever that there was a different view entertained by the six judges of the Court of Errors and Appeals who affirmed the conviction. And it strains the imagination to say that the ordinance itself would warrant any other interpretation.

Nevertheless, in this Court the requisite majority for affirmance of appellant's conviction is composed in part of Justices who give the New Jersey ordinance a construction different from that given it by the state courts. That is not all. Affirmance here means that the appellant will be punished for an offense with which he was not charged, to prove which no evidence was offered, and of which he was not convicted, according to the only New Jersey court which affirmed with opinion. At the last term of court, we held that the Arkansas Supreme Court had denied an appellant due process because it had failed to appraise the validity of a conviction "on consideration of the case as it was tried and as the issues were determined in the trial court." I am unable to distinguish the action taken by this Court today from the action of the Arkansas Supreme Court which we declared denied a defendant due process of law.

The New Jersey ordinance is on its face, and as construed and applied in this case by that state's courts, an absolute and unqualified prohibition of amplifying devices on any of Trenton's streets at any time, at any place, for any purpose, and without regard to how noisy they may be.

In *Saia* v. *New York,* we had before us an ordinance of the City of Lockport, New York, which forbade the use of sound amplification devices except with permission of the chief of police. The ordinance was applied to keep a minister from using an amplifier while preaching in a public park. We held that the ordinance, aimed at the use of an amplifying device, invaded the area of free speech guaranteed the people by the First and Fourteenth Amendments. The ordinance, so we decided, amounted to censorship in its baldest form. And our conclusion rested on the fact that the chief of police was given arbitrary power to prevent the use of speech amplifying devices at all times and places in the city without regard to the volume of the sound. We pointed out the indispensable function performed by loud speakers in modern public speaking. We then placed use of loud speakers in public streets and parks on the same constitutional level as freedom to speak on streets without such devices, freedom to speak over radio, and freedom to distribute literature.

In this case the Court denies speech amplifiers the constitutional shelter recognized by our decisions and holding in the *Saia Case.* This is true because the Trenton, New Jersey, ordinance here sustained goes beyond a mere prior censorship of all loud speakers with authority in the censor to prohibit some of them. This Trenton ordinance wholly bars the use of all loud speakers mounted upon any vehicle in any of the city's public streets.

In my view this repudiation of the prior *Saia* opinion makes a dangerous and unjustifiable breach in the constitutional barriers designed to insure freedom of expression. Ideas and beliefs are today chiefly disseminated to the masses of people through the press, radio, moving pictures, and public address systems. To some extent at least there is competition of ideas between and within these groups. The basic premise of the First Amendment is that all present instruments of communication, as well as others that inventive genius may bring into being, shall be free from governmental censorship or prohibition. Laws which hamper the free use of some instruments of communication thereby favor competing channels. Thus, unless constitutionally prohibited, laws like this Trenton ordinance can give an overpowering influence to views of owners of legally favored instruments of communication. This favoritism, it seems to me, is the inevitable result of today's decision. For the result of today's opinion in upholding this statutory prohibition of amplifiers would surely not be reached by this Court if such channels of communication as the press, radio, or moving pictures were similarly attacked.

There are many people who have ideas that they wish to disseminate but who do not have enough money to own or control publishing plants, newspapers, radios, moving picture studios, or chains of show places. Yet everybody knows the vast reaches of these powerful channels of communication which from the very nature of our economic system must be under the control and guidance of comparatively few people. On the other hand, public speaking is done by many men of divergent minds with no centralized control over the ideas they entertain so as to limit the causes they espouse. It is no reflection on the value of preserving freedom for dissemination of the ideas of publishers of newspapers, magazines, and other literature, to believe that transmission of ideas through public speaking is also essential to the sound thinking of a fully informed citizenry.

It is of particular importance in a government where people elect their officials that the fullest opportunity be afforded candidates to express and voters to hear their views. It is of equal importance that criticism of governmental action not be limited to criticisms by press, radio, and moving pictures. In no other way except public speaking can the desirable objective of widespread public discussion be assured. For the press, the radio, and the moving picture owners have their favorites, and it assumes the impossible to suppose that these agencies will at all times be equally fair as between the candidates and officials they favor and those whom they vigorously oppose. And it is an obvious fact that public speaking today without the sound amplifiers is a wholly inadequate way to reach the people on a large scale. Consequently, to tip the scales against transmission of ideas through public speaking, as the Court does today, is to deprive the people of a large part of the basic advantages of the receipt of ideas that the First Amendment was designed to protect.

There is no more reason that I can see for wholly prohibiting one useful instrument of communication than another. If Trenton can completely bar the streets to the advantageous use of loud speakers, all cities can do the same. In that event preference in the dissemination of ideas is given those who can obtain the support of newspapers, etc., or those who have money enough to buy advertising from newspapers, radios, or moving pictures. This Court should no more permit this invidious prohibition against the dissemination of ideas by speaking than it would permit a complete blackout of the press, the radio, or moving pictures. It is wise for all who cherish freedom of expression to reflect upon the plain fact that a holding that the audiences of public speakers can be constitutionally prohibited is not unrelated to a like prohibition in other fields. And the right to freedom of expression should be protected from absolute censorship for persons without, as for persons with, wealth and power. At least, such is the theory of our society.

I am aware that the "blare" of this new method of carrying ideas is susceptible of abuse and may under certain circumstances constitute an intolerable nuisance. But ordinances can be drawn which adequately protect a community from unreasonable use of public speaking devices without absolutely denying to the community's citizens all information that may be disseminated or received through this new avenue for trade in ideas. I would agree without reservation to the sentiment that "unrestrained use throughout a municipality of all sound amplifying devices would be intolerable." And, of course, cities may restrict or absolutely ban the use of amplifiers on busy streets in the business area. A city ordinance that reasonably restricts the volume of sound, or the hours during which an amplifier may be used, does not, in my mind, infringe the constitutionally protected area of free speech. It is because this ordinance does none of these things, but is instead an absolute prohibition of all uses of an amplifier on any of the streets of Trenton at any time that I must dissent.

I would reverse the judgment.

Wolf v. Colorado

338 U.S. 25

Decided June 27, 1949

In deciding cases based on the Fourth Amendment's prohibition of "unreasonable searches and seizures," the Supreme Court has compiled a record that is marked by frequent change and inconsistency. In the landmark case of Weeks v. United States, *the Court in 1914 decided by unanimous vote that a federal trial court's denial of a pretrial motion for the return of papers seized unlawfully was a prejudicial error. Speaking for the Court, Justice Day held that if the documents in question could be used as evidence in a criminal prosecution, then the Fourth Amendment's protection against unreasonable search and seizure might as well be removed from the Constitution.*

Through the last quarter century, divisions within the Court on search and seizure tests have been close and sharp. In 1947 Justice Black supported Chief Justice Vinson's 5-to-4 majority opinion in Harris v. United States, *which sustained a prosecution and conviction for draft evasion on evidence that was not being sought for but was found incidentally in a search for evidence relating to an allegedly forged check. The next year Justice Black dissented in* Trupiano v. United States, *wherein Justice Murphy's 5-to-4 majority opinion held that evidence seized by federal liquor agents should have been suppressed on the ground that the search was made without a warrant although there was ample time to obtain a warrant.*

The matter of state acceptance or rejection of the Court's rule in the Weeks Case *came up in* Julius A. Wolf v. People of the State of Colorado. *Dividing 6 to 3, with a majority opinion by Justice Frankfurter, joined by Chief Justice Vinson and Justices Reed, Jackson, and Burton, the Court held that the Constitution does not forbid, in a state criminal case, the use of evidence obtained by an unreasonable search and seizure. Justice Black concurred separately. Justices Douglas, Murphy, and Rutledge in their dissenting opinions took the position that the Constitution prohibits, in state as well as federal courts, admission of evidence obtained by unreasonable searches and seizures.*

MR. JUSTICE BLACK, concurring

In this case, petitioner was convicted of a crime in a state court on evidence obtained by a search and seizure conducted in a manner that this Court has held "unreasonable" and therefore in violation of the Fourth Amendment. And under a rule of evidence adopted by this Court evidence so obtained by federal officers cannot be used against defendants in federal courts. For reasons stated in my dissenting opinion in *Adamson* v. *California*, I agree with the conclusion of the Court that the Fourth Amendment's prohibition of "unreasonable searches and seizures" is enforceable against the States. Consequently, I should be for reversal of this case if I thought the Fourth Amendment not only prohibited "unreasonable searches and seizures," but also, of itself, barred the use of evidence so unlawfully obtained. But I agree with what appears to be a plain implication of the Court's opinion that the federal exclusionary rule is not a command of the Fourth Amendment but is a judicially created rule of evidence which Congress might negate. This leads me to concur in the Court's judgment of affirmance.

It is not amiss to repeat my belief that the Fourteenth Amendment was intended to make the Fourth Amendment in its entirety applicable to the States. The Fourth Amendment was designed to protect people against unrestrained searches and seizures by sheriffs, policemen, and other law enforcement officers. Such protection is an essential in a free society. And I am unable to agree that the protection of people from overzealous or ruthless state officers is any less essential in a country of "ordered liberty" than is the protection of people from overzealous or ruthless federal officers. Certainly there are far more state than federal enforcement officers and their activities, up to now, have more frequently and closely touched the intimate daily lives of people than have the activities of federal officers. A state officer's "knock at the door . . . as a prelude to a search, without authority of law," may be, as our experience shows, just as ominous to "ordered liberty" as though the knock were made by a federal officer.

United States v. Alpers

338 U.S. 680

Decided February 6, 1950

When Congress wrote the words "or other matter of indecent character" into Section 245 of the Federal Criminal Code, did it mean to add phonograph records to a specific list of prohibited "obscene" articles, including "obscene" books, pamphlets, pictures, and films? This was the question before the Supreme Court in United States of America *v.* Alexander Lawrence Alpers.

Alpers was convicted in a United States District Court in California for having made an interstate shipment of phonograph records "of indecent character." Justice Minton, in a 5-to-3 majority opinion, upheld the conviction under the general provisions of the statute, and thus reversed the Court of Appeals, which had previously reversed the District Court. Chief Justice Vinson and Justices Reed, Burton, and Clark joined his opinion.

Justice Black, joined by Justices Frankfurter and Jackson, dissented. Justice Douglas took no part in the case. The Black dissent reflected his deeply held belief that the Supreme Court should construe Acts of Congress with utmost care when censorship results. The opinion provided a striking example of Justice Black's devotion to principle at a time when the majority was engaged in so-called practical considerations.

MR. JUSTICE BLACK, *with whom* MR. JUSTICE FRANKFURTER *and* MR. JUSTICE JACKSON *concur, dissenting*

I am unable to agree that the conduct of this respondent was made an offense by the language of the statutory provision on which his conviction rests. That provision forbids deposit with an express company, for interstate carriage, of "any obscene, lewd, or lascivious, or any filthy book, pamphlet, picture, motion-picture film, paper, letter, writing, print, or other matter of indecent character. . . ." The crime with which respondent was charged involved phonograph records, which do not come under any specific category listed in the statute. Consequently, the information against respondent could only charge violation of the provision's general language barring shipment of "other matter of indecent character." The Court sustains the conviction here by reasoning that a phonograph record is "matter" within the meaning of this congressional prohibition.

Our system of justice is based on the principle that criminal statutes shall be couched in language sufficiently clear to apprise people of the precise conduct that is prohibited. Judicial interpretation deviates from this salutary principle when statutory language is expanded to include conduct that Congress might have barred, but did not, by the language it used.

The reluctance of courts to expand the coverage of criminal statutes is particularly important where, as here, the statute results in censorship. According to dictionary definitions, "matter" undeniably includes phonograph records and the substances of which they are made. Indeed, dictionaries tell us that "matter" encompasses all tangibles and many intangibles, including material treated or to be treated in a book, speech, legal action, or the like; matter for discussion, argument, exposition, etc.; and material treated in the medieval metrical romances. The many meanings of "matter" are warning signals against giving the word the broad construction adopted by the Court.

History is not lacking in proof that statutes like this may readily be converted into instruments for dangerous abridgments of freedom of expression. People of varied temperaments and beliefs have always differed among themselves concerning what is "indecent." Sculpture, paintings, and literature, ranked among the classics by some, deeply offend the religious and moral sensibilities of others. And those which offend, however priceless or irreplaceable, have often been destroyed by honest zealots convinced that such destruction was necessary to preserve morality as they saw it.

Of course, there is a tremendous difference between cultural treasures and the phonograph records here involved. But our decision cannot be based on that difference. Involved in this case is the vital question of whether courts should give the most expansive construction to general terms in legislation providing for censorship of publications or pictures found to be "indecent," "obscene," etc. Censorship in any field may so readily encroach on constitutionally protected liberties that courts should not add to the list of items banned by Congress.

In the provision relied on, as well as elsewhere in the Act, Congress used language carefully describing a number of "indecent" articles and forbade their shipment in interstate commerce. This specific list applied censorship only to articles that people could read or see; the Court now adds to it articles capable of use to produce sounds that people can hear. The judicial addition here may itself be small. But it is accomplished by a technique of broad interpretation which too often may be successfully invoked by the many people who want the law to proscribe what other people may say, write, hear, see, or read. I cannot agree to any departure from the sound practice of narrowly construing statutes which by censorship restrict liberty of communication.

Since Congress did not specifically ban the shipment of phonograph records, this Court should not do so.

United States v. Rabinowitz

339 U.S. 56

Decided February 20, 1950

Indication of the growing confusion in cases involving the Fourth Amendment's protective stand against "unreasonable searches and seizures" appeared in Wolf v. Colorado *(page 200). This confusion was aggravated by the 5-to-3 decision in the federal case of* United States of America v. Albert J. Rabinowitz, *which expressly reversed in large part the 5-to-4 decision in* Trupiano v. United States, *handed down about twenty months earlier. In the* Trupiano *Case, the Court held that evidence seized by federal liquor agents should have been suppressed on the ground that the search was made without a warrant even though there was ample time to obtain a warrant. In the* Rabinowitz *Case, federal agents, seeking forged and altered government stamps, searched without a warrant the desk, safe, and file cabinets in the one-room office of a New York man whose arrest had been validly ordered.*

The evidence obtained without a warrant was used against Rabinowitz at his trial and became the basis for his conviction. The United States Court of Appeals in New York, however, reversed the conviction on the strength of the Trupiano *Decision. Then, in still another turn-around, the Supreme Court reversed the Court of Appeals in a majority opinion by Justice Minton with whom Chief Justice Vinson and Justices Reed, Clark, and Burton joined. The dissenters, Justices Black, Frankfurter, and Jackson, took the position that in the interest of the law's stability the* Trupiano *Decision should not be reversed. Justice Douglas did not take part.*

Justice Black's plea for stability, notwithstanding his own dissent in Trupiano, *was strongly supported by Justice Frankfurter who concluded his* Rabinowitz *dissent with these strong words: "In overruling* Trupiano *we overrule the underlying principle of a whole series of recent cases . . . These are not outmoded decisions eroded by time. Even under normal circumstances, the Court ought not to overrule such a series of decisions where no mischief flowing from them has been made manifest. Respect for continuity in law where reasons for change are wanting, alone requires adherence to* Trupiano *and the other decisions. Especially ought the Court not re-enforce needlessly the instabilities of our day by giving fair ground for the belief that Law is the expression of chance—for instance, of unexpected changes in the Court's composition and the contingencies in the choice of successors."*

MR. JUSTICE BLACK, *dissenting*

Trupiano v. *United States* was decided on the unarticulated premise that the Fourth Amendment of itself barred the use of evidence obtained by what the Court considered an "unreasonable" search. I dissented in that case. Later, concurring in this Court's decision in *Wolf* v. *Colorado*, I stated my agreement with the "plain implication" of the *Wolf* opinion that "the federal exclusionary rule is not a command of the Fourth Amendment but is a judicially created rule of evidence which Congress might negate." In the light of the *Wolf Case*, the *Trupiano* rule is not a constitutional command, but rather an evidentiary policy adopted by this Court in the exercise of its supervisory powers over federal courts. The present case comes within that rule: the trial court admitted certain evidence procured by a search and seizure without a search warrant although the officers had ample time and opportunity to get one. Whether this Court should adhere to the *Trupiano* principle making evidence so obtained inadmissible in federal courts now presents no more than a question of what is wise judicial policy. Although the rule does not in all respects conform to my own ideas, I think that the reasons for changing it are outweighed by reasons against its change.

American Communications Association v. Douds

339 U.S. 382

Decided May 8, 1950

*Few important decisions in the last quarter century have been so
unsatisfactory as the decision sustaining the anti-Communist affidavit required for officers of labor unions that utilized the Labor Relations Act of 1947. In the first place, for one reason or another,
three Justices, Douglas, Clark, and Minton, did not participate in
the combined cases—American Communications Association,
C.I.O., et al. v. Charles T. Douds, Regional Director of the National Labor Relations Board, and United Steelworkers of America
et al. v. National Labor Relations Board. Thus a Court reduced to
only two thirds of its membership ruled on the issues.*

*Of the six members taking part, five joined in an opinion up-
holding the requirement of disclosure of any Communist affiliation
on the part of a union official. The Court's opinion was written by
Chief Justice Vinson and supported by Justices Reed, Frankfurter,
Jackson, and Burton. Of the five, however, only Chief Justice
Vinson and Justices Reed and Burton sustained the statute in its
demand that the union official state that he does not believe in and
is not a member of nor supports any organization that believes in
or teaches the overthrow of the Government by force. Justice
Frankfurter found that section too uncertain to be constitutional.*

Justice Jackson objected to the section as a trespass by Congress on freedom of speech.

As the sole out-and-out dissenter, Justice Black took the strong stand that the law in question in its entirety violated the right of free speech in that it penalized belief through the imposition of civil disabilities. Test oaths, whether political or religious, are, he said, "implacable foes of free thought." In this significant decision, with its portent of things to come, Justice Black demonstrated his capacity to stand alone in his championship of freedom for the individual.

Mr. Justice Black, *dissenting*

We have said that "Freedom to think is absolute of its own nature; the most tyrannical government is powerless to control the inward workings of the mind." But people can be, and in less democratic countries have been, made to suffer for their admitted or conjectured thoughts. Blackstone recalls that Dionysius is "recorded to have executed a subject barely for dreaming that he had killed him; which was held for a sufficient proof that he had thought thereof in his waking hours." Such a result, while too barbaric to be tolerated in our nation, is not illogical if a government can tamper in the realm of thought and penalize "belief" on the ground that it might lead to illegal conduct. Individual freedom and governmental thought-probing cannot live together. As the Court admits even today, under the First Amendment "Beliefs are inviolate."

Today's decision rejects that fundamental principle. The Court admits, as it must, that the "proscriptions" of Section 9 (h) of the National Labor Relations Act, as amended by the Taft-Hartley Act, rest on "beliefs and political affiliations," and that "Congress has undeniably discouraged the lawful exercise of political freedoms" which are "protected by the First Amendment." These inescapable facts should compel a holding that Section 9 (h) conflicts with the First Amendment.

Crucial to the Court's contrary holding is the premise that congressional power to regulate trade and traffic includes power to proscribe "beliefs and political affiliations." No case cited by the Court provides the least vestige of support for thus holding that the Commerce Clause restricts the right to think. On the contrary, the First Amendment was added after adoption of the Constitution for the express purpose of barring Congress from using previously granted powers to abridge belief or its expression. Freedom to think is inevitably abridged when beliefs are penalized by imposition of civil disabilities.

Since Section 9 (h) was passed to exclude certain beliefs from one arena of the national economy, it was quite natural to utilize the test oath as a weapon. History attests the efficacy of that instrument for inflicting penalties and disabilities on obnoxious minorities. It was one of the major devices used against the Huguenots in France, and against "heretics" during the Spanish Inquisition. It helped English rulers identify and outlaw Catholics, Quakers, Baptists, and Congregationalists—groups considered dangerous for political as well as religious reasons. And wherever the test oath was in vogue, spies and informers found rewards far more tempting than truth. Painful awareness of the evils of thought espionage made such oaths "an abomination to the founders of this nation." Whether religious, political, or both, test oaths are implacable foes of free thought. By approving their imposition, this Court has injected compromise into a field where the First Amendment forbids compromise.

The Court assures us that today's encroachment on liberty is just a small one, that this particular statutory provision "touches only a relative handful of persons, leaving the great majority of persons of the identified affiliations and beliefs completely free from restraint." But not the least of the virtues of the First Amendment is its protection of each member of the smallest and most unorthodox minority. Centuries of experience testify that laws aimed at one political or religious group, however rational these laws may be in their beginnings, generate hatreds and prejudices which rapidly spread beyond control. Too often it is fear which inspires such passions, and nothing is more reckless or contagious. In the resulting hysteria, popular indignation tars with the same brush all those who have ever been associated with any member of the group under attack or who hold a view which, though supported by revered Americans as essential to democracy, has been adopted by that group for its own purposes.

Under such circumstances, restrictions imposed on proscribed groups are seldom static, even though the rate of expansion may not move in geometric progression from discrimination to armband to ghetto and worse. Thus I cannot regard the Court's holding as one which merely bars Communists from holding union office and nothing more. For its reasoning would apply just as forcibly to statutes barring Communists and their suspected sympathizers from election to political office, mere membership in unions, and in fact from getting or holding any jobs whereby they could earn a living.

The Court finds comfort in its assurance that we need not fear too much legislative restriction of political belief or association "while this Court sits." That expression, while felicitous, has no validity in this particular constitutional field. For it springs from the assumption that individual mental freedom can be constitutionally abridged whenever any majority of this Court finds a satisfactory legislative reason. Never before has this Court held that the Government could for any reason attaint persons for their political beliefs or affiliations. It does so today.

Today the "political affiliation" happens to be the Communist Party: testimony of an ex-Communist that some Communist union officers had called "political strikes" is held sufficient to uphold a law coercing union members not to elect any Communist as an officer. Under this reasoning, affiliations with other political parties could be proscribed just as validly. Of course, there is no practical possibility that either major political party would turn this weapon on the other, even though members of one party were accused of "political lockouts" a few years ago and members of the other are now charged with fostering a "welfare state" alien to our system. But with minor parties the possibility is not wholly fanciful. One, for instance, advocates Socialism; another allegedly follows the Communist "line"; still another is repeatedly charged with a desire and purpose to deprive Negroes of equal job opportunities. Under today's opinion, Congress could validly bar all members of these parties from officership in unions or industrial corporations; the only showing required would be testimony that some members in such positions had, by attempts to further their party's purposes, unjustifiably fostered industrial strife which hampered interstate commerce.

It is indicated, although the opinion is not thus limited and is based on threats to commerce rather than to national security, that members of the Communist Party or its "affiliates" can be individually attainted without danger to others because there is some evidence that as a group they act in obedience to the commands of a foreign power. This was the precise reason given in Sixteenth

Century England for attainting all Catholics unless they subscribed
to test oaths wholly incompatible with their religion. Yet in the
hour of crisis, an overwhelming majority of the English Catholics
thus persecuted rallied loyally to defend their homeland against
Spain and its Catholic troops. And in our own country, Jefferson
and his followers were earnestly accused of subversive allegiance to
France. At the time, imposition of civil disability on all members of
his political party must have seemed at least as desirable as does
Section 9(h) today. For at stake, so many believed, was the survival of a newly founded nation, not merely a few potential inter-
ruptions of commerce by strikes "political" rather than economic
in origin.

These experiences underline the wisdom of the basic constitutional precept that penalties should be imposed only for a person's
own conduct, not for his beliefs or for the conduct of others with
whom he may associate. Guilt should not be imputed solely from
association or affiliation with political parties or any other organization, however much we abhor the ideas which they advocate. Like
anyone else, individual Communists who commit overt acts in violation of valid laws can and should be punished. But the postulate
of the First Amendment is that our free institutions can be maintained without proscribing or penalizing political belief, speech,
press, assembly, or party affiliation. This is a far bolder philosophy
than despotic rulers can afford to follow. It is the heart of the system on which our freedom depends.

Fears of alien ideologies have frequently agitated the nation
and inspired legislation aimed at suppressing advocacy of those
ideologies. At such times the fog of public excitement obscures the
ancient landmarks set up in our Bill of Rights. Yet then, of all
times, should this Court adhere most closely to the course they
mark. This was done in *De Jonge* v. *Oregon*, where the Court
struck down a state statute making it a crime to participate in a
meeting conducted by Communists. It had been stipulated that the
Communist Party advocated violent overthrow of the Government. Speaking through Chief Justice Hughes, a unanimous Court
calmly announced time-honored principles that should govern this
Court today:

> The greater the importance of safeguarding the community from
> incitements to the overthrow of our institutions by force and vio-
> lence, the more imperative is the need to preserve inviolate the
> constitutional rights of free speech, free press and free assembly in

order to maintain the opportunity for free political discussion, to the end that government may be responsive to the will of the people and that changes, if desired, may be obtained by peaceful means. Therein lies the security of the Republic, the very foundation of constitutional government.

Feiner v. New York

340 U.S. 315

Decided January 15, 1951

The case of Irving Feiner *v.* People of the State of New York *stirred Justice Black profoundly, as his dissent shows. A young student, distressed by racial discrimination, spoke to a crowd in Syracuse, New York, through a sound amplifying system from a box on the sidewalk. The burden of his remarks was that Negroes were discriminated against in the matter of rights and that they should insist on fair treatment. Because the police regarded the address as being too derogatory to public officials and too likely to produce trouble, Feiner was ordered to stop speaking and arrested when he did not stop. He was tried for disorderly conduct, convicted, and sentenced to the New York Penitentiary.*

The Supreme Court upheld the State conviction in an opinion by Chief Justice Vinson, with whom Justices Reed, Jackson, Burton, and Clark joined and Justice Frankfurter concurred. Justices Douglas and Minton dissented on the ground that the facts showed no present danger of a riot. Justice Black believed that it was up to the police to maintain law and order at the meeting so the speaker might present his views to the public. The essence of his dissent is that the student was sentenced because of the unpopularity of his views and hence this was a violation of his constitutional rights.

Mr. Justice Black, *dissenting*

The record before us convinces me that petitioner, a young college student, has been sentenced to the penitentiary for the unpopular views he expressed on matters of public interest while lawfully making a street-corner speech in Syracuse, New York. Today's decision, however, indicates that we must blind ourselves to this fact because the trial judge fully accepted the testimony of the prosecution witnesses on all important points. Many times in the past this Court has said that despite findings below, we will examine the evidence for ourselves to ascertain whether federally protected rights have been denied; otherwise review here would fail of its purpose in safeguarding constitutional guarantees. Even a partial abandonment of this rule marks a dark day for civil liberties in our Nation.

But still more has been lost today. Even accepting every "finding of fact" below, I think this conviction makes a mockery of the free speech guarantees of the First and Fourteenth Amendments. The end result of the affirmance here is to approve a simple and readily available technique by which cities and states can with impunity subject all speeches, political or otherwise, on streets or elsewhere, to the supervision and censorship of the local police. I will have no part or parcel in this holding which I view as a long step toward totalitarian authority.

Considering only the evidence which the state courts appear to have accepted, the pertinent "facts" are: Syracuse city authorities granted a permit for O. John Rogge, a former assistant attorney general, to speak in a public school building on March 8, 1948, on the subject of racial discrimination and civil liberties. On March 8th, however, the authorities canceled the permit. The Young Progressives, under whose auspices the meeting was scheduled, then arranged for Mr. Rogge to speak at the Hotel Syracuse. The gathering on the street where petitioner spoke was held to protest the cancellation and to publicize the meeting at the hotel. In this connection, petitioner used derogatory but not profane language with reference to the city authorities, President Truman, and the American Legion. After hearing some of these remarks, a policeman, who had been sent to the meeting by his superiors, reported to Police Headquarters by telephone. To whom he reported or what was said does not appear in the record, but after returning from the call, he and another policeman started through the crowd toward petitioner. Both officers swore they did not intend to make an arrest when they started, and the trial court accepted their statements. They also said, and the court believed, that they heard and saw "angry mutterings," "pushing," "shoving and milling around," and "restlessness." Petitioner spoke in a "loud, high pitched voice." He said that "colored people don't have equal rights and they should rise up in arms and fight for them." One man who heard this told the officers that if they did not take that "S . . . O . . . B . . ." off the box, he would. The officers then approached petitioner for the first time. One of them first "asked" petitioner to get off the box, but petitioner continued urging his audience to attend Rogge's speech. The officer next "told" petitioner to get down, but he did not. The officer finally "demanded" that petitioner get down, telling him he was under arrest. Petitioner then told the crowd that "the law had arrived and would take over" and asked why he was arrested. The officer first replied that the charge was "unlawful assembly" but later changed the ground to "disorderly conduct."

The Court's opinion apparently rests on this reasoning: The policeman, under the circumstances detailed, could reasonably conclude that serious fighting or even riot was imminent; therefore he could stop petitioner's speech to prevent a breach of peace; accordingly, it was "disorderly conduct" for petitioner to continue speaking in disobedience of the officer's request. As to the existence of a dangerous situation on the street corner, it seems far-fetched to suggest that the "facts" show any imminent threat of riot or uncontrollable disorder. It is neither unusual nor unexpected that some people at public street meetings mutter, mill about, push, shove, or disagree, even violently, with the speaker. Indeed, it is rare where controversial topics are discussed that an outdoor crowd does not do some or all of these things. Nor does one isolated threat to assault the speaker forebode disorder. Especially should the danger be discounted where, as here, the person threatening was a man whose wife and two small children accompanied him and who, so far as the record shows, was never close enough to petitioner to carry out the threat.

Moreover, assuming that the "facts" did indicate a critical situation, I reject the implication of the Court's opinion that the police had no obligation to protect petitioner's constitutional right to talk. The police of course have power to prevent breaches of the peace. But if, in the name of preserving order, they ever can interfere with a lawful public speaker, they first must make all reasonable efforts to protect him. Here the policeman did not even pretend to try to protect petitioner. According to the officers' testimony, the crowd was restless but there is no showing of any attempt to quiet it; pedestrians were forced to walk into the street, but there was no effort to clear a path on the sidewalk; one person threatened to assault petitioner but the officers did nothing to discourage this when even a word might have sufficed. Their duty was to protect petitioner's right to talk, even to the extent of arresting the man who threatened to interfere. Instead, they shirked that duty and acted only to suppress the right to speak.

Finally, I cannot agree with the Court's statement that petitioner's disregard of the policeman's unexplained request amounted to such "deliberate defiance" as would justify an arrest or conviction for disorderly conduct. On the contrary, I think that the policeman's action was a "deliberate defiance" of ordinary official duty as well as of the constitutional right of free speech. For at least where time allows, courtesy and explanation of commands are basic elements of good official conduct in a democratic society. Here petitioner was "asked" then "told" then "commanded" to stop speaking, but a man making a lawful address is certainly not required to be silent merely because an officer directs it. Petitioner was entitled to know why he should cease doing a lawful act. Not once was he told. I understand that people in authoritarian countries must obey arbitrary orders. I had hoped that there was no such duty in the United States.

In my judgment, today's holding means that as a practical matter, minority speakers can be silenced in any city. Hereafter, despite the First and Fourteenth Amendments, the policeman's club can take heavy toll of a current administration's public critics. Criticism of public officials will be too dangerous for all but the most courageous. This is true regardless of the fact that in two other cases decided this day, *Kunz* v. *New York*, and *Niemotko* v. *Maryland*, a majority, in obedience to past decisions of this Court, provides a theoretical safeguard for freedom of speech. For whatever is thought to be guaranteed in *Kunz* and *Niemotko* is taken away by what is done here. The three cases read together mean that while previous restraints probably cannot be imposed on an unpopular speaker, the police have discretion to silence him as soon as the customary hostility to his views develops.

In this case I would reverse the conviction, thereby adhering to the great principles of the First and Fourteenth Amendments as announced for this Court in 1940 by Mr. Justice Roberts:

> In the realm of religious faith and in that of political belief, sharp differences arise. In both fields, the tenets of one man may seem the rankest error to his neighbor. To persuade others to his own point of view, the pleader, as we know, at times, resorts to exaggeration, to vilification of men who have been, or are, prominent in church or state, and even to false statement. But the people of this nation have ordained in the light of history, that, in spite of the probability of excesses and abuses, these liberties are, in the long view, essential to enlightened opinion and right conduct on the part of the citizens of a democracy.

I regret my inability to persuade the Court not to retreat from this principle.

Joint Anti-Fascist Refugee Committee v. McGrath

341 U.S. 123

Decided April 30, 1951

One of the earliest struggles in the Cold War on the home front arose from the blacklisting of allegedly Communist organizations by Attorney General Tom C. Clark in November 1947, under an Executive Order on loyalty issued by President Truman earlier the same year. There was neither notice to nor hearing for the blacklisted organizations before their names were turned over to the Loyalty Review Board of the Civil Service Commission. This had the effect of convicting all the listed organizations of disloyalty in a public announcement which received widespread attention. Subsequently the list was transmitted, as required by the Executive Order, to all government departments and boards, for use in administrative proceedings for the discharge of government employees held to be disloyal.

Three organizations sued the Attorney General for relief and asked that their names be taken from the list. They asserted that they were charitable, not in any way disoyal, and that their activities had been harmed by inclusion on the blacklist. Lower courts granted the Government's motions to dismiss these suits and the organizations appealed. The three cases—Joint Anti-Fascist Refugee Committee v. J. Howard McGrath, Attorney General of the United States, National Council of American-Soviet Friendship, Inc., et al. *v.* McGrath, *and* International Workers Order, Inc., and Arthur Lowndes Drayton *v.* McGrath—*were joined in the Supreme Court and reversed by five Justices. Justice Clark, as former Attorney General, did not participate. Justice Burton delivered the opinion that announced the judgment of the Court. Supporting the Burton judgment in the conclusion that the complaining organizations had standing to sue were Justices Black, Frankfurter, Douglas, and Jackson. Chief Justice Vinson and Justices Reed and Minton dissented. The decision produced five opinions.*

His separate concurrence deserves to be ranked among Justice Black's most telling opinions.

MR. JUSTICE BLACK, *concurring*

Without notice or hearing and under color of the President's Executive Order No. 9835, the Attorney General found petitioners guilty of harboring treasonable opinions and designs, officially branded them as Communists, and promulgated his findings and conclusions for particular use as evidence against government employees suspected of disloyalty. In the present climate of public opinion it appears certain that the Attorney General's much publicized findings, regardless of their truth or falsity, are the practical equivalents of confiscation and death sentences for any blacklisted organization not possessing extraordinary financial, political, or religious prestige and influence. The Government not only defends the power of the Attorney General to pronounce such deadly edicts but also argues that individuals or groups so condemned have no standing to seek redress in the courts, even though a fair judicial hearing might conclusively demonstrate their loyalty. My basic reasons for rejecting these and other contentions of the Government are in summary the following:

(1) I agree with Mr. Justice Burton that petitioners have standing to sue for the reason among others that they have a right to conduct their admittedly legitimate political, charitable, and business operations free from unjustified governmental defamation. Otherwise, executive officers could act lawlessly with impunity. And, assuming that the President may constitutionally authorize the promulgation of the Attorney General's list, I further agree with Mr. Justice Burton that this Court should not attribute to the President a purpose to vest in a cabinet officer the power to destroy political, social, religious, or business organizations by "arbitrary

fiat," and thus the methods employed by the Attorney General exceed his authority under Executive Order No. 9835.

(2) Assuming, though I deny, that the Constitution permits the Executive officially to determine, list and publicize individuals and groups as traitors and public enemies, I agree with Mr. Justice Frankfurter that the Due Process Clause of the Fifth Amendment would bar such condemnation without notice and a fair hearing. My views previously expressed under similar circumstances are relevant here.

(3) More fundamentally, however, in my judgment the Executive has no constitutional authority, with or without a hearing, officially to prepare and publish the lists challenged by petitioners. In the first place, the system adopted effectively punishes many organizations and their members merely because of their political beliefs and utterances, and to this extent smacks of a most evil type of censorship. This cannot be reconciled with the First Amendment as I interpret it. Moreover, officially prepared and proclaimed governmental blacklists possess almost every quality of bills of attainder, the use of which was from the beginning forbidden to both national and state governments. It is true that the classic bill of attainder was a condemnation by the Legislature following investigation by that body, while in the present case the Attorney General performed the official tasks. But I cannot believe that the authors of the Constitution, who outlawed the bill of attainder, inadvertently endowed the Executive with power to engage in the same tyrannical practices that had made the bill such an odious institution.

There is argument that Executive power to issue these pseudo-bills of attainder can be implied from the undoubted power of the Government to hire and discharge employees and to protect itself against treasonable individuals or organizations. Our basic law, however, wisely withheld authority for resort to Executive investigations, condemnations, and blacklists as a substitute for imposition of legal types of penalties by courts following trial and conviction in accordance with procedural safeguards of the Bill of Rights.

In this day when prejudice, hate, and fear are constantly invoked to justify irresponsible smears and persecution of persons even faintly suspected of entertaining unpopular views, it may be futile to suggest that the cause of internal security would be fostered, not hurt, by faithful adherence to our constitutional guarantees of individual liberty. Nevertheless, since prejudice manifests itself in much the same way in every age and country and since what has happened before can happen again, it surely should not be amiss to call attention to what has occurred when dominant governmental groups have been left free to give uncontrolled rein to their prejudices against unorthodox minorities. As specific illustration, I am adding as an appendix Macaulay's account of a parliamentary proscription which took place when popular prejudice was high; this is only one out of many similar instances that readily can be found. Memories of such events were fresh in the minds of the Founders when they forbade the use of the bill of attainder.

Dennis v. United States

341 U.S. 494

Decided June 4, 1951

Justice Black's devotion to free speech and thought met one of its severest tests in the midst of the Korean war. The occasion was the Supreme Court's review of the conviction of the eleven leaders of the American Communist Party. The case was that of Eugene Dennis, John B. Williamson, Jacob Stachel, Robert G. Thompson, Benjamin J. Davis, Jr., Henry Winston, John Gates, Irving Potash, Gilbert Green, Carl Winter, and Gus Hall *v.* United States of America. *Indicted in the presidential election year of 1948, the eleven were found guilty of violating the 1940 Smith Act, which prohibited conspiracy to teach or advocate the overthrow of the Government by force or violence. The convictions in Judge Harold R. Medina's United States District Court were upheld in the Court of Appeals in an opinion by Chief Judge Learned Hand.*

In the Supreme Court, Chief Justice Vinson accepted the Hand conclusions for a 6-to-2 decision. The essence of the Vinson opinion, joined by Justices Reed, Burton, and Minton, was that a clear and present danger existed and that Congress had the right to legislate against it. Justices Frankfurter and Jackson concurred in separate opinions, each of which found the Smith Act valid insofar as it was at issue. Justice Clark, as a recent Attorney General, did not participate. Justices Black and Douglas dissented in separate opinions, each strongly worded. Neither found any basis for the conclusion that there was a danger clear and present. Each held that the restriction on freedom of speech was without justification.

The Black dissent in the Dennis Case *recalled Charles Evans Hughes's description of "a dissent in a court of last resort" as "an appeal to the brooding spirit of the law, to the intelligence of a future day, when a later decision may possibly correct the error into which the dissenting judge believes the court to have been betrayed." For Justice Black raised just such an appeal, particularly in the last paragraph, as he looked to the future. The "calmer time" to which he addressed himself came just six years later* (Yates *v.* United States, *page 308). Here is the* Dennis *dissent that foretold its coming.*

Mr. Justice Black, *dissenting*

Here again, as in *Breard* v. *Alexandria,* decided this day, my basic disagreement with the Court is not as to how we should explain or reconcile what was said in prior decisions but springs from a fundamental difference in constitutional approach. Consequently, it would serve no useful purpose to state my position at length.

At the outset I want to emphasize what the crime involved in this case is, and what it is not. These petitioners were not charged with an attempt to overthrow the Government. They were not charged with overt acts of any kind designed to overthrow the Government. They were not even charged with saying anything or writing anything designed to overthrow the Government. The charge was that they agreed to assemble and to talk and publish certain ideas at a later date: The indictment is that they conspired to organize the Communist Party and to use speech or newspapers and other publications in the future to teach and advocate the forcible overthrow of the Government. No matter how it is worded, this is a virulent form of prior censorship of speech and press, which I believe the First Amendment forbids. I would hold Section 3 of the Smith Act authorizing this prior restraint unconstitutional on its face and as applied.

But let us assume, contrary to all constitutional ideas of fair criminal procedure, that petitioners, although not indicted for the crime of actual advocacy, may be punished for it. Even on this radical assumption, the other opinions in this case show that the only way to affirm these convictions is to repudiate directly or indirectly the established "clear and present danger" rule. This the Court does in a way which greatly restricts the protections afforded by the First Amendment. The opinions for affirmance indicate that the chief reason for jettisoning the rule is the expressed fear that advocacy of Communist doctrine endangers the safety of the Republic. Undoubtedly, a governmental policy of unfettered communication of ideas does entail dangers. To the Founders of this Nation, however, the benefits derived from free expression were worth the risk. They embodied this philosophy in the First Amendment's command that Congress "shall make no law abridging . . . the freedom of speech, or of the press. . . ." I have always believed that the First Amendment is the keystone of our Government, that the freedoms it guarantees provide the best insurance against destruction of all freedom. At least as to speech in the realm of public matters, I believe that the "clear and present danger" test does not "mark the furthermost constitutional boundaries of protected expression" but does "no more than recognize a minimum compulsion of the Bill of Rights."

So long as this Court exercises the power of judicial review of legislation, I cannot agree that the First Amendment permits us to sustain laws suppressing freedom of speech and press on the basis of Congress' or our own notions of mere "reasonableness." Such a doctrine waters down the First Amendment so that it amounts to little more than an admonition to Congress. The Amendment as so construed is not likely to protect any but those "safe" or orthodox views which rarely need its protection. I must also express my objection to the holding because, as Mr. Justice Douglas's dissent shows, it sanctions the determination of a crucial issue of fact by the judge rather than by the jury. Nor can I let this opportunity pass without expressing my objection to the severely limited grant of *certiorari* in this case which precluded consideration here of at least two other reasons for reversing these convictions: (1) the record shows a discriminatory selection of the jury panel which prevented trial before a representative cross section of the community; (2) the record shows that one member of the trial jury was violently hostile to petitioners before and during the trial.

Public opinion being what it now is, few will protest the conviction of these Communist petitioners. There is hope, however, that in calmer times, when present pressures, passions, and fears subside, this or some later Court will restore the First Amendment liberties to the high preferred place where they belong in a free society.

Breard v. Alexandria

341 U.S. 622

Decided June 4, 1951

Although a highly placed jurist, far removed from the practice of daily journalism, Justice Black has shown himself to be more concerned with the basic guarantee of freedom of the press than many newspaper editors and publishers have demonstrated themselves to be. The clarity with which he has seen the mission and methods of the press comes out in his dissent in Jack H. Breard v. City of Alexandria, Louisiana. *At issue was a municipal ordinance which barred canvassers or peddlers from calling at private homes without first having been invited or requested to make the call. The appellant contended that the ordinance violated the Due Process Clause by depriving canvassers of their means of livelihood, that it violated the Commerce Clause, and that, as applied to solicitors of subscriptions to magazines, it violated the constitutional guarantee of freedom of the press.*

All these contentions were rejected by six members of the Supreme Court—Justice Reed, who delivered the majority opinion, and Justices Frankfurter, Clark, Minton, Jackson, and Burton, who supported Justice Reed. Chief Justice Vinson, joined by Justice Douglas, dissented on the ground that the ordinance was not regulatory but prohibitive and as a consequence discriminated against interstate commerce in favor of local merchants. Justice Black's dissent, also joined by Justice Douglas, took the position that, when applied to canvassers for periodicals, the ordinance violated freedom of the press. In his dissent he referred to Jones v. Opelika *being reversed without "forthright overruling." This was a reference, not to the 1942 decision in* Jones v. Opelika *(page 97) but to a subsequent decision in the same case, handed down after the Court ordered a rehearing.*

This would not be the only time that Justice Black would find himself in the minority after having earlier enjoyed the satisfaction of being in the majority on the same issue in a Bill of Rights test.

Mr. Justice Black, *with whom* Mr. Justice Douglas *joins, dissenting*

On May 3, 1943, this Court held that cities and states could not enforce laws which impose flat taxes on the privilege of door-to-door sales of religious literature, or which make it unlawful for persons to go from home to home knocking on doors and ringing doorbells to invite occupants to religious, political, or other kinds of public meetings. Over strong dissents, these laws were held to invade liberty of speech, press, and religion in violation of the First and Fourteenth Amendments. Today a new majority adopts the position of the former dissenters and sustains a city ordinance forbidding door-to-door solicitation of subscriptions to the *Saturday Evening Post, Newsweek,* and other magazines. Since this decision cannot be reconciled with the *Jones v. Opelika, Murdock* v. *Pennsylvania,* and *Martin* v. *Struthers Cases,* it seems to me that good judicial practice calls for their forthright overruling. But whether this is done or not, it should be plain that my disagreement with the majority of the Court as now constituted stems basically from a different concept of the reach of the constitutional liberty of the press rather than from any difference of opinion as to what former cases have held.

Today's decision marks a revitalization of the judicial views which prevailed before this Court embraced the philosophy that the First Amendment gives a preferred status to the liberties it protects. I adhere to that preferred position philosophy. It is my belief that the freedom of the people of this Nation cannot survive even a little governmental hobbling of religious or political ideas, whether they be communicated orally or through the press.

The constitutional sanctuary for the press must necessarily include liberty to publish and circulate. In view of our economic system, it must also include freedom to solicit paying subscribers

Of course, homeowners can if they wish forbid newsboys, reporters, or magazine solicitors to ring their doorbells. But when the homeowner himself has not done this, I believe that the First Amendment, interpreted with due regard for the freedoms it guarantees, bars laws like the present ordinance which punish persons who peacefully go from door to door as agents of the press.

Garner v. Board of Public Works of Los Angeles

341 U.S. 716

Decided June 4, 1951

The Los Angeles City Charter barred from public employment persons who advise, advocate, or teach the violent overthrow of the Government or who are members of a group so pledged. Pursuant to this provision an ordinance was enacted to require every employee of the city to take an oath that within a period subsequent to the adoption of the charter provision he had not been a member of or become affiliated with such a group. The ordinance also required the employee to execute an affidavit to the same effect.

Some city employees took the oath, but would not execute the affidavit. Some refused to do either. When they were discharged they sought reinstatement on the ground that their constitutional rights had been violated. Upholding the denial of relief in the state courts, the Supreme Court, in a 5-to-4 decision in Ray H. Garner et al v. Board of Public Works of the City of Los Angeles et al., *ruled that neither the oath nor the affidavit violated the constitutional provisions relating to free speech, free assembly, the right of petition, bills of attainder,* ex post facto *laws, and due process. Justice Clark delivered the majority opinion and was joined by Chief Justice Vinson and Justices Reed, Jackson, and Minton.*

Justices Frankfurter and Burton dissented as to the constitutionality of the oath requirement, but Justices Black and Douglas dissented on the ground that the Los Angeles ordinance was wholly invalid. Justice Black's dissent recorded his awareness that the Court's opinion in United States v. Lovett (page 135), which he delivered five years earlier, was now seriously damaged. It also showed his vigilance against what he believed to be the misreading of a decision relied on by the majority.

MR. JUSTICE BLACK, *dissenting*

I agree with the dissenting opinion of Mr. Justice Douglas but wish to emphasize two objections to the opinion of the Court:

1. Our *per curiam* opinion in *Gerende* v. *Board of Supervisors* in no way stands for the principle for which the Court cites it today. In *Gerende*, we upheld a Maryland law that had been interpreted by the highest court of that state to require only an oath that a candidate "is not a person who is engaged 'in one way or another in the attempt to overthrow the government *by force or violence*,' and that he is not knowingly a member of an organization engaged in such an attempt." The oath and affidavit in the present case are obviously not so limited.

2. The opinion of the Court creates considerable doubt as to the continued vitality of three of our past decisions: *Cummings* v. *Missouri; Ex parte Garland;* and *United States* v. *Lovett.* To this extent it weakens one more of the Constitution's great guarantees of individual liberty. See, for example, *Dennis* v. *United States* and *Breard* v. *Alexandria* decided this day.

Rochin v. California

342 U.S. 165

Decided January 2, 1952

Justice Frankfurter, who wrote the Court's opinion in Antonio
Richard Rochin v. People of the State of California, *summarized
its essential facts as follows. Having "some information that [the
petitioner here] was selling narcotics," three deputy sheriffs of
Los Angeles County, on July 1, 1949, went to the house in which
Rochin lived. Finding the outside door open, they entered and
then forced open the door to Rochin's upstairs room. Rochin,
partly dressed, was sitting on the side of the bed on which his wife
was lying. On a stand beside the bed the deputies saw two capsules.
When asked "Whose stuff is this?" Rochin seized the capsules and
put them in his mouth. A struggle ensued. The officers jumped on
Rochin and tried to extract the capsules, but were unable to re-
cover them. Rochin was then handcuffed and taken to a hospital
where, at the direction of one of the officers, a physician forced an
emetic solution through a tube into Rochin's stomach against his
will. This caused him to vomit and in the vomited matter were
found two capsules which contained morphine.*

*Rochin was convicted on a charge of violating the California
Health and Safety Code and sentenced to sixty days imprisonment.
The chief evidence against him was the two capsules, which were
admitted over his objection and with full knowledge of how they
were obtained. The California Supreme Court, without giving an
opinion, denied Rochin a hearing, but two Justices strongly dissented, saying they found "no valid ground of distinction between*

a verbal confession extracted by physical abuse and a confession wrested from defendant's body by physical abuse."

Justice Frankfurter's opinion was supported by Chief Justice Vinson and Justices Reed, Jackson, Burton, and Clark. Justice Minton did not take part. Justices Black and Douglas concurred separately on the ground that the Fifth Amendment's bar against self-incrimination applies to the States as well as to the Federal Government. The Frankfurter argument can be understood from Justice Black's opinion, which is directed at the Court's willingness to rely on "nebulous standards" when a plain command of the Bill of Rights is at hand.

MR. JUSTICE BLACK, concurring

Adamson v. *California* sets out reasons for my belief that state as well as federal courts and law enforcement officers must obey the Fifth Amendment's command that "No person . . . shall be compelled in any criminal case to be a witness against himself." I think a person is compelled to be a witness against himself not only when he is compelled to testify, but also when as here, incriminating evidence is forcibly taken from him by a contrivance of modern science. California convicted this petitioner by using against him evidence obtained in this manner, and I agree with Mr. Justice Douglas that the case should be reversed on this ground.

In the view of a majority of the Court, however, the Fifth Amendment imposes no restraint of any kind on the States. They nevertheless hold that California's use of this evidence violated the Due Process Clause of the Fourteenth Amendment. Since they hold as I do in this case, I regret my inability to accept their interpretation without protest. But I believe that faithful adherence to the specific guarantees in the Bill of Rights insures a more permanent protection of individual liberty than that which can be afforded by the nebulous standards stated by the majority.

What the majority hold is that the Due Process Clause empowers this Court to nullify any state law if its application "shocks the conscience," offends "a sense of justice," or runs counter to the "decencies of civilized conduct." The majority emphasize that these statements do not refer to their own consciences or to their senses of justice and decency. For we are told that "we may not draw on our merely personal and private notions"; our judgment must be grounded on "considerations deeply rooted in reason, and in the compelling traditions of the legal profession." We are further admonished to measure the validity of state practices, not by our reason, or by the traditions of the legal profession, but by "the community's sense of fair play and decency"; by the "traditions and consciences of our people"; or by "those canons of decency and fairness which express the notions of justice of English-speaking peoples." These canons are made necessary, it is said, because of "interests of society pushing in opposite directions."

If the Due Process Clause does vest this Court with such unlimited power to invalidate laws, I am still in doubt as to why we should consider only the notions of English-speaking peoples to determine what are immutable and fundamental principles of justice. Moreover, one may well ask what avenues of investigation are open to discover "canons" of conduct so universally favored that this Court should write them into the Constitution? All we are told is that the discovery must be made by an "evaluation based on a disinterested inquiry pursued in the spirit of science on a balanced order of facts."

Some constitutional provisions are stated in absolute and unqualified language such, for illustration, as the First Amendment stating that no law shall be passed prohibiting the free exercise of religion or abridging the freedom of speech or press. Other constitutional provisions do require courts to choose between competing policies, such as the Fourth Amendment which, by its terms, necessitates a judicial decision as to what is an "unreasonable" search or seizure. There is, however, no express constitutional language granting judicial power to invalidate *every* state law of *every* kind deemed "unreasonable" or contrary to the Court's notion of civilized decencies; yet the constitutional philosophy used by the majority has, in the past, been used to deny a state the right to fix the price of gasoline, and even the right to prevent bakers from palming off smaller for larger loaves of bread. These cases, and others, show the extent to which the evanescent standards of the majority's philosophy have been used to nullify state legislative programs passed to suppress evil economic practices. What paralyzing role this same philosophy will play in the future economic affairs of this country is impossible to predict. Of even graver concern, however, is the use of the philosophy to nullify the Bill of Rights. I long ago concluded that the accordion-like qualities of this philosophy must inevitably imperil all the individual liberty safeguards specifically enumerated in the Bill of Rights. Reflection and recent decisions of this Court sanctioning abridgment of the freedom of speech and press have strengthened this conclusion.

Adler v. Board of Education

342 U.S. 485

Decided March 3, 1952

Under the impetus of the Cold War with Communism, New York State enacted the so-called Feinberg law. This statute provided that a person who teaches or advocates or is knowingly a member of an organization that teaches or advocates the overthrow of the Government by force or violence shall be disqualified from holding a position in the New York public school system. The law also made it the responsibility of the New York Board of Regents to determine the organizations engaged in such activities, to list them, after notice and hearing, and to issue regulations that membership in a listed organization shall be sufficient cause for disqualification.

Before a test arose under the law, an action was brought for a declaration that it was invalid and for an injunction restraining the Board of Education in New York from enforcing it. The highest court in New York State decided in favor of the Feinberg law's validity. The case went to the Supreme Court as Irving Adler, George Friedlander, Mark Friedlander, et al. *v.* Board of Education of the City of New York.

Justice Minton, in a 6-to-3 majority opinion joined by Chief Justice Vinson and Justices Reed, Jackson, Burton, and Clark, ruled that the law did not trespass on the Bill of Rights guarantees of free speech, free assembly, and due process. Justice Frankfurter dissented on the jurisdictional ground that the adjudication involved a speculation to be avoided in a court charged with weighing questions of constitutionality.

Justices Black and Douglas in their dissenting opinions made it clear that the school systems are not to be cells for Communist activities nor the classrooms forums for propagandizing the Marxist creed. But the dissenters held resolutely to the belief that any judgment of guilt against a teacher should be based on overt acts. Justice Black found in the majority opinion a compelling influence for intellectual conformity.

Mr. Justice Black, *dissenting*

While I fully agree with the dissent of Mr. Justice Douglas, the importance of this holding prompts me to add these thoughts.

This is another of those rapidly multiplying legislative enactments which make it dangerous—this time for school teachers—to think or say anything except what a transient majority happen to approve at the moment. Basically these laws rest on the belief that government should supervise and limit the flow of ideas into the minds of men. The tendency of such governmental policy is to mold people into a common intellectual pattern. Quite a different governmental policy rests on the belief that government should leave the mind and spirit of man absolutely free. Such a governmental policy encourages varied intellectual outlooks in the belief that the best views will prevail. This policy of freedom is in my judgment embodied in the First Amendment and made applicable to the States by the Fourteenth. Because of this policy public officials cannot be constitutionally vested with powers to select the ideas people can think about, censor the public views they can express, or choose the persons or groups people can associate with. Public officials with such powers are not public servants; they are public masters.

I dissent from the Court's judgment sustaining this law which effectively penalizes school teachers for their thoughts and their associates.

Sacher v. United States

343 U.S. 1

Decided March 10, 1952

United States Judge Harold R. Medina, who presided at the District Court trial of the eleven Communist leaders out of which came Dennis v. United States *(page 223), held all the lawyers for the defendants in criminal contempt at the end of the proceedings in his court. Judge Medina's many specifications of misconduct against the defense lawyers amounted to charging them with conspiracy to impede the trial. In effect he charged them, tried them, and found them guilty all in one act. As punishment he sentenced the lawyers, and also a layman who acted as his own attorney, to jail terms up to six months.*

The case went to the Supreme Court as Harry Sacher, Richard Gladstein, George W. Crockett, Jr., et al. v. United States of America. *The question was whether Judge Medina was authorized under Rule 42(a) of the Federal Rules of Criminal Procedure to decide contempt guilt or innocence and to impose punishment, or whether the charges should be adjudged only under Rule 42(b) by another judge after giving the defendants notice, a hearing, and an opportunity to answer for themselves and to present evidence.*

Justice Jackson, speaking also for Chief Justice Vinson and Justices Reed, Burton, and Minton, decided that the trial judge had acted legally in imposing the summary conviction and punishment. The majority also ruled that it was proper for Judge Medina to withhold his contempt decree until the end of the trial. Justice Clark, as former Attorney General, did not participate. Justices

Black, Frankfurter, and Douglas dissented in separate opinions,
with Justice Douglas concurring also in the opinions of Justices
Black and Frankfurter.

MR. JUSTICE BLACK, *dissenting*

I would reverse these convictions because of my belief that
(1) the Judge should not have passed on the contempt charges he
preferred; (2) whatever judge considered the charges, guilt should
not have been summarily decided as it was—without notice, without a hearing, and without an opportunity for petitioners to defend
themselves; (3) petitioners were constitutionally entitled to have
their guilt or innocence of criminal contempt decided by a jury.

After a nine months' trial of leaders of the Communist Party,
a jury brought in a verdict of guilty and was discharged. Immediately, presiding Judge Medina asked all the defendants' lawyers to
stand up, then read them a very minor part of a lengthy "contempt
certificate" in which they were alleged to have committed many
acts of contempt at various times during the protracted trial. Without affording any of them a chance to say a word before he acted,
the presiding Judge held all of them guilty of contempt and sentenced each one to prison.

First. I think it was a grave error for the Judge to pass on the
charges he brought. Reasons why he should not have done so have
been forcefully presented by Mr. Justice Frankfurter here and
by Judge Charles Clark in the Court of Appeals. Their arguments
that Judge Medina should not have made these adjudications are
vividly buttressed by the collection of trial episodes placed in the
appendix to Mr. Justice Frankfurter's opinion. These episodes be-
speak an attitude of distrust of the lawyers and, I regret to add, of
hostility to them, generally deemed inconsistent with that complete
impartiality the process of judging demands. Facts that appear of
special importance to me in considering what were the Judge's
personal feelings toward those he convicted are these:

The presiding Judge was convinced that the lawyers had deliberately and calculatingly badgered and insulted him throughout
the long months of trial. Among these insults, so the Judge believed
and declared, were insolent, sarcastic, impudent, and disrespectful
charges that he angled for newspaper headlines; connived with the
United States Attorney; entertained racial prejudice; judicially
acted with "bias, prejudice, corruption, and partiality." He found

and repeatedly declared that these lawyers were acting in concerted agreement in an attempt to create confusion, provoke incidents and break down his health. As the trial progressed, the record shows that the Judge expressed stronger and stronger fears that the alleged conspiracy to destroy his health was about to succeed. This belief may explain his sharp and somewhat heated repartee in his frequent controversies with counsel. But whatever the provocation, the record shows a constantly growing resentment of the Judge against the lawyers.

The Judge's distrust of and disrespect for the lawyers clearly appear from his frequent charges that their statements were false and unreliable. These repeated accusations, as particularly shown by the following colloquy, impress me as showing such bitter hostility to the lawyers that the accuser should be held disqualified to try them:

> *Mr. Sacher:* I am offended on these constant aspersions on the veracity of representations that I make. I am an officer of this court and I resent these—
>
> *The Court:* There was an instance when you deliberately lied to me when they were passing these press releases. You said that they were not and you were caught red-handed.
>
> *Mr. Sacher:* That is the most offensive charge that can be made against an officer of the court. . . . What has a lawyer got but his honor.
>
> *The Court:* . . . You were caught red-handed.
>
> *Mr. Sacher:* That is the most detestable thing I ever heard from a judge. I resent that and I urge that it be expunged from the record. . . . I will defend my honor as a member of the bar against your honor or anybody else. . . . I think an idiot resorts to lying. I don't have to do it.
>
> *The Court:* You did it.
>
> We better let these little amenities go. I can see from your belligerent manner if you thought you could, you might physically come up to the bench and physically attack me. I know your manner and it doesn't frighten me in the slightest degree.

Liar ordinarily is a fighting word spoken in anger to express bitter personal hostility against another. I can think of no other reason for its use here, particularly since the Judge's charge was baseless. And the Judge's personal feeling toward these lawyers, Sacher in particular, is further indicated by an occurrence immediately *after* they had been sentenced. Sacher asked and was granted the privilege of making a brief statement. This statement was relevant and dignified. Nevertheless, the Judge interrupted him and used this language to a lawyer he had just abruptly and summarily sentenced to prison: "You continue in the same *brazen* manner that you used throughout the whole trial. . . . despite all kinds of warnings throughout the case, you continue with the same old *mealy-mouth* way of putting it which I have been listening to throughout the case." (Emphasis supplied.) Candor compels me to say that in this episode the decorum and dignity of the lawyer who had just been sentenced to prison loses nothing by comparison with others.

Certainly repeatedly calling a lawyer a liar marks a drastic deviation from the desirable judicial standard. A judge who does this should no more be permitted to try the lawyer he accuses than a judge should be permitted to try his own case. No man should be forced to trial before a judge who has previously publicly attacked his personal honor and integrity. The risk to impartial justice is too great.

Second. Before sentence and conviction these petitioners were accorded no chance at all to defend themselves. They were not even afforded an opportunity to challenge the sufficiency or the accuracy of the charges. Their sentences were read to them but the full charges were not. I cannot reconcile this summary blasting of legal careers with a fair system of justice. Such a procedure constitutes an overhanging menace to the security of every courtroom advocate in America. The menace is most ominous for lawyers who are obscure, unpopular, or defenders of unpopular persons or unorthodox causes.

Conviction without trial is not only inherently unfair in the first court, but the unfairness is carried up to the appellate level. This case proves that. A fair review requires scrutiny of 13,000 pages of evidence, most of which is irrelevant. For the contempt certificate states: "As isolated quotations from or references to the transcript can give but a partial view of the acts, statements, and conduct above referred to, I hereby make the entire record part of these proceedings." Such a record obscured the lawyers' trial conduct in a maze of evidence that has nothing to do with their own guilt or innocence. It is not surprising that this Court shrinks from reading such a record; it refuses to do so. No assertion is made that the Court of Appeals waded through it. Consequently, there is every indication that the Court of Appeals appraised the factual accuracy of Judge Medina's charges on a basis deemed by him as "inadequate" because presenting only "a partial view" of the numerous court-lawyer controversies. Such an "inadequate" basis of review is to be expected since no hearing was held which could have framed concrete issues and focused attention on evidence relevant to them.

There are other manifest elements of unfairness in a system which calls on appellate courts to judge the trial conduct of lawyers, accused of contempt, on the basis of all evidence introduced against their clients in a prior criminal case. This unfairness is particularly emphasized here. The root of Judge Medina's charges was that these lawyers followed a concerted course deliberately designed to bring the whole judicial system into public contempt and disgrace. Their clients were Communist leaders. Much of the 13,000 pages of evidence was offered to show that they planned to subvert and destroy all governmental institutions, including courts. Unless we are to depart from high traditions of the bar, evil purposes of their clients could not be imputed to these lawyers whose duty it was to represent them with fidelity and zeal. Yet from the very parts of the record which Judge Medina specified, it is difficult to escape the impression that his inferences against the lawyers were colored, however unconsciously, by his natural abhorrence for the unpatriotic and treasonable designs attributed to their Communist leader clients. It appears to me that if there have ever been, or can ever be, cases in which lawyers are entitled to a full hearing before their liberty is forfeited and their professional hopes are blighted, these are such cases. . . .

Third. Article 3, Section 2 of the Constitution provides that "The Trial of all Crimes . . . shall be by Jury." Not satisfied with this single protection for jury trial, the Founders re-emphasized the guaranty by declaring in the Sixth Amendment that "In all criminal prosecutions, the accused shall enjoy the right to a speedy and public trial, by an impartial jury. . . ." And the Fifth Amendment provides that "No person shall be held to answer for a capital, or otherwise infamous crime, unless on a presentment or indictment of a Grand Jury. . . ." These contempt proceedings are "criminal prosecutions" brought to avenge an alleged public wrong. Petitioners were imprisoned for terms up to six months, but these terms could have been longer. The Government's position in *United States* v. *United Mine Workers of America* was that the amount of punishment for the crime of contempt can be fixed at a judge's discretion, with no limit but the Eighth Amendment's prohibition against cruel and unusual punishment. Certainly, petitioners have been sentenced for crimes. Consequently, these lawyers have been wrongfully deprived of the jury benefits of the foregoing constitutional provisions unless they are inapplicable to the crime of contempt.

There are undoubtedly sayings in some past opinions of this Court broad enough to justify what was done here. Indeed judges, and perhaps lawyers, pretty generally subscribe to the doctrine that judicial institutions would be imperiled if judges were without power summarily to convict and punish for court room offenses. Our recent decisions, however, have expressed more cautious views about the judicial authority to punish for contempt. Returning to the early views of this Court, we have marked the limits of that authority as being "the least possible power adequate to the end proposed." The "end proposed" is "power adequate" in the court to preserve order and decorum and to compel obedience to valid court orders. To achieve these ends—decorum and obedience to orders—courts must have power to act immediately, and upon this need the power of contempt rests. Measured by this test, as Judge Charles Clark's dissenting opinion pointed out, there was no necessity here for Judge Medina's summary action, because the trial was over and the danger of obstructing it was passed. For the same reason there was no longer need, so far as that trial was concerned, to try petitioners for their courtroom conduct without benefit of the Bill of Rights procedural safeguards.

A concurring judge in the Court of Appeals feared that it might bring about "demoralization of the court's authority" should any one other than Judge Medina try the case. The reason given was: "For instance, in all likelihood, at a trial of the lawyers, Sacher would introduce the testimony of himself and others in an effort to prove that he was not 'angrily shouting,' as charged in Specification VII, and did not speak 'in an insolent manner,' as charged in Specification VIII; Gladstein would similarly seek to prove there he did not 'angrily' advance 'toward the bench' or make remarks in a 'truculent manner,' as charged in Specification VIII, and did not speak to the judge 'in a sarcastic and impertinent manner,' as charged in Specification XI; etc., etc." What would be wrong with this? Are defendants accused by judges of being offensive to them to be conclusively presumed guilty on the theory that judges' observations and inferences must be accepted as infallible? There is always a possibility that a judge may be honestly mistaken. Unfortunately history and the existence of our Bill of Rights indicate that judicial errors may be from worse causes.

The historic power of summary contempt grew out of the need for judicial enforcement of order and decorum in the courtroom and to compel obedience to court orders. I believe the idea of judges having unrestricted power to bypass the Bill of Rights in relation to criminal trials and punishments is an illegitimate offspring of this historic coercive contempt power. It has been said that such a "summary process of the Star Chamber slipped into the common law courts," and that the alleged ancient history to support its existence is "fiction." With the specific reservation that I think summary contempt proceedings may be employed solely to enforce obedience and order, and not to impose unconditional criminal punishment, I agree with this statement of Mr. Justice Holmes: "I would go as far as any man in favor of the sharpest and most summary enforcement of order in Court and obedience to decrees, but when there is no need for immediate action contempts are like any other breach of law and should be dealt with as the law deals with other illegal acts."

I believe these petitioners were entitled to a jury trial. I believe a jury is all the more necessary to obtain a fair trial when the alleged offense relates to conduct that has personally affronted a judge. The majority here and the majority below appear to have affirmed these convictions on the assumption that appellate review so fully guarantees a fair trial that it is an adequate substitute for trial by jury. While I agree that the power of lawyer-judges to set aside convictions deemed prejudicial or erroneous is one vital safeguard of liberty, I cannot agree that it affords the full measure of security which the Constitution has provided against unjust convictions. Preference for trial by a jury of laymen over trial by lawyer-judges lies behind the constitutional guarantee of trial by jury. I am among those who still believe in trial by jury as one of the indispensable safeguards of liberty.

Beauharnais v. *Illinois*

343 U.S. 250

Decided April 28, 1952

As president of the White Circle League of America, Inc., Joseph
Beauharnais, on January 6, 1950, passed out bundles of anti-Negro
leaflets to volunteers for distribution on downtown street corners
in Chicago. The printed matter called on "One million self-respecting white people in Chicago to unite" as a means of preventing "the
white race from becoming mongrelized by the Negro." It made
other related appeals. Beauharnais was convicted in the Municipal
Court of Chicago for violating an Illinois law that in effect prohibits "group libel," and was fined $200. He challenged the statute
as an abridgment of freedom of speech and of the press. The Illinois
Supreme Court upheld the conviction and the United States Supreme Court affirmed the result in a 5-to-4 decision in Joseph
Beauharnais v. People of the State of Illinois.

Justice Frankfurter wrote the majority opinion, joined by
Chief Justice Vinson and Justices Burton, Clark, and Minton. The
majority cited the history of violence associated with the race issue
in Illinois from the assassination of Elijah Parish Lovejoy, abolition-
ist editor, in 1837, to the World War I riots in East St. Louis and
the riots in Cicero in 1951. The majority also disassociated itself
from any consideration of the wisdom of the Illinois statute in its
conclusion that the law was within the authority of the Illinois Legislature to enact.

Each of the dissenters—Justices Black, Reed, Douglas, and
Jackson—filed his own views. Justice Jackson agreed with the

majority that a state may bring classes "of any race, color, creed or religion" under libel law protection, but found no "clear and present danger" in this case and moreover found that basic safeguards for the accused had been disregarded. Justice Reed, joined by Justice Douglas, objected to the "ambiguous meaning" of much of the terminology of the law. Justice Douglas underscored his belief that free speech has a preferred position in terms of the rights of citizens generally. Justice Black, joined by Justice Douglas, held that the law and the proceedings under it gravely violated freedom of speech.

MR. JUSTICE BLACK, *with whom* MR. JUSTICE DOUGLAS *concurs, dissenting*

This case is here because Illinois inflicted criminal punishment on Beauharnais for causing the distribution of leaflets in the city of Chicago. The conviction rests on the leaflet's contents, not on the time, manner, or place of distribution. Beauharnais is head of an organization that opposes amalgamation and favors segregation of white and colored people. After discussion, an assembly of his group decided to petition the mayor and council of Chicago to pass laws for segregation. Volunteer members of the group agreed to stand on street corners, solicit signers to petitions addressed to the city authorities, and distribute leaflets giving information about the group, its beliefs, and its plans. In carrying out this program, a solicitor handed out a leaflet which was the basis of this prosecution. Since the Court opinion quotes only parts of the leaflet, I am including all of it as an appendix to this dissent.

I

That Beauharnais and his group were making a genuine effort to petition their elected representatives is not disputed. Even as far back as 1689, the Bill of Rights exacted of William and Mary said: "It is the right of the subjects to petition the King; and all commitments and prosecutions for such petitioning are illegal." And 178 years ago the Declaration of Rights of the Continental Congress proclaimed to the monarch of that day that his American subjects had "a right peaceably to assemble, consider of their grievances, and petition the King; and that all prosecutions, prohibitory proclamations, and commitments for the same, are illegal." After independence was won, Americans stated as the first unequivocal command of their Bill of Rights: "Congress shall make no law . . . abridging the freedom of speech, or of the press; or the right of the people peaceably to assemble, and to petition the Government for a redress of grievances." Without distortion, this First Amendment could not possibly be read so as to hold that Congress has power to punish Beauharnais and others for petitioning Congress as they have here sought to petition the Chicago authorities. And we have held in a number of prior cases that the Fourteenth Amendment makes the specific prohibitions of the First Amendment equally applicable to the States.

In view of these prior holdings, how does the Court justify its holding today that states can punish people for exercising the vital freedoms intended to be safeguarded from suppression by the First Amendment? The prior holdings are not referred to; the Court simply acts on the bland assumption that the First Amendment is wholly irrelevant. It is not even accorded the respect of a passing mention. This follows logically, I suppose, from recent constitutional doctrine which appears to measure state laws solely by this Court's notions of civilized "canons of decency," reasonableness, etc. Under this "reasonableness" test, State laws abridging First Amendment freedoms are sustained if found to have a "rational basis." . . .

Today's case degrades First Amendment freedoms to the "rational basis" level. It is now a certainty that the new "due process" coverall offers far less protection to liberty than would adherence to our former cases compelling states to abide by the unequivocal First Amendment command that its defined freedoms shall not be abridged.

The Court's holding here and the constitutional doctrine behind it leave the rights of assembly, petition, speech, and press almost completely at the mercy of state legislative, executive, and judicial agencies. I say "almost" because state curtailment of these freedoms may still be invalidated if a majority of this Court conclude that a particular infringement is "without reason," or is "a wilful and purposeless restriction unrelated to the peace and well being of the State." But lest this encouragement should give too much hope as to how and when this Court might protect these basic freedoms from state invasion, we are cautioned that state legislatures must be left free to "experiment" and to make "legislative" judgments. We are told that mistakes may be made during the legislative process of curbing public opinion. In such event the

Court fortunately does not leave those mistakenly curbed, or any of us for that matter, unadvised. Consolation can be sought and must be found in the philosophical reflection that state legislative error in stifling speech and press "is the price to be paid for the trial-and-error inherent in legislative efforts to deal with obstinate social issues." My own belief is that no legislature is charged with the duty or vested with the power to decide what public issues Americans can discuss. In a free country that is the individual's choice, not the State's. State experimentation in curbing freedom of expression is startling and frightening doctrine in a country dedicated to self-government by its people. I reject the holding that either State or Nation can punish people for having their say in matters of public concern.

II

The Illinois statute upheld by the Court makes it a crime:

1. for "any person, firm or corporation,"

2. to "manufacture, sell, or offer for sale, advertise or publish, present or exhibit in any public place,"

3. any "lithograph [construed to include any printed matter] moving picture, play, drama or sketch,"

4. which portrays "depravity, criminality, unchastity, or lack of virtue,"

5. of "a class of citizens, of any race, color, creed or religion,"

6. and exposes such a class to "contempt, derision, or obloquy,"

7. *or* "is productive of breach of the peace or riots."

This statute imposes state censorship over the theater, moving pictures, radio, television, leaflets, magazines, books, and newspapers. No doubt the statute is broad enough to make criminal the "publication, sale, presentation or exhibition" of many of the world's great classics, both secular and religious.

The Court condones this expansive state censorship by painstakingly analogizing it to the law of criminal libel. As a result of this refined analysis, the Illinois statute emerges labeled a "group libel law." This label may make the Court's holding more palatable for those who sustain it, but the sugar-coating does not make the censorship less deadly. However tagged, the Illinois law is not that criminal libel which has been "defined, limited, and constitutionally recognized time out of mind." For as "constitutionally recognized,"

that crime has provided for punishment of false, malicious, scurril-
ous charges against individuals, not against huge groups. This
limited scope of the law of criminal libel is of no small importance.
It has confined state punishment of speech and expression to the
narrowest of areas involving nothing more than purely private
feuds. Every expansion of the law of criminal libel so as to punish
discussions of matters of public concern means a corresponding
invasion of the area dedicated to free expression by the First
Amendment.

Prior efforts to expand the scope of criminal libel beyond its
traditional boundaries have not usually met with widespread
popular acclaim. "Seditious libel" was such an expansion and it
did have its day, particularly in the English Court of Star Chamber.
But the First Amendment repudiated seditious libel for this country. And one need only glance through the parliamentary discussion of Fox's Libel Law passed in England in 1792, to sense the
bad odor of criminal libel in that country even when confined
to charges against individuals only.

The Court's reliance on *Chaplinsky* v. *New Hampshire* is also
misplaced. New Hampshire had a State law making it an offense to
direct insulting words at an *individual* on a public street. Chaplinsky
had violated that law by calling a man vile names "face-to-face."
We pointed out in that context that the use of such "fighting
words" was not an essential part of exposition of ideas. Whether
the words used in their context here are "fighting" words in the
same sense is doubtful, but whether so or not they are not addressed
to or about *individuals*. Moreover, the leaflet used here was also
the means adopted by an assembled group to enlist interests in their
efforts to have legislation enacted. And the fighting words were
but a part of arguments on questions of wide public interest and
importance. Freedom of petition, assembly, speech, and press
could be greatly abridged by a practice of meticulously scrutiniz-
ing every editorial, speech, sermon, or other printed matter to
extract two or three naughty words on which to hang charges of
"group libel." The *Chaplinsky Case* makes no such broad inroads
on First Amendment freedoms. Nothing Mr. Justice Murphy
wrote for the Court in that case or in any other case justifies any
such inference.

Unless I misread history, the majority is giving libel a more
expansive scope and more respectable status than it was ever
accorded even in the Star Chamber. For here it is held to be

punishable to give publicity to any picture, moving picture, play, drama or sketch, or any printed matter which a judge may find unduly offensive to any race, color, creed, or religion. In other words, in arguing for or against the enactment of laws that may differently affect huge groups, it is now very dangerous indeed to say something critical of one of the groups. And any "person, firm or corporation" can be tried for this crime. "Person, firm or corporation" certainly includes a book publisher, newspaper, radio or television station, candidate, or even a preacher.

It is easy enough to say that none of this latter group have been proceeded against under the Illinois Act. And they have not —yet. But emotions bubble and tempers flare in racial and religious controversies, the kind here involved. It would not be easy for any court, in good conscience, to narrow this Act so as to exclude from it any of those I have mentioned. Furthermore, persons tried under the Act could not even get a jury trial except as to the bare fact of publication. Here, the court simply charged the jury that Beauharnais was guilty if he had caused distribution of the leaflet. Such trial by judge rather than by jury was outlawed in England in 1792 by Fox's Libel Law.

This Act sets up a system of state censorship which is at war with the kind of free government envisioned by those who forced adoption of our Bill of Rights. The motives behind the State law may have been to do good. But the same can be said about most laws making opinions punishable as crimes. History indicates that urges to do good have led to the burning of books and even to the burning of "witches."

No rationalization on a purely legal level can conceal the fact that state laws like this one present a constant overhanging threat to freedom of speech, press, and religion. Today Beauharnais is punished for publicly expressing strong views in favor of segregation. Ironically enough, Beauharnais, convicted of crime in Chicago, would probably be given a hero's reception in many other localities, if not in some parts of Chicago itself. Moreover, the same kind of State law that makes Beauharnais a criminal for advocating segregation in Illinois can be utilized to send people to jail in other states for advocating equality and non-segregation. What Beauharnais said in his leaflet is mild compared with usual arguments on both sides of racial controversies.

We are told that freedom of petition and discussion are in no danger "while this Court sits." This case raises considerable doubt.

Since those who peacefully petition for changes in the law are not to be protected "while this Court sits," who is? I do not agree that the Constitution leaves freedom of petition, assembly, speech, press, or worship at the mercy of a case-by-case, day-by-day majority of this Court. I had supposed that our people could rely for their freedom on the Constitution's commands, rather than on the grace of this Court on an individual case basis. To say that a legislative body can, with this Court's approval, make it a crime to petition for and publicly discuss proposed legislation seems as farfetched to me as it would be to say that a valid law could be inacted to punish a candidate for President for telling the people his views. I think the First Amendment, with the Fourteenth, "absolutely" forbids such laws without any "ifs" or "buts" or "whereases." Whatever the danger, if any, in such public discussions, it is a danger the Founders deemed outweighed by the danger incident to the stifling of thought and speech. The Court does not act on this view of the Founders. It calculates what it deems to be the danger of public discussion, holds the scales are tipped on the side of state suppression, and upholds state censorship. This method of decision offers little protection to First Amendment liberties "while this Court sits."

If there be minority groups who hail this holding as their victory, they might consider the possible relevancy of this ancient remark:

Another such victory and I am undone.

Zorach v. Clauson

343 U.S. 306

Decided April 28, 1952

Justice Black's majority opinion in the 1947 school transportation case from New Jersey (page 147) was the first in a series of Black opinions relating to Church and State in terms of questions associated with school attendance. The decision in that case, Everson v. Board of Education, *was followed in 1948 by the decision in* Illinois ex rel. McCollum v. Board of Education *(page 182), with Justice Black speaking again for the majority. The* Everson *and* McCollum *Decisions were widely read, studied, debated, and controverted. They were both applauded and criticized.*

One result was to start more or less related cases through the courts. Among these was Tessim Zorach and Esta Gluck v. Andrew G. Clauson, Jr., et al. Constituting the Board of Education of the City of New York. *The* Zorach Case *raised the question of the constitutionality of New York's released-time system for religious instruction outside the public school buildings as distinguished from the released-time arrangement inside the public school buildings, which was found unconstitutional in the* McCollum Case.

In one of their relatively few separations in major Bill of Rights tests, Justice Douglas handed down the Zorach *majority opinion, while Justice Black dissented. The position of the majority, which also included Chief Justice Vinson and Justices Reed, Burton, Clark, and Minton, was that release of public school pupils for religious instruction outside the school buildings was not a violation of the First Amendment.*

Justice Black in his dissent saw no "significant" distinction be-
tween the facts in the New York and Illinois cases. The two other
dissenters were Justices Frankfurter and Jackson. The former ob-
jected particularly to a procedure that did not permit a showing of
the coercive character of the New York program. The latter pro-
duced one of his most acid dissents, for it concluded with these
words: "Today's judgment will be more interesting to students of
psychology and of the judicial processes than to students of con-
stitutional law."

The dissent of Justice Black shows an understanding of the
basis of freedom of religion not always displayed by clergymen
and its other professional beneficiaries.

Mr. Justice Black, *dissenting*

Illinois ex rel. McCollum v. *Board of Education* held invalid
as an "establishment of religion" an Illinois system under which
school children, compelled by law to go to public schools, were
freed from some hours of required school work on condition that
they attend special religious classes held in the school buildings.
Although the classes were taught by sectarian teachers, neither
employed nor paid by the State, the State did use its power to
further the program by releasing some of the children from
regular class work, insisting that those released attend the religious
classes, and requiring that those who remained behind do some
kind of academic work while the others received their religious
training. We said this about the Illinois system:

> Pupils compelled by law to go to school for secular education are
> released in part from their legal duty upon the condition that they
> attend the religious classes. This is beyond all question a utilization
> of the tax-established and tax-supported public school system to
> aid religious groups to spread their faith. And it falls squarely un-
> der the ban of the First Amendment. . . .

I see no significant difference between the invalid Illinois
system and that of New York here sustained. Except for the use of
the school buildings in Illinois, there is no difference between the
systems which I consider even worthy of mention. In the New
York program, as in that of Illinois, the school authorities release
some of the children on the condition that they attend the religious
classes, get reports on whether they attend, and hold the other
children in the school building until the religious hour is over. As

we attempted to make categorically clear, the *McCollum Decision* would have been the same if the religious classes had not been held in the school buildings. We said:

> Here *not only* are the State's tax-supported public school buildings used for the dissemination of religious doctrines. The State *also* affords sectarian groups an invaluable aid in that it helps to provide pupils for their religious classes through the use of the State's compulsory public school machinery. *This* is not separation of Church and State. (Emphasis supplied.)

McCollum thus held that Illinois could not constitutionally manipulate the compelled classroom hours of its compulsory school machinery so as to channel children into sectarian classes. Yet that is exactly what the Court holds New York can do.

I am aware that our *McCollum Decision* on separation of Church and State has been subjected to a most searching examination throughout the country. Probably few opinions from this Court in recent years have attracted more attention or stirred wider debate. Our insistence on "a wall between Church and State which must be kept high and impregnable" has seemed to some a correct exposition of the philosophy and a true interpretation of the language of the First Amendment to which we should strictly adhere. With equal conviction and sincerity, others have thought the *McCollum Decision* fundamentally wrong and have pledged continuous warfare against it. The opinions in the court below and the briefs here reflect these diverse viewpoints. In dissenting today, I mean to do more than give routine approval to our *McCollum Decision*. I mean also to reaffirm my faith in the fundamental philosophy expressed in *McCollum* and in *Everson* v. *Board of Education*. That reaffirmance can be brief because of the exhaustive opinions in those recent cases.

Difficulty of decision in the hypothetical situations mentioned by the Court, but not now before us, should not confuse the issues in this case. Here the sole question is whether New York can use its compulsory education laws to help religious sects get attendants presumably too unenthusiastic to go unless moved to do so by the pressure of this state machinery. That this is the plan, purpose, design, and consequence of the New York program cannot be denied. The State thus makes religious sects beneficiaries of its power to compel children to attend secular schools. Any use of such coercive power by the State to help or hinder some religious sects or to prefer all religious sects over non-believers or vice versa is just what I think the First Amendment forbids. In considering whether a state has entered this forbidden field the question is not whether it has entered too far but whether it has entered at all. New York is manipulating its compulsory education laws to help religious sects get pupils. This is not separation but combination of Church and State.

The Court's validation of the New York system rests in part on its statement that Americans are "a religious people whose institutions presuppose a Supreme Being." This was at least as true when the First Amendment was adopted; and it was just as true when eight Justices of this Court invalidated the released time system in *McCollum* on the premise that a state can no more "aid all religions" than it can aid one. It was precisely because Eighteenth Century Americans were a religious people divided into many fighting sects that we were given the constitutional mandate to keep Church and State completely separate. Colonial history had already shown that, here as elsewhere, zealous sectarians entrusted with governmental power to further their causes would sometimes torture, maim, and kill those they branded "heretics," "atheists," or "agnostics." The First Amendment was therefore to insure that no one powerful sect or combination of sects could use political or governmental power to punish dissenters whom they could not convert to their faith. Now as then, it is only by wholly isolating the State from the religious sphere and compelling it to be completely neutral, that the freedom of each and every denomination and of all non-believers can be maintained. It is this neutrality the Court abandons today when it treats New York's coercive system as a program which *merely* "encourages religious instruction or cooperates with religious authorities." The abandonment is all the more dangerous to liberty because of the Court's legal exaltation of the orthodox and its derogation of unbelievers.

Under our system of religious freedom, people have gone to their religious sanctuaries not because they feared the law but because they loved their God. The choice of all has been as free as the choice of those who answered the call to worship moved only by the music of the old Sunday morning church bells. The spiritual mind of man has thus been free to believe, disbelieve, or doubt, without repression, great or small, by the heavy hand of government. Statutes authorizing such repression have been stricken. Before today, our judicial opinions have refrained from drawing invidious distinctions between those who believe in no religion and those who do believe. The First Amendment has lost much if the religious follower and the atheist are no longer to be judicially regarded as entitled to equal justice under law.

State help to religion injects political and party prejudices into a holy field. It too often substitutes force for prayer, hate for love, and persecution for persuasion. Government should not be allowed, under cover of the soft euphemism of "co-operation," to steal into the sacred area of religious choice.

Separate Opinion of Mr. Justice Black

violation...

Public Utilities Commission
v. Pollak

343 U.S. 451

Decided May 26, 1952

Are the people who ride on public transportation "a captive audience" if they are made the targets of commercial broadcasting? Are the First Amendment's free speech protections violated by such a system of radio programs? These questions came up in the District of Columbia, where the street railway company installed loud speakers on its vehicles to transmit radio programs, consisting chiefly of music, interlarded with advertising.

Six members of the Supreme Court—Justice Burton who wrote the majority opinion and Chief Justice Vinson and Justices Reed, Jackson, Clark, and Minton—found no unconstitutional act on the part of either the transit company or the Commission that allowed the broadcasting. The facts in the case, however, so moved Justice Frankfurter, himself "a victim of the practice in controversy," that he did not trust himself to participate. The case, Public Utilities Commission of the District of Columbia, Capital Transit Company and Washington Transit Radio, Inc. v. Franklin S. Pollak and Guy Martin and a companion proceeding involving the same litigants, brought a strong dissent from Justice Douglas.

Justice Black's statement of his views in his separate opinion is as compact as it is clear.

Separate Opinion of Mr. Justice Black

I concur in the Court's holding that this record shows no violation of the Due Process Clause of the Fifth Amendment. I also agree that Capital Transit's musical programs have not violated the First Amendment. I am of the opinion, however, that subjecting Capital Transit's passengers to the broadcasting of news, public speeches, views, or propaganda of any kind and by any means would violate the First Amendment. To the extent, if any, that the Court holds the contrary, I dissent.

Wieman v. Updegraff

344 U.S. 183

Decided December 15, 1952

A law of Oklahoma required all state employees to take an oath concerning, among other things, membership in or association with certain organizations held to be disloyal or subversive or dangerous to the national security. Knowledge, at the time of membership, of the nature and purpose of a blacklisted organization, was not made a factor to be considered in the interpretation of the required test oath.

A group of staff and faculty members at Oklahoma State College objected to the oath and did not take it in the time allowed by law. The Oklahoma courts sustained the law, but the Supreme Court, in the case of Robert M. Wieman et al. v. Paul W. Updegraff *et al., reversed the Oklahoma Supreme Court and held the oath law was invalid as an infringement of the Fourteenth Amendment. The Court's opinion, written by Justice Clark, found that the requirement of the oath created a conclusive presumption of disloyalty of one who had been a member of or affiliated with a proscribed organization without regard for what the member might or might not have known about the organization at the time of membership. Joining with Justice Clark were Chief Justice Vinson and Justices Reed and Minton.*

In a separate concurring opinion, supported by Justice Douglas, Justice Black took a very strong stand against all test oaths. He condemned them as unconstitutional on the ground that they violate the Constitution's guarantees of freedom of thought, speech, and the press. Justice Frankfurter, with Justice Douglas's support, concurred in the Court's opinion, but underscored the urgency of constitutional protection of rights on which the Oklahoma law trespassed. Justice Burton supported the decision's result, while Justice Jackson did not participate.

His Wieman *opinion is one of Justice Black's most impressive statements in behalf of First Amendment freedoms.*

MR. JUSTICE BLACK, *concurring*

I concur in all the Court says in condemnation of Oklahoma's test oath. I agree that the State Act prescribing that test oath is fatally offensive to the due process guarantee of the United States Constitution.

History indicates that individual liberty is intermittently subjected to extraordinary perils. Even countries dedicated to government by the people are not free from such cyclical dangers. The first years of our Republic marked such a period. Enforcement of the Alien and Sedition Laws by zealous patriots who feared ideas made it highly dangerous for people to think, speak, or write critically about government, its agents, or its policies, either foreign or domestic. Our constitutional liberties survived the ordeal of this regrettable period because there were influential men and powerful organized groups bold enough to champion the undiluted right of individuals to publish and argue for their beliefs however unorthodox or loathsome. Today, however, few individuals and organizations of power and influence argue that unpopular advocacy has this same wholly unqualified immunity from governmental interference. For this and other reasons the present period of fear seems more ominously dangerous to speech and press than was that of the Alien and Sedition Laws. Suppressive laws and practices are the fashion. The Oklahoma oath statute is but one manifestation of a national network of laws aimed at coercing and controlling the minds of men. Test oaths are notorious tools of tyranny. When used to shackle the mind they are, or at least they should be, unspeakably odious to a free people. Test oaths are made still more dangerous when combined with bills of attainder which, like this Oklahoma statute, impose pains and penalties for past lawful associations and utterances.

Governments need and have ample power to punish treasonable acts. But it does not follow that they must have a further power to punish thought and speech as distinguished from acts. Our own free society should never forget that laws which stigmatize and penalize thought and speech of the unorthodox have a way of reaching, ensnaring and silencing many more people than at first intended. We must have freedom of speech for all or we will in the long run have it for none but the cringing and the craven. And I cannot too often repeat my belief that the right to speak on matters of public concern must be wholly free or eventually be wholly lost.

It seems self-evident that all speech criticizing government rulers and challenging current beliefs may be dangerous to the status quo. With full knowledge of this danger the Framers rested our First Amendment on the premise that the slightest suppression of thought, speech, press, or public assembly is still more dangerous. This means that individuals are guaranteed an undiluted and un-equivocal right to express themselves on questions of current public interest. It means that Americans discuss such questions as of right and not on sufferance of legislatures, courts, or any other govern-mental agencies. It means that courts are without power to appraise and penalize utterances upon their notion that these utterances are dangerous. In my view this uncompromising interpretation of the Bill of Rights is the one that must prevail if its freedoms are to be saved. Tyrannical totalitarian governments cannot safely allow their people to speak with complete freedom. I believe with the Framers that our free Government can.

Shaughnessy v. United States ex rel. Mezei

345 U.S. 206

Decided March 16, 1953

The alien exclusion case of Ignatz Mezei is one of the most amazing in the long history of the Supreme Court. Pertinent facts appear to be as follows: Mezei was born in Gibraltar, on board ship in the harbor, of Hungarian-Rumanian parents. He came to the United States in 1923 and lived creditably as a resident alien in Buffalo, New York, from that year until 1948. Learning that his mother was near death in Rumania, he sailed for Europe in May 1948. He was denied entry into Rumania and stayed for some 19 months in Hungary because of "difficulty in securing an exit permit."

Finally, Mezei obtained a quota immigration visa from the American Consul in Budapest and boarded a ship in Le Havre for the United States to return to his wife and home in Buffalo. He arrived in New York, on February 9, 1950, but was temporarily excluded from the United States by an immigration inspector. While his case was being considered he was sent to Ellis Island, where he was held for two years. On May 10, the Attorney General ordered that the exclusion be made permanent without a hearing on the "basis of information of a confidential nature, the disclosure of which would be prejudicial to the public interest."

To get himself off Ellis Island, the hapless Mezei tried to enter both England and France, only to be refused admission. The State

Department attempted unsuccessfully to persuade Hungary to re-admit him. He asked about a dozen Latin-American countries to take him in but all refused. In June 1951, Mezei advised the Immigration Service that he would make no further efforts to leave Ellis Island. There he stayed, excluded from this country and refused admission to any other.

Mezei's plight began to attract attention and, aided by some who felt that a serious injustice was being done him, he applied for a writ of habeas corpus. The United States District Court in New York City sustained the writ partly on the ground that further detention, after 21 months on Ellis Island, could be held justified only on a showing that Mezei's presence in the United States would be dangerous to national security. No such showing was made and the District Court directed that Mezei be conditionally paroled on bond. The Court of Appeals affirmed by divided vote and the case went to the Supreme Court as Edward J. Shaughnessy, District Director of Immigration and Naturalization v. United States of America ex rel. Ignatz Mezei.

By a 5-to-4 division, the Supreme Court reversed the lower courts. Justice Clark, in an opinion joined by Chief Justice Vinson and Justices Reed, Burton, and Minton, concluded that Mezei's continued exclusion did not deprive him of "any statutory or constitutional right." Justice Black wrote a dissenting opinion, in which Justice Douglas joined. Justice Jackson wrote a dissent, in which Justice Frankfurther joined. The patent inhumanity of the case led Justice Jackson to call for "a fair hearing with fair notice of the charges" and to say: "It is inconceivable to me that this measure of simple justice and fair dealing would menace the security of this country. No one can make me believe that we are that far gone."

Justice Black found the proceedings more like arbitrary imprisonments under Communist and Nazi regimes than like a fair trial based on due process of law.

Mr. Justice Black, *with whom* Mr. Justice Douglas *concurs, dissenting*

Mezei came to this country in 1923 and lived as a resident alien in Buffalo, New York, for twenty-five years. He made a trip to Europe in 1948 and was stopped at our shore on his return in 1950. Without charge of or conviction for any crime, he was for two years held a prisoner on Ellis Island by order of the Attorney General. Mezei sought *habeas corpus* in the District Court. He wanted to go to his wife and home in Buffalo. The Attorney

General defended the imprisonment by alleging that it would be dangerous to the Nation's security to let Mezei go home even temporarily on bail. Asked for proof of this, the Attorney General answered the judge that all his information was "of a confidential nature" so much so that telling any of it or even telling the names of any of his secret informers would jeopardize the safety of the Nation. Finding that Mezei's life as a resident alien in Buffalo had been "unexceptional" and that no facts had been proven to justify his continued imprisonment, the District Court granted bail. The Court of Appeals approved. Now this Court orders Mezei to leave his home and go back to his island prison to stay indefinitely, perhaps for life.

Mr. Justice Jackson forcefully points out the danger in the Court's holding that Mezei's liberty is completely at the mercy of the unreviewable discretion of the Attorney General. I join Mr. Justice Jackson in the belief that Mezei's continued imprisonment without a hearing violates due process of law.

No society is free where government makes one person's liberty depend upon the arbitrary will of another. Dictatorships have done this since time immemorial. They do now. Russian laws of 1934 authorized the People's Commissariat to imprison, banish, and exile Russian citizens as well as "foreign subjects who are socially dangerous." Hitler's secret police were given like powers. German courts were forbidden to make any inquiry whatever as to the information on which the police acted. Our Bill of Rights was written to prevent such oppressive practices. Under it this Nation has fostered and protected individual freedom. Its Founders abhorred arbitrary one-man imprisonments. Their belief was—our constitutional principles are—that no person of any faith, rich or poor, high or low, native or foreigner, white or colored, can have his life, liberty or property taken "without due process of law." This means to me that neither the federal police nor federal prosecutors nor any other governmental officials can put or keep people in prison without accountability to courts of justice. It means that individual liberty is too highly prized in this country to allow executive officials to imprison and hold people on the basis of information kept secret from courts. It means that Mezei should not be deprived of his liberty indefinitely except as the result of a fair open court hearing in which evidence is appraised by the court, not by the prosecutor.

Isserman v. Ethics Committee

345 U.S. 927

Denied April 6, 1953

A consequence of the decision in the contempt case of Sacher v.
United States *(page 223) was that one of the defending lawyers
for the eleven Communist leaders, Abraham J. Isserman, was ordered disbarred permanently from practice of law in New Jersey
by the Supreme Court of that state. The disbarred lawyer brought
action in New Jersey, where he lost, and then appealed to the
United States Supreme Court for a writ of* certiorari, *which the
Supreme Court denied in* Abraham J. Isserman v. Ethics Committee of the Essex County Bar Association.

*Usually there is no written opinion when a petition for a writ
of* certiorari *is turned down. In this instance, however, Justice
Black felt strongly enough about the failure to hear the case that
he filed a memorandum for the record saying that he would have
granted the writ and thus made it possible for the lawyer to have
his case reviewed by the Supreme Court. Justice Douglas agreed
with Justice Black. Justice Clark took no part.*

MR. JUSTICE BLACK, *with whom* MR. JUSTICE DOUGLAS *agrees*

I would grant this *certiorari*. It involves an order of the New
Jersey Supreme Court permanently disbarring petitioner from the
practice of law in that State. The Court's order rests on petitioner's
conviction of contempt in a Federal District Court, affirmed by

this Court in *Sacher* v. *United States*. The record of the New Jersey proceedings before us leaves me with the belief that the State failed to afford petitioner the kind of a hearing required by the Due Process Clause of the Fourteenth Amendment. Although petitioner was allowed to appear before a local bar committee and to present a formal answer and make oral argument before the State Supreme Court, the full record persuades me that he was denied an adequate opportunity to confront witnesses against him and to offer evidence in his behalf. Instead of hearing evidence and making its own findings, the state court's order was based on findings made by a federal district judge who had summarily convicted petitioner of contempt without a hearing. I believe that a lawyer is denied due process when he is expelled from his profession without ever having been afforded an opportunity to confront his accusers and present evidence to deny, explain, or extenuate the charges against him.

Stein v. New York

346 U.S. 156

Decided June 15, 1953

If it is deeply satisfying to see the Supreme Court strengthen the application of the guarantees of liberty in the Bill of Rights, it is, on the other hand, the more disheartening to watch our highest tribunal weaken protections and safeguards that have been applied in the past. The three joined cases of Harry A. Stein v. People of the State of New York, Nathan Wissner v. People of the State of New York, *and* Calman Cooper v. People of the State of New York *illustrate the weakening process at work.*

The three defendants were tried in New York on charges of felony murder, found guilty by a jury, and sentenced to death. The evidence included confessions by two defendants which implicated all three. All the defendants objected to the use of the confessions on the ground that they were coerced. The evidence on the issue of coercion was heard by the trial court in the presence of the jury. The New York Court of Appeals affirmed.

The convictions were upheld in a 6-to-3 decision in the Supreme Court, with Justice Jackson giving the majority opinion, joined by Chief Justice Vinson and Justices Reed, Burton, Clark, and Minton. Justices Black, Frankfurter, and Douglas wrote dissenting opinions holding that confessions resulting from coercive police pressure were sufficient in themselves to cause the convictions to be set aside.

Justice Black found in the decision a blow, perhaps fatal, to his early unanimous opinion in Chambers v. Florida *(page 62).*

MR. JUSTICE BLACK, *dissenting*

I concur in MR. JUSTICE DOUGLAS's opinion.

More constitutional safeguards go here—one, the right of a person to be free from arbitrary seizure, secret confinement, and police bludgeoning to make him testify against himself in absence of relative, friend, or counsel; another, the right of an accused to confront and cross-examine witnesses who swear he is guilty of crime. Tyrannies have always subjected life and liberty to such secret inquisitorial and oppressive practices. But in many cases, beginning at least as early as *Chambers* v. *Florida,* this Court set aside state convictions as violative of due process when based on confessions extracted by state police while suspects were held incommunicado. That line of cases is greatly weakened if not repudiated by today's sanction of the arbitrary seizure and secret questioning of the defendants here. State police wishing to seize and hold people incommunicado are now given a green light. Moreover, the Court actually holds (unnecessarily, I think) that states are free to deny defendants an opportunity to confront and cross-examine witnesses who testify against them, even in death cases. This also runs counter to what we have said due process guarantees an accused. Lastly, today's opinion takes this opportunity to narrow the scope this Court has previously given the Fifth Amendment's guarantee that no person "shall be compelled in any criminal case to be a witness against himself." *Bram* v. *United States* held that this constitutional provision forbids federal officers to "browbeat" an accused, or to "push him into a corner, and entrap him into fatal contradictions. . . ." The Court adds the *Bram Case* to those it repudiates today, apparently agreeing with Professor Wigmore that Mr. Justice White's opinion there represents "the height of absurdity. . . ."

In short, the Court's holding and opinion break down barriers that have heretofore stood in the way of secret and arbitrary governmental action directed against persons suspected of crime or political unorthodoxy. My objection to such action by any governmental agent or agency has been set out in many opinions. See for illustration, *Chambers* v. *Florida* and *Ashcraft* v. *Tennessee* (alleged confessions extracted without violence while suspects held incommunicado at the mercy of police officers); *In re Oliver* (secret conviction based on incommunicado questioning by three judges where the accused had neither relative, friend, or counsel present); *Joint Anti-Fascist Refugee Committee* v. *McGrath* (Attorney General's public condemnation of groups as treasonable and subversive based on secret information without notice or hearing); dissenting opinions, *Gallegos* v. *Nebraska* (arbitrary arrest, secret imprisonment and systematic questioning to obtain an alleged confession); *Carlson* v. *Landon* (Attorney General's denial of bail based on secret charges by secret informers without affording accused a hearing); *Ludecke* v. *Watkins* (Attorney General's judicially unreviewable banishment of an alien based on secret undisclosed information and without a hearing); *Shaughnessy* v. *United States ex rel. Mezei* (Attorney General's judicially unreviewable imprisonment and denial of bail to an alien based on secret undisclosed information and without a hearing).

I join MR. JUSTICE FRANKFURTER and MR. JUSTICE DOUGLAS in protesting the Court's action in these cases.

Irvine v. California

347 U.S. 128

Decided February 8, 1954

The case of Patrick E. Irvine *v.* People of the State of California *presented a set of facts so flagrant in disregard of the rights of the privacy of a citizen that two members of the Supreme Court—Chief Justice Warren and Justice Jackson—made the apparently unprecedented proposal that the Clerk of the Supreme Court be directed to forward a copy of the record, together with a copy of the decision, for the attention of the Attorney General. The facts were summarized by Justice Jackson as follows.*

Long Beach police suspected Irvine of illegal bookmaking operations but lacked proof necessary for arrest and prosecution. On December 1, 1951, while Irvine and his wife were absent from their home, an officer arranged to have a locksmith go there and make a door key. Two days later, again in the absence of occupants, officers and a technician made entry into the home by the use of this key and installed a concealed microphone in the hall. A hole was bored in the roof of the house and wires were strung to transmit to a neighboring garage whatever sounds the microphone might pick up.

Since the results of this eavesdropping were not satisfactory to the officers who had hidden in the garage, a week later police again made surreptitious entry and moved the microphone to a concealed place in the bedroom. Then twenty days later the police once more entered the house and shifted the device to a closet where it remained "until its purpose of enabling the officers to overhear incriminating statements was accomplished." At the trial the snatches of conversation which the prosecution thought useful were received in evidence. This was objected to on the ground that such testimony was inadmissible because it was obtained by methods which violated the Fourteenth Amendment.

As to the conduct of the entering police, Justice Jackson, whose opinion upholding the conviction of Irvine was joined by Chief Justice Warren and Justices Reed and Minton, spoke these strong words:

> Each of these repeated entries of petitioner's home without a search warrant or other process was a trespass, and probably a burglary, for which any unofficial person should be, and probably would be, severely punished. Science has perfected amplifying and recording devices to become frightening instruments of surveillance and invasion of privacy, whether by the policeman, the blackmailer, or the busybody. That officers of the law would break and enter a home, secrete such a device, even in a bedroom, and listen to the conversation of the occupants for over a month would be almost incredible if it were not admitted. Few police measures have come to our attention that more flagrantly, deliberately, and persistently violated the fundamental principle declared by the Fourth Amendment as a restriction on the Federal Government that "The right of the people to be secure in their persons, houses, papers, and effects, against unreasonable searches and seizures, shall not be violated . . .

Calling attention to Section 242 of 18 United States Code (Supplement III), Justice Jackson concluded:

> This section provides that whoever, under color of any law, statute, ordinance, regulation or custom, willfully subjects any inhabitant of any state to the deprivation of any rights, privileges or immunities secured or protected by the Constitution of the United States shall be fined or imprisoned. It does not appear that the statute of limitations yet bars prosecutions. We believe the Clerk of this Court should be directed to forward a copy of the record in this case, together with a copy of this opinion, for the attention of the Attorney General of the United States. However, Mr. Justice Reed and Mr. Justice Minton do not join in this paragraph. Judgment affirmed.

In a separate concurring opinion, Justice Clark said: "In the light of the 'incredible' activity of the police here, it is with great reluctance that I follow Wolf. Perhaps strict adherence to the tenor of that decision may produce needed converts for its extinction. Thus I merely concur in the judgment of affirmance."

This sustaining of Patrick Irvine's conviction in circumstances that flagrantly violated the Constitution brought very strong protests from the four dissenters, Justices Black, Frankfurter, Douglas, and Burton. Justice Douglas, who concurred in the Black dissent, also dissented separately in an opinion that included these words: "The search and seizure conducted in this case smack of the police state, not the free America the Bill of Rights envisaged. . . . What transpired here was as revolting as the abuses arising out of the Writs of Assistances against which James Otis complained. . . . We should throw our weight on the side of the citizen and against the lawless police. We should be alert to see that no unconstitutional *evidence is used to convict any person in America."*

Justice Frankfurter, joined by Justice Burton, said: ". . . by reason of the exclusion of evidence derived from the unfair aspects of the . . . prosecution a guilty defendant may escape. But the people can avoid such miscarriages of justice. A sturdy, self-respecting democratic community should not put up with lawless police and prosecutors."

The Irvine Decision came in Chief Justice Warren's first term on the Supreme Court. It marks the only major occasion when he tipped the scales against individual liberty in a close test arising under the Bill of Rights.

MR. JUSTICE BLACK, *with whom* MR. JUSTICE DOUGLAS *concurs, dissenting*

I would reverse this conviction because the petitioner Irvine was found guilty of a crime and sentenced to prison on evidence extorted from him by the Federal Government in violation of the Fifth Amendment.

Federal law makes it a crime punishable by fine, imprisonment, or both, for a person to run a gambling business without making a report to the Government and buying a federal wagering tax stamp, both of which reveal his gambling operations. Petitioner made the necessary report of his gambling activities in California and bought the required tax stamp. The information he gave and the stamp he bought were used in this case to convict and sentence him to prison for violating California's antigambling law. For reasons given in my dissent in *United States* v. *Kahriger*, I believe the federal law that extracted the disclosures and required the tax stamp violates the Fifth Amendment's command that a person shall not be compelled to be a witness against himself. But even though the law is valid, as the Court held, *use* of such forced confessions to convict the confessors still amounts to compelling a person to testify against himself in violation of the Fifth Amendment.

The Fifth Amendment forbids the Federal Government and the agents through which it acts—courts, grand juries, prosecutors, marshals, or other officers—to use physical torture, psychological pressure, threats of fines, imprisonment or prosecution, or other governmental pressure to force a person to testify against himself. And if the Federal Government does extract incriminating testimony, as the Court has held it may in compelling gamblers to confess, the immunity provided by the Amendment should at the very least prevent the use of such testimony in any court, federal or state. The use of such testimony is barred, even though the Fifth Amendment may not of itself prohibit the States or their agents from extorting incriminating testimony. The Amendment does plainly prohibit all federal agencies from using their power to force self-incriminatory statements. Consequently, since the Amendment is the supreme law of the land and is binding on all American judges, the use of federally coerced testimony to convict a person of crime in any court, state or federal, is forbidden.

The Fifth Amendment not only forbids agents of the Federal Government to compel a person to be a witness against himself; it forbids federal courts to convict persons on their own forced testimony, whatever "sovereign"—federal or state—may have compelled it. Otherwise, the constitutional mandate against self-incrimination is an illusory safeguard that collapses whenever a confession is extorted by anyone other than the Federal Government.

Though not essential to disposition of this case, it seems appropriate to add that I think the Fourteenth Amendment makes the Fifth Amendment applicable to states and that state courts like federal courts are therefore barred from convicting a person for crime on testimony which either state or federal officers have compelled him to give against himself. The construction I give to the Fifth and Fourteenth Amendment makes it possible for me to adhere to what we said in *Ashcraft* v. *Tennessee*, that "The Constitution of the United States stands as a bar against the conviction of any individual in an American court by means of a coerced confession."

So far as this case is concerned it is enough for me that Irvine was convicted in a state court on a confession coerced by the Federal Government. I believe this frustrates a basic purpose of the Fifth Amendment—to free Americans from fear that federal power could be used to compel them to confess conduct or beliefs in order to take away their life, liberty, or property. For this reason I would reverse Irvine's conviction.

It has been suggested that the Court should call on the Attorney General to investigate this record in order to start criminal prosecutions against certain California officers. I would strongly object to any such action by this Court. It is inconsistent with my own view of the judicial function in our Government. Prosecution, or anything approaching it, should, I think, be left to government officers whose duty that is.

Barsky v. Board of Regents

347 U.S. 442

Decided April 26, 1954

It is hard to find satisfaction of any kind in the outcome of the case of Dr. Edward A. Barsky v. Board of Regents of the University of the State of New York. Dr. Barsky was one of many Americans who believed that the Spanish Civil War provided a proving ground against Western democracies in pre-World War II days when Hitler and Mussolini were trying out arms and troops on the side of Franco against Loyalist Spain. Dr. Barsky cared enough about the outcome to lead an American hospital unit to the battle zone. After his return to New York, where he practiced medicine, he served as chairman of a committee designed to assist Spanish refugees.

When his organization came under the fire of the House Un-American Activities Committee, Dr. Barsky declined to produce papers and records in an effort to test the authority of the House Committee to compel the delivery of such items. He was found guilty in the District of Columbia, and sentenced to jail, where he served five months. When he had completed his imprisonment, he was again placed under attack, this time by the medical profession's disciplinary committee under a New York law authorizing such action against a physician who has been convicted of a crime. A complicated set of proceedings concluded with his suspension for six months.

Dr. Barsky lost in the New York courts and appealed to the Supreme Court, where he lost still another time—by a 6-to-3 de-

cision. A majority opinion by Justice Burton, joined by Chief Justice Warren and Justices Reed, Jackson, Clark, and Minton, asserted that due process had not been denied. It found the revocation of the physician's license within the authority of the State under the circumstances. Justices Black and Douglas wrote dissenting opinions and each joined the opinion of the other. Justice Frankfurter, who also dissented, based his opposition to the majority opinion on the ground that in this case the use of the Attorney General's list of allegedly subversive organizations violated due process of law.

MR. JUSTICE BLACK, *with whom* MR. JUSTICE DOUGLAS *concurs, dissenting*

Dr. Barsky has been a practicing physician and surgeon since his graduation from the medical college of Columbia University in 1919, except for time spent doing postgraduate work in Europe. Beginning with his internship he has been almost continuously on the staff of Beth Israel Hospital in New York, the city of his birth. During the Spanish Civil War, Dr. Barsky and others became actively concerned with the medical needs of Loyalist soldiers. The doctor went over to Spain to head an American hospital for the Loyalist wounded. Following his return to practice in New York, Dr. Barsky became chairman of the Joint Anti-Fascist Refugee Committee, an organization founded in 1942 to help with problems of Spanish refugees from the Franco government. In 1945 the House Committee on Un-American Activities began an investigation of the Refugee Committee to see if it was spreading political propaganda. Dr. Barsky and other members of the organization's executive board were summoned before the congressional Committee and asked to produce the records of contributions and disbursements of the Refugee Committee. Dr. Barsky and the others refused, explaining that many contributors had relatives in Spain whose lives might be endangered if the contributors' names were given out publicly. Instead, the organization was willing to give the required information to the President's War Relief Control Board. In making his refusal, Dr. Barsky had the advice of attorneys that his action was justified because the congressional Committee's subpoena transcended its constitutional powers. Concededly, this advice was reasonable and in accord with the legal opinion of many lawyers and jurists throughout the country. Moreover, the Refugee Committee was advised that the only way to raise its constitutional claim and test the subpoena's validity was for its executives to risk jail by refusing to produce the requested papers. Dr. Barsky was sentenced to six months in jail as punishment for his disobedience of the order to produce, and the Court of Appeals affirmed his sentence, overruling his constitutional arguments. This Court denied *certiorari* without approving or disapproving the constitutional contentions.

When Dr. Barsky was released from jail and ready to resume his practice, an agent of the Board of Regents of the University of the State of New York served him with a complaint demanding that his license to practice medicine be revoked. This action was not based on any alleged failing of Dr. Barsky in his abilities or conduct as a physician or surgeon. The sole allegation was that he had been convicted of a crime—refusal to produce papers before Congress. New York law authorizes revocation or suspension of a physician's license if he is convicted of a crime. Hearings were held before a Grievance Committee of physicians appointed by the Regents, and there was much testimony to the effect that Dr. Barsky was both a skillful surgeon and a good citizen. No witness testified to any conduct of Dr. Barsky which in any way reflected on his personal or professional character. Nothing was proven against him except that he had refused to produce papers. In reviewing the findings of fact, pursuant to Section 211 of the State's Education Law, the Regents' Discipline Committee reported that Dr. Barsky's refusal to produce the Refugee Committee's papers was shown to be due to a desire to preserve the constitutional rights of his organization, that his offense involved no moral turpitude whatever, and that he had already been punished. The right to test the constitutional power of a Committee is itself a constitutionally protected right in this country. But despite all these things the Regents suspended Dr. Barsky's medical license for six months, giving no reason for their action.

I have no doubt that New York has broad power to regulate the practice of medicine. But the right to practice is, as Mr. Justice Douglas shows, a very precious part of the liberty of an individual physician or surgeon. It may mean more than any property. Such a right is protected from arbitrary infringement by our Constitution, which forbids any state to deprive a person of liberty or property without due process of law. Accordingly, we brought this case here to determine if New York's action against Dr. Barsky violates the requirements of the Federal Constitution.

This record reveals, in my opinion, that New York has contravened the Constitution in at least one, and possibly two respects. First, it has used in place of probative evidence against Dr. Barsky an attainder published by the Attorney General of the United States in violation of the Constitution. Second, it has permitted Dr. Barsky to be tried by an agency vested with intermingled legislative-executive-judicial powers so broad and so devoid of legislative standards or guides that it is in effect not a tribunal operating within the ordinary safeguards of law but an agency with arbitrary power to decide, conceivably on the basis of suspicion, whim or caprice, whether or not physicians shall lose their licenses.

First. At the hearing before a subcommittee of the Medical Grievance Committee, appointed by the Regents, the lawyer for the Regents introduced evidence that the Refugee Committee headed by Dr. Barsky had been listed by the Attorney General of the United States as subversive. Pages and pages of the record are devoted to this listing, to arguments about its meaning, and to other innuendoes of suspected Communistic associations of Dr. Barsky without a single word of legal or credible proof. Excerpts from the record are printed in the Appendix to this opinion. The Grievance Committee made a formal finding of fact that the Refugee Committee had been listed as subversive. This Court, however, has held that the Attorney General's list was unlawful (*Joint Anti-Fascist Refugee Committee* v. *McGrath*). My view was and is that the list was the equivalent of a bill of attainder which the Constitution expressly forbids. The Regents' own reviewing Committee on Discipline recognized the illegality of the list and advised the Regents that no weight should be given to it. This reviewing committee also recommended that the Regents not accept the Grievance Committee's recommendation of a six months' suspension but instead give no suspension at all. The Regents, however, accepted and sustained the determination of the Grievance Committee. Dr. Barsky sought review in the Court of Appeals, but New York's highest court said it was without power to review the use of the Attorney General's list. Our responsibility is, however, broader. We must protect those who come before us from unconstitutional deprivation of their rights, whether the state court is empowered to do so or not. The record shows that the Grievance Committee made a finding of fact that "Ever since 1947, the [Refugee] Committee has been listed as subversive by the Attorney General of the United States." It seems perfectly natural for the Grievance Committee to rely on this list, for the Regents are charged with the duty of making up their own list of "subversive" organizations for the purpose of dismissing teachers, and New York law authorizes the Regents to make use of the Attorney General's list. Dr. Barsky had a constitutional right to be free of any imputations on account of this illegal list. That reason alone should in my judgment require reversal of this case.

Second. Even if the evidence considered by the Regents and the Grievance Committee had been proper, I would still have grave doubts that Dr. Barsky was tried by procedures meeting constitutional requirements. The Regents who tried and suspended him exercise executive, legislative, and judicial powers. The Regents have broad supervisory and disciplinary controls over schools, school boards, and teachers. They also have powers over libraries and library books, and they censor movies. Doctors, dentists, veterinarians, accountants, surveyors, and other occupational groups are also subject to discipline by the Regents and must obey their rules. For example the Department of Education, headed by the Regents, has its own investigators, detectives, and lawyers to get evidence and develop cases against doctors. Persons appointed by the Department prefer charges and testify against an accused before a committee of doctors appointed by the Regents. This committee, after hearing evidence presented by departmental prosecutors, makes findings and recommendations which are reviewed by another Regents' committee with power to make its own findings and recommendations. Then the Regents themselves, apparently bound in no way by the recommendations of either of their committees, make the final decision as to doctors' professional fate.

A doctor is subject to discipline by the Regents whenever he is convicted of a "crime" within or without the State. Whether his "crime" is the most debasing or the most trivial, the Regents have complete discretion to impose any measure of discipline from mere reprimand to full revocation of the doctor's license. No legislative standards fetter the Regents in this respect. And no court in New York can review the exercise of their "discretion," if it is shown that the Regents had authority to impose any discipline at all. Should they see fit or let a doctor repeatedly guilty of selling narcotics to his patients continue to practice, they could do so and at the same time bar for life a doctor guilty of a single minor infraction having no bearing whatever on his moral or professional character. They need give no reasons. Indeed the Regents might discipline a doctor for wholly indefensible reasons, such as his race, religion, or suspected political beliefs, without any effective checks on their decisions.

In this case one can only guess why the Regents overruled their Discipline Committee and suspended Dr. Barsky. Of course, it may be possible that the Regents thought that *every* doctor who refuses to testify before a congressional committee should be suspended from practice. But so far as we know the suspension may rest on the Board's unproven suspicions that Dr. Barsky had associated with Communists. This later ground, if the basis of the Regents' action, would indicate that in New York a doctor's right to practice rests on no more than the will of the Regents. This Court, however, said many years ago that "the nature and theory of our institutions of government . . . do not mean to leave room for the play and action of purely personal and arbitrary power. . . . For, the very idea that one man may be compelled to hold his life, or the means of living, or any material right essential to the enjoyment of life, at the mere will of another, seems intolerable in any country where freedom prevails. . . ."

Galvan v. Press

347 U.S. 522

Decided May 24, 1954

*Should brief and disillusioning membership in the Communist
Party subject an otherwise exemplary alien to deportation, and
hence separation from his wife and children unless they abandon
their country? This question arose in the case of* Robert Norbert
Galvan *v.* U. L. Press, *Officer in Charge, Immigration and Naturalization Service, etc.* Galvan, *a native of Mexico, was ordered deported under Section 22 of the Internal Security (McCarran) Act
of 1950 because of Communist affiliation from 1944 to 1946. His
defense was that he did not know the Communist Party advocated
violent action, and also that the law applied to only those who were
fully conscious of that policy.*

*Seven members of the Supreme Court upheld the application
of the law and came to the conclusion that the deportation proceeding was valid under it. According to their broad interpretation of the statute, it did not require demonstrated knowledge of
the Communist Party's advocacy of violence. Justice Frankfurter
delivered the majority opinion and was joined by Chief Justice
Warren and Justices Reed, Jackson, Burton, Clark, and Minton.
Commenting on the majority opinion, Justice Reed noted a reservation about the weight given, in their construction of a statute, to a
memorandum placed by a sponsor of the law in the* Congressional
Record.

*Justices Black and Douglas filed dissenting opinions and sup-
ported each other in these. In essence they took the view that the*

Constitution's prohibition against bills of attainder and its safe-guards of free speech, due process, and equal protection of the laws were sufficient to prevent the deportation of an alien who joined a political organization that was recognized at the time as legal by both the Federal Government and the State of California, where Galvan lived.

MR. JUSTICE BLACK, *with whom* MR. JUSTICE DOUGLAS *concurs, dissenting*

Petitioner has lived in this country thirty-six years, having come here from Mexico in 1918 when only seven years of age. He has an American wife to whom he has been married for twenty years, four children all born here, and a stepson who served this country as a paratrooper. Since 1940 petitioner has been a laborer at the Van Camp Sea Food Company in San Diego, California. In 1944 petitioner became a member of the Communist Party. Decid-ing that he no longer wanted to belong to that party he got out sometime around 1946 or 1947. As pointed out in the Court's opinion, during the period of his membership the Communist Party functioned "as a distinct and active political organization." Party candidates appeared on California election ballots, and no Federal law then frowned on Communist Party political activities. Now in 1954, however, petitioner is to be deported from this country solely because of his past lawful membership in that party. And this is to be done without proof or finding that petitioner knew that the party had any evil purposes or that he agreed with any such purposes that it might have had. On the contrary, there is strong evidence that he was a good, law-abiding man, a steady worker, and a devoted husband and father loyal to this country and its form of government.

For joining a lawful political group years ago—an act which he had no possible reason to believe would subject him to the slightest penalty—petitioner now loses his job, his friends, his home, and maybe even his children, who must choose between their father and their native country. Perhaps a legislative Act penalizing political activities legal when engaged in is not a bill of attainder. But see *United States* v. *Lovett*. Conceivably an Act prescribing exile for prior innocent conduct does not violate the constitutional prohibition of *ex post facto* laws. It may be possible that this deportation order for engaging in political activities does not violate the First Amendment's clear ban against abridgment of political speech and assembly. Maybe it is not even a denial of due process and equal protection of the laws. But see dissenting opinions in *Carlson* v. *Landon* and *Harisiades* v. *Shaughnessy.* I am unwilling to say, however, that despite these constitutional safeguards this man may be driven from our land because he joined a political party that California and the Nation then recognized as perfectly legal.

Rice v. Sioux City Cemetery

349 U.S. 70

Decided May 9, 1955

Supreme Court cases involving racial discrimination usually arise when Negroes, in certain adverse situations, seek to exercise their constitutional rights as American citizens. But such a test may concern the original peoples of this continent, the North American Indians. The case of Evelyn Rice *v.* Sioux City Memorial Park Cemetery, Inc., et al. *grew out of the attempt of Mrs. Rice to bury her deceased husband in a cemetery where she owned a lot. Funeral services were conducted at the grave site and the burial party disbanded. Then, because the body was that of an American who was also a Winnebago Indian, the cemetery refused to proceed with the interment. It based its refusal on a provision in the contract of sale of the burial lot which stated that "burial privileges accrue only to members of the Caucasian race."*

Mrs. Rice sued for damages to compensate her for mental suffering growing out of her experience. She contended that the racial restriction in the cemetery contract was void under the Constitutions of Iowa and the United States and was also a violation of the United Nations Charter. The case was dismissed in the first court and the Iowa Supreme Court affirmed the dismissal. The United States Supreme Court sustained the Iowa decision by an even division, on November 15, 1954. A petition for rehearing took the case back to the Supreme Court. On May 9, 1955, the rehearing was granted and the writ for certiorari *was dismissed as "improvidently granted."*

The majority opinion was by Justice Frankfurter, who was joined by Justices Reed, Burton, Clark, and Minton. The majority pointed out that after the start of the Rice Case, Iowa enacted a law which prohibited cemeteries from denying burial on account of race or color, but which did not apply to pending cases. This led the majority of five to declare that the writ of certiorari had been "improvidently granted." Justice Black, joined by Chief Justice Warren and Justice Douglas—Justice Harlan did not participate—dissented on the ground that the dismissal was not justified and that the petitioner was entitled to have the still unanswered questions decided.

MR. JUSTICE BLACK, *with whom* THE CHIEF JUSTICE *and* MR. JUSTICE DOUGLAS *join, dissenting*

We think that only very unusual circumstances can justify dismissal of cases on the ground that *certiorari* was improvidently granted. Our objections to such dismissals are stronger when, as here, a case has already been argued and decided by the Court. We do not agree that the circumstances relied on by the Court justify this dismissal. We granted *certiorari* because serious questions were raised concerning a denial of the equal protection of the laws guaranteed by the Fourteenth Amendment. Those questions remain undecided. The Court dismisses the case because the Iowa Legislature has provided that every person in Iowa except one who has already filed a suit can prosecute claims like this. Apparently this law leaves everyone in Iowa free to vindicate this kind of right except the petitioner. This raises a new question of denial of equal protection of the laws equally as grave as those which prompted us to take this case originally. We cannot agree that this dismissal is justified merely because this petitioner is the only one whose rights may have been unconstitutionally denied.

Peters v. Hobby

349 U.S. 331

Decided June 6, 1955

Is it better for the Supreme Court to decide a case narrowly, perhaps on a technical point, or to decide it broadly in terms of the constitutional issues which may be involved? Justice Black's position is that generally it is better not to decide constitutional questions if the case can be disposed of adequately on non-constitutional grounds. But he would not be bound by an inflexible rule for he believes there are occasions when it is better judicial practice to reach the constitutional issue and to decide it notwithstanding the availability of a non-constitutional determination.

Such a case was John P. Peters v. Oveta Culp Hobby et al. *The petitioner was a professor of medicine at Yale. Because of his eminence in his field, he was employed as a special consultant in the United States Public Health Service of the Federal Security Agency, whose functions were transferred in 1953 to the then new Department of Health, Education, and Welfare. His consultant duties consisted of giving advice on proposals to grant federal assistance to medical research institutions. He neither had nor needed access to classified material and nothing that he did in this capacity was confidential.*

Twice in security checks the question of Professor Peters's loyalty came up and twice he was cleared by the loyalty review board of his agency. The Federal Loyalty Review Board then conducted a "post-audit" of the agency review board's findings and came to the conclusion that there was a reasonable question about his loyalty. This conclusion was based on information provided by informants whose identity was not made known to Professor Peters. In some instances the identity of the informants was not made known to the Federal Loyalty Review Board. The information was not given under oath, but it was accepted to the extent that the chairman of the Review Board notified Professor Peters that he was barred from federal service for three years.

Professor Peters sued the Secretary of the Department of Health, Education, and Welfare, Mrs. Hobby, in an effort to obtain a declaration that his removal and debarment from Government employment were not valid. He argued that Executive Order No. 9835, which established the Loyalty Review Board, was violated in the action against him and that the Constitution was violated in that he had no opportunity to meet and cross-examine those who had accused him in secret.

Seven members of the Supreme Court participated in the majority holding: Chief Justice Warren, who gave the majority opinion; Justices Frankfurter, Clark, Minton, and Harlan, who joined it; and Justices Black and Douglas, who concurred separately. The majority opinion did not reach the constitutional issues, raised for determination by Professor Peters, but contented itself with a finding that the Loyalty Review Board exceeded its presidentially conferred powers when it reviewed, on its own initiative, a loyalty case already decided in the employee's favor. Justice Black, in his separate concurrence, doubted the power of the President to issue the order in question, and Justice Douglas, also concurring separately, took the position that the Loyalty Review Board, when it relied on "faceless informers," deprived Professor Peters of his liberty within the meaning of the Fifth Amendment. Justice Reed, joined by Justice Burton, dissented from the holding of the majority that the Loyalty Review Board had exceeded its authority under the presidential order. The dissenters did not take up the constitutional questions.

Mr. Justice Black, concurring

I would prefer to decide this case on the constitutional questions discussed by Mr. Justice Douglas or on some of the other constitutional questions necessarily involved. I agree that it is generally better for this Court not to decide constitutional questions in cases which can be adequately disposed of on non-constitutional grounds. But this generally accepted practice should not be treated as though it were an inflexible rule to be inexorably followed under all circumstances. Here, as in the *Youngstown Case*, I think it would be better judicial practice to reach and decide the constitutional issues, although I agree with the Court that the Presidential Order can justifiably be construed as denying the Loyalty Review Board the power exercised in this case. For this reason I join the opinion of the Court. But I wish it distinctly understood that I have grave doubt as to whether the Presidential Order has been authorized by any Act of Congress. That order and others associated with it embody a broad, far-reaching espionage program over government employees. These orders look more like legislation to me than properly authorized regulations to carry out a clear and explicit command of Congress. I also doubt that the Congress could delegate power to do what the President has attempted to do in the Executive Order under consideration here. And of course the Constitution does not confer lawmaking power on the President.

I have thought it necessary to add these statements to the Court's opinion in order that the President's power to issue the order might not be considered as having been decided *sub silentio*.

Michel v. Louisiana

350 U.S. 91

Decided December 5, 1955

Justice Black's capacity for going straight to the heart of a case and finding there its central issue, while others may be stopping short, marked his dissent in the joined cases of John Michel v. State of Louisiana *and* Clifton Alton Poret and Edgar Labat v. State of Louisiana. *The three Negro men were sentenced to death in Louisiana courts on charges of aggravated rape. They challenged the justice of the procedure on the ground that Negroes had been systematically excluded from the jury panel.*

It was clear that the challenges came after the time limit set for challenges and a majority of six decided that the indictments were valid. Justice Clark wrote the Court's opinion, which was joined by Justices Reed, Frankfurter, Burton, Minton, and Harlan. Chief Justice Warren and Justices Black and Douglas dissented in opinions written by Black and Douglas, which all the dissenters joined. Justice Black did not stop with answering the question whether the time limit for challenging the composition of the grand jury had expired. He went on to ask whether the right to have an impartial jury could be waived any more than the right to be tried by an unbiased judge could be waived.

The trial court's question of the guilt or innocence of the accused did not enter into the Black statement of the issue before the Supreme Court. Under our system, as he put it, "even a bad man is entitled to have his case considered at every stage by a fair tribunal."

MR. JUSTICE BLACK, *with whom* THE CHIEF JUSTICE *and*
MR. JUSTICE DOUGLAS *concur, dissenting*

Petitioners, who are colored, were indicted, convicted, and
sentenced to death in a Louisiana state court. The grand jury
indicting the petitioners was drawn from the parish of Orleans
where 32 percent of the population is colored. Only once within
the memory of people living in that parish had a colored person
been selected as a grand juror. That juror, who happened to look
like a white man, was selected under the mistaken idea that he was
one. The foregoing facts are not disputed here.

Each of the petitioners challenges the validity of the indictment against him on the ground that the failure to have colored
people on the grand jury was the result of systematic and deliberate
exclusion on account of race. In 1875, Congress made it a crime for
state or federal officers to disqualify citizens from grand or petit
jury service on account of race or color. And, since the adoption
of the Fourteenth Amendment, this Court has consistently held that
systematic exclusion of Negroes from grand jury service violates
the Federal Constitution. The Court holds, however, that these
petitioners had a reasonable opportunity to challenge the composition of the grand jury indicting them but failed to do so, thereby
waiving their constitutional and statutory rights to have the
charges against them considered by a fair and legal grand jury.
Without going into the facts of each particular case, I think that the
record shows that there was no such reasonable opportunity
afforded to petitioners Michel and Poret or their counsel. I shall
add a few words, however, about the supposed opportunity of
petitioner Poret to challenge the validity of the indicting grand
jury.

The state courts have found that Poret fled from Louisiana
after allegedly committing the crime for which he was indicted.
But the time allowed Poret by State law to challenge the validity
of his grand jury expired long before he was arrested and brought
back to Louisiana. It is apparent therefore that after his arrest Poret
never had any opportunity at all to challenge the grand jury. It is
true that if Poret had not fled and had been arrested and had the
benefit of counsel early enough he could have challenged the grand
jury's composition. For this reason the Court holds that he forfeited
his federally guaranteed right to have his case considered by an
unpacked grand jury. I cannot agree that the right to the kind of

fair trial guaranteed by the Federal Constitution and congressional enactment can be thus denied by a state. If Poret can be denied this constitutional right, why not others? Could a state statute of limitations like this one declare that anyone under indictment who flees the State has thereby waived his right to counsel or his right to be tried by an unbiased judge?

Poret could have been charged with a federal crime under 62 Stat. 755, 18 U.S.C. Section 1073 for fleeing from one state to another to avoid prosecution. But he could not have been convicted until after adequate notice and a fair trial on an indictment returned by a fair grand jury selected without regard to race or color. And certainly Congress did not by this statute authorize state courts to forfeit the federally protected rights of an accused because he had violated the federal law against fleeing. I suppose Congress would have no power to do such a thing. Under our system even a bad man is entitled to have his case considered at every stage by a fair tribunal.

No sound reasons have been advanced supporting the power of a state to use the device here contrived to justify trial of defendants on indictments returned by grand juries in flagrant violation of the Federal Constitution. The arguments advanced by the Court find no substantial support in any of our prior decisions. On the contrary, this Court has strongly asserted the right of defendants to raise defenses permitted others despite their guilt or innocence of charges that are separate and distinct from those upon which they are tried. The Court's opinion here appears to me to give far too little weight to the constitutional and statutory rights of an accused to be indicted and tried by juries selected without racial discrimination.

I would reverse the convictions of Poret and Michel. Since Labat and Poret were jointly indicted by the same unconstitutionally selected grand jury, I would vacate the conviction of Poret's co-defendant Labat.

Nilva v. United States

352 U.S. 385

Decided February 25, 1957

Justice Black's vigilance and care in his desire to see that each defendant receives fair dealing in the courts have marked many of his opinions, and especially his dissent in Allen I. Nilva v. United States of America. *Nilva, a lawyer, was convicted in Federal Court in North Dakota of criminal contempt on charges of disobeying a subpoena to produce company records bearing on an alleged conspiracy involved in interstate commerce. The Court of Appeals upheld the conviction and so did the United States Supreme Court in a 5-to-4 decision.*

Justice Burton delivered the majority opinion, which Justices Frankfurter, Clark, Harlan, and Whittaker joined. Since two of the three specifications of contempt on which Nilva was convicted were conceded by the Government to be of doubtful validity, the majority remanded the case to the trial court for it to reconsider the sentence of one year and a day. The possibility of a lighter sentence did not touch the issue of justice in the proceedings for Justice Black, nor for the three other dissenters who joined him, Chief Justice Warren and Justices Douglas and Brennan.

The Nilva *dissent may sound technical at first, but the further the reader follows Justice Black's analysis of the facts and the application of the pertinent law, including a rule which the Supreme Court itself promulgated, the more the case becomes a matter of elemental fairness in courts of justice.*

MR. JUSTICE BLACK, *with whom* THE CHIEF JUSTICE, MR. JUSTICE DOUGLAS, *and* MR. JUSTICE BRENNAN *join, dissenting*

This conviction for criminal contempt should be reversed and the case should be remanded to the District Court with directions that it be tried before some district judge other than the one who preferred the charges against the petitioner and then convicted him. There have probably been few cases in the annals of this Court where the proceedings below were afflicted with so many flagrant errors. The Government has confessed most of these errors, but contends that enough can be salvaged from the record to sustain the conviction.

Petitioner, who is a lawyer, was a vice president of the Mayflower Distributing Company. Apparently he served largely as a nominal officer and performed only minor functions for this company. He was indicted with the president of the company and another man on a charge that they had conspired unlawfully to transport gambling devices in interstate commerce. A jury acquitted petitioner but failed to reach a verdict on the charge against the other two defendants. Subsequently a new trial was ordered for these two defendants. Prior to this new trial, the Government procured the issuance of two very broad subpoenas that directed the Mayflower Distributing Company to produce a large number of its corporate records, which the Government anticipated might show illegal transactions in interstate commerce. These subpoenas were served on the company's secretary, but since he was occupied elsewhere he asked the petitioner to produce the material demanded by the subpoenas. On rather short notice petitioner produced a substantial number of records in compliance with these orders.

However, the Government, believing that all of the company's records called for by the subpoenas had not been produced, examined petitioner under oath before the trial judge in an effort to determine the extent of his compliance. Petitioner testified that he had produced as many of the records demanded as he could locate by a diligent search; nevertheless, the trial judge ordered that all of the company's records be impounded. Government agents took charge of these impounded records and examined them. The Government claims that this material included books and documents called for by the subpoenas but not produced by the petitioner.

The trial judge issued an order under Rule 42 (b) of the

Federal Rules of Criminal Procedure for petitioner to show cause why he should not be held in criminal contempt of the court. This charge of contempt was based on three specifications: (1) that petitioner had testified falsely and evasively when asked under oath whether he had produced all the materials called for by the subpoenas; (2) that he had failed to comply with the first subpoena by not producing five items; and (3) that he had disobeyed the second subpoena by failing to produce twenty-two items. Four days after this order was issued, a hearing on the contempt charge was held before the same trial judge who sat in the retrial of the two other defendants and who preferred the charge against the petitioner. The judge found petitioner guilty on all three specifications of contempt and sentenced him to one year and one day imprisonment. The Court of Appeals affirmed the judgment.

The Government confesses that the conviction on the first two specifications of contempt cannot be sustained. As it concedes, there was not only insufficient evidence to support the charges made in these specifications but the trial court admitted and relied on evidence which was clearly incompetent. In addition, petitioner was denied his constitutional right to confront and cross-examine witnesses whose testimony was used against him. And in regard to the first specification alleging false and evasive testimony under oath, petitioner's conduct, at most, only involved perjury, a crime that cannot be punished by use of the contempt power. Nevertheless, the Government would have us uphold the conviction and sentence below on the basis of the finding of guilt on the third specification alone, the alleged failure to comply with the second subpoena.

A fundamental premise of our criminal law is that the prosecution has the burden of proving beyond a reasonable doubt that the accused committed the offense charged. And this Court has repeatedly emphasized that a prosecution for criminal contempt should be treated the same as any other criminal prosecution in this respect. Before petitioner could be found guilty of criminal contempt for failing to comply with a subpoena, the prosecution had the burden of showing beyond a reasonable doubt that he intentionally refused to obey the court's order by not producing the materials demanded even though they were available to him. In this case the record does not contain enough competent evidence for the trier of fact to find that petitioner intentionally refused to comply with the second subpoena or even that the books and documents demanded by that subpoena were available to him.

Only four of the twenty-two documents referred to in the third specification were introduced in evidence and, as the Government recognizes, the conviction must rest on petitioner's intentional refusal to produce these four documents. The only competent evidence in the record which even tends to support an inference that petitioner knew the location of any of these four documents or that they were accessible to him was his comment that he had "previously" examined two of them. But by itself this solitary ambiguous fragment is clearly insufficient to justify finding beyond a reasonable doubt that the records were available to petitioner at the time when he was supposed to comply with the second subpoena. Since the prosecution offered no admissible evidence at the trial, this obscure remark constitutes the sole case on this point against petitioner. It is the only shred of admissible evidence that the majority has been able to glean from the record. On the other hand, petitioner testified that as far as he knew most of the company's records were stored in the basement of its office and that he had made a diligent search through these records in an effort to produce the material demanded by the subpoena. And he was not the custodian of the company's records, but only a nominal officer.

Similarly, there was almost nothing before the trial court which even suggested that petitioner intentionally refused to produce the records demanded. He stated under oath that he was not trained in accounting and was not familiar with the company's accounting records. He repeatedly testified that he had attempted in good faith to comply with the subpoena. The Government contends that a *prima facie* case of intentional refusal can be made out circumstantially from such evidence as is contained in the record. But since the competent evidence does not even support an inference that petitioner knew the location of the four crucial documents or that they were accessible to him, it is hard to see how an intentional refusal to obey can be implied at all, let alone beyond a reasonable doubt.

The trial judge compounded his error in convicting petitioner on such a striking insufficiency of competent evidence by relying on inadmissible hearsay statements which were not subject to cross-examination. The Government introduced in evidence, over objection, a transcript of an FBI agent's testimony at a prior trial in which petitioner was not a party. . . .

The judge's position was manifestly wrong. A trial for criminal contempt is a proceeding wholly separate from any prior trial out of which the alleged contempt arose. A conviction for contempt in a Rule 42 (b) proceeding must stand on the evidence properly introduced in that proceeding. Where a trial judge bases his decision in part on evidence which, although material, is inadmissible, the conviction cannot stand even though an appellate court might conclude after expunging the bad evidence that enough good remained to support the conviction. The defendant is entitled to a decision by the trial judge based on that judge's evaluation of the proper evidence. It is no answer to say that the trial judge could have found the defendant guilty solely on the good evidence. He did not and the defendant is entitled to a retrial. The danger of prejudice from inadmissible hearsay was particularly grave in this case since the admissible evidence before the trial court was so grossly inadequate.

The erroneous admission of portions of the record from the earlier trial accentuated another impropriety in the proceedings below. I believe that it is wrong in a Rule 42 (b) proceeding for the same judge who issued the orders allegedly disobeyed and who preferred the charges of contempt on his own initiative and based on his own knowledge to sit in judgment on the accused. In essence, this allows a man who already believes that another person has disobeyed his command to act as both prosecutor and judge in a proceeding to "decide" formally whether that person disobeyed him and should be punished. It is contrary to elemental principles of justice to place such power in the hands of any man. At the very least, another judge should be called upon to try the contempt charges. Here, besides issuing the orders allegedly disobeyed and then citing petitioner for contempt, the trial judge was intimately involved in earlier proceedings from which the contempt charge developed and in which evidence relevant to that charge was presented. Under such circumstances he would have been superhuman not to have held preconceived views as to petitioner's guilt.

The record discloses several incidents which specifically indicate that petitioner was not accorded a fair trial. At the outset, the judge informed the petitioner that the burden was on him to proceed. This is completely inconsistent with the presumption of innocence which exists in favor of a person charged with criminal contempt. Rather, the prosecutor carries the burden of establishing beyond a reasonable doubt that the alleged contemnor committed the offense charged. The almost total absence of any attempt by the Government to introduce evidence at petitioner's trial in support of the accusations of contempt indicates that it relied on the trial judge's personal knowledge of the case. And as the majority points out several times, the trial judge repeatedly indicated prior to the trial that he believed that petitioner was guilty of false and evasive testimony—the offense charged in the first specification of contempt. There is nothing which suggests that he did not have similar preconceived views on the other two specifications. Surely every defendant is entitled to an impartial trial by one who has not prejudged his case but instead decides only on the evidence introduced at the trial. Application of this simple principle is just as necessary in contempt cases as in others.

Under Rule 42 (b) of the Federal Rules of Criminal Procedure when the alleged contempt involves "disrespect to or criticism of a judge" that judge shall be disqualified. Rule 42 (b) contains no provision with respect to disqualification in other circumstances. The majority relies on this silence to reject petitioner's contention that the trial judge here should have stepped aside. But at most, Rule 42 (b) only permits a negative inference that a judge who prefers contempt charges for violations of his orders and who is intimately involved in related proceedings bearing on these charges can sit in judgment on the alleged contempt. In any event, Rule 42 (b) is a rule promulgated by this Court, and where it is not explicit we should not interpret it in a manner to deny a fair trial before an impartial arbiter. Even if the majority were correct in saying that an "abuse of discretion" must be shown before this Court will compel a judge to disqualify himself, the record in this case clearly shows that it was an "abuse of discretion" for the trial judge not to step aside.

If the preceding errors and improprieties are not flagrant enough, the Court of Appeals contributed additional error by relying on a so-called "supplemental record" to affirm the conviction. This "supplemental record" included material which was not introduced at the trial and which was not even made a part of the record on appeal by the trial judge. The Government now concedes that it was improper for the appellate court to rely on this material. But as its first opinion shows, the Court of Appeals referred to the "supplemental record" to support its conclusion that there was sufficient evidence for the trial judge to find that the papers called for were available to petitioner, that he failed to produce them, and that this failure was in bad faith. And on rehearing, the Court of Appeals added still further error. After conceding that there were grave doubts about the admissibility of the FBI agent's uncrossexamined hearsay statements, it nevertheless stated that the conviction was not reversible because the contempt could have been prosecuted under the summary procedures of Rule 42 (a). But as the Government points out, petitioner could not conceivably have been convicted under that rule.

And there are even more matters tainting the proceedings below. For example, petitioner was rushed to trial with an unduly short period to prepare his defense to the contempt charge. He was informed of the specifications of contempt on a Friday and told to appear the next Tuesday for trial. Since the subpoenas were extremely broad and vague and the specifications involved a large number of documents petitioner faced a formidable task in preparing a defense. He had four days, over a week-end, to secure a lawyer and familiarize him with the case, to examine a great volume of records, to talk with those having relevant knowledge about these records, and to secure witnesses. And when at the trial his lawyer requested a reasonable continuance, the judge gave only a few hours respite.

This Court should not sanction a conviction where the whole proceedings below were riddled with so many basic errors of serious magnitude. Sending the case back for a new sentence, even if it turns out to be a smaller one, seems to me to fall far short of according this petitioner the kind of justice every defendant has a right to expect from our courts. While somehow there is an idea that procedural safeguards required in other criminal trials are not available in trials for criminal contempt, due process certainly requires that one charged with such contempt be given a fair trial before an impartial judge. Here petitioner is to be deprived of his liberty and perhaps his professional career without having received that essential prerequisite to justice.

Konigsberg v. State Bar of California

353 U.S. 252

Decided May 6, 1957

One of the most gratifying of Justice Black's majority opinions in the Bill of Rights field was that in the 5-to-3 decision in Raphael Konigsberg *v.* State Bar of California and Committee of the Bar Examiners of the State of California.

At the height of McCarthyism in 1953, Konigsberg, an overseas veteran of World War II, passed the bar examination in California. Yet he was excluded from membership in the legal profession there on the ground that his refusal to answer questions about his political affiliations kept him from proving that he was of good moral character and that he did not advocate overthrow of the Governments of the United States and California. He said under oath that he did not believe in the overthrow of the Government by force or violence, but he objected to questions concerning party membership or affiliation because he regarded them as offensive to the First and Fourteenth Amendments. Not wanting to weaken those Amendments and their vital guarantees of freedom, he declined to answer certain questions.

The Konigsberg Case *and the somewhat similar case of* Rudolph Schware *v.* Board of Bar Examiners of the State of New Mexico *were argued about the same time in the Supreme Court and both were decided on the same day. Moreover, Justice Black gave the majority opinion in the 8-to-0 Schware Decision as well as that in the Konigsberg Case. In Schware it was held that admitted past membership in the Communist Party did not justify an inference of bad moral character fifteen years later. The Schware holding in turn became a basis for the decision in the Konigsberg Case. Joining with Justice Black in Konigsberg were Chief Justice Warren and Justices Douglas, Burton, and Brennan. Justices Clark and Harlan dissented in an opinion by the latter, and Justice Frankfurter dissented separately. The question of jurisdiction was raised by the dissenters. Justice Whittaker did not take part.*

Nevertheless, this was not the end of the Konigsberg controversy. The conflict continued in California and four years later it was back in the Supreme Court. Justice Black spoke again, but the second time in strong dissent (page 397). Here is his first Konigsberg opinion.

Mr. Justice Black *delivered the opinion of the Court*

The petitioner, Raphael Konigsberg, graduated from the Law School of the University of Southern California in 1953 and four months later satisfactorily passed the California bar examination. Nevertheless, the State Committee of Bar Examiners, after several hearings, refused to certify him to practice law on the ground he had failed to prove (1) that he was of good moral character and (2) that he did not advocate overthrow of the Government of the United States or California by unconstitutional means. As permitted by State law, Konigsberg asked the California Supreme Court to review the Committee's refusal to give him its certification. He contended that he had satisfactorily proved that he met all the requirements for admission to the bar, and that the Committee's action deprived him of rights secured by the Fourteenth Amendment to the United States Constitution. The State Supreme Court, without opinion, and with three of its seven justices dissenting, denied his petition for review. We granted *certiorari* because the constitutional questions presented were substantial. . . .

. . . While this is not a criminal case, its consequences for Konigsberg take it out of the ordinary run of civil cases. The Committee's action prevents him from earning a living by practicing law. This deprivation has grave consequences for a man who has spent years of study and a great deal of money in preparing to be a lawyer.

In view of the grounds relied on in Konigsberg's petition for review, his repeated assertions throughout the hearings of various federal constitutional rights, and the practices of the California Supreme Court, we cannot conclude that that court, with three of its seven justices dissenting, intended to uphold petitioner's exclusion from the practice of law because his lawyer failed to elaborate in his brief the constitutional claims set forth in his petition for review and in the record of the hearings. Our conclusion is that the constitutional issues are before us, and we must consider them.

We now turn to the merits. In passing on Konigsberg's application, the Committee of Bar Examiners conducted a series of hearings. At these hearings Konigsberg was questioned at great length about his political affiliations and beliefs. Practically all of these questions were directed at finding out whether he was or ever had been a member of the Communist Party. Konigsberg declined to respond to this line of questioning, insisting that it was an intrusion into areas protected by the Federal Constitution. He also objected on the ground that California law did not require him to divulge his political associations or opinions in order to qualify for the Bar and that questions about these matters were not relevant. . . .

In Konigsberg's petition for review to the State Supreme Court there is no suggestion that the Committee had excluded him merely for failing to respond to its inquiries. Nor did the Committee in its answer indicate that this was the basis for its action. After responding to Konigsberg's allegations, the Bar Committee set forth a defense of its action which in substance repeated the reasons it had given Konigsberg in the formal notice of denial for rejecting his application. . . .

If it were possible for us to say that the Board had barred Konigsberg solely because of his refusal to respond to its inquiries into his political associations and his opinions about matters of public interest, then we would be compelled to decide far-reaching and complex questions relating to freedom of speech, press, and assembly. There is no justification for our straining to reach these difficult problems when the Board itself has not seen fit, at any time, to base its exclusion of Konigsberg on his failure to answer. If and when a state makes failure to answer a question an independent ground for exclusion from the bar, then this Court, as the cases arise, will have to determine whether the exclusion is constitutionally permissible. We do not mean to intimate any view on that problem here nor do we mean to approve or disapprove Konigsberg's refusal to answer the particular questions asked him.

We now pass to the issue which we believe is presented in this case: Does the evidence in the record support any reasonable doubts about Konigsberg's good character or his loyalty to the Governments of State and Nation? In considering this issue, we must, of course, take into account the Committee's contention that Konigsberg's failure to respond to questions was evidence from which some inference of doubtful character and loyalty can be drawn.

Konigsberg claims that he established his good moral character by overwhelming evidence and carried the burden of proving that he does not advocate overthrow of the Government. He contends here, as he did in the California court, that there is no evidence in the record which rationally supports a finding of doubt about his character or loyalty. If this contention is correct, he has been denied the right to practice law although there was no basis for the finding that he failed to meet the qualifications which the State demands of a person seeking to become a lawyer. If this is true, California's refusal to admit him is a denial of due process and of equal protection of the laws because both arbitrary and discriminatory. After examination of the record, we are compelled to agree with Konigsberg that the evidence does not rationally support the only two grounds upon which the Committee relied in rejecting his application for admission to the California Bar.

A. *Good Moral Character*. The term "good moral character" has long been used as a qualification for membership in the bar and has served a useful purpose in this respect. However the term, by itself, is unusually ambiguous. It can be defined in an almost unlimited number of ways, for any definition will necessarily reflect the attitudes, experiences, and prejudices of the definer. Such a vague qualification, which is easily adapted to fit personal views and predilections, can be a dangerous instrument for arbitrary and discriminatory denial of the right to practice law.

While we do not have the benefit of a definition of "good moral character" by the California Supreme Court in this case, counsel for the State tells us that the definition of that term adopted in California "stresses elements of honesty, fairness and respect for the rights of others and for the laws of the state and nation." The decisions of California courts cited here do not support so broad a definition as claimed by counsel. These cases instead appear to define "good moral character" in terms of an absence of proven conduct or acts which have been historically considered as manifestations of "moral turpitude." . . . It should be emphasized that neither the definition proposed by counsel nor those appearing in the California cases equates unorthodox political beliefs or membership in lawful political parties with bad moral character. . . .

A person called on to prove his character is compelled to turn to the people who know him. Here, forty-two individuals who had known Konigsberg at different times during the past twenty years attested to his excellent character. These testimonials came from persons in every walk of life. Included among them were a Catholic priest, a Jewish rabbi, lawyers, doctors, professors, businessmen, and social workers. The following are typical of the statements made about Konigsberg:

An instructor at the University of Southern California Law School:

> He seems to hold the Constitution in high esteem and is a vigorous supporter of civil rights. . . . He indicated to me an open-mindedness seemingly inconsistent with any calculated disregard of his duty as a loyal and conscientious citizen.

A rabbi:

> I unreservedly recommend Mr. Konigsberg as a person who is morally and ethically qualified to serve as a member of [the bar].

A lawyer:

> I recommend Mr. Konigsberg unreservedly as a person of high moral principle and character. . . . He is a much more profound person than the average bar applicant and exhibits a social consciousness which, in my opinion, is unfortunately too rare among applicants.

A Catholic Monsignor:

> I do not hesitate to recommend him to you. I am satisfied that he will measure up to the high requirements established for members of the legal profession.

Other witnesses testified to Konigsberg's belief in democracy and devotion to democratic ideas, his principled convictions, his honesty and integrity, his conscientiousness and competence in his work, his concern and affection for his wife and children, and his loyalty to the country. These, of course, have traditionally been the kind of qualities that make up good moral character. The significance of the statements made by these witnesses about Konigsberg is enhanced by the fact that they had known him as an adult while he was employed in responsible professional positions. Even more significant, not a single person has testified that Konigsberg's moral character was bad or questionable in any way.

Konigsberg's background, which was also before the Committee, furnished strong proof that his life had always been honest and upright. Born in Austria in 1911, he was brought to this country when eight years old. After graduating from Ohio State University in 1931, he taught American history and literature for a time in a Cleveland high school. In 1934 he was given a scholarship to Ohio State University and there received his Master of Arts degree in Social Administration. He was then employed by the District of Columbia as a supervisor in its Department of Health. In 1936 he went to California where he worked as an executive for several social agencies and at one time served as District Supervisor for the California State Relief Administration. With our entry into the Second World War, he volunteered for the Army and was commissioned a second lieutenant. He was selected for training as an orientation officer in the Army's information and education program and in that capacity served in North Africa, Italy, France, and Germany. He was promoted to captain and while in Germany was made orientation officer for the entire Seventh Army. As an orientation officer one of his principal functions was to explain to soldiers the advantages of democracy as compared with totalitarianism. After his honorable discharge in 1946, he resumed his career in social work. In 1950, at the age of thirty-nine, Konigsberg entered the Law School of the University of Southern California and was graduated in 1953. There is no criticism in the record of his professional work, his military service, or his performance at the law school.

Despite Konigsberg's forceful showing of good moral character and the fact that there is no evidence that he has ever been convicted of any crime or has ever done anything base or depraved, the State nevertheless argues that substantial doubts were raised about his character by: (1) the testimony of an ex-Communist that Konigsberg had attended meetings of a Communist Party unit in 1941; (2) his criticism of certain public officials and their policies; and (3) his refusal to answer certain questions about his political associations and beliefs. When these items are analyzed, we believe that it cannot rationally be said that they support substantial doubts about Konigsberg's moral fitness to practice law.

(1) *Testimony of the Ex-Communist.* The suspicion that Konigsberg was or had been a Communist was based chiefly on the testimony of a single ex-Communist that Konigsberg had attended meetings of a Communist Party unit in 1941. From the witness' testimony it appears that this unit was some kind of discussion group. On cross-examination she conceded that her sole basis for believing that Konigsberg was a member of that party was his attendance at these meetings. Her testimony concerned events that occurred many years before and her identification of Konigsberg was not very convincing. She admitted that she had not known him personally and never had any contact with him except at these meetings in 1941. Konigsberg denied that he had ever seen her or known her. And in response to a Bar Examiner's question as to whether he was a communist, in the philosophical sense, as distinguished from a member of the Communist Party, Konigsberg replied: "If you want a categorical answer to 'Are you a communist?' the answer is no."

Even if it be assumed that Konigsberg was a member of the Communist Party in 1941, the mere fact of membership would not support an inference that he did not have good moral character. There was no evidence that he ever engaged in or abetted any unlawful or immoral activities—or even that he knew of or supported any actions of this nature. It may be, although there is no evidence in the record before us to that effect, that some members of that party were involved in illegal or disloyal activities, but petitioner cannot be swept into this group solely on the basis of his alleged membership in that party. In 1941 the Communist Party was a recognized political party in the State of California. Citizens of that State were free to belong to that party if they wanted to do so. The State had not attempted to attach penalties of any kind to membership in the Communist Party. Its candidates' names were on the ballots California submitted to its voters. Those who accepted the State at its word and joined that party had a right to expect that the State would not penalize them, directly or indirectly, for doing so thereafter.

(2) *Criticism of Certain Public Officials and Their Policies.* In 1950 Konigsberg wrote a series of editorials for a local newspaper. In these editorials he severely criticized, among other things,

this country's participation in the Korean War, the actions and policies of the leaders of the major political parties, the influence of "big business" in American life, racial discrimination, and this Court's decisions in *Dennis* and other cases. When read in the light of the ordinary give-and-take of political controversy, the editorials Konigsberg wrote are not unusually extreme and, fairly interpreted, only say that certain officials were performing their duties in a manner that, in the opinion of the writer, was injurious to the public. We do not believe that an inference of bad moral character can rationally be drawn from these editorials. Because of the very nature of our democracy such expressions of political views must be permitted. Citizens have a right under our constitutional system to criticize government officials and agencies. Courts are not, and should not be, immune to such criticism. Government censorship can no more be reconciled with our national constitutional standard of freedom of speech and press when done in the guise of determining "moral character," than if it should be attempted directly.

(3) *Refusal to Answer Questions.* During the prolonged hearings before the Committee of Bar Examiners, Konigsberg was not asked directly about his honesty, trustworthiness, or other traits which are generally thought of as related to good character. Almost all of the Bar Examiners' questions concerned his political affiliations, editorials, and beliefs. Konigsberg repeatedly declined to answer such questions, explaining that his refusal was based on his understanding that under the First and Fourteenth Amendments to the United States Constitution a State could not inquire into a person's political opinions or associations and that he had a duty not to answer. Essentially, this is the same stand he had taken several years before when called upon to answer similar questions before the Tenney Committee.

The State argues that Konigsberg's refusal to tell the Examiners whether he was a member of the Communist Party or whether he had associated with persons who were members of that party or groups which were allegedly Communist dominated tends to support an inference that he is a member of the Communist Party and therefore a person of bad moral character. We find it unnecessary to decide if Konigsberg's constitutional objections to the Committee's questions were well founded. Prior decisions by this Court indicate that his claim that the questions were improper was not frivolous, and we find nothing in the record which indicates that his position was not taken in good faith. Obviously the State could not draw unfavorable inferences as to his truthfulness, candor or his moral character in general if his refusal to answer was based on a belief that the United States Constitution prohibited the type of inquiries which the Committee was making. On the record before us, it is our judgment that the inferences of bad moral character which the Committee attempted to draw from Konigsberg's refusal to answer questions about his political affiliations and opinions are unwarranted.

B. *Advocating the Overthrow of Government by Force.* The Committee also found that Konigsberg had failed to prove that he did not advocate the overthrow of the Government of the United States or California by force and violence. Konigsberg repeatedly testified under oath before the Committee that he did not believe in nor advocate the overthrow of any government in this country by any unconstitutional means. For example, in response to one question as to whether he advocated overthrowing the Government, he emphatically declared: "I answer specifically I do not, I never did or never will." No witness testified to the contrary. As a matter of fact, many of the witnesses gave testimony which was utterly inconsistent with the premise that he was disloyal. And Konigsberg told the Committee that he was ready at any time to take an oath to uphold the Constitution of the United States and the Constitution of California.

Even if it be assumed that Konigsberg belonged to the Communist Party in 1941, this does not provide a reasonable basis for a belief that he presently advocates overthrowing the Government by force. The ex-Communist, who testified that Konigsberg attended meetings of a Communist unit in 1941, could not remember any statements by him or anyone else at those meetings advocating the violent overthrow of the Government. And certainly there is nothing in the newspaper editorials that Konigsberg wrote that tends to support a finding that he champions violent overthrow. Instead, the editorials expressed hostility to such a doctrine. For example, Konigsberg wrote:

It is vehemently asserted that advocacy of force and violence is a danger to the American government and that its proponents should be punished. With this I agree. Such advocacy is un-

American and does undermine our democratic processes. Those
who preach it must be punished.

Counsel for California offers the following editorial as evidence that Konigsberg advocates overthrow of the government by
force and violence:

> Loyalty to America, in my opinion, has always meant adherence to
> the basic principles of our Constitution and Declaration of In-
> dependence—not loyalty to any man or group of men. Loyalty to
> America means belief in and militant support of her noble ideals
> and the faith of her people. Loyalty to America today, therefore,
> must mean opposition to those who are betraying our country's
> traditions, who are squandering her manpower, her honor and her
> riches.

On its surface this editorial does not appear to be a call for
armed revolution. To the contrary, it manifests a strongly held
conviction for our constitutional system of government. However, the State attempts to draw an inference adverse to Konigsberg from his use of the word "militant" which it points out in one
sense means "warlike." To us it seems far-fetched to say that ex-
hortation to "militant" support of America's "noble ideals" demonstrates a willingness to overthrow our democratic institutions.
We recognize the importance of leaving States free to select
their own bars, but it is equally important that the State not exercise this power in an arbitrary or discriminatory manner nor in
such way as to impinge on the freedom of political expression or
association. A bar composed of lawyers of good character is a
worthy objective, but it is unnecessary to sacrifice vital freedoms
in order to obtain that goal. It is also important both to society and
the bar itself that lawyers be unintimidated—free to think, speak,
and act as members of an Independent Bar. In this case we are compelled to conclude that there is no evidence in the record which
rationally justifies a finding that Konigsberg failed to establish his
good moral character or failed to show that he did not advocate
forceful overthrow of the Government. Without some authentic
reliable evidence of unlawful or immoral actions reflecting adversely upon him, it is difficult to comprehend why the State Bar
Committee rejected a man of Konigsberg's background and character as morally unfit to practice law. As we said before, the mere
fact that Konigsberg's past membership in the Communist Party,
if true, without anything more, is not an adequate basis for conclud-

ing that he is disloyal or a person of bad character. A lifetime of good citizenship is worth very little if it is so frail that it cannot withstand the suspicions which apparently were the basis for the Committee's action.

The judgment of the court below is reversed and the case remanded for further proceedings not inconsistent with this opinion.

Reversed and remanded.

Yates v. United States

354 U.S. 298

Decided June 17, 1957

*The conviction of the top echelon of the Communist Party in the
United States was sustained in 1951 in* Dennis v. United States *with
Justice Black one of only two dissenters. In his* Dennis *opinion
(page 223), Justice Black expressed the hope that in "calmer times"
the Supreme Court would "restore the First Amendment liberties
to the high preferred place where they belong in a free society."
That calmer time came, at least partially, six years later when the
cases of fourteen "second-string" Communists from California
were decided in* Oleta O'Connor Yates, Harry Steinberg, Loretta
Starvus Stack et al. v. United States of America; William Schneiderman v. United States of America; *and* Al Richmond and Philip
Marshall Connelly v. United States of America.*

*The defendants were charged under the 1940 Smith Act with
conspiring to advocate and teach the overthrow of the Government
by force and violence and to organize, in the Communist Party in
the United States, an instrument for those who advocate and teach
violent overthrow. The Supreme Court decision, in an opinion by
Justice Harlan, reversed the convictions and returned the cases to
the United States District Court for Southern California with instructions to enter judgments of acquittal for five of the defendants,
because of insufficient evidence, and to grant a new trial for nine.
As it turned out, the Justice Department did not pursue the prosecution of the nine and the cases were dropped.*

In the Court's opinion, Justice Harlan distinguished between mere teaching and advocacy of the doctrine of forcible overthrow and overt acts to that end. Doing so, he substantially reduced the standing of the Dennis *Decision, and some students of both* Dennis *and* Yates *found elements of reversal in the latter. Justice Clark, the one outright dissenter in* Yates, *spoke of the majority's distinctions as too subtle and difficult for him to grasp. Chief Justice Warren and Justices Black, Frankfurter, Douglas, and Burton supported all or parts of the majority opinion. Justices Black and Douglas dissented in important respects, for they found the defendants were tried for their political views on evidence so flimsy that all should have been acquitted. The Black opinion said that the prosecutions appeared to be more in line with the philosophy of authoritarian rule than with the principle of freedom expressed by the First Amendment. Justices Brennan and Whittaker did not participate.*

Four years later the membership provision of the Smith Act brought that much controverted law before the Supreme Court still another time. Justice Black's dissent in that case, Scales *v.* United States *(page 431), would show him yet more firmly attached to the freedoms guaranteed in the Bill of Rights.*

MR. JUSTICE BLACK, *with whom* MR. JUSTICE DOUGLAS *joins, concurring in part and dissenting in part*

I

I would reverse everyone of these convictions and direct that all the defendants be acquitted. In my judgment the statutory provisions on which these prosecutions are based abridge freedom of speech, press, and assembly in violation of the First Amendment to the United States Constitution.

The kind of trials conducted here are wholly dissimilar to normal criminal trials. Ordinarily these "Smith Act" trials are prolonged affairs lasting for months. In part this is attributable to the routine introduction in evidence of massive collections of books, tracts, pamphlets, newspapers, and manifestoes discussing Communism, Socialism, Capitalism, Feudalism, and governmental institutions in general, which, it is not too much to say, are turgid, diffuse, abstruse, and just plain dull. Of course, no juror can or is expected to plow his way through this jungle of verbiage. The testimony of witnesses is comparatively insignificant. Guilt or innocence may turn on what Marx or Engels or someone else wrote or advocated as much as a hundred or more years ago. Elaborate, refined distinctions are drawn between "Communism," "Marxism," "Leninism," "Trotskyism," and "Stalinism." When the propriety of obnoxious or unorthodox views about government is in reality made the crucial issue, as it must be in cases of this kind, prejudice makes conviction inevitable except in the rarest circumstances.

I I

Since the Court proceeds on the assumption that the statutory provisions involved are valid, however, I feel free to express my views about the issues it considers.

First. I agree with Part I of the Court's opinion that deals with the statutory term, "organize," and holds that the organizing charge in the indictment was barred by the three-year statute of limitations.

Second. I also agree with the Court insofar as it holds that the trial judge erred in instructing that persons could be punished under the Smith Act for teaching and advocating forceful overthrow as an abstract principle. But on the other hand, I cannot agree that the instruction which the Court indicates it might approve is constitutionally permissible. The Court says that persons can be punished for advocating action to overthrow the Government by force and violence, where those to whom the advocacy is addressed are urged "to *do* something, now or in the future, rather than merely to *believe* in something." Under the Court's approach, defendants could still be convicted simply for agreeing to talk as distinguished from agreeing to act. I believe that the First Amendment forbids Congress to punish people for talking about public affairs, whether or not such discussion incites to action, legal or illegal. As the Virginia Assembly said in 1785, in its "Statute for Religious Liberty," written by Thomas Jefferson, "it is time enough for the rightful purposes of civil government, for its officers to interfere when principles break out into overt acts against peace and good order. . . ."

Third. I also agree with the Court that petitioners, Connelly, Kusnitz, Richmond, Spector, and Steinberg, should be ordered acquitted since there is no evidence that they have ever engaged in anything but "wholly lawful activities." But in contrast to the Court, I think the same action should also be taken as to the remaining nine defendants. The Court's opinion summarizes the strongest evidence offered against these defendants. This summary reveals a pitiful inadequacy of proof to show beyond a reasonable doubt that the defendants were guilty of conspiring to incite persons to act to overthrow the Government. The Court says:

> In short, while the record contains evidence of little more than a general program of educational activity by the Communist Party which included advocacy of violence as a theoretical matter, we are not prepared to say, at this stage of the case, that it would be impossible for a jury, resolving all conflicts in favor of the Government and giving the evidence as to these San Francisco and Los Angeles episodes its utmost sweep, to find that advocacy of action was also engaged in when the group involved was thought particularly trustworthy, dedicated, and suited for violent tasks.

It seems unjust to compel these nine defendants, who have just been through one four-month trial, to go through the ordeal of another trial on the basis of such flimsy evidence. As the Court's summary demonstrates, the evidence introduced during the trial against these defendants was insufficient to support their conviction. Under such circumstances, it was the duty of the trial judge to direct a verdict of acquittal. If the jury had been discharged so that the Government could gather additional evidence in an attempt to convict, such a discharge would have been a sound basis for a plea of former jeopardy in a second trial. I cannot agree that "justice" requires this Court to send these cases back to put these defendants in jeopardy again in violation of the spirit if not the letter of the Fifth Amendment's provision against double jeopardy.

Fourth. The section under which this conspiracy indictment was brought, 18 U.S.C. Section 371, requires proof of an overt act done "to effect the object of the conspiracy." Originally, eleven such overt acts were charged here. These eleven have now dwindled to two, and as the Court says:

> Each was a public meeting held under Party auspices at which speeches were made by one or more of the petitioners extolling leaders of the Soviet Union and criticizing various aspects of the foreign policy of the United States. At one of the meetings an appeal for funds was made. Petitioners contend that these meetings do not satisfy the requirement of the statute that there be shown an act done by one of the conspirators "to effect the object of the conspiracy." The Government concedes that nothing unlawful was shown to have been said or done at these meetings, but contends that these occurrences nonetheless suffice as overt acts under the jury's findings.

The Court holds that attendance at these lawful and orderly meetings constitutes an "overt act" sufficient to meet the statutory requirements. I disagree.

The requirement of proof of an overt act in conspiracy cases is no mere formality, particularly in prosecutions like these which in many respects are akin to trials for treason. Article III, Section 3, of the Constitution provides that "No Person shall be convicted of Treason unless on the Testimony of two witnesses to the same overt Act, or on Confession in open Court." One of the objects of this provision was to keep people from being convicted of disloyalty to Government during periods of excitement when passions and prejudices ran high, merely because they expressed "unacceptable" views. The same reasons that make proof of overt acts so important in treason cases apply here. The only overt act which is now charged against these defendants is that they went to a constitutionally protected public assembly where they took part in lawful discussion of public questions, and where neither they nor anyone else advocated or suggested overthrow of the United States Government. Many years ago this Court said that "The very idea of a government, republican in form, implies a right on the part of its citizens to meet peaceably for consultation in respect to public affairs and to petition for a redress of grievances." In my judgment defendants' attendance at these public meetings cannot be viewed as an overt act to effectuate the object of the conspiracy charged.

III

In essence, petitioners were tried upon the charge that they believe in and want to foist upon this country a different and to us a despicable form of authoritarian government in which voices criticizing the existing order are summarily silenced. I fear that the present type of prosecutions are more in line with the philosophy of authoritarian government than with that expressed by our First Amendment.

Doubtlessly, dictators have to stamp out causes and beliefs which they deem subversive to their evil regimes. But governmental suppression of causes and beliefs seems to me to be the very antithesis of what our Constitution stands for. The choice expressed in the First Amendment in favor of free expression was made against a turbulent background by men such as Jefferson, Madison, and Mason—men who believed that loyalty to the provisions of this Amendment was the best way to assure a long life for this new nation and its Government. Unless there is complete freedom for expression of all ideas, whether we like them or not, concerning the way government should be run and who shall run it, I doubt if any views in the long run can be secured against the censor. The First Amendment provides the only kind of security system that can preserve a free government—one that leaves the way wide open for people to favor, discuss, advocate, or incite causes and doctrines however obnoxious and antagonistic such views may be to the rest of us.

Trop v. *Dulles*

356 U.S. 86

―――

Decided March 31, 1958

How far can military authorities legally go in depriving soldiers of civic rights following a court-martial conviction? This was the question in Albert L. Trop *v.* John Foster Dulles, *as Secretary of State of the United States. Dividing 5 to 4, the Supreme Court answered by holding that Section 401 (g) of the Nationality Act of 1940 was invalid and could not be used as the statutory basis for taking away the citizenship of a soldier who had been found guilty of desertion in wartime.*

Chief Justice Warren, supported by Justices Black, Douglas, and Whittaker, took the position that citizenship could not be so divested under the Constitution. Justice Brennan, concurring, found no relevant connection between expatriation on the ground of wartime desertion and the war power, or indeed any other power, of Congress. Justice Frankfurter, in a dissenting opinion joined by Justices Burton, Clark, and Harlan, contended that the law was within the constitutional authority of Congress to enact.

Justices Black and Douglas, in a separate concurrence by the former, said with utmost candor that "nothing in the Constitution or its history" supported any such claim for military control.

MR. JUSTICE BLACK, *whom* MR. JUSTICE DOUGLAS *joins, concurring*

While I concur in the opinion of THE CHIEF JUSTICE, there is one additional thing that needs to be said.

Even if citizenship could be involuntarily divested, I do not believe that the power to denationalize may be placed in the hands of military authorities. If desertion or other misconduct is to be a basis for forfeiting citizenship, guilt should be determined in a civilian court of justice where all the protections of the Bill of Rights guard the fairness of the outcome. Such forfeiture should not rest on the findings of a military tribunal. Military courts may try soldiers and punish them for military offenses, but they should not have the last word on the soldier's right to citizenship. The statute held invalid here not only makes the military's finding of desertion final but gives military authorities discretion to choose which soldiers convicted of desertion shall be allowed to keep their citizenship and which ones shall thereafter be stateless. Nothing in the Constitution or its history lends the slightest support for such military control over the right to be an American citizen.

Speiser v. Randall

357 U.S. 513

Decided June 30, 1958

With eloquent and moving words, Justice Black set forth his basic patriotic creed in his concurrence in Lawrence Speiser v. Justin A. Randall, as Assessor of Contra Costa County, State of California. *It at once became one of his outstanding opinions, well worth publication in full in every newspaper across the country and equally worth reading aloud to every religious and secular organization, association, or group. The* Speiser Case *was joined with* Daniel Prince v. City and County of San Francisco, *and these two were companion cases with* First Unitarian Church of Los Angeles v. County of Los Angeles, City of Los Angeles, H. L. Byram, County of Los Angeles Tax Collector *and also with* Valley Unitarian-Universalist Church v. County of Los Angeles, City of Los Angeles, H. L. Byram, County Tax Collector, *decided the same day and by the same division of the Justices. The Black concurrence was joined by Justice Douglas.*

The Constitution of California orders that tax exemption be denied to all who favor unlawful overthrow of the Government of a State or the Nation. To make this effective, the California Legislature passed a legal requirement that all who claim tax-exemption must sign a statement on their tax returns disavowing the prohibited advocacy. In the Speiser Case, *a veteran, who refused to file the oath, was denied the exemption as a veteran from the property tax. The Superior Court of Contra Costa County held that both the state constitutional provision and the statute under it were uncon-*

*stitutional restrictions on freedom of speech. That judgment was
reversed by the California Supreme Court.*

*In the United States Supreme Court, Justice Brennan handed
down a decision that held that the statutory provision denied the
veterans free speech without affording them due process under the
Fourteenth Amendment. The Brennan opinion did not pass on the
validity of the pertinent section of the California Constitution. In
some part, the majority opinion reflected the views of six members
of the Court. In addition to Justice Brennan, they were Justices
Black, Frankfurter, Douglas, Harlan, and Whittaker. Justices
Black and Douglas wrote concurring opinions, with each joining
the opinion of the other. Justice Burton concurred in the result,
Justice Clark dissented, and Chief Justice Warren did not participate.*

MR. JUSTICE BLACK, *whom* MR. JUSTICE DOUGLAS *joins, concurring*

California, in effect, has imposed a tax on belief and expression. In my view, a levy of this nature is wholly out of place in this
country; so far as I know such a thing has never even been attempted before. I believe that it constitutes a palpable violation of
the First Amendment, which of course is applicable in all its particulars to the States. The mere fact that California attemps to exact
this ill-concealed penalty from individuals and churches and that
its validity has to be considered in this Court only emphasizes how
dangerously far we have departed from the fundamental principles
of freedom declared in the First Amendment. We should never
forget that the freedoms secured by that Amendment—speech,
press, religion, petition, and assembly—are absolutely indispensable
for the preservation of a free society in which government is based
upon the consent of an informed citizenry and is dedicated to the
protection of the rights of all, even the most despised minorities.

This case offers just another example of a wide-scale effort by
government in this country to impose penalties and disabilities on
everyone who is or is suspected of being a "Communist" or who is
not ready at all times and all places to swear his loyalty to State and
Nation. Government employees, lawyers, doctors, teachers,
pharmacists, veterinarians, subway conductors, industrial workers, and a multitude of others have been denied an opportunity to
work at their trade or profession for these reasons. Here a tax is
levied unless the taxpayer makes an oath that he does not and will

not in the future advocate certain things; in Ohio those without jobs have been denied unemployment insurance unless they are willing to swear that they do not hold specific views; and Congress has even attempted to deny public housing to needy families unless they first demonstrate their loyalty. These are merely random samples; I will not take time here to refer to innumerable others, such as oaths for hunters and fishermen, wrestlers and boxers, and junk dealers.

I am convinced that this whole business of penalizing people because of their views and expressions concerning government is hopelessly repugnant to the principles of freedom upon which this Nation was founded and which have helped to make it the greatest in the world. As stated in prior cases, I believe "that the First Amendment grants an absolute right to believe in any governmental system, [to] discuss all governmental affairs, and [to] argue for desired changes in the existing order. This freedom is too dangerous for bad, tyrannical governments to permit. But those who wrote and adopted our First Amendment weighed those dangers against the dangers of censorship and deliberately chose the First Amendment's unequivocal command that freedom of assembly, petition, speech and press shall not be abridged. I happen to believe this was a wise choice and that our free way of life enlists such respect and love that our Nation cannot be imperiled by mere talk."

Loyalty oaths, as well as other contemporary "security measures," tend to stifle all forms of unorthodox or unpopular thinking or expression—the kind of thought and expression which has played such a vital and beneficial role in the history of this Nation. The result is a stultifying conformity which in the end may well turn out to be more destructive to our free society than foreign agents could ever hope to be. The course which we have been following the last decade is not the course of a strong, free, secure people, but that of the frightened, the insecure, the intolerant. I am certain that loyalty to the United States can never be secured by the endless proliferation of "loyalty" oaths; loyalty must arise spontaneously from the hearts of people who love their country and respect their government. I also adhere to the proposition that the "First Amendment provides the only kind of security system that can preserve a free government—one that leaves the way wide open for people to favor, discuss, advocate, or incite causes and doctrines however obnoxious and antagonistic such views may be to the rest of us."

If it be assumed however, as Mr. Justice Brennan does for purposes of this case, that California may tax the expression of certain views, I am in full agreement with him that the procedures it has provided to determine whether petitioners are engaged in "taxable" advocacy violate the requirements of due process.

Bartkus v. Illinois

359 U.S. 121

Decided March 30, 1959

The Fifth Amendment says: ". . . nor shall any person be subject for the same offense to be twice put in jeopardy of life or limb . . ." The command is all-out, absolute, unequivocal, without qualification or reservation of any kind. Justice Black thinks that it means what it says, and so, apparently, do Americans generally. And yet in the case of Alfonse Bartkus v. People of the State of Illinois, the Supreme Court decided, 5 to 4, that an alleged robber, after being acquitted in a federal court, could be tried in a state court, found guilty, and sentenced to life imprisonment. Bartkus's defense was that he was in a barber shop getting a hair cut several miles from the scene of the robbery; this was corroborated by the owner of the barber shop, his son, and other witnesses.

 The record in the Supreme Court makes clear that the issue, whether the Fifth Amendment barred the second prosecution on the same offense, was a difficult one for the highest tribunal to decide. The case was first argued in the Supreme Court on November 19, 1957. Eight Justices participated with the result that they divided equally, 4 to 4, and the affirmance of the Illinois State Supreme Court was allowed to stand. Since this was an unsatisfactory way to leave the question, the case was restored to the docket for reargument, on May 26, 1958. It was then reargued on October 21 and 22 of that year, and decided more than five months later.

 Justice Frankfurter, speaking also for Justices Clark, Harlan, Whittaker, and Stewart, held that the Fifth Amendment did not *apply to the States and that the second trial, in the Illinois state court, did not constitute double jeopardy under the Constitution. The majority also took the position that Bartkus was not denied due process of law. To his opinion, Justice Frankfurter attached a nine-page appendix citing state constitutional provisions. Justice Black wrote a dissenting opinion, which Chief Justice Warren and Justice Douglas joined, and Justice Brennan also wrote a dissent, which the Chief Justice and Justice Douglas joined.*

The Black opinion sought to answer the majority's arguments, and, with the Justice's reading of the constitutional provisions and the decisions and laws in question, this dissent became one of his most impressive. For its length it was one of Justice Black's most heavily documented, with many citations in the text and additional documentary material in some 34 footnotes. The first footnote began with the sentence: "While I participated in the Court's holding and opinion in Palko *I have since expressed my disagreement with both, as has Mr. Justice Douglas." The last footnote reprinted the news item to which Justice Black referred in the last paragraph of his dissent. It was a dispatch from Moscow printed in* The New York Times, *October 22, 1958, and it reported the second trial given a 19-year-old Russian whose punishment for the first conviction was protested as being too lenient. The youth was then tried again and sentenced to death.*

Justice Brennan, in his dissent, found so many federal officers taking part in the State trial that it became in actuality a second federal prosecution. This removed any doubt for Justice Brennan and those who joined him whether double jeopardy was involved. Justice Frankfurter's majority opinion was criticized widely over the country and corrective action in Illinois came quickly. Prohibitory legislation, with bi-partisan sponsorship, passed the Illinois Legislature in short order. The bill was signed, within four months of the decision, by Governor William G. Stratton, who also commuted Bartkus's life sentence to the seven years already served. Meantime the United States Attorney General announced that the Department of Justice would no longer participate in State trials of defendants who had been freed in federal courts.

MR. JUSTICE BLACK, *with whom* THE CHIEF JUSTICE *and* MR. JUSTICE DOUGLAS *concur, dissenting*

Petitioner, Bartkus, was indicted in a United States District Court for bank robbery. He was tried by a jury and acquitted. So far as appears the trial was conducted fairly by an able and conscientious judge. Later, Bartkus was indicted in an Illinois state court for the same bank robbery. This time he was convicted and sentenced to life imprisonment. His acquittal in the federal court would have barred a second trial in any court of the United States because of the provision in the Fifth Amendment that no person "shall be subject for the same offense to be twice put in jeopardy of life or limb." The Court today rejects Bartkus's contention that his state conviction after a federal acquittal violates the Fourteenth Amendment to our Constitution. I cannot agree.

The Court's holding further limits our already weakened constitutional guarantees against double prosecutions. *United States v. Lanza*, decided in 1922, allowed federal conviction and punishment of a man who had been previously convicted and punished for the identical acts by one of our states. Today, for the first time in its history, this Court upholds the state conviction of a defendant who has been *acquitted* of the same offense in the federal courts. I would hold that a federal trial following either state acquittal or conviction is barred by the Double Jeopardy Clause of the Fifth Amendment. And, quite apart from whether that clause is as fully binding on the States as it is on the Federal Government, I would hold that Bartkus's conviction cannot stand. For I think double prosecutions for the same offense are so contrary to the spirit of our free country that they violate even the prevailing view of the Fourteenth Amendment, expressed in *Palko* v. *Connecticut*.

The Fourteenth Amendment, this Court said in *Palko*, does not make all of the specific guarantees of the Bill of Rights applicable to the States. But, the Court noted, some of "the privileges and immunities" of the Bill of Rights, "have been taken over . . . and brought within the Fourteenth Amendment by a process of absorption." The Court indicated that incorporated in due process were those "principle[s] of justice so rooted in the traditions and conscience of our people as to be ranked as fundamental." It then held that a statute allowing a state to appeal in a criminal case did not violate such fundamental principles. But it expressly left open the question of whether "the state [could be] permitted after a trial free from error to try the accused over again." That question is substantially before us today.

Fear and abhorrence of governmental power to try people twice for the same conduct is one of the oldest ideas found in Western civilization. Its roots run deep into Greek and Roman times. Even in the Dark Ages, when so many other principles of justice were lost, the idea that one trial and one punishment were enough remained alive through the canon law and the teachings of the early Christian writers. By the thirteenth century it seems to have been firmly established in England, where it came to be considered as a "universal maxim of the common law." It is not surprising, therefore, that the principle was brought to this country by the earliest settlers as part of their heritage of freedom, and that it has been recognized here as fundamental again and again. Today it is found, in varying forms, not only in the Federal Constitution, but in the jurisprudence or constitutions of every state, as well as most foreign nations. It has, in fact, been described as a part of all advanced systems of law and as one of those universal principles "of reason, justice, and conscience, of which Cicero said: 'Nor is it one thing at Rome and another at Athens, one now and another in the future, but among all nations it is the same.'" While some writers have explained the opposition to double prosecutions by emphasizing the injustice inherent in two punishments for the same act, and others have stressed the dangers to the innocent from allowing the full power of the State to be brought against them in two trials, the basic and recurring theme has always simply been that it is wrong for a man to "be brought into Danger for the same Offence more than once." Few principles have been more deeply "rooted in the traditions and conscience of our people."

The Court apparently takes the position that a second trial for the same act is somehow less offensive if one of the trials is conducted by the Federal Government and the other by a state. Looked at from the standpoint of the individual who is being prosecuted, this notion is too subtle for me to grasp. If double punishment is what is feared, it hurts no less for two "Sovereigns" to inflict it than for one. If danger to the innocent is emphasized, that danger is surely no less when the power of State and Federal Governments is brought to bear on one man in two trials, than when one of these "Sovereigns" proceeds alone. In each case, inescapably, a man is forced to face danger twice for the same conduct.

The Court, without denying the almost universal abhorrence of such double prosecutions, nevertheless justifies the practice here in the name of "federalism." This, it seems to me, is a misuse and desecration of the concept. Our Federal Union was conceived and created "to establish Justice" and to "secure the Blessings of Liberty," not to destroy any of the bulwarks on which both freedom and justice depend. We should, therefore, be suspicious of any supposed "requirements" of "federalism" which result in obliterating ancient safeguards. I have been shown nothing in the history of our Union, in the writings of its Founders, or elsewhere, to indicate that individual rights deemed essential by both State and Nation were to be lost through the combined operations of the two governments. Nor has the Court given any sound reason for thinking that the successful operation of our dual system of government depends in the slightest on the power to try people twice for the same act.

Implicit in the Court's reliance on "federalism" is the premise that failure to allow double prosecutions would seriously impair law enforcement in both State and Nation. For one jurisdiction might provide minor penalties for acts severely punished by the other and, by accepting pleas of guilty, shield wrongdoers from justice. I believe this argument fails on several grounds. In the first place, it relies on the unwarrented assumption that State and Nation will seek to subvert each other's laws. It has elsewhere been persuasively argued that most civilized nations do not and have not needed the power to try people a second time to protect themselves even when dealing with foreign lands. It is inconceivable to me, as it was to the Constitutional Court of South Carolina in 1816, that "If this prevails among nations who are strangers to each other, [it could] fail to [prevail] with us who are so intimately bound by political ties."

The Court's argument also ignores the fact that our Constitution allocates power between local and federal governments in such a way that the basic rights of each can be protected without double trials. The Federal Government is given power to act in limited areas only, but in matters properly within its scope it is supreme. It can retain exclusive control of such matters, or grant the States concurrent power on its own terms. If the States were to subvert federal laws in these areas by imposing inadequate penalties, Congress would have full power to protect the national interest, either by defining the crime to be punished and establishing minimum penalties applicable in both state and federal courts, or by excluding the States altogether. Conversely, in purely local matters the power of the States is supreme and exclusive. State courts can and should, therefore, protect all essentially local interests in one trial without federal interference. In areas, however, where the Constitution has vested power in the Federal Government the States necessarily act only to the extent Congress permits, and it is no infringement on their basic rights if Congress chooses to fix penalties smaller than some of them might wish. In fact, this will rarely occur, for Congress is not likely to use indirect means to limit state power when it could accomplish the same result directly by pre-empting the field.

Ultimately the Court's reliance on federalism amounts to no more than the notion that, somehow, one act becomes two because two jurisdictions are involved. Hawkins, in his Pleas of the Crown, long ago disposed of a similar contention made to justify two trials for the same offense by different counties as "a mere Fiction or Construction of Law, which shall hardly take Place against a Maxim made in Favour of Life." It was discarded as a dangerous fiction then, it should be discarded as a dangerous fiction now.

To bolster its argument that successive state and federal prosecutions do not violate basic principles of justice, the Court cites many cases. It begins with eight early state decisions which, it says, "clarified the issue by stating opposing arguments." Four of these cases held that prosecution by one government must bar subsequent prosecutions elsewhere. Two of the remaining four refused to hold that concurrent jurisdiction could exist since they feared that such a holding might bring about two trials for the same offense, a result they considered too shocking to tolerate. "This is against natural justice," said the North Carolina Superior Court in 1794, "and therefore I cannot believe it to be law. The seventh case cited is an inconclusive discussion coming from a state whose highest court had previously stated unequivocally that a bar against double prosecutions would exist. Thus only one of these early state cases actually approves the doctrine the Court today advances, and that approval is in dicta. Significantly, the highest court of the same state later expressed the view that such double trials would virtually never occur in our country.

The Court relies mainly, however, on a later line of decisions starting with *Fox* v. *Ohio*. Most of these, like *Fox* itself, involved only the question of whether both State and Federal Governments could make the same conduct a crime. Although some, in dicta, admitted the possibility that double prosecutions might result from such concurrent power, others did not discuss the question. Many, especially among the earlier cases, pointed out that double punishment violates the genius of our free country and therefore would never occur. As Chief Justice Taney, on circuit, said in one of them, "Yet in all civilized countries it is recognized as a fundamental principle of justice that a man ought not to be punished twice for the same offense; and if this party had been punished . . . in the state tribunal, the court would have felt it to be its duty to suspend sentence, and to represent the facts to the president, to give him an opportunity of . . . granting pardon." While a limited number of cases after *Fox* are cited in which a double conviction was upheld, in several of these the second court was so troubled by the result that only nominal sentences were imposed. In fact, before *United States* v. *Lanza,* where this Court upheld and encouraged the practice, the cases of actual double punishment found are so few, in relation to the great mass of criminal cases decided, that one can readily discern an instinctive unwillingness to impose such hardships on defendants.

Despite its exhaustive research, the Court has cited only three cases before *Lanza* where a new trial after an *acquittal* was upheld. In one of these, *United States* v. *Barnhart,* the state court in which the defendant had been acquitted did not have jurisdiction of the action. The Federal Circuit Court relied on this lack of jurisdiction in allowing a retrial, but made an alternate holding based on the same general arguments used by the Court today. The *Barnhart* opinion also intimated that the first trial may have been a sham. Sham trials, as well as those by courts without jurisdiction, have been considered by courts and commentators not to be jeopardy, and might therefore not bar subsequent convictions. In the second case cited by the Court, the state conviction followed acquittal by a federal court-martial at a time when, as the state court seemed to recognize, a military trial was thought by many not to be a trial for the purpose of double jeopardy even when both trials were conducted by the same "Sovereign." The third case relied on, a 1915 decision from the State of Washington, is the only one of the three where it can fairly be said that a defendant acquitted in a proper jury trial was subsequently tried again by a jury and convicted.

One may, I think, infer from the fewness of the cases that retrials after acquittal have been considered particularly obnoxious, worse even, in the eyes of many, than retrials after conviction. I doubt, in fact, if many practices which have been found to violate due process can boast of so little actual support. Yet it is on this meager basis that the Court must ultimately rest its finding that

Bartkus's retrial does not violate fundamental principles "rooted in the traditions and conscience of our peoples." Nor are these scattered and dubious cases unchallenged, for, balanced against them, we have a firm holding by this Court sustaining an extremely narrow construction of a federal statute in order to make a state acquittal conclusive in the federal courts and thereby avoid the evil approved today [*United States* v. *Mason*]. That case, as well as the "sacred duty . . . to maintain unimpaired those securities for the personal rights of the individual which have received for ages the sanction of the jurist and the statesman" [*Ex parte Lange*], should make us doubly hesitant to encourage so blatant a violation of constitutional policies against double trials by giving an "illiberal construction . . . to the words of the fundamental law in which they are embodied."

Since *Lanza*, people have apparently become more accustomed to double trials, once deemed so shocking, just as they might, in time, adjust themselves to all other violations of the Bill of Rights should they be sanctioned by this Court. The Court is therefore able to find a 1943 state case, as well as four federal cases in the last five years, in which a conviction following acquittal was sustained. Thus this practice, which for some 150 years was considered so undesirable that the Court must strain to find examples, is now likely to become a commonplace. For, after today, who will be able to blame a conscientious prosecutor for failing to accept a jury verdict of acquittal when he believes a defendant guilty and knows that a second try is available in another jurisdiction and that such a second try is approved by the Highest Court in the Land? Inevitably, the victims of such double prosecutions will most often be the poor and the weak in our society, individuals without friends in high places who can influence prosecutors not to try them again. The power to try a second time will be used, as have all similar procedures, to make scapegoats of helpless, political, religious, or racial minorities and those who differ, who do not conform, and who resist tyranny.

There are some countries that allow the dangerous practice of trying people twice. I am inserting below a recent news item about a man who was tried, convicted, sentenced to prison and then was tried again, convicted and sentenced to death. Similar examples are not hard to find in lands torn by revolution or crushed by dictatorship. I had thought that our constitutional protections embodied in the Double Jeopardy and Due Process Clauses would have barred any such things happening here. Unfortunately, last year's holdings by this Court in *Ciucci* v. *Illinois* and *Hoag* v. *New Jersey* and to-day's affirmance of the convictions of Bartkus and Abbate cause me to fear that in an important number of cases it can happen here.

I would reverse.

Barenblatt v. United States

360 U.S. 109

Decided June 8, *1959*

The exceedingly controversial House Committee on Un-American Activities has been taking cases to court and has been taken there itself through much of its stormy lifetime. Justice Black's majority opinion in United States v. Lovett *(page 135) held unconstitutional an Act of Congress sponsored by the Committee early in its career. In 1957 in* Watkins v. United States, *a majority opinion by Chief Justice Warren plainly declared that the Committee did not have the power to expose for exposure's sake; that, on the contrary, to be valid the inquiries of the Committee must be pertinent to legislation under consideration or in prospect. In the* Watkins Case, *the Warren opinion held that the evidence did not show that the question under legislative inquiry at the time was ever made known to the witness, John T. Watkins, a labor union official in Illinois.*

The Chief Justice was joined in that important opinion by Justices Black, Douglas, Harlan, and Brennan. Justice Frankfurter concurred in a separate opinion that the witness was entitled to be protected against the hazards of vagueness in the enforcement of the criminal process, and that clear definition was lacking. The single dissenter, Justice Clark, contended that there was sufficient showing of pertinency of the questions to the purpose of enacting legislation. Justices Burton and Whittaker did not take part in Watkins.

Another major case arising from an investigation conducted by the House Committee on Un-American Activities reached the

Supreme Court in Lloyd Barenblatt *v.* United States of America. *The defendant, professionally a college teacher of psychology, refused to answer questions about alleged Communist affiliation on the ground that the First Amendment protects privacy of individual belief. He expressly disclaimed reliance on the Fifth Amendment. In a 5-to-4 decision, which many students of the Supreme Court found substantially in conflict with the* Watkins *ruling, Justice Harlan delivered a majority opinion joined by Justices Frankfurter, Clark, Whittaker, and Stewart. It held, among other things, that the investigation was authorized, and that the authority was not assailable because of vagueness, that the defendant was adequately advised as to the pertinency of the questions, that these questions did not trespass on constitutional rights, and that it was immaterial if the purpose of the investigation was exposure.*

This wrenching change from Watkins *to* Barenblatt *brought from Justice Black one of his greatest opinions in his long service on the Nation's highest tribunal. In his dissent he was joined by Chief Justice Warren and Justice Douglas. He also had the support of Justice Brennan, who in a separate dissent, said he could find no purpose in the record "except exposure purely for the sake of exposure," and that, said Justice Brennan "is outside the constitutional pale of congressional inquiry."*

Justice Black's Barenblatt *dissent is reproduced in full, including all citations, all footnotes, and his appendix, which contains a selection of statements by the House Committee. Inclusion of this additional material, which is a part of the opinion in the* United States Reports, *will enable the reader to appreciate more fully the vast amount of study, reasoning, and work that went into answering the five-Justice majority and in stating the case for adherence to historic principles. In particular, he addressed himself to the "balancing" test stated by the majority, but not, as Justice Black found, applied in the decision. He also concerned himself with the evident encroachment on the judiciary by legislative committees that in effect indict, try, and punish, and he could not have been plainer in stating the aim of the House Committee on Un-American Activities. Surely this is one of the major state papers of our times.*

MR. JUSTICE BLACK, with whom THE CHIEF JUSTICE, and MR. JUSTICE DOUGLAS concur, dissenting

On May 28, 1954, petitioner Lloyd Barenblatt, then thirty-one years old, and a teacher of psychology at Vassar College, was summoned to appear before a Subcommittee of the House Committee on Un-American Activities. After service of the summons, but before Barenblatt appeared on June 28, his four-year contract with Vassar expired and was not renewed. He, therefore, came to the Committee as a private citizen without a job. Earlier that day, the Committee's interest in Barenblatt had been aroused by the testimony of an ex-Communist named Crowley. When Crowley had first appeared before the Un-American Activities Committee, he had steadfastly refused to admit or deny Communist affiliations or to identify others as Communists. After the House reported this refusal to the United States Attorney for prosecution, Crowley "voluntarily" returned and asked to testify. He was sworn in and interrogated, but not before he was made aware by various Committee members of Committee policy to "make an appropriate recommendation" to protect any witness who "fully cooperates with the Committee." He then talked at length, identifying by name, address, and occupation, whenever possible, people he claimed had been Communists. One of these was Barenblatt, who, according to Crowley, had been a Communist during 1947–1950 while a graduate student and teaching fellow at the University of Michigan. Though Crowley testified in great detail about the small group of Communists who had been at Michigan at that time and though the Committee was very satisfied with his testimony, it sought repetition of much of the information from Barenblatt. Barenblatt, however, refused to answer their questions and filed a long statement outlining his constitutional objections. He asserted that the Committee was violating the Constitution by abridging freedom of speech, thought, press, and association, and by conducting legislative trials of known or suspected Communists which trespassed on the exclusive power of the judiciary. He argued that however he answered questions relating to membership in the Communist Party his position in society and his ability to earn a living would be seriously jeopardized; that he would, in effect, be subjected to a bill of attainder despite the twice-expressed constitutional mandate against such legislative punishments.[1] This would occur, he pointed out, even if he did no more than invoke the protection of clearly applicable provisions of the Bill of Rights as a reason for refusing to answer.

---

[1] Bills of attainder are among the few measures explicitly forbidden to both State and Federal Governments by the body of the Constitution itself. U.S. Const., Art. 1, 9, cl. 3, states "No Bill of Attainder or *ex post facto* Law shall be passed." U.S. Const., Art. 1, 10, cl. 1, reads in part "No State shall . . . pass any Bill of Attainder (or) *ex post facto* Law . . ."

He repeated these, and other objections, in the District Court as a reason for dismissing an indictment for contempt of Congress. His position, however, was rejected at the trial and in the Court of Appeals for the District of Columbia Circuit over the strong dissents of Chief Judge Edgerton and Judges Bazelon, Fahy, and Washington. The Court today affirms, and thereby sanctions, the use of the contempt power to enforce questioning by congressional committees in the realm of speech and association. I cannot agree with this disposition of the case for I believe that the resolution establishing the House Un-American Activities Committee and the questions that Committee asked Barenblatt violate the Constitution in several respects. (1) Rule XI creating the Committee authorizes such a sweeping, unlimited, all-inclusive, and undiscriminating compulsory examination of witnesses in the field of speech, press, petition, and assembly that it violates the procedural requirements of the Due Process Clause of the Fifth Amendment. (2) Compelling an answer to the questions asked Barenblatt abridges freedom of speech and association in contravention of the First Amendment. (3) The Committee proceedings were part of a legislative program to stigmatize and punish by public identification and exposure all witnesses considered by the Committee to be guilty of Communist affiliations, as well as all witnesses who refused to answer Committee questions on constitutional grounds; the Committee was thus improperly seeking to try, convict, and punish suspects, a task which the Constitution expressly denies to Congress and grants exclusively to the courts, to be exercised by them only after indictment and in full compliance with all the safeguards provided by the Bill of Rights.

I

It goes without saying that a law to be valid must be clear enough to make its commands understandable. For obvious reasons, the standard of certainty required in criminal statutes is more exacting than in non-criminal statutes.[2] This is simply because it would be unthinkable to convict a man for violating a law he could not understand. This Court has recognized that the stricter standard is as much required in criminal contempt cases as in all other criminal

[2] E.g., *Lanzetta* v. *New Jersey*, 306 U.S. 451, 83 L. ed. 888, 59 S. Ct. 618; *Winters* v. *New York*, 333 U.S. 507, 515, 92 L. ed. 840, 849, 68 S. Ct. 665; *Jordan* v. *De George*, 341 U.S. 223, 230, 231, 95 L. ed. 886, 891, 892, 71 S. Ct. 703.

cases,[3] and has emphasized that the "vice of vagueness" is especially pernicious where legislative power over an area involving speech, press, petition, and assembly is involved.[4] In this area the statement that a statute is void if it "attempts to cover so much that it effectively covers nothing," see *Musser* v. *Utah,* 333 U.S. 95, 97, 92 L. ed. 562, 565, 68 S. Ct. 397, takes on double significance. For a statute broad enough to support infringement of speech, writings, thoughts, and public assemblies, against the unequivocal command of the First Amendment necessarily leaves all persons to guess just what the law really means to cover, and fear of a wrong guess inevitably leads people to forego the very rights the Constitution sought to protect above all others.[5] Vagueness becomes even more intolerable in this area if one accepts, as the Court today does, a balancing test to decide if First Amendment rights shall be protected. It is difficult at best to make a man guess—at the penalty of imprisonment—whether a court will consider the State's need for certain information superior to society's interest in unfettered freedom. It is unconscionable to make him choose between the right to keep silent and the need to speak when the statute supposedly establishing the "state's interest" is too vague to give him guidance. Cf. *Scull* v. *Virginia,* 359 U.S. 344, 3 L. ed. 2d 865, 79 S. Ct. 838.

Measured by the foregoing standards, Rule XI cannot support any conviction for refusal to testify. In substance it authorizes the Committee to compel witnesses to give evidence about all "un-American propaganda," whether instigated in this country or abroad.[6] The word "propaganda" seems to mean anything that people say, write, think, or associate together about. The term "un-

[3] E.g., *Watkins* v. *United States,* 354 U.S. 178, 207, 208, 1 L. ed. 2d 1273, 1295, 77 S. Ct. 1173; *Flaxer* v. *United States,* 358 U.S. 147, 3 L. ed. 2d 183, 79 S. Ct. 191; *Scull* v. *Virginia,* 359 U.S. 344, 3 L. ed. 2d 865, 79 S. Ct. 838.

[4] See, e.g., *Herndon* v. *Lowry,* 301 U.S. 242, 81 L. ed. 1066, 57 S. Ct. 732; *Winters* v. *New York,* 333 U.S. 507, 92 L. ed. 840, 68 S. Ct. 665; *Watkins* v. *United States,* 354 U.S. 178, 1 L. ed. 2d 1273, 77 S. Ct. 1173; *Scull* v. *Virginia,* 359 U.S. 344, 3 L. ed. 2d 865, 79 S. Ct. 838.

[5] *Thornhill* v. *Alabama,* 310 U.S. 88, 97, 98, 84 L. ed. 1093, 1099, 1100, 60 S. Ct. 736. Cf. *Herndon* v. *Lowry,* 301 U.S. 242, 81 L. ed. 1066, 57 S. Ct. 732.

[6] Rule XI in relevant part reads, "The Committee on Un-American Activities, as a whole or by subcommittee, is authorized to make from time to time investigations of (1) the extent, character, and objects of un-American propaganda activities in the United States, (2) the diffusion within the United States of subversive and un-American propaganda that is instigated from foreign countries or of a domestic origin and attacks the principle of the form of government as guaranteed by our Constitution, and (3) all other questions in relation thereto

American" is equally vague. As was said in *Watkins* v. *United States*, 354 U.S. 178, 202, 1 L. ed. 2d 1273, 1292, 77 S. Ct. 1173, "Who can define (its) meaning . . . ? What is that single, solitary 'principle of the form of government as guaranteed by our Constitution'?" I think it clear that the boundaries of the Committee are, to say the least, "nebulous." Indeed, "It would be difficult to imagine a less explicit authorizing resolution." Ibid.

The Court—while not denying the vagueness of Rule XI—nevertheless defends its application here because the questions asked concerned Communism, a subject of investigation which had been reported to the House by the Committee on numerous occasions. If the issue were merely whether Congress intended to allow an investigation of Communism, or even of Communism in education, it may well be that we could hold the data cited by the Court sufficient to support a finding of intent. But that is expressly not the issue. On the Court's own test, the issue is whether Barenblatt can know with sufficient certainty, at the time of his interrogation, that there is so compelling a need for his replies that infringement of his rights of free association is justified. The record does not disclose where Barenblatt can find what that need is. There is certainly no clear congressional statement of in Rule XI. Perhaps if Barenblatt had had time to read all the reports of the Committee to the House, and in addition had examined the appropriations made to the Committee he, like the Court, could have discerned an intent by Congress to allow an investigation of Communism in education. Even so he would be hard put to decide what the need for this investigation is since Congress expressed it neither when it enacted Rule XI nor when it acquiesced in the Committee's assertions of power. Yet it is knowledge of this need—what is wanted from him and why it is wanted—that a witness must have if he is to be in a position to comply with the Court's rule that he balance individual rights against the requirements of the State. I cannot see how that knowledge can exist under Rule XI.

But even if Barenblatt could evaluate the importance to the Government of the information sought, Rule XI would still be too broad to support his conviction. For we are dealing here with governmental procedures which the Court itself admits reach to the very fringes of congressional power. In such cases more is required

---

that would aid Congress in any necessary remedial legislation." H. Res. 5, 83d Cong., 1st Sess., 99 Cong. Rec., 15, 18, 24. See also H. Res. 7, 86th Cong., 1st Sess., Cong. Rec., Jan. 7, 1959, p. 13.

of legislatures than a vague delegation to be filled in later by mute acquiescence.[7] If Congress wants ideas investigated, if it even wants them investigated in the field of education, it must be prepared to say so expressly and unequivocally. And it is not enough that a court through exhaustive research can establish, even conclusively, that Congress wished to allow the investigation. I can find no such unequivocal statement here.

For all these reasons, I would hold that Rule XI is too broad to be meaningful and cannot support petitioner's conviction.[8]

II

The First Amendment says in no equivocal language that Congress shall pass no law abridging freedom of speech, press, assembly, or petition.[9] The activities of this Committee, authorized by Congress, do precisely that, through exposure, obloquy, and public scorn. See *Watkins* v. *United States,* 354 U.S. 178, 197, 198, 1 L. ed. 2d 1273, 1289, 1290, 77 S. Ct. 1173. The Court does not really deny this fact but relies on a combination of three reasons for permitting the infringement: (A) The notion that despite the First Amendment's

[7] See, e.g., *Panama Ref. Co.* v. *Ryan,* 293 U.S. 388, 79 L. ed. 446, 55 S. Ct. 241; *A.L.A. Schechter Poultry Corp.* v. *United States,* 295 U.S. 495, 551, 79 L. ed. 1570, 1591, 55 S. Ct. 837, 97 A.L.R. 947 (concurring opinion); *Berra* v. *United States,* 351 U.S. 131, 135, 100 L. ed. 1013, 1018, 76 S. Ct. 685 (dissenting opinion); *Watkins* v. *United States,* 354 U.S. 178, 203–205, 1 L. ed. 2d 1273, 1292–4, 77 S. Ct. 1173; *Sweezy* v. *New Hampshire,* 354 U.S. 234, 1 L. ed. 2d 1311, 77 S. Ct. 1203. Cf. *United States* v. *Rumely,* 345 U.S. 41, 97 L. ed. 770, 73 S. Ct. 543; *Kent* v. *Dulles,* 357 U.S. 116, 2 L. ed. 2d 1204, 78 S. Ct. 1113. These cases show that when this Court considered that the legislative measures involved were of doubtful constitutionality substantively, it required explicit delegations of power.

[8] It is, of course, no answer to Barenblatt's claim that Rule XI is too vague, to say that if it had been too vague it would have been so held in *Watkins* v. *United States,* 354 U.S. 178, 1 L. ed. 2d 1273, 77 S. Ct. 1173. It would be a strange rule, indeed, which would imply the invalidity of a broad ground of decision from the fact that this Court decided an earlier case on a narrower basis.

[9] The First Amendment reads: "Congress shall make no law respecting an establishment of religion, or prohibiting the free exercise thereof; or abridging the freedom of speech, or of the press; or the right of the people peaceably to assemble, and to petition the Government for a redress of grievances." There can be no doubt that the same Amendment protects the right to keep silent. See *West Virginia Board of Education* v. *Barnette,* 319 U.S. 624, 87 L. ed. 1628, 63 S. Ct. 1178, 147 A.L.R. 674; *National Asso. for Advancement of Colored People* v. *Alabama,* 357 U.S. 449, 460–66, 2 L. ed. 2d 1488, 1498–1502, 78 S. Ct. 1163; *Sweezy* v. *New Hampshire,* 354 U.S. 234, 255, 1 L. ed. 2d 1311, 1327, 77 S. Ct. 1203 (concurring opinion); *Watkins* v. *United States,* 354 U.S. 178, 1 L. ed. 2d 1273, 77 S. Ct. 1173; *Scull* v. *Virginia,* 359 U.S. 344, 3 L. ed. 2d 865, 79 S. Ct. 838. Cf. *United States* v. *Rumely,* 345 U.S. 41, 97 L. ed. 770, 73 S. Ct. 543.

command Congress can abridge speech and association if this Court decides that the governmental interest in abridging speech is greater than an individual's interest in exercising that freedom, (B) the Government's right to "preserve itself," (C) the fact that the Committee is only after Communists or suspected Communists in this investigation.

(A) I do not agree that laws directly abridging First Amendment freedoms can be justified by a congressional or judicial balancing process. There are, of course, cases suggesting that a law which primarily regulates conduct but which might also indirectly affect speech can be upheld if the effect on speech is minor in relation to the need for control of the conduct. With these cases I agree. Typical of them are *Cantwell* v. *Connecticut*, 310 U.S. 296, 84 L. ed. 1213, 60 S. Ct. 900, 128 A.L.R. 1352, and *Schneider* v. *Irvington*, 308 U.S. 147, 84 L. ed. 155, 60 S. Ct. 146. Both of these involved the right of a city to control its streets. In *Cantwell*, a man had been convicted of breach of the peace for playing a phonograph on the street. He defended on the ground that he was disseminating religious views and could not, therefore, be stopped. We upheld his defense, but in so doing we pointed out that the city did have substantial power over conduct on the streets even where this power might to some extent affect speech. A State, we said, might "by general and non-discriminatory legislation regulate the times, the places, and the manner of soliciting upon its streets and holding meetings thereon." 310 U.S. at 304. But even such laws governing conduct, we emphasized, must be tested, though only by a balancing process, if they indirectly affect ideas. On one side of the balance, we pointed out, is the interest of the United States in seeing that its fundamental law protecting freedom of communication is not abridged; on the other, the obvious interest of the State to regulate conduct within its boundaries. In *Cantwell* we held that the need to control the streets could not justify the restriction made on speech. We stressed the fact that where a man had a right to be on a street, "he had a right peacefully to impart his views to others." 310 U.S., at 308. Similar views were expressed in *Schneider*, which concerned ordinances prohibiting the distribution of handbills to prevent littering. We forbade application of such ordinances when they affected literature designed to spread ideas. There were other ways, we said, to protect the city from littering which would not sacrifice the right of the people to be informed. In so holding, we, of course, found it necessary to "weigh the circumstances." 308 U.S., at 161. But we did not in *Schneider*, any more than in *Cantwell*, even remotely suggest that a law directly aimed at curtailing speech and political persuasion could be saved through a balancing process. Neither these cases, nor any others, can be read as allowing legislative bodies to pass laws abridging freedom of speech, press, and association merely because of hostility to views peacefully expressed in a place where the speaker had a right to be. Rule XI, on its face and as here applied, since it attempts inquiry into beliefs, not action—ideas and associations, not conduct, does just that.[10]

To apply the Court's balancing test under such circumstances is to read the First Amendment to say "Congress shall pass no law abridging freedom of speech, press, assembly and petition, unless Congress and the Supreme Court reach the joint conclusion that on balance the interests of Government in stifling these freedoms is greater than the interest of the people in having them exercised." This is closely akin to the notion that neither the First Amendment nor any other provision of the Bill of Rights should be enforced unless the Court believes it is *reasonable* to do so. Not only does this violate the genius of our *written* Constitution, but it runs expressly counter to the injunction to Court and Congress made by Madison when he introduced the Bill of Rights. "If they [the First Ten Amendments] are incorporated into the Constitution, independent tribunals of justice will consider themselves in a peculiar manner the guardians of those rights; they will be an impenetrable bulwark against *every* assumption of power in the Legislative or Executive; they will be naturally led to resist *every* encroachment upon rights expressly stipulated for in the Constitution by the declaration of rights." [11] Unless we return to this view of our judi-

---

[10] I do not understand the Court's opinion in *Watkins* v. *United States*, 354 U.S. 178, 198, 1 L. ed. 2d 1273, 1290, 77 S. Ct. 1173, to approve the type of balancing process adopted in the Court's opinion here. We did discuss in that case "the weight to be ascribed to . . . the interest of the Congress in demanding disclosures from an unwilling witness." As I read, and still read, the Court's discussion of this problem in Watkins it was referring to the problems raised by *Kilbourn* v. *Thompson*, 103 U.S. 168, 26 L. ed. 377, which held that legislative committees could not make roving inquiries into the private business affairs of witnesses. The Court, in *Kilbourn*, held that the courts must be careful to insure that, on balance, Congress did not unjustifiably encroach on an individual's private business affairs. Needless to say, an individual's right to silence in such matters is quite a different thing from the public's interest in freedom of speech and the test applicable to one has little, if anything, to do with the test applicable to the other.

[11] 1 Annals of Cong. 439 (1789). (Italics supplied.)

cial function, unless we once again accept the notion that the Bill
of Rights means what it says and that this Court must enforce that
meaning, I am of the opinion that our great charter of liberty will
be more honored in the breach than in the observance.

But even assuming what I cannot assume, that some balancing
is proper in this case, I feel that the Court after stating the test ignores it completely. At most it balances the right of the Government to preserve itself, against Barenblatt's right to refrain from
revealing Communist affiliations. Such a balance, however, mistakes the factors to be weighed. In the first place, it completely
leaves out the real interest in Barenblatt's silence, the interest of
the people as a whole in being able to join organizations, advocate
causes, and make political "mistakes" without later being subjected
to governmental penalties for having dared to think for themselves.
It is this right, the right to err politically, which keeps us strong as
a Nation. For no number of laws against Communism can have as
much effect as the personal conviction which comes from having
heard its arguments and rejected them, or from having once accepted its tenets and later recognized their worthlessness. Instead,
the obloquy which results from investigations such as this not only
stifles "mistakes" but prevents all but the most courageous from
hazarding any views which might at some later time become dis-
favored. This result, whose importance cannot be overestimated, is
doubly crucial when it affects the universities, on which we must
largely rely for the experimentation and development of new ideas
essential to our country's welfare. It is these interests of society,
rather than Barenblatt's own right to silence, which I think the
Court should put on the balance against the demands of the Government, if any balancing process is to be tolerated. Instead they
are not mentioned, while on the other side the demands of the
Government are vastly overstated and called "self preservation."
It is admitted that this Committee can only seek information for
the purpose of suggesting laws, and that Congress' power to make
laws in the realm of speech and association is quite limited, even
on the Court's test. Its interest in making such laws in the field of
education, primarily a state function, is clearly narrower still. Yet
the Court styles this attenuated interest self-preservation and allows it to overcome the need our country has to let us all think,
speak, and associate politically as we like and without fear of reprisal. Such a result reduces "balancing" to a mere play on words
and is completely inconsistent with the rules this Court has previ-

ously given for applying a "balancing test," where it is proper: "[T]he courts should be *astute* to examine the *effect* of the challenged legislation. Mere *legislative preferences or beliefs* . . . may well support regulation directed at other personal activities, but be insufficient to justify such as diminishes the exercise of rights so vital to the maintenance of democratic institutions." *Schneider* v. *Irvington*, 308 U.S. 147, 161, 84 L. ed. 155, 164, 60 S. Ct. 146. (Italics supplied.)

(B) Moreover, I cannot agree with the Court's notion that First Amendment freedoms must be abridged in order to "preserve" our country. That notion rests on the unarticulated premise that this Nation's security hangs upon its power to punish people because of what they think, speak, or write about, or because of those with whom they associate for political purposes. The Government, in its brief, virtually admits this position when it speaks of the "communication of unlawful ideas." I challenge this premise, and deny that ideas can be proscribed under our Constitution. I agree that despotic governments cannot exist without stifling the voice of opposition to their oppressive practices. The First Amendment means to me, however, that the only constitutional way our Government can preserve itself is to leave its people the fullest possible freedom to praise, criticize, or discuss, as they see fit, all governmental policies and to suggest, if they desire, that even its most fundamental postulates are bad and should be changed; "Therein lies the security of the Republic, the very foundation of constitutional government." [12] On that premise this land was created, and on that premise it has grown to greatness. Our Constitution assumes that the common sense of the people and their attachment to our country will enable them, after free discussion, to withstand ideas that are wrong. To say that our patriotism must be protected against false ideas by means other than these is, I think, to make a baseless charge. Unless we can rely on these qualities—if, in short, we begin to punish speech—we cannot honestly proclaim ourselves to be a free Nation and we have lost what the

[12] "The greater the importance of safeguarding the community from incitements to the overthrow of our institutions by force and violence, the more imperative is the need to preserve inviolate the constitutional rights of free speech, free press and free assembly in order to maintain the opportunity for free political discussion, to the end that government may be responsive to the will of the people and that changes, if desired, may be obtained by peaceful means. Therein lies the security of the Republic, the very foundation of constitutional government," *De Jonge* v. *Oregon*, 299 U.S. 353, 365, 81 L. ed. 278, 284, 57 S. Ct. 255,

Founders of this land risked their lives and their sacred honor to defend.

(C) The Court implies, however, that the ordinary rules and requirements of the Constitution do not apply because the Committee is merely after Communists and they do not constitute a political party but only a criminal gang. "[T]he long and widely accepted view," the Court says, is "that the tenets of the Communist Party include the ultimate overthrow of the Government of the United States by force and violence." [13] This justifies the investigation undertaken. By accepting this charge and allowing it to support treatment of the Communist Party and its members which would violate the Constitution if applied to other groups, the Court, in effect, declares that Party outlawed. It has been only a few years since there was a practically unanimous feeling throughout the country and in our courts that this could not be done in our free land. Of course, it has always been recognized that members of the Party who, either individually or in combination, commit acts in violation of valid laws can be prosecuted. But the Party as a whole and innocent members of it could not be attainted merely because it had some illegal aims and because some of its members were lawbreakers. Thus in *De Jonge* v. *Oregon*, 299 U.S. 353, 357, 81 L. ed. 278, 280, 57 S. Ct. 255, on stipulated facts that the Communist Party advocated criminal syndicalism—"crime, physical violence, sabotage or any unlawful acts or methods as a means of accomplishing or effecting industrial or political change or revolution"—a unanimous Court, speaking through Chief Justice Hughes, held that a Communist addressing a Communist rally could be found guilty of no offense so long as no violence or crime was urged at the meeting. The Court absolutely refused to concede that either De Jonge or the Communist Party forfeited the protections of the First and Fourteenth Amendments because one of the Party's purposes was to effect a violent change of government. See also *Herndon* v. *Lowry*, 301 U.S. 242, 81 L. ed. 1066, 57 S. Ct. 732.

Later, in 1948, when various bills were proposed in the House and Senate to handicap or outlaw the Communist Party, leaders of the bar who had been asked to give their views rose up to contest

---

[13] Cf. statement of Sir Richard Nagle presenting a bill of attainder against between two and three thousand persons for political offenses, " 'Many of the persons here attainted,' said he, 'have been proved traitors by such evidence as satisfies us. As to the rest we have followed common fame.' " Cited in *Joint Anti-Fascist Committee* v. *McGrath*, 341 U.S. 123, 142, 148 (concurring opinion).

the constitutionality of the measures. The late Charles Evans Hughes, Jr., questioned the validity, under both the First and Fifth Amendments, of one of these bills, which in effect outlawed the Party. The late John W. Davis attacked it as lacking an ascertainable standard of guilt under many of this Court's cases.[14] And the Attorney General of the United States not only indicated that such a measure would be unconstitutional but declared it to be unwise even if valid. He buttressed his position by citing a statement by J. Edgar Hoover, Director of the Federal Bureau of Investigation, and the declaration of this Court in *West Virginia State Board of Education* v. *Barnette,* 319 U.S. 624, 642, 87 L. ed. 1628, 1639, 63 S. Ct. 1178, 147 A.L.R. 674, that:

"If there is any fixed star in our constitutional constellation, it is that no official, high or petty, can prescribe what shall be orthodox in politics, nationalism, religion, or other matters of opinion or force citizens to confess by word or faith or act their faith therein." [15]

Even the proponent of the bill disclaimed any aim to outlaw the Communist Party and pointed out the "disadvantages" of such a move by stating that "the Communist Party was illegal and outlawed in Russia when it took over control of the Soviet Union." [16] Again, when the Attorney General testified on a proposal to bar

[14] See Hearings, Senate Committee on the Judiciary on H.R. 5852, 80th Cong., 2d Sess. 415–20, 420–22.

[15] Id. at 422–5. See also Hearings, Subcommittee on Legislation of the House Committee on Un-American Activities on H.R. 4422, H.R. 4581, 80th Cong., 2d Sess. 16–37.

[16] Hearings, Subcommittee on Legislation of the Committee on Un-American Activities on H.R. 4422, H.R. 4581, 80th Cong., 2d Sess. 13. This statement was relied on by the Honorable Thomas E. Dewey, then a candidate for the presidency of the United States, in a speech given in Portland, Oregon, in May, 1948. Mr. Dewey went on to say, in opposing outlawry of the Communist Party:

"I am against it because it is a violation of the Constitution of the United States and of the Bill of Rights, and clearly so. I am against it because it is immoral and nothing but totalitarianism itself. I am against it because I know from a great many years' experience in the enforcement of the law that the proposal wouldn't work, and instead it would rapidly advance the cause of communism in the United States and all over the world. . . .

"There is an American way to do this job, a perfectly simple American way . . . outlawing every conceivable *act* of subversion against the United States. . . .

"Now, times are too grave to try any expedients and fail. This expedient has failed, this expedient of outlawing has failed in Russia. It failed in Europe, it failed in Italy, it failed in Canada. . . .

"Let us not make such a terrific blunder in the United States. . . . Let us go forward as Free Americans. Let us have the courage to be Free." XIV *Vital Speeches of the Day,* 486, 487. (Italics supplied.)

the Communist Party from the ballot he said, "an organized group, whether you call it political or not, could hardly be barred from the ballot without jeopardizing the constitutional guarantees of all other political groups and parties." [17]

All these statements indicate quite clearly that no matter how often or how quickly we repeat the claim that the Communist Party is not a political party, we cannot outlaw it, as a group, without endangering the liberty of all of us. The reason is not hard to find, for mixed among those aims of Communism which are illegal are perfectly normal political and social goals. And muddled with its revolutionary tenets is a drive to achieve power through the ballot, if it can be done. These things necessarily make it a political party whatever other, illegal, aims it may have. Cf. *Gerende* v. *Board of Supervisors*, 341 U.S. 56, 95 L. ed. 745, 71 S. Ct. 565. Significantly, until recently the Communist Party was on the ballot in many states. When that was so, many Communists undoubtedly hoped to accomplish its lawful goals through support of Communist candidates. Even now some such may still remain.[18] To attribute to them, and to those who have left the Party, the taint of the group is to ignore both our traditions that guilt like belief is "personal and not a matter of mere association" and the obvious fact that "men adhering to a political party or other organization notoriously do not subscribe unqualifiedly to all of its platforms or asserted principles." *Schneiderman* v. *United States*, 320 U.S. 118, 136, 87 L. ed. 1796, 1808, 63 S. Ct. 1333. See also *Dennis* v. *United States*, 341 U.S. 494, 579, 581, 95 L. ed. 1137, 1188, 1190, 71 S. Ct. 857 (dissenting opinions).

The fact is that once we allow any group which has some political aims or ideas to be driven from the ballot and from the battle for men's minds because some of its members are bad and some of its tenets are illegal, no group is safe. Today we deal with Communists or suspected Communists. In 1920, instead, the New York Assembly suspended duly elected legislators on the ground

[17] Hearings, Subcommittee on Legislation of the Committee on Un-American Activities on H.R. 4422, H.R. 4581, 80th Cong., 2d Sess. 20. Compare statement of John Lilburne, "what is done unto any one, may be done unto every one." Note 39, *infra*.

[18] S. Doc. No. 97, 85th Cong., 2d Sess. 149, lists the States with laws relating to the Communist Party and the ballot. See also, Fund For the Republic, Digest of the Public Record of Communism in the United States, 324–43. For a discussion of State laws requiring a minimum percentage of the votes cast to remain on the ballot, see Note, 57 *Yale L.J.* 1276.

that, being Socialists, they were disloyal to the country's principles.[19] In the 1830's the Masons were hunted as outlaws and subversives, and abolitionists were considered revolutionaries of the
most dangerous kind in both North and South.[20] Earlier still, at
the time of the universally unlamented Alien and Sedition laws,
Thomas Jefferson's party was attacked and its members were deri-
sively called "Jacobins." Fisher Ames described the party as a
"French faction" guilty of "subversion" and "officered, regimented
and formed to subordination." Its members, he claimed, intended
to "take arms against the laws as soon as they dare." [21] History
should teach us then, that in times of high emotional excitement
minority parties and groups which advocate extremely unpopular
social or governmental innovations will always be typed as criminal gangs and attempts will always be made to drive them out.[22]
It was knowledge of this fact, and of its great dangers, that caused
the Founders of our land to enact the First Amendment as a guarantee that neither Congress nor the people would do anything to
hinder or destroy the capacity of individuals and groups to seek
converts and votes for any cause, however radical or unpalatable
their principles might seem under the accepted notions of the time.
Whatever the States were left free to do, the First Amendment
sought to leave Congress devoid of any kind or quality of power
to direct any type of national laws against the freedom of individuals to think what they please, advocate whatever policy they
choose, and join with others to bring about the social, religious,
political, and governmental changes which seem best to them.[23] To-

---

[19] See O'Brian, "Loyalty Tests and Guilt by Association," 61 *Harv. L. Rev.*
592, 593. Significantly the action of the New York Assembly was strongly condemned by Charles Evans Hughes, then a former Associate Justice of this Court,
and later its Chief Justice.

[20] See generally, McCarthy, *The Anti-masonic Party; A Study of Political
Anti-masonry in the United States, 1827–1840.* H.R. Doc. No. 461 57th Cong., 2d
Sess. 365, Nye, *William Lloyd Garrison,* 88–105; Korngold, *Two Friends of Man,*
82–104. Cf. St. George Tucker, Appendix, 1 *Blackstone* (Tucker ed. 1803) 315,
discussing English laws "for suppressing assemblies of free-masons" and pointing
out that similar laws cannot be enacted under our Constitution.

[21] Ames, *Laocoon,* printed in *Works of Fisher Ames* (1809 ed.), 94, 97, 101,
106. See also *American Communications Asso. CIO* v. *Douds,* 339 U.S. 382, 445,
94 L. ed. 925, 968, 70 S. Ct. 674 (dissenting opinion).

[22] Cf. Mill, *On Liberty* (1885 ed.), 30 (criticizing laws restricting the right
to advocate tyrannicide).

[23] Cf. St. George Tucker, Appx., 1 *Blackstone Commentaries* (Tucker ed.
1803) 299. "[T]he judicial courts of the respective states are open to all persons
alike for the redress of injuries of this nature [libel]; . . . . But the genius of our

day's holding, in my judgment, marks another major step in the progressively increasing retreat from the safeguards of the First Amendment.

It is, sadly, no answer to say that this Court will not allow the trend to overwhelm us; that today's holding will be strictly confined to "Communists," as the Court's language implies. This decision can no more be contained than could the holding in *American Communications Asso. CIO* v. *Douds*, 339 U.S. 382, 94 L. ed. 925, 70 S. Ct. 674. In that case the Court sustained as an exercise of the commerce power an Act which required labor union officials to take an oath that they were not members of the Communist Party. The Court rejected the idea that the *Douds* holding meant that the Party and all its members could be attainted because of their Communist beliefs. It went to great lengths to explain that the Act held valid "touches only a relative handful of persons, leaving the great majority of persons of the identified affiliations and beliefs completely free from restraint." "[W]hile this Court sits," the Court proclaimed, no wholesale proscription of Communists or their Party can occur, 339 U.S., at 404, 410. I dissented and said:

"Under such circumstances, restrictions imposed on proscribed groups are seldom static, even though the rate of expansion may not move in geometric progression from discrimination to armband to ghetto and worse. Thus I cannot regard the Court's holding as one which merely bars Communists from holding union office and nothing more. For its reasoning would apply just as forcibly to statutes barring Communists and their respective sympathizers from election to political office, mere membership in unions, and in fact from getting or holding any job whereby they could earn a living." 339 U.S., at 449.

My prediction was all too accurate. Today, Communists or suspected Communists have been denied an opportunity to work as government employees, lawyers, doctors, teachers, pharmacists, veterinarians, subway conductors, industrial workers, and in just about any other job. See *Speiser* v. *Randall*, 357 U.S. 513, 531, 2 L. ed. 2d 1460, 1476, 78 S. Ct. 1332 (concurring opinion). Cf. *Barsky* v. *Board of Regents*, 347 U.S. 442, 456, 467, 472, 98 L. ed. 829, 841, 847, 849, 74 S. Ct. 650 (dissenting opinions). In today's holding

government will not permit the federal legislature to interfere with the subject; and the federal courts are, I presume, equally restrained by the principles of the constitution, and the amendments which have since been adopted."

they are singled out and, as a class, are subjected to inquisitions which the Court suggests would be unconstitutional but for the fact of "Communism." Nevertheless, this Court still sits! [24]

III

Finally, I think Barenblatt's conviction violates the Constitution because the chief aim, purpose, and practice of the House Un-American Activities Committee, as disclosed by its many reports, is to try witnesses and punish them because they are or have been Communists or because they refuse to admit or deny Communist affiliations. The punishment imposed is generally punishment by humiliation and public shame. There is nothing strange or novel about this kind of punishment. It is in fact one of the oldest forms of governmental punishment known to mankind; branding, the pillory, ostracism, and subjection to public hatred being but a few examples of it.[25] Nor is there anything strange about a court's reviewing the power of a congressional committee to inflict punishment. In 1880 this Court nullified the action of the House of Representatives in sentencing a witness to jail for failing to answer questions of a congressional committee. *Kilbourn* v. *Thompson,* 103 U.S. 168, 26 L. ed. 377. The Court held that the Committee in its investigation of the Jay Cooke bankruptcy was seeking to exercise judicial power, and this, it emphatically said, no committee could do. It seems to me that the proof that the Un-American Activities Committee is here undertaking a purely judicial function is overwhelming, far stronger, in fact, than it was in the Jay Cooke investigation, which, moreover, concerned only business transactions, not freedom of association.

The Un-American Activities Committee was created in 1938.

[24] The record in this very case indicates how easily such restrictions spread. During the testimony of one witness an organization known as the Americans for Democratic Action was mentioned. Despite testimony that this organization did not admit Communists, one member of the Committee insisted that it was a Communist front because "it followed a party line, almost identical in many particulars with the Communist Party line." Presumably if this accusation were repeated frequently and loudly enough that organization, or any other, would also be called a "criminal gang." Cf. *Feiner* v. *New York,* 340 U.S. 315, 321, 329, 95 L. ed. 295, 300, 304, 71 S. Ct. 303, 328 (dissenting opinions).

[25] See generally, XII *Encyclopedia of the Social Sciences,* 714; Barnes, *The Story of Punishment,* 62–4; Lowie, *Primitive Society,* 398; Andrews, *Old-Time Punishments* (1890 ed.), 1–145, 164–87; IV *Plutarch's Lives* (Clough, New Nat. ed. 1914) 43–4.

It immediately conceived of its function on a grand scale as one of ferreting out "subversives" and especially of having them removed from government jobs.[26] It made many reports to the House urging removal of such employees.[27] Finally, at the instigation of the Committee, the House put a rider on an appropriation bill to bar three government workers from collecting their salary.[28] The House action was based on Committee findings that each of the three employees was a member of, or associated with, organizations deemed undesirable and that the "views and philosophies" of these workers "as expressed in various statements and writings constitute subversive activity within the definition adopted by your committee, and that [they are], therefore, unfit for the present to continue in Government employment." [29] The Senate and the President agreed to the rider, though not without protest. We held that statute void

[26] In its very first report it stated, "The Committee has felt that it is its sworn duty and solemn obligation to the people of this country to focus the spotlight of publicity upon every individual and organization engaged in subversive activities regardless of politics or partisanship." It further claimed that, "While Congress does not have the power to deny to citizens the right to believe in, teach, or advocate, communism, fascism, and nazism, it does have the right to focus the spotlight of publicity upon their activities." H.R. Rep. No. 2, 76th Cong., 1st Sess. 9–10, 13. See also the statement of the Committee's first Chairman, "I am not in a position to say whether we can legislate effectively in reference to this matter, but I do know that exposure in a democracy of subversive activities is the most effective weapon that we have in our possession." 83 Cong. Rec. 7570 (1938).

[27] See, e.g., H.R. Rep. No. 2747, 77th Cong., 2d Sess. 5. "On September 6, 1941, the chairman of this Committee wrote the President a letter, accompanied by 43 exhibits, detailing the Communist affiliation and background of the following officials . . . and suggested that they be dismissed from their positions." "On November 28, 1941 . . . the chairman called the attention of the members to the case of [the] principal economist in the Department of Agriculture"; "On January 15, 1942, the chairman of the Committee . . . called attention to . . . one Malcolm Cowley. . . . Several weeks later Mr. Cowley resigned his position with the Federal Government"; "On March 28, 1942, the chairman wrote a letter to the . . . Chairman of the Board of Economic Welfare and called attention to . . . eight of its employees and made particular reference to one Maurice Parmelee. . . . The following week, Mr. Parmelee was dismissed. . . ." Id. at 6. "In the Chairman's speech of September 24 (1942) he also presented to the House the names of 19 officials of the Government. . . . Yet, to the Committee's knowledge, no action has been taken in the cases of the 19 officials." Id. at 8.

[28] Section 304 of the Urgent Deficiency Appropriation Act, 1943, 57 Stat. 431, 450. The history of this rider is detailed in *United States* v. *Lovett*, 328 U.S. 303, 90 L. ed. 1252, 66 S. Ct. 1073.

[29] See, e.g., H.R. Rep. No. 448, 78th Cong., 1st Sess. 6, 8. The Un-American Activities Committee did not actually undertake the trials of these government employees. That task fell to a special Subcommittee of the Committee on Appropriations which was created in response to a speech by the Chairman of the Un-American Activities Committee, Id. at 3.

as a bill of attainder in *United States* v. *Lovett,* 328 U.S. 303, 90 L. ed. 1252, 66 S. Ct. 1073 (1946), stating that its "effect was to inflict punishment without the safeguards of a judicial trial" and that this "cannot be done either by a State or by the United States." 328 U.S., at 316, 317.

Even after our *Lovett* holding, however, the Committee continued to view itself as the "only agency of government that has the power of exposure," and to work unceasingly and sincerely to identify and expose all suspected Communists and "subversives" in order to eliminate them from virtually all fields of employment.[30] How well it has succeeded in its declared program of "pitiless publicity and exposure" is a matter of public record. It is enough to cite the experience of a man who masqueraded as a Communist for the FBI and who reported to this same Committee that since 1952 when his "membership" because known he has been unable to hold any job.[31] To accomplish this kind of result, the Committee has called witnesses who are suspected of Communist affiliation, has subjected them to severe questioning and has insisted that each tell the name of every person he has ever known at any time to

[30] Virtually every report of the Committee emphasizes that its principal function is exposure and that once exposed subversives must be driven out. Space, however, prevents listing more than a random sampling of statements by the Committee. These are given in an Appendix to this opinion, *infra,* p. 1149. For other similar statements by the Committee and its members, see, e.g., notes 26, 27, *supra;* 31–7, *infra; Watkins* v. *United States,* 354 U.S. 178, 1 L. ed. 2d 1273, 77 S. Ct. 1173; *United States* v. *Josephson* (C.A. 2 N.Y.) 165 F2d 82, 93 (dissenting opinion); *Barsky* v. *United States,* 83 App. D.C. 127, 138, 167 F2d 241, 252 (dissenting opinion).

[31] This evidence was given before the Committee on May 7, 1959, in Chicago, Ill. It has not yet been published.

Even those the Committee does not wish to injure are often hurt by its tactics, so all-pervasive is the effect of its investigations:

"It has been brought to the attention of the Committee that many persons so subpenaed . . . have been subjected to ridicule and discrimination as a result of having received such subpenas"; "The Committee . . . has met with many obstacles and difficulties. Not the least of these has been the reluctance of former Communists to give testimony before the Committee which might bring upon them public censure and economic retaliation"; "To deny to these *co-operative* witnesses a full opportunity for social, economic, and political rehabilitation . . . will . . . render more difficult the obtaining of authentic . . . information." H.R. Rep. No. 2431, 82d Cong., 2d Sess. 5. (Italics added.)

"While the American people . . . were fortunate to have this testimony, some of the witnesses themselves were not. Instances have come to the Committee's attention where several of these witnesses have been forced from gainful employment after testifying. Some have been released from the employment which they competently held for years prior to their testimony." H.R. Rep. No. 2516, 82d Cong., 2d Sess. 3.

have been a Communist, and, if possible, to give the addresses and occupations of the people named. These names are then indexed, published, and reported to Congress, and often to the press.[32] The same technique is employed to cripple the job opportunities of those who strongly criticize the Committee or take other actions it deems undesirable.[33] Thus, in 1949, the Committee reported that it had indexed and printed some 335,000 names of people who had signed "Communist" petitions of one kind or another.[34] All this the Committee did and does to punish by exposure the many phases of "un-American" activities that it reports cannot be reached by legislation, by administrative action, or by any other agency of Government, which, of course, includes the courts.

The same intent to expose and punish is manifest in the Committee's investigation which led to Barenblatt's conviction. The declared purpose of the investigation was to identify to the people of Michigan the individuals responsible for the, alleged, Communist success there.[35] The Committee claimed that its investigation "uncovered" members of the Communist Party holding positions in the school systems in Michigan; that most of the teachers subpoenaed before the Committee refused to answer questions on the

[32] Descriptions of the size and availability of Committee's files as well as the efficiency of its cross-indexing system can be found in most of its reports. See, e.g., H.R. Rep. No. 2742, 79th Cong., 2d Sess. 16–17; H.R. Rep. No. 1950, 81st Cong., 2d Sess. 18–23; H.R. Rep. No. 2431, 82d Cong., 2d Sess. 24–8.

[33] It is impossible even to begin to catalogue people who have been stigmatized by the Committee for criticizing it. In 1942 the Committee reported "Henry Luce's *Time* magazine has been drawn sucker-fashion into this movement to alter our form of government. . . ." H.R. Rep. No. 2277, 77th Cong., 2d Sess. 2. In 1946 Harold Laski and Socialists generally were attacked for their "impertinence in suggesting that the United States should trade its system of free economy for some brand of Socialism." The Committee deemed it "imperative" that it ascertain the "methods used to enable Mr. Laski to broadcast to [a] rally." H.R. Rep. No. 2231, 79th Cong., 2d Sess. 46–7. In 1951 a full report was issued on a "Communist lobby"—a committee formed to urge defeat of a Communist control bill before Congress. Among the distinguished sponsors of the group listed by the Committee was the late Prof. Zechariah Chafee. The Committee, nevertheless, advised "the American public that individuals who knowingly and actively support such a propaganda outlet . . . are actually aiding and abetting the Communist program in the United States." H.R. Rep. No. 3248, 81st Cong., 2d Sess. 1, 11–12, 15. See also, Gellhorn, *Report on a Report of the House Committee on Un-American Activities*, 60 Harv. L. Rev. 1193.

[34] H.R. Rep. No. 1950, 81st Cong., 2d Sess. 19.

[35] "The 1954 hearings were set up by the Committee in order to demonstrate to the people of Michigan the fields of concentration of the Communist Party in the Michigan area, and the identity of those individuals responsible for its success." H.R. Rep. No. 57, 84th Cong., 1st Sess. 15.

ground that to do so might result in self-incrimination, and that most of these teachers had lost their jobs. It then stated that "the Committee on Un-American Activities approves of this action. . . ." [36] Similarly, as a result of its Michigan investigation, the Committee called upon American labor unions to amend their constitutions, if necessary, in order to deny membership to any Communist Party member.[37] This would, of course, prevent many workers from getting or holding the only kind of jobs their particular skills qualified them for. The Court, today, barely mentions these statements, which, especially when read in the context of past reports by the Committee, show unmistakably what the Committee was doing. I cannot understand why these reports are deemed relevant to a determination of a congressional intent to investigate Communism in education, but irrelevant to any finding of congressional intent to bring about exposure for its own sake or for the purposes of punishment.

I do not question the Committee's patriotism and sincerity in doing all this.[38] I merely feel that it cannot be done by Congress under our Constitution. For, even assuming that the Federal Government can compel witnesses to testify as to Communist affiliations in order to subject them to ridicule and social and economic retaliation, I cannot agree that this is a legislative function. Such publicity is clearly punishment, and the Constitution allows only one way in which people can be convicted and punished. As we said in *Lovett,* "Those who wrote our Constitution well knew the danger inherent in special legislative acts which take away the life, liberty or property of particular named persons because the legislature thinks them guilty of conduct which deserves punishment. *They intended to safeguard the people of this country from punishment without trial by duly constituted courts.*" 328 U.S., at 317. (Italics added.) Thus if Communism is to be made a crime, and Communists are to be subjected to "pains and penalties," I would still hold this conviction bad, for the crime of Communism, like

---

[36] Id. at 17.

[37] "[T]he Committee on Un-American Activities calls upon the American labor movement . . . to amend its constitutions where necessary in order to deny membership to a member of the Communist Party or any other group which dedicates itself to the destruction of America's way of life." Ibid.

[38] Sincerity and patriotism do not, unfortunately, insure against unconstitutional acts. Indeed, some of the most lamentable and tragic deaths of history were instigated by able, patriotic, and sincere men. See generally Mill, *On Liberty* (1885 ed.) 43–8.

all others, can be punished only by court and jury after a trial with all judicial safeguards.

It is no answer to all this to suggest that legislative committees should be allowed to punish if they grant the accused some rules of courtesy or allow him counsel. For the Constitution proscribes *all* bills of attainder by State or Nation, not merely those which lack counsel or courtesy. It does this because the Founders believed that punishment was too serious a matter to be entrusted to any group other than an independent judiciary and a jury of twelve men acting on previously passed, unambiguous laws, with all the procedural safeguards they put in the Constitution as essential to a fair trial—safeguards which included the right to counsel, compulsory process for witnesses, specific indictments, confrontation of accusers, as well as protection against self-incrimination, double jeopardy, and cruel and unusual punishment—in short, due process of law. Cf. *Chambers* v. *Florida*, 309 U.S. 227, 84 L. ed. 716, 60 S. Ct. 472. They believed this because not long before, worthy men had been deprived of their liberties, and indeed their lives, through parliamentary trials without these safeguards. The memory of one of these, John Lilburne—banished and disgraced by a parliamentary committee on penalty of death if he returned to his country—was particularly vivid when our Constitution was written. His attack on trials by such committees and his warning that "what is done unto any one, may be done unto every one" [39] was part of the his-

---

[39] "For certainly it cannot be denied, but if he be really an offender, he is such by the breach of some law, made and published before the fact, and ought by due process of law, and verdict of 12 men, to be thereof convict, and found guilty of such crime; unto which the law also hath prescribed such a punishment agreeable to that our fundamental liberty; which enjoineth than no freeman of England should be adjudged of life, limb, liberty, or estate, but by Juries; a freedom which parliaments in all ages contended to preserve from violation; as the birthright and chief inheritance of the people, as may appear most remarkably in the Petition of Right, which you have stiled that most excellant law.

"And therefore we trust upon second thoughts, being the parliament of England, you will be so far from bereaving us, who have never forfeited our right, of this our native right, and way of Trials by Juries, (for what is done unto any one, may be done unto every one), that you will preserve them entire to us, and to posterity, from the encroachments of any that would innovate upon them. . . .

"And it is believed, that . . . had [the cause] at any time either at first or last been admitted to a trial at law, and had passed any way by verdict of twelve sworn men; all the trouble and inconveniences arising thereupon had been prevented; the way of determination by major votes of committees, being neither so certain nor so satisfactory in any case as by way of Juries, the benefit of challenges and exceptions, and unanimous consent, being all essential privileges in the latter; whereas committees are tied to no such rules, but are at liberty to be present or absent at pleasure. Besides, Juries being birthright, and the other but new and

tory of the times which moved those who wrote our Constitution to determine that no such arbitrary punishments should ever occur here. It it is the protection from arbitrary punishments through the right to a judicial trial with all these safeguards which over the years has distinguished America from lands where drumhead courts and other similar "tribunals" deprive the weak and the unorthodox of life, liberty, and property without due process of law. It is this same right which is denied to Barenblatt, because the Court today fails to see what is here for all to see—that exposure and punishment is the aim of this Committee and the reason for its existence. To deny this is to ignore the Committee's own claims and the reports it has issued ever since it was established. I cannot believe that the nature of our judicial office requires us to be so blind, and must conclude that the Un-American Activities Committee's "identification" and "exposure" of Communists and suspected Communists, like the activities of the Committee in *Kilbourn* v. *Thompson,* amount to an encroachment on the judiciary which bodes ill for the liberties of the people of this land.

Ultimately all the questions in this case really boil down to one —whether we as a people will try fearfully and futilely to preserve democracy by adopting totalitarian methods, or whether in accordance with our traditions and our Constitution we will have the confidence and courage to be free.

I would reverse this conviction.

APPENDIX TO OPINION OF MR. JUSTICE BLACK, DISSENTING

RANDOM SELECTION OF STATEMENTS BY THE HOUSE
UN-AMERICAN ACTIVITIES COMMITTEE ON EXPOSURE
AND PUNISHMENT OF "SUBVERSIVES"

"[T]o inform the American people of the activities of any such organizations . . . is the real purpose of the House Commit-

---

temporary, men do not, nor, as we humbly conceive, ever will acquiesce in the one as in the other; from whence it is not altogether so much to be wondered at, if upon dissatisfactions, there have been such frequent printing of men's cases, and dealings of Committees, as there have been; and such harsh and inordinate heats and expressions between parties interested, such sudden and importunate appeals to your authority, being indeed all alike out of the true English road, and leading into nothing but trouble and perplexity, breeding hatred and enmities between worthy families, affronts and disgust between persons of the same public affection and interest, and to the rejoicing of none but public adversaries. All which, and many more inconveniences, can only be avoided, by referring all such cases to the usual Trials and final determinations of law." *5 Howell's State Trials,* 411–12, Statement of John Lilburne (1653).

tee." "The purpose of this Committee is the task of protecting our constitutional democracy by turning the light of pitiless publicity on [these] organizations." H.R. Rep. No. 1476, 76th Cong., 3d Sess. 1–2, 24.

"The very first exposure which our Committee undertook in the summer of 1938 was that of the German-American Bund"; "Other organizations . . . have been greatly crippled . . . as a result of our exposures. The American Youth Congress once enjoyed a very considerable prestige. . . . Today many of its distinguished former sponsors refuse to be found in its company. . . . We kept the spotlight of publicity focused upon the American Youth Congress, and today it is clear to all that, in spite of a degree of participation in its activities by many fine people, it was never at its core anything less than a tool of Moscow." "This Committee is the only agency of Government that has the power of exposure. . . . There are many phases of un-American activities that cannot be reached by legislation or administrative action. We believe that the Committee has shown that fearless exposure . . . is the . . . answer." H.R. Rep. No. 1, 77th Cong., 1st Sess. 21–2, 24.

"Our investigation has shown that a steady barrage against Congress comes . . . from *The New Republic*, one of whose editors . . . was recently forced out of an $8,000 Government job by the exposure of his Communist activities." H.R. Rep. No. 2277, 77th Cong., 2d Sess. 3.

"[T]he House Committee on Un-American Activities is empowered to explore and expose activities by un-American individuals and organizations which, while sometimes being legal, are nonetheless inimical to our American concepts." The Committee recommends that Congress "discharge . . . any employee or official of the Federal Government whose loyalty to the United States is found to be in doubt." H.R. Rep. No. 2742, 79th Cong., 2d Sess. 16, 17.

"Index of Persons and Organizations." (Six pages of names follow.) H.R. Rep. No. 2233, 79th Cong., 2d Sess. III–VIII.

"Early in 1947 the Committee adopted the following eight point program. . . .

"1. To expose and ferret out the Communists and Communist sympathizers in the Federal Government.

"2. To spotlight the spectacle of . . . Communists . . . in American labor."

"In a sense the storm of opposition to the activities of the Committee is a tribute to its achievements in the field of exposure." Report of the Committee on Un-American Activities to the United States House of Representatives, 80th Cong., 2d Sess., Dec. 31, 1948, 2, 3 (Committee print).

"The Committee would like to remind the Congress that its work is part of an 11-year continuity of effort that began . . . in August 1938. The Committee would also like to recall that at no time in those 11 years has it ever wavered from a relentless pursuit and exposure." "In the course of its investigations . . . the Committee has made available a large, completely indexed, and readily accessible reference collection of lists of signers of Communist Party election petitions." H.R. Rep. No. 1950, 81st Cong., 2d Sess. 15, 19.

"To conduct the exposé . . . it was necessary for the investigative staff to interview over 100 persons. . . .

"The same tedious investigation of details was necessary prior to the successful exposure . . . in the Territory of Hawaii." "As a result of the investigation and hearings held by the Committee, Dolivet's contract with the United Nations has not been renewed, and it is the Committee's understanding that he was removed from editorship of the *United Nations World*." H.R. Rep. No. 3249, 81st Cong., 2 Sess. 4, 5.

"During 1951 the Committee's hearings disclosed the positive identification of more individuals . . . than during any preceding year." "If Communism in Hollywood is now mythical, it is only because this Committee conducted three investigations to bring it about. The industry itself certainly did not accomplish this." "The Committee's investigation . . . was concerned almost entirely with the problem of exposure of the actual members of the Communist Party and did not deal, except in a few instances, with . . . fellow travelers." "On the question of fellow travelers, suffice it to say . . . 'The time has come now when even the fellow traveler must get out.'" "Dr. Struik was identified as a Communist teacher. . . . Nevertheless he was permitted to teach . . . until this year." "With individuals like . . . Struik . . . teaching in our leading universities, your Committee wonders who the Professor Struiks were . . . who led Alger Hiss along the road of Communism." H.R. Rep. No. 2431, 82d Cong., 2d Sess. 6, 8–9, 16–17.

"In this annual report the Committee feels that the Congress and the American people will have a much clearer and fuller picture . . . by having set forth the names and, where possible, the positions occupied by individuals who have been identified as Communists, or former Communists, during the past year." "The Committee considers the failure of certain trade-unionists to rid themselves of Communists to be a national disgrace." "The following persons were identified." (Approximately fifty pages of names follow.) H.R. Rep. No. 2516, 82d Cong., 2 Sess. 6–7, 12–27, 28–34, 36–40, 41–56, 58–67 (similar lists can be found in various other reports).

"The focal point of the investigation into the general area of education was to the individual who had been identified." "The question has been asked as to what purpose is served by the disclosure of the names of individuals who may long ago have left the conspiracy." "The Committee has no way of knowing the status of his membership at present until he is placed under oath and the information is sought to be elicited." H.R. No. 1192, 83d Cong., 2d Sess. 1, 7.

Kingsley International Pictures Corporation v. Regents

360 U.S. 684

—————

Decided June 29, 1959

The case of Burstyn *v.* Wilson, *decided in 1952, is a landmark in the Supreme Court's application of the First Amendment's protection of free expression. In it, for the first time, the freedom that is guaranteed to the press was extended to motion pictures. At issue was the exhibition in New York City of Roberto Rossellini's film* The Miracle, *which was produced, directed, and acted in Italy by Roman Catholics, with Anna Magnani in the leading role. After generally favorable reviews in the Italian press, including L'Osservatore Romano,* the Vatican newspaper, The Miracle *was shown freely in Italy. When exhibition was undertaken in New York, Cardinal Spellman condemned the film as "vile," "despicable," and "sacrilegious." At masses in St. Patrick's Cathedral, on Sunday, January 7, 1951, he read a statement calling on "all right-thinking citizens" to boycott the theater and to join in tightening censorship laws. The controversy, which included the picketing of the theater by groups of Roman Catholics and the banning of the film by municipal and state authorities, went through the New York courts. With two dissents, the New York Court of Appeals upheld the ban.*

By its unanimous decision, which demonstrated strikingly the role of the Supreme Court as protector of our basic liberties, the highest tribunal reversed the New York courts. Justice Clark, speaking also for Chief Justice Vinson and Justices Black, Douglas, and Minton, held that the constitutional guarantee of free speech and press prevented a state from suppressing a film on the basis of a conclusion by a censor that the film was "sacrilegious." Justice Reed concurred, but noted that the Court's opinion did not foreclose a licensing system for motion pictures. Justice Frankfurter, in a concurrence joined by Justices Jackson and Burton, found the term "sacrilegious" too vague.

Two years later the New York Legislature amended its motion-picture licensing law in an effort to make it more specific and thus meet the objections of the Supreme Court. Under the revised statute, a film version of D. H. Lawrence's novel Lady Chatterley's Lover *was refused a license by the New York Education Department's Motion Picture Division on the ground that three scenes were "immoral" within the meaning of the amended law. The New York courts divided sharply on the issue. The 4-to-3 ruling of the New York Court of Appeals, which upheld the refusal to license, however, unanimously and explicitly rejected any notion that the film was obscene.*

This new test of film censorship reached the Supreme Court in Kingsley International Pictures Corporation *v.* Regents of the University of the State of New York. *Six of the nine Justices wrote opinions. Justice Stewart, speaking also for Chief Justice Warren and Justices Black, Douglas, and Brennan, reversed the New York ban and held, moreover, that the New York statute, as interpreted by the New York Court of Appeals, was unconstitutional under the First and Fourteenth Amendments. Justices Black and Douglas, in concurring opinions, made it plain that they believed all prior censorship of motion pictures violates the Constitution. Justice Frankfurter, concurring separately, agreed that the State trespassed on free expression, but said that he thought the Court's opinion exceeded appropriate limits in the ground it covered. Also concurring, Justice Clark held that the statute, after its amendment, was still too vague to be constitutional. Justice Harlan, joined by Justices Frankfurter and Whittaker, concurred in the result, saying that New York had gone beyond constitutional bounds in banning* Lady Chatterley's Lover, *but that the decision went too far in voiding the law. The belief that the Supreme Court must necessarily handle these censorship controversies on a "case-by-case" basis was expressed in several of these opinions.*

This multiplicity of opinions in one case, with the expression of so many individual views on film censorship, including support for instance-by-instance appraisal by judges, led Justice Black to deliver a short but fundamental reflection on the role of the Supreme Court with respect to censorship of ideas and morals among a free people.

Mr. Justice Black, *concurring*

I concur in the Court's opinion and judgment but add a few words because of concurring opinions by several Justices who rely on their appraisal of the movie *Lady Chatterley's Lover* for holding that New York cannot constitutionally bar it. Unlike them, I have not seen the picture. My view is that stated by Mr. Justice Douglas, that prior censorship of moving pictures, like prior censorship of newspapers and books, violates the First and Fourteenth Amendments. If despite the Constitution, however, this Nation is to embark on the dangerous road of censorship, my belief is that this Court is about the most inappropriate Supreme Board of Censors that could be found. So far as I know, judges possess no special expertise providing exceptional competency to set standards and to supervise the private morals of the Nation. In addition, the Justices of this Court seem especially unsuited to make the kind of value judgments—as to what movies are good or bad for local communities—which the concurring opinions appear to require. We are told that the only way we can decide whether a state or municipality can constitutionally bar movies is for this Court to view and appraise each movie on a case-by-case basis. Under these circumstances, every member of the Court must exercise his own judgment as to how bad a picture is, a judgment which is ultimately based at least in large part on his own standard of what is immoral. The end result of such decisions seems to me to be a purely personal determination by individual Justices as to whether a particular picture viewed is too bad to allow it to be seen by the public. Such an individualized determination cannot be guided by reasonably fixed and certain standards. Accordingly, neither States nor moving picture makers can possibly know in advance, with any fair degree of certainty, what can or cannot be done in the field of movie making and exhibiting. This uncertainty cannot easily be reconciled with the rule of law which our Constitution envisages.

The different standards which different people may use to decide about the badness of pictures are well illustrated by the contrasting standards mentioned in the opinion of the New York Court of Appeals and the concurring opinion of Mr. Justice Frankfurter here. As I read the New York court's opinion, this movie was held immoral and banned because it makes adultery too alluring. Mr. Justice Frankfurter quotes Mr. Lawrence, author of the book from which the movie was made, as believing censorship should be applied only to publications that make sex look ugly, that is, as I understand it, less alluring.

In my judgment, this Court should not permit itself to get into the very center of such policy controversies, which have so little in common with lawsuits.

Smith v. California

361 U.S. 147

Decided December 14, 1959

A city ordinance made it unlawful for any person in Los Angeles, California, to have in his possession any obscene or indecent book in any place where books were sold or kept for sale. As the proprietor of a bookstore, Eleazar Smith was charged and convicted under the ordinance in a Municipal Court where the ordinance was interpreted as imposing a "strict" criminal liability without requiring knowledge by the defendant of the contents of the book in his possession as obscene. Smith's contention that this construing of the ordinance was in conflict with the Bill of Rights was rejected on appeal in California.

In the United States Supreme Court, where the case appeared as Eleazar Smith v. People of the State of California, *all nine members found the conviction invalid and reversed it. Justice Brennan wrote the Court's opinion, which was joined by Chief Justice Warren and Justices Clark, Whittaker, and Stewart. This opinion held that the ordinance, in failing to require knowledge on the part of the bookseller of the obscene matter in the book, had so great a tendency to restrict free expression as to render the ordinance unconstitutional.*

Justices Black, Frankfurter, and Douglas wrote separate concurring opinions and Justice Harlan filed an opinion that was partly concurring and partly dissenting. The Frankfurter and Harlan opinions took notice of the fact that the trial court excluded appropriately offered testimony through qualified witnesses about the prevailing literary standards in Los Angeles and relevant literary and moral criteria for books. In his opinion, Justice Black stated as plainly as words could his deep-seated belief that censorship is the enemy of progress and that the Constitution was wise to bar it.

MR. JUSTICE BLACK, *concurring*

The appellant was sentenced to prison for possessing in his bookstore an "obscene" book in violation of a Los Angeles city ordinance. I concur in the judgment holding that ordinance unconstitutional, but not for the reasons given in the Court's opinion.

The Court invalidates the ordinance solely because it penalizes a bookseller for mere possession of an "obscene" book, even though he is unaware of its obscenity. The grounds on which the Court draws a constitutional distinction between a law that punishes possession of a book with knowledge of its "obscenity" and a law that punishes without such knowledge are not persuasive to me. Those grounds are that conviction of a bookseller for possession of an "obscene" book when he is unaware of its obscenity "will tend to restrict the books he sells to those he has inspected," and therefore "may tend to work a substantial restriction on freedom of speech." The fact is, of course, that prison sentences for possession of "obscene" books will seriously burden freedom of the press whether punishment is imposed with or without knowledge of the obscenity. The Court's opinion correctly points out how little extra burden will be imposed on prosecutors by requiring proof that a bookseller was aware of a book's contents when he possessed it. And if the Constitution's requirement of knowledge is so easily met, the result of this case is that one particular bookseller gains his freedom, but the way is left open for state censorship and punishment of all other booksellers by merely adding a few new words to old censorship laws. Our constitutional safeguards for speech and press therefore gain little. Their victory, if any, is a Pyrrhic one.

That it is apparently intended to leave the way open for both Federal and State Governments to abridge speech and press (to the extent this Court approves) is also indicated by the following statements in the Court's opinion: " 'The door barring federal and state intrusion into this area [freedom of speech and press] cannot be left ajar; it must be kept tightly closed and opened only the slightest crack necessary to prevent encroachment upon more important interests.' . . . . This ordinance opens that door too far."

This statement raises a number of questions for me. What are the "more important" interests for the protection of which constitutional freedom of speech and press must be given second place? What is the standard by which one can determine when abridgment of speech and press goes "too far" and when it is slight enough to be constitutionally allowable? Is this momentous decision to be left to a majority of this Court on a case-by-case basis? What express provision or provisions of the Constitution put freedom of speech and press in this precarious position of subordination and insecurity?

Certainly the First Amendment's language leaves no room for inference that abridgments of speech and press can be made just because they are slight. That Amendment provides, in simple words, that "Congress shall make no law . . . abridging the freedom of speech, or of the press." I read "no law abridging" to mean *no law abridging*. The First Amendment, which is the supreme law of the land, has thus fixed its own value on freedom of speech and press by putting these freedoms wholly "beyond the reach" of *federal* power to abridge. No other provision of the Constitution purports to dilute the scope of these unequivocal commands of the First Amendment. Consequently, I do not believe that any federal agencies, including Congress and this Court, have power or authority to subordinate speech and press to what they think are "more important interests." The contrary notion is, in my judgment, court-made not Constitution-made.

State intrusion or abridgment of freedom of speech and press raises a different question, since the First Amendment by its terms refers only to laws passed by Congress. But I adhere to our prior decisions holding that the Fourteenth Amendment made the First applicable to the States. It follows that I am for reversing this case because I believe that the Los Angeles ordinance sets up a censorship in violation of the First and Fourteenth Amendments.

If, as it seems, we are on the way to national censorship, I think it timely to suggest again that there are grave doubts in my mind as to the desirability or constitutionality of this Court's becoming a Supreme Board of Censors—reading books and viewing television performances to determine whether, if permitted, they might adversely affect the morals of the people throughout the many diversified local communities in this vast country. It is true that the ordinance here is on its face only applicable to "obscene or indecent writing." It is also true that this particular kind of censorship is considered by many to be "the obnoxious thing in its mildest and least repulsive form . . ." But "illegitimate and unconstitutional practices get their first footing in that way. . . . It is the duty of courts to be watchful for the constitutional rights of the citizen, and against any stealthy encroachments thereon." While it is "obscenity and indecency" before us today, the experience of mankind—both ancient and modern—shows that this type of elastic phrase can, and most likely will, be synonymous with the political, and maybe with the religious unorthodoxy of tomorrow.

Censorship is the deadly enemy of freedom and progress. The plain language of the Constitution forbids it. I protest against the judiciary giving it a foothold here.

Bates v. Little Rock

361 U.S. 516

Decided February 23, 1960

One consequence of the application of the Supreme Court's decision in the school desegregation cases joined in Brown v. Board of Education of Topeka *(1954) was a series of controversies and court tests in Little Rock, Arkansas. Under ordinances that levied an occupation license tax in Little Rock and North Little Rock, organizations operating in the communities were required to submit to municipal authorities the names of all their members. Officers of the Little Rock organization of the National Association for the Advancement of Colored People refused to submit a list of its membership. They were convicted in a state court and the convictions were upheld in the Arkansas Supreme Court, two justices dissenting.*

The case went to the United States Supreme Court as Daisy Bates et al. *v.* City of Little Rock et al. *on certiorari and the Arkansas courts were unanimously reversed in a decision handed down by Justice Stewart. The basis of the ruling was that the defendants had not enjoyed due process under the Fourteenth Amendment inasmuch as the cities of Little Rock and North Little Rock had failed to demonstrate a controlling justification for the deterrence of free association which compulsory disclosure of the membership rolls would produce. Joining with Justice Stewart were Chief Justice Warren and Justices Frankfurter, Clark, Harlan, Brennan, and Whittaker.*

Justices Black and Douglas concurred in the Court's judgment

*and agreed substantially with the opinion, but they wrote a sepa-
rate concurrence expressing the view that the ordinances of the
two communities as applied were in violation of free speech and
free assembly and so in conflict with the First Amendment made
applicable to the States by the Fourteenth Amendment.*

MR. JUSTICE BLACK *and* MR. JUSTICE DOUGLAS, *concurring*

We concur in the judgment and substantially with the opinion
because we think the facts show that the ordinances as here applied
violate freedom of speech and assembly guaranteed by the First
Amendment, which this Court has many times held was made applicable to the States by the Fourteenth Amendment.

Moreover, we believe, as we indicated in *United States* v.
Rumely, that First Amendment rights are beyond abridgment
either by legislation that directly restrains their exercise or by
suppression or impairment through harassment, humiliation, or
exposure by government. One of those rights, freedom of assembly,
includes of course freedom of association; and it is entitled to
no less protection than any other First Amendment right as
N.A.A.C.P. v. *Alabama* and *DeJonge* v. *Oregon* hold. These are
principles applicable to all people under our Constitution irrespective of their race, color, politics, or religion. That is, for us, the
essence of the present opinion of the Court.

Talley v. California

362 U.S. 60

Decided March 7, 1960

City councils, although operating with good intentions, all too frequently have trespassed on the Constitution's protection of freedom of speech, press, and religion. This has happened in many instances because the municipal authorities have passed ordinances designed to regulate the distribution of handbills in the interest, for example, of unlittered sidewalks and streets. But not a few of these handbill ordinances have called for censorship or license in the areas of thought and expression and as a consequence have been held invalid.

Such a test arose in Los Angeles where the ordinance prohibited anonymous or fictitiously signed political advertising on handbills or leaflets. For the case, Manuel D. Talley v. California, Justice Black delivered the majority opinion, which found the ordinance invalid on its face. Supporting the Court's opinion were Chief Justice Warren and Justices Douglas, Brennan, and Stewart. Justice Harlan concurred in a separate opinion, and Justice Clark wrote a dissenting opinion, which Justices Frankfurter and Whittaker joined.

In a footnote, Justice Black pointed out that "some of Thomas Paine's pamphlets were signed with pseudonyms."

Mr. Justice Black *delivered the opinion of the Court*

The question presented here is whether the provisions of a Los Angeles City ordinance restricting the distribution of handbills "abridge the freedom of speech and of the press secured against state invasion by the Fourteenth Amendment of the Constitution." The ordinance, Section 28.06 of the Municipal Code of the City of Los Angeles, provides:

> No person shall distribute any hand-bill in any place under any circumstances, which does not have printed on the cover, or the face thereof, the name and address of the following:
>
> (a) The person who printed, wrote, compiled or manufactured the same.
>
> (b) The person who caused the same to be distributed; provided, however, that in the case of a fictitious person or club, in addition to such fictitious name, the true names and addresses of the owners, managers or agents of the person sponsoring said handbill shall also appear thereon.

The petitioner was arrested and tried in a Los Angeles Municipal Court for violating this ordinance. It was stipulated that the petitioner had distributed handbills in Los Angeles, and two of them were presented in evidence. Each had printed on it the following:

> National Consumers Mobilization,
> Box 6533,
> Los Angeles 55, Calif.
> PLeasant 9–1576.

The handbills urged readers to help the organization carry on a boycott against certain merchants and businessmen, whose names were given, on the ground that, as one set of handbills said, they carried products of "manufacturers who will not offer equal employment opportunities to Negroes, Mexicans, and Orientals." There also appeared a blank, which, if signed, would request enrollment of the signer as a "member of National Consumers Mobilization," and which was preceded by a statement that "I believe that every man should have an equal opportunity for employment no matter what his race, religion, or place of birth."

The Municipal Court held that the information printed on the handbills did not meet the requirements of the ordinance, found the petitioner guilty as charged, and fined him $10. The Appellate Department of the Superior Court of the County of Los Angeles affirmed the conviction, rejecting petitioner's contention, timely made in both state courts, that the ordinance invaded his freedom of speech and press in violation of the Fourteenth and First Amendments to the Federal Constitution. Since this was the highest state court available to petitioner, we granted *certiorari* to it to consider this constitutional contention.

In *Lovell* v. *Griffin*, we held void on its face an ordinance that comprehensively forbade any distribution of literature at any time or place in Griffin, Georgia, without a license. Pamphlets and leaflets, it was pointed out, "have been historic weapons in the defense of liberty" and enforcement of the Griffin ordinance "would restore the system of license and censorship in its baldest form." A year later we had before us four ordinances each forbidding distribution of leaflets—one in Irvington, New Jersey, one in Los Angeles, California, one in Milwaukee, Wisconsin, and one in Worcester, Massachusetts. Efforts were made to distinguish these four ordinances from the one held void in the *Griffin Case*. The chief grounds urged for distinction were that the four ordinances had been passed to prevent either frauds, disorder, or littering, according to the records in these cases, and another ground urged was that two of the ordinances applied only to certain city areas. This Court refused to uphold the four ordinances on those grounds pointing out that there were other ways to accomplish these legitimate aims without abridging freedom of speech and press. Frauds, street littering, and disorderly conduct could be denounced and punished as offenses, the Court said. Several years later we followed the *Griffin* and *Schneider Cases* in striking down a Dallas, Texas, ordinance which was applied to prohibit the dissemination of information by the distribution of handbills. We said that although a city could punish any person for conduct on the streets if he violates a valid law, "one who is rightfully on a street . . . carries with him there as elsewhere the constitutional right to express his views in an orderly fashion . . . by handbills and literature as well as by the spoken word."

The broad ordinance now before us, barring distribution of "any hand-bill in any place under any circumstances," falls precisely under the ban of our prior cases unless this ordinance is saved by the qualification that handbills can be distributed if they have printed on them the names and addresses of the persons who prepared, distributed, or sponsored them. For, as in *Griffin*, the ordinance here is not limited to handbills whose content is "obscene or offensive to public morals or that advocates unlawful conduct." Counsel has urged that this ordinance is aimed at providing a way to identify those responsible for fraud, false advertising, and libel. Yet the ordinance is in no manner so limited, nor have we been referred to any legislative history indicating such a purpose. Therefore, we do not pass on the validity of an ordinance limited to prevent these or any other supposed evils. This ordinance simply bars all handbills under all circumstances anywhere that do not have the printed names and addresses on them in the place the ordinance requires.

There can be no doubt that such an identification requirement would tend to restrict freedom to distribute information and thereby freedom of expression. "Liberty of circulating is as essential to that freedom as liberty of publishing; indeed, without the circulation, the publication would be of little value."

Anonymous pamphlets, leaflets, brochures, and even books have played an important role in the progress of mankind. Persecuted groups and sects from time to time throughout history have been able to criticize oppressive practices and laws either anonymously or not at all. The obnoxious press licensing law of England, which was also enforced on the Colonies was due in part to the knowledge that exposure of the names of printers, writers, and distributors would lessen the circulation of literature critical of the government. The old seditious libel cases in England show the lengths to which government had to go to find out who was responsible for books that were obnoxious to the rulers. John Lilburne was whipped, pilloried, and fined for refusing to answer questions designed to get evidence to convict him or someone else for the secret distribution of books in England. Two Puritan Ministers, John Penry and John Udall, were sentenced to death on charges that they were responsible for writing, printing, or publishing books. Before the Revolutionary War colonial patriots frequently had to conceal their authorship or distribution of literature that easily could have brought down on them prosecutions by English-controlled courts. Along about that time the Letters of Junius were written and the identity of their author is unknown to this day. Even the Federalist Papers, written in favor of the adoption of our Constitution, were published under fictitious names. It is plain that anonymity has sometimes been assumed for the most constructive purposes.

We have recently had occasion to hold in two cases that there are times and circumstances when States may not compel members of groups engaged in the dissemination of ideas to be publicly identified. The reason for those holdings was that identification and fear of reprisal might deter perfectly peaceful discussions of public matters of importance. This broad Los Angeles ordinance is subject to the same infirmity. We hold that it, like the Griffin, Georgia, ordinance, is void on its face.

The judgment of the Appellate Department of the Superior Court of the State of California is reversed and the cause is remanded to it for further proceedings not inconsistent with this opinion.

It is so ordered.

Thompson v. Louisville

362 U.S. 199

Decided March 21, 1960

Sam Thompson is one American who knows what the Supreme Court can do in protecting the rights of a rank-and-file citizen of little means. A long-time Negro resident of Louisville, Kentucky, he was convicted under a local ordinance that made it unlawful for any person without visible means of support or unable to give a satisfactory account of himself to "loaf or trespass in any premises" without first having obtained the consent of the owner or controller of the place. How the petitioner happened to be arrested, tried, and found guilty and why the Supreme Court reversed the judgment all are clearly stated in the unanimous opinion in Sam Thompson v. City of Louisville. *Written during a period when Justice Black so often found it necessary to break from the majority in Bill of Rights tests, this opinion happily enjoyed the support of all his brethren on the highest bench: Chief Justice Warren and Justices Douglas, Frankfurter, Clark, Harlan, Brennan, Whittaker, and Stewart.*

MR. JUSTICE BLACK *delivered the opinion of the Court*

Petitioner was found guilty in the Police Court of Louisville, Kentucky, of two offenses—loitering and disorderly conduct. The ultimate question presented to us is whether the charges against petitioner were so totally devoid of evidentiary support as to render his conviction unconstitutional under the Due Process Clause of the Fourteenth Amendment. Decision of this question turns not on the sufficiency of the evidence, but on whether this conviction rests upon any evidence at all.

The facts as shown by the record are short and simple. Petitioner, a long-time resident of the Louisville area, went into the Liberty End Cafe about 6:20 on a Saturday evening, January 24, 1959. In addition to selling food, the cafe was licensed to sell beer to the public and some 12 to 30 patrons were present during the time petitioner was there. When petitioner had been in the cafe about half an hour, two Louisville police officers came in on a "routine check." Upon seeing petitioner "out there on the floor dancing by himself," one of the officers, according to his testimony, went up to the manager who was sitting on a stool nearby and asked him how long petitioner had been in there and if he had bought anything. The officer testified that upon being told by the manager that petitioner had been there "a little over a half-hour and that he had not bought anything," he accosted Thompson and "asked him what was his reason for being in there and he said he was waiting on a bus." The officer then informed petitioner that he was under arrest and took him outside. This was the arrest for loitering. After going outside, the officer testified, petitioner "was very argumentative—he argued with us back and forth and so then we placed a disorderly conduct charge on him." Admittedly the disorderly conduct conviction rests solely on this one sentence description of petitioner's conduct after he left the cafe.

The foregoing evidence includes all that the city offered against him, except a record purportedly showing a total of 54 previous arrests of petitioner. Before putting on his defense, petitioner moved for a dismissal of the charges against him on the ground that a judgment of conviction on this record would deprive him of property and liberty without due process of law under the Fourteenth Amendment in that (1) there was no evidence to support findings of guilt and (2) the two arrests and prosecutions were reprisals against him because petitioner had employed counsel and demanded a judicial hearing to defend himself against prior and allegedly baseless charges by the police. This motion was denied.

Petitioner then put in evidence on his own behalf, none of which in any way strengthened the city's case. He testified that he bought, and one of the cafe employees served him, a dish of macaroni and a glass of beer and that he remained in the cafe waiting for a bus to go home. Further evidence showed without dispute that at the time of his arrest petitioner gave the officers his home address; that he had money with him, and a bus schedule showing that a bus to his home would stop within half a block of the cafe at about 7:30; that he owned two unimproved lots of land; that in addition to work he had done for others, he had regularly worked one day or more a week for the same family for thirty years; that he paid no rent in the home where he lived and that his meager income was sufficient to meet his needs. The cafe manager testified that petitioner had frequently patronized the cafe, and that he had never told petitioner that he was unwelcome there. The manager further testified that on this very occasion he saw petitioner "standing there in the middle of the floor and patting his foot," and that he did not at any time during petitioner's stay there object to anything he was doing. There is no evidence that anyone else in the cafe objected to petitioner's shuffling his feet in rhythm with the music of the juke box or that his conduct was boisterous or offensive to anyone present. At the close of his evidence, petitioner repeated his motion for dismissal of the charges on the ground that a conviction on the foregoing evidence would deprive him of liberty and property without due process under the Fourteenth Amendment. The court denied the motion, convicted him of both offenses, and fined him $10 on each charge. A motion for new trial, on the same grounds, also was denied, which exhausted petitioner's remedies in the police court.

Since police court fines of less than $20 on a single charge are not appealable or otherwise reviewable in any other Kentucky court, petitioner asked the police court to stay the judgments so that he might have an opportunity to apply for *certiorari* to this Court (before his case became moot) to review the due process contentions he raised. The police court suspended judgment for 24 hours, during which time petitioner sought a longer stay from the Kentucky Circuit Court. That court, after examining the police court's judgments and transcript, granted a stay concluding that "there appears to be merit" in the contention that "there is no evidence upon which conviction and sentence by the Police Court could be based" and that petitioner's "Federal Constitutional claims are substantial and not frivolous." On appeal by the city, the Kentucky Court of Appeals held that the Circuit Court lacked the power to grant the stay it did, but nevertheless went on to take the extraordinary step of granting its own stay, even though petitioner had made no original application to that court for such a stay. Explaining its reason, the Court of Appeals took occasion to agree with the Circuit Court that petitioner's "Federal Constitutional claims are substantial and not frivolous." The Court of Appeals then went on to say that petitioner

> appears to have a real question as to whether he has been denied due process under the Fourteenth Amendment of the Federal Constitution, yet this substantive right cannot be tested unless we grant him a stay of execution because his fines are not appealable and will be satisfied by being served in jail before he can prepare and file his petition for certiorari. Appellee's substantive right of due process is of no avail to him unless this court grants him the ancillary right whereby he may test same in the Supreme Court.

Our examination of the record presented in the petition for *certiorari* convinced us that although the fines here are small, the due process questions presented are substantial and we therefore granted *certiorari* to review the police court's judgments.

The city correctly assumes here that if there is no support for these convictions in the record they are void as denials of due process. The pertinent portion of the city ordinance under which petitioner was convicted of loitering reads as follows:

> It shall be unlawful for any person . . . , without visible means of support, or who cannot give a satisfactory account of himself, . . . to sleep, lie, loaf, or trespass in or about any premises, building, or other structure in the City of Louisville, without first having obtained the consent of the owner or controller of said premises, structure, or building; . . . (Section 85–12, Ordinances of the City of Louisville).

In addition to the fact that petitioner proved he had "visible means of support," the prosecutor at trial said: "This is a loitering charge here. There is no charge of no visible means of support." Moreover, there is no suggestion that petitioner was sleeping, lying, or trespassing in or about this cafe. Accordingly, he could only have been convicted for being unable to give a satisfactory account of himself while loitering in the cafe, without the consent of the manager. Under the words of the ordinance itself, if the evidence fails to prove all three elements of this loitering charge, the conviction is not supported by evidence, in which event it does not comport with due process of law. The record is entirely lacking in evidence to support any of the charges.

Here, petitioner spent about half an hour on a Saturday evening in January in a public cafe which sold food and beer to the public. When asked to account for his presence there, he said he was waiting for a bus. The city concedes that the is no law making it an offense for a person in such a cafe to "dance," "shuffle," or "pat" his feet in time to music. The undisputed testimony of the manager, who did not know whether petitioner had bought macaroni and beer or not but who did see the patting, shuffling, or dancing, was that petitioner was welcome there. The manager testified that he did not, at any time during petitioner's stay in the cafe, object to anything petitioner was doing and that he never saw petitioner do anything that would cause any objection. Surely this is implied consent, which the city admitted in oral argument satisfies the ordinance. The arresting officer admitted that there was nothing in any way "vulgar" about what he called petitioner's "ordinary dance," whatever relevance, if any, vulgarity might have to a charge of loitering. There simply is no semblance of evidence from which any person could reasonably infer that petitioner could not give a satisfactory account of himself or that he was loitering or loafing there (in the ordinary sense of the words) without "the consent of the owner or controller" of the cafe.

Petitioner's conviction for disorderly conduct was under Section 85–8 of the city ordinance which, without definition, provides that "whoever shall be found guilty of disorderly conduct in the City of Louisville shall be fined . . ." etc. The only evidence of "disorderly conduct" was the single statement of the policeman that after petitioner was arrested and taken out of the cafe he was very argumentative. There is no testimony that petitioner raised his voice, used offensive language, resisted the officers, or engaged in any conduct of any kind likely in any way to adversely affect the good order and tranquillity of the City of Louisville. The only information the record contains on what the petitioner was "argumentative" about is his statement that he asked the officers "what they arrested me for." We assume, for we are justified in assuming, that merely "arguing" with a policeman is not, because it could not be, "disorderly conduct" as a matter of the substantive law of Kentucky. Moreover, Kentucky law itself seems to provide that if a man wrongfully arrested fails to object to the arresting officer, he waives any right to complain later that the arrest was unlawful.

Thus we find no evidence whatever in the record to support these convictions. Just as "Conviction upon a charge not made would be sheer denial of due process," so is it a violation of due process to convict and punish a man without evidence of his guilt.

The judgments are reversed and the cause is remanded to the Police Court of the City of Louisville for proceedings not inconsistent with this opinion.

Reversed and remanded.

Uphaus v. Wyman

364 U.S. 388

Decided November 14, 1960

One of the most distressing cases in Justice Black's quarter century on the Supreme Court was that of Willard Uphaus, a teacher of religious education and a Christian peace advocate who, at the age of seventy, served a year in jail rather than bear, as he saw it, "false witness against his neighbor." In addition to the facts given in the opinion, it may be noted that this Methodist lay leader was born to religious parents on a farm near Muncie, Indiana; that he attended both Earlham College, a Quaker institution, and Indiana University, where he received a degree in 1917, by working his way through; that he volunteered for the Army in World War I but was rejected for physical reasons. He received a master's degree in religious education at Yale University in 1922 and a doctorate in 1925.

He taught at Vanderbilt, Howard, and Hastings College in Nebraska. At Hastings his theological views brought on a conflict with the college authorities. When he was asked to resign, six of his associates on the faculty resigned in a joint protest. He then returned to Yale as a professor of religion and higher education. In the New Deal years, he was executive secretary of the Religion and Labor Foundation, which was designed to bring the churches and working people closer together. After World War II, he attended peace sessions abroad, including one in Warsaw for which he was criticized because it was behind the Iron Curtain. His wife, the former Ola Hawkins Dudley, was a missionary in China for seventeen years before their marriage in 1938.

Dr. Uphaus became executive director of World Fellowship, Inc., in 1953, and it was in connection with that organization's public discussion program at a summer camp near Conway, New Hampshire, that he entered constitutional history as a "First Amendment defendant." He freely answered questions about himself in the one-man investigation of alleged subversive activities conducted by Louis C. Wyman, as Attorney General of New Hampshire. But his respectful though unshakable refusal to give Wyman the names of the camp's guests brought him a citation for contempt, which was upheld by the New Hampshire Supreme Court 3 to 2, and also by the United States Supreme Court in the 5-to-4 decision of Willard Uphaus v. Louis C. Wyman *(360 U.S. 72), delivered June 8, 1959. Justice Clark wrote the majority opinion, supported by Justices Frankfurter, Harlan, Whittaker, and Stewart. Justice Brennan's strong dissent was joined by Chief Justice Warren and Justices Black and Douglas.*

On December 14, 1959, Dr. Uphaus began serving his indefinite term in the Merrimack County Jail, Boscawen, New Hampshire, and efforts to clear him continued. One proceeding was based on a change in the pertinent New Hampshire law after the contempt finding. Out of this came a nine-line per curiam *decision by the Supreme Court that dismissed the appeal for "want of jurisdiction." Although Justice Brennan held to his view of the 1959 case, he now stated he could not see a "substantial federal question" in the 1960 case. The summary dismissal of the new proceeding deeply disturbed Justice Black, who wrote one of his most memorable dissents, with the concurrence of Chief Justice Warren and Justice Douglas. This opinion takes a high place among Justice Black's testaments to freedom.*

MR. JUSTICE BLACK, *with whom* THE CHIEF JUSTICE *and* MR. JUSTICE DOUGLAS *concur, dissenting*

I concur in the dissent of Mr. Justice Douglas and agree with him that since the New Hampshire law upheld by this Court in *Uphaus* v. *Wyman*, 360 U.S. 72, has now been changed, new federal questions are presented which cannot be dismissed as involving only the correctness of a ruling on local law, and that we consequently should not dismiss this appeal but should note jurisdiction, grant bail, and hear arguments. The recent amendment withdrew the power, involved in the previous appeal, which authorized the

Attorney General of New Hampshire "to determine whether subversive persons . . . are presently located within" the State, and
thus took away the very power under which the Attorney General
was acting when he demanded the names of guests at the summer
camp in New Hampshire managed by the appellant, Dr. Willard
Uphaus. Notwithstanding that fact, the New Hampshire courts
have held that the State still has an interest in those names sufficient
to justify the continued imprisonment of Dr. Uphaus for his refusal
to comply with the demand to produce them. This appeal therefore raises federal questions as to whether this latter holding violates
the Federal Constitution. I think that the Court's action today in
treating those federal questions as insubstantial is wrong in at least
two different respects.

First, I think this action is inconsistent with the Court's own
test as set forth in its opinion on the prior appeal and there used to
square the imprisonment of Dr. Uphaus with the First Amendment.
That test was stated in these terms: "The interest of the guests at
World Fellowship in their associational privacy having been asserted, we have for decision the federal question of whether the
public interests overbalance these conflicting private ones." This
required the Court to weigh the interest of those guests against
the interest of the State, as broadly expressed by its legislature, in
knowing "whether subversive persons . . . are presently located
within" the State, a balancing process which there resulted in the
conclusion that the state interest must prevail. Now, however, it
is clear that the interest of the State so weighed no longer exists
and a new balance must be made if the invasion of "associational
privacy" previously sanctioned is to be permitted to continue. But
this the Court refuses to do, apparently on the theory that the present appeal is controlled by the previous disposition. It seems to me
that "balancing" which refuses to take note of such an important
change in the interest of the State is little balancing at all—a mere
illusion, in fact.

Secondly, it seems to me that the record as it now stands before this Court requires a reappraisal of the question whether the
actions of the State of New Hampshire constitute a bill of attainder
in violation of Article I, Section 10, of the Constitution. On the
prior appeal, the majority of this Court held that the record *as it
then stood* would not justify such a conclusion. The present record,
however, presents new facts relevant to that issue. For here we are
confronted with a situation in which the courts of New Hampshire

have stated that it was the intention of the legislature of that State to permit the Attorney General to single out Dr. Uphaus and any others (if, indeed, there are any others) against whom investigative proceedings had already been commenced and to pursue those proceedings, not in furtherance of any general aim of the State—that general aim, if it ever existed, has been abandoned by the amendment—but apparently for the sole purpose of setting these people off for special treatment. What this special treatment is to be is clearly shown by the brief filed before this Court in this appeal by the State Attorney General himself, who administers the Act. That brief states unequivocally that "[t]hose who voluntarily and knowingly appear with, consult with, confer with, attend functions with and otherwise act in concert with Communists or former Communists in America cannot possibly have any reasonable right of privacy in regard to such activities. . . ." In the light of all these new facts, the decision upon the former appeal is not and cannot properly be held to be dispositive of the question whether *this* record shows that New Hampshire is unconstitutionally imposing a bill of attainder upon Dr. Uphaus.

I think the summary dismissal of this appeal without even so much as the benefit of oral argument, when the abridgment of the rights of free speech and assembly is so obvious, is a sad indication of just how far this Court has already departed from the protections of the Bill of Rights and an omen of things yet to come. Such retrogression, of course, follows naturally from the Court's recent trend toward substituting for the plain language of the commands of the Bill of Rights elastic concepts which permit the Court to uphold direct abridgments of liberty unless the Court views those abridgments as "arbitrary," "unreasonable," "offensive to decency" or "unjustified on balance," for these concepts reduce the absolute commands of the Constitution to mere admonitions. I think it is time for all who cherish the liberties guaranteed by the Bill of Rights to look closely at the disastrous consequences upon those liberties which have resulted from the Court's use of such concepts. In my mind, the present case graphically illustrates those consequences when it is stripped of the ambiguous legal formulations which have been imposed upon it and considered in the context in which it actually arose—the conduct of Dr. Uphaus as an individual.

He is a citizen of this country by birth. Throughout the nearly seventy years of his life, evidently from early boyhood, he has been a deeply religious person. The record shows his active membership in and official service for various Methodist churches in the communities where he has lived. The value of that membership and those services is attested by affidavits filed by the pastors of those churches. The record further indicates, without dispute, that he is a man whose life has been dedicated to the principles of his religion. He holds a degree as a Doctor of Theology. He taught religious education at Yale University and was associated with the Religion and Labor Foundation for a number of years. Over the years, his religious faith manifested itself in an increasing opposition to war. It was this belief which led him, in 1952, to become the Director of World Fellowship, Inc., a summer camp operated, he says, in the interest of promoting the ideas of pacifism.

Almost immediately upon his arrival at World Fellowship, Dr. Uphaus came under the fire of an investigation being conducted by the Attorney General of New Hampshire, apparently on the theory that World Fellowship was frequented by "subversive" persons. Eventually, as the Director of World Fellowship, he was called before the Attorney General to testify. At the very outset of the hearing before the Attorney General, he expressed a complete willingness to answer any question concerning himself, including any views he might hold or any actions he might have taken with regard to any subject. In addition, he expressed a willingness to give the Attorney General any information which might be wanted in regard to the subject matter of any speeches made at World Fellowship. But he absolutely refused to give the Attorney General: (1) a list of the non-professional employees of the camp; (2) a list of all the guests who had stayed at the camp; and (3) his personal correspondence with the speakers who had appeared at the camp. Upon being met with this refusal, the Attorney General sought a court order requiring Dr. Uphaus to produce these items. At the resulting hearing, the court, apparently viewing the request of the Attorney General for the names of the camp's dishwashers and floor sweepers as totally unreasonable and being uncertain as to the legal amenability to subpoena of the correspondence, ordered Dr. Uphaus to produce only the names of the guests. This, Dr. Uphaus persisted, he could not do, resting his refusal upon the following reasons, to which he has adhered throughout this long ordeal: (1) because "by the direct teachings of the Bible . . . it is wrong to bear false witness against my brother; and inasmuch as I have no reason to believe that any of these persons whose names have been called for have in any sense hurt this state or our country, I have reason to believe that they should not be in the possession of the Attorney General"; (2) because "the social teachings of the Methodist Church . . . condemn guilt by association"; and (3) because "I love this document [the Bill of Rights] and I propose to uphold it with the full strength and power of my spirit and intelligence."

Nonetheless, the order to produce was upheld and Dr. Uphaus was imprisoned for his failure to comply with it. As a result, he has been in jail since last December 14 under a judgment which sentenced him to imprisonment for one year or until such time as he would comply with the order to produce. His plight, however, is even worse than would normally be indicated by that sentence in that there can be no assurance at all that he will be released at the end of the year specified. The Attorney General of New Hampshire insists, notwithstanding the recent legislation reducing his powers, that he has a right to continue all investigations presently pending, and the Supreme Court of New Hampshire apparently agrees with him. This Court, by its action today, necessarily takes the position that this serious abridgment of the rights of free speech and peaceable assembly does not even raise a substantial federal question. As a result, it is entirely possible that Dr. Uphaus will be subjected to new questioning and forced into a new "contempt" as soon as he serves out this year's imprisonment. The brief filed by the Attorney General of New Hampshire makes it appear that he has every intention of doing just that. Thus, a distinct possibility exists that this man who, at least so far as these records show, has never committed a single crime, nor even so much as an immoral act, faces imprisonment for the rest of his life. This simply because he has refused to violate his religious principles and sacrifice his constitutional rights by disclosing the names of those with whom he has peaceably assembled to discuss public affairs in this country.

In this respect, the predicament of Dr. Uphaus may be likened to that of the defendant in the famous *Sheriff's Case* before the House of Lords in 1767. There the City of London sought to prosecute a religious dissenter for refusing to serve in the office of sheriff as required by its by-laws. The defense was that the Corporation Act would have made it a crime for a dissenter to serve in that office, for it required an oath from all officeholders that they had taken the sacraments of the Church of England within the year. The dilemma of the dissenter was vividly described by Lord Mansfield in stating his views on the case:

> Make a law to render them incapable of office; make another, to punish them for not serving. . . . If they accept, punish them; if they refuse, punish them; if they say, yes, punish them; if they say, no, punish them. My Lords, this is a most exquisite dilemma, from which there is no escaping; it is a trap a man cannot get out of; it is as bad persecution as the bed of Procrustes: If they are too short, stretch them; if they are too long, lop them.

This technique of putting unorthodox groups into a position where their only real choice is between various alternative punishments (a technique the prevalence of which today extends far beyond the borders of New Hampshire) is strikingly similar to that being utilized here against Dr. Uphaus. If he testifies, his friends will suffer; if he refuses to testify, he goes to jail. The dilemma is truly one "from which there is no escaping" for a man who, like Dr. Uphaus or like the religious dissenter in the *Sheriff's Case*, cannot bring himself to sacrifice either his religious principles or his legal rights.

That case also serves to highlight a most unfortunate aspect of the decision in this case. For there, nearly two hundred years ago and in England where there was no Bill of Rights, the House of Lords refused to countenance the use of that technique. They held it to be inconsistent with the Toleration Act by which Parliament had guaranteed religious freedom even though the terms of that guarantee were far less sweeping and more limited in application than the absolute commands of our First Amendment. In my view, the majority's disposition of this case, reducing as it does those absolute commands to mere admonitions, means that our First Amendment amounts to something less as a charter of freedom than England's Toleration Act was held to be. This in the very face of the indisputable historical fact that one of the primary reasons for the establishment of this country was the desire of early settlers to escape religious persecution.

I do not suggest, of course, that this imprisonment of Dr. Uphaus is without precedent in history. Indeed, I am painfully aware that there are a multitude of such precedents extending from many centuries back in the past and continuing forward in an almost unbroken line to the present day. There is, for example, the case of the Puritan minister John Udall in 1590, a case which

bears a strong similarity to that of Dr. Uphaus. Udall was called
before a court in connection with the investigation of the authorship of certain religious tracts which, in the words of one of the
judges, "tend[ed] to the overthrowing of the State, and the moving of Rebellion." That court sought to force Udall to disclose the
identity of other Puritans so that it might question them as to the
authorship of the tracts. In refusing to divulge the demanded
names, Udall gave his reasons in a statement not unlike that of Dr.
Uphaus before the New Hampshire court. "I will take an oath of
allegiance to her majesty, wherein I will acknowledge her supremacy according to statute, and promise my obedience as be-
cometh a subject; but to swear to accuse myself or others, I think
you have no law for it." Udall, like Dr. Uphaus, was sentenced to
jail for civil contempt under a judgment which ordered his imprisonment until such time as he would consent to testify. But
such coercion was as ineffective in that case as it has been to date
in this. Udall's dauntless spirit was never broken even though his
body was. He died in prison within a few years.

It would not be difficult to point out many other cases such
as that of Udall, but I will content myself with one other. Some
seventy years after John Udall's experiences, there was a dissenting
preacher in England named John Bunyan. He was arrested for
preaching and efforts were made to get him to agree not to preach
any more. He refused to be coerced into silence. The result was
that he was put through a kind of trial and sentenced to prison for
holding "several unlawful [religious] meetings . . . to the great
disturbance and distraction of the good subjects of this kingdom. . . ." In Bunyan's case the imprisonment lasted twelve
years, and it was during those twelve years that he gave to the
world *The Pilgrim's Progress.* One of the judges who acquiesced
in the imprisonment of Bunyan was Sir Matthew Hale, later Lord
Chief Justice Hale, a man described by Lord Campbell as "one of
the most pure, the most pious, the most independent, and the most
learned" Chief Justices England ever had. That this description is
not entirely unjustified, despite the fact that his record was also
marred by the part he took in the conviction and sentencing to
death of two unfortunate women as witches, is, I think, a tragic
commentary upon the record of the judiciary, throughout the centuries, in discharging its duty to protect civil liberties. It is perhaps
one of the ironies of history that the name of John Bunyan, a poor
tinker and preacher, is at least as well known and respected today

as that of the great Chief Justice of England who permitted him to languish in jail.

My guess is that history will look with no more favor upon the imprisonment of Willard Uphaus than it has upon that of Udall, Bunyan or the many others like them. For this is another of that ever-lengthening line of cases where people have been sent to prison and kept there for long periods of their lives because their beliefs were inconsistent with the prevailing views of the moment. I believe the First and Fourteenth Amendments were intended to prevent any such imprisonments in this country. The grounds urged by the Attorney General of New Hampshire here are, as shown by the cases of Udall and Bunyan, precisely those that have always been urged for throwing dissenters in jail, namely, that they are a menace to the community and it is dangerous to leave them free. It may be true, as the Attorney General of New Hampshire suspects, that Dr. Uphaus has at some time been in the company of Communists, or that the people who have been in his camp have been in the company of Communists. But even if it is true and those associates are as bad as they are suspected to be, it is my belief that our Constitution with its Bill of Rights absolutely forbids the imposition of pains and penalties upon him for peaceably assembling with them. That great charter was drafted by men who were well aware of the constant danger to individual liberty in a country where public officials are permitted to harass and punish people on nothing more than charges that they associate with others labeled by the Government as publicans and sinners.

Wilkinson v. United States

365 U.S. 399

Decided February 27, 1961

Largely on the strength of the Supreme Court's decision in Watkins
v. United States *forbidding exposure for exposure's sake, Frank
Wilkinson declined to answer questions about his personal beliefs
and associations put to him by the House Committee on Un-
American Activities. Wilkinson was an avowed critic of the Committee and had been urging its abolition to audiences at public
meetings. He was found guilty of contempt of Congress and the
conviction was affirmed by the United States Court of Appeals.
While his case was in litigation, the Supreme Court handed down
its decision in* Barenblatt v. United States *(page 329), which substantially undercut* Watkins, *if indeed it did not reverse* Watkins
in large part.

When the case of Frank Wilkinson v. United States *was decided by the Supreme Court in a 5-to-4 ruling, the* Barenblatt *Decision was cited as controlling. The majority opinion in the* Wilkinson *Case was handed down by Justice Stewart, joined by Justices
Frankfurter, Clark, Harlan, and Whittaker. Justice Black delivered
a dissent, joined by Chief Justice Warren and Justice Douglas, and
a dissent by Justice Douglas was joined by Chief Justice Warren
and Justice Black. Justice Brennan's dissent was joined by Justice
Douglas.*

*The dissenters found that no authority had been given to a
congressional committee to investigate persons who criticized the
committee and, furthermore, that the purpose of their unauthorized*

*investigation was not to lay the basis for legislation but to attempt
to expose for that purpose primarily.*

MR. JUSTICE BLACK, *with whom* THE CHIEF JUSTICE *and*
MR. JUSTICE DOUGLAS *concur, dissenting*

In July 1958 the House Un-American Activities Committee
announced its intention to conduct a series of hearings in Atlanta,
Georgia, ostensibly to obtain information in aid of the legislative
function of the House of Representatives. Petitioner, a long-time
opponent of the Committee, decided to go to Atlanta for the
purpose of lending his support to those who were fighting against
the hearings. He arrived in Atlanta and registered in a hotel there
on July 23 as a representative of the Emergency Civil Liberties
Committee, a New York organization which was working for the
abolition of the Un-American Activities Committee. Within an
hour of his registration, petitioner was served with a subpoena
requiring his appearance before the Committee. When he appeared
in response to this subpoena, petitioner was told that he had been
subpoenaed because the Committee was informed that "you were
sent to this area by the Communist Party for the purpose of
developing a hostile sentiment to this Committee and to its work
for the purpose of undertaking to bring pressure upon the United
States Congress to preclude these particular hearings." A number
of questions were then put to petitioner all of which related to his
personal beliefs and associations, but petitioner refused to answer
any of these questions on the ground that they violated his rights
under the First Amendment. For this, he was convicted under
2 U.S.C. Section 192 and sentenced to jail for twelve months.

On these facts, which are undisputed in the record, the majority upholds petitioner's conviction as "indistinguishable" from
that upheld in *Barenblatt* v. *United States*. On this point, I find
myself only partially in disagreement with the majority. I think
this case could and should be distinguished from *Barenblatt* on the
ground urged by Mr. Justice Douglas—that the resolution authorizing the Un-American Activities Committee does not authorize
that Committee to interrogate a person for criticizing it. I therefore
join in the dissent filed by Mr. Justice Douglas on that ground. On
the other hand, I must agree with the majority that so far as
petitioner's constitutional claims are concerned, *Barenblatt* is "indistinguishable." Unlike the majority, however, I regard this rec-

ognition of the unlimited sweep of the decision in the *Barenblatt Case* a compelling reason, not to reaffirm that case, but to overrule it.

In my view, the majority by its decision today places the stamp of constitutional approval upon a practice as clearly inconsistent with the Constitution, and indeed with every ideal of individual freedom for which this country has so long stood, as any that has ever come before this Court. For, like Mr. Justice Douglas, I think it clear that this case involves nothing more nor less than an attempt by the Un-American Activities Committee to use the contempt power of the House of Representatives as a weapon against those who dare to criticize it. The majority does not and, in reason, could not deny this for the conclusion is all but inescapable for anyone who will take the time to read the record. They say instead that it makes no difference whether the Committee was harassing petitioner solely by reason of his opposition to it or not because "it is not for us to speculate as to the motivations that may have prompted the decision of individual members of the subcommittee to summon the petitioner." The clear thrust of this sweeping abdication of judicial power is that the Committee may continue to harass its opponents with absolute impunity so long as the "protections" of *Barenblatt* are observed. Since this is to be the rule under which the Committee will be permitted to operate, I think it necessary in the interest of fairness to those who may in the future wish to exercise their constitutional right to criticize the Committee that the true nature of those "protections" be clearly set forth.

The first such "protection" relates to the question of whom the Committee may call before it. Is there any limitation upon the power of the Committee to subpoena and compel testimony from anyone who attacks it? On this point, the majority, relying upon the fact that at a previous hearing the Committee was told by a paid informant that petitioner was a Communist and upon statements by the Committee's counsel to the effect that the Committee had information that petitioner had been sent to Atlanta by the Communist Party, says simply: "It is to be emphasized that the petitioner was not summoned to appear as the result of an indiscriminate dragnet procedure, lacking in probable cause for belief that he possessed information which might be helpful to the subcommittee." Significantly, the majority does not say just how much its "emphasis" on this point is worth, if anything. Thus, for all that appears in the majority opinion, there is no assurance that the Committee will be required to produce any information at all as a prerequisite to the exercise of its subpoena and contempt powers. Assuming for the sake of argument, however, that such a requirement will be imposed, it then becomes relevant to inquire as to just how much this requirement will mean in terms of genuine protection for those who in good faith wish to criticize the Committee.

That inquiry is, to my mind, satisfactorily settled by a look at the facts of this case. So far as appears from this record, the only information the Committee had with regard to petitioner was the testimony of a paid informant at a previous Committee hearing. The only evidence to the effect that petitioner was in fact a member of the Communist Party that emerges from that testimony is a flat conclusory statement by the informant that it was so. No testimony as to particular happenings upon which such a conclusion could rationally be based was given at that hearing. When this fact is considered in conjunction that the fact that petitioner was not accorded the opportunity to cross-examine the informant or the protection of the statute permitting inspection of statements given to the FBI by paid informants, it seems obvious to me that such testimony is almost totally worthless for the purpose of establishing probable cause. For all we know, the informant may have had no basis at all for her conclusion and, indeed, the possibility of perjury cannot, in view of its frequent recurrence in these sorts of cases, be entirely discounted. Thus, in my view, the "protection" afforded by a requirement of some sort of probable cause, even if imposed, is almost totally worthless. In the atmosphere existing in this country today, the charge that someone is a Communist is so common that hardly anyone active in public life escapes it. Every member of this Court has, on one occasion or another, been so designated. And a vast majority of the members of the other two branches of Government have fared no better. If the mere fact that someone has been called a Communist is to be permitted to satisfy a requirement of probable cause, I think it plain that such a requirement is wholly without value. To impose it would only give apparent respectability to a practice which is inherently in conflict with our concepts of justice and due process.

The other such "protection" afforded to critics of the Un-American Activities Committee under these decisions is included in the majority's so-called balancing test. Under that test, we are told, this Court will permit only those abridgments of personal beliefs and associations by Committee inquiry that the Court believes so important in terms of the need of the Committee for information that such need outweighs the First Amendment rights of the witness and the public. For my part, I need look no further than this very case to see how little protection this high-sounding slogan really affords. For in this case the majority is holding that the interest of the Committee in the information sought outweighs that of the witness and the public in free discussion, while, at the same time, it disclaims any power to determine whether the Committee is in fact interested in the information at all. The truth of the matter is that the balancing test, at least as applied to date, means that the Committee may engage in *any* inquiry a majority of this Court happens to think could possibly be for a legitimate purpose whether that "purpose" be the true reason for the inquiry or not. And under the tests of legitimacy that are used in this area, any first-year law school student worth his salt could construct a rationalization to justify almost any question put to any witness at any time.

Thus, in my view, the conclusion is inescapable that the only real limitation upon the Committee's power to harass its opponents is the Committee's own self-restraint, a characteristic which probably has not been predominant in the Committee's work over the past few years. The result of all this is that from now on anyone who takes a public position contrary to that being urged by the House Un-American Activities Committee should realize that he runs the risk of being subpoenaed to appear at a hearing in some far off place, of being questioned with regard to every minute detail of his past life, of being asked to repeat all the gossip he may have heard about any of his friends and acquaintances, of being accused by the Committee of membership in the Communist Party, of being held up to the public as a subversive and a traitor, of being jailed for contempt if he refuses to co-operate with the Committee in its probe of his mind and associations, and of being branded by his neighbors, employer, and erstwhile friends as a menace to society *regardless of the outcome of that hearing.* With such a powerful weapon in his hands, it seems quite likely that the Committee will weather all criticism, even though justifiable, that may be directed toward it. For there are not many people in our society who will have the courage to speak out against such a formidable opponent. If the present trend continues, this already small number will necessarily dwindle as their ranks are thinned by the jails.

Government by consent will disappear to be replaced by government by intimidation because some people are afraid that this country cannot survive unless Congress has the power to set aside the freedoms of the First Amendment at will.

I can only reiterate my firm conviction that these people are tragically wrong. This country was not built by men who were afraid and it cannot be preserved by such men. Our Constitution, in unequivocal terms, gives the right to each of us to say what we think without fear of the power of the Government. That principle has served us so well for so long that I cannot believe it necessary to allow any governmental group to reject it in order to preserve its own existence. Least of all do I believe that such a privilege should be accorded the House Un-American Activities Committee. For I believe that true Americanism is to be protected, not by committees that persecute unorthodox minorities, but by strict adherence to basic principles of freedom that are responsible for this Nation's greatness. Those principles are embodied for all who care to see in our Bill of Rights. They were put there for the specific purpose of preventing just the sort of governmental suppression of criticism that the majority upholds here. Their ineffectiveness to that end stems, not from any lack of precision in the statement of the principles, but from the refusal of the majority to apply those principles as precisely stated. For the principles of the First Amendment are stated in precise and mandatory terms, and unless they are applied in those terms, the freedoms of religion, speech, press, assembly and petition will have no effective protection. Where these freedoms are left to depend upon a balance to be struck by this Court in each particular case, liberty cannot survive. For under such a rule, there are no constitutional rights that cannot be "balanced" away.

Braden v. United States

365 U.S. 431

Decided February 27, 1961

In 1954 Carl and Anne Braden were indicted for sedition by the State of Kentucky and he was found guilty and sentenced to prison for fifteen years. His offense was that he had helped a Negro family buy a home in an all-white suburb of Louisville. In 1956 the Supreme Court held in Pennsylvania v. Nelson *that the Federal Smith Act superseded enforceability of state legislation against sedition. Braden was then released and the State charges against him and his wife were dismissed. After he resumed his activities against segregation, he was called before a subcommittee of the House Committee on Un-American Activities at a hearing in Atlanta, Georgia. He relied on the* Watkins Decision, *as* Wilkinson *did after him, and he refused to answer questions that violated First Amendment guarantees, on the ground that his political views and personal associations were his private concerns. Cited for contempt, he was convicted and the judgment was affirmed by the Court of Appeals.*

The case was a companion to Wilkinson v. United States *(page 385), and the Supreme Court decided it by the same division and on much the same basis. Justice Stewart, joined by Justices Frankfurter, Clark, Harlan, and Whittaker, found no violation of Braden's constitutional freedoms. The majority also held that it was no valid defense that he took his stand on a previous decision of the Supreme Court. The dissenters held diametrically opposite views. Justice Black wrote a dissent joined by Chief Justice War-*

*ren and Justice Douglas, and Justice Douglas wrote one joined by
Chief Justice Warren and Justices Black and Brennan. In particular, the dissenters held that Braden was entitled to rely on earlier
Supreme Court decisions with respect to his First Amendment
rights.*

*Braden, like Wilkinson, yielded himself to federal authorities.
Together they were committed to prison for a year. Almost at
once petitions for presidential pardons took form, but clemency
was not extended.*

Mr. Justice Black, *with whom* The Chief Justice *and*
Mr. Justice Douglas *concur, dissenting*

The petitioner in this case, as is shown by the facts set forth in
the dissenting opinion of Mr. Justice Douglas, in which I concur,
has for some time been at odds with strong sentiment favoring
racial segregation in his home State of Kentucky. A white man
himself, the petitioner has nonetheless spoken out strongly against
that sentiment. This activity, which once before resulted in his
being charged with a serious crime, seems also to have been the
primary reason for his being called before the Un-American Activities Committee. For the occasion of that Committee's compelling
petitioner to go from Rhode Island, where he was vacationing, to
Atlanta for questioning appears from the record to have been the
circulation of two letters, both in the nature of petitions to Congress, urging that certain legislative action be taken which, in the
view of the signers of the petitions, would help those working
against segregation. One of these petitions, signed by petitioner
and his wife, asked those who read it to urge their representatives
in Congress to vote against proposed legislation which would have
empowered the States to enact antisedition statutes, because, in the
view of the signers, those statutes could too readily be used against
citizens working for integration. The other petition, bearing the
signature of 200 southern Negroes, was sent directly to the House
of Representatives and requested that body not to allow the Un-
American Activities Committee to conduct hearings in the South
because, so the petition charged, "all of its [the Committee's]
activities in recent years suggest that it is much more interested in
harassing and labeling as 'subversive' any citizen who is inclined to
be liberal or an independent thinker." The record shows that the
Committee apparently believed that petitioner had drafted both of

these petitions and that he had circulated them, not—as would appear from the face of the petitions—for the purpose of further-ing the cause of integration, but for the purpose of furthering the interests of the Communist Party, of which the Committee claimed to have information that he was a member, by fomenting racial strife and interfering with the investigations of the Un-American Activities Committee.

When petitioner appeared in response to this subpoena, he was asked a number of questions regarding his personal beliefs and associations, culminating in the question of whether he was a member of the Communist Party at "the instant" he affixed his signature to the petition urging defeat of the statute authorizing State antisedition laws. Petitioner refused to answer these questions on the grounds, first, that the Committee had no power to ask the questions it put to him, and, secondly, that he could properly refuse to answer such questions under the First Amendment. For this refusal to answer he, like Frank Wilkinson who followed him on the witness stand at the Atlanta hearing, was convicted under 2 U.S.C. Section 192 and sentenced to twelve months in jail. And, as was the case with the conviction of Wilkinson, the majority here affirms petitioner's conviction "[u]pon the reasoning and author-ity" of *Barenblatt* v. *United States*.

Again I must agree with the majority that insofar as the con-viction is attacked on constitutional grounds, the decision in *Barenblatt* constitutes ample authority for its action, even though it cannot be denied that the Committee's conduct constitutes a direct abridgment of the right of petition. Indeed, I think the majority might well have, with equal justification, relied upon a much earlier decision of this Court, that in *Beauharnais* v. *Illinois*. For it was there that a majority of this Court first applied to the right of petition the flexible constitutional rule upon which the decision in this case is based—the rule that the right of petition, though guaranteed in precise and mandatory terms by the First Amendment, may be abandoned at any time Government can offer a reason for doing so that a majority of this Court finds sufficiently compelling. Ironically, the need there asserted by the State of Illinois and accepted by a majority of this Court as sufficiently compelling to warrant abridgment of the right of petition was the need to protect Negroes against what was subsequently labeled "libel . . . of a racial group," although it was actually nothing more than the circulation of a petition seeking governmental and public support for a program of racial segregation. Thus, the decision in *Beauharnais* had all the outward appearances of being one which would aid the underprivileged Negro minority. This decision, however, is a dramatic illustration of the shortsightedness of such an interpretation of that case. For the very constitutional philosophy that gave birth to *Beauharnais* today gives birth to a decision which may well strip the Negro of the aid of many of the white people who have been willing to speak up in his behalf. If the House Un-American Activities Committee is to have the power to interrogate everyone who is called a Communist, there is one thing certain beyond the peradventure of a doubt—no legislative committee, state or federal, will have trouble finding cause to subpoena all persons anywhere who take a public stand for or against segregation. The lesson to be learned from these two cases is, to my mind, clear. Liberty, to be secure for any, must be secure for all—even for the most miserable merchants of hated and unpopular ideas.

Both *Barenblatt* and *Beauharnais* are offspring of a constitutional doctrine that is steadily sacrificing individual freedom of religion, speech, press, assembly and petition to governmental control. There have been many other such decisions and the indications are that this number will continue to grow at an alarming rate. For the presently prevailing constitutional doctrine, which treats the First Amendment as a mere admonition, leaves the liberty-giving freedoms which were intended to be protected by that Amendment completely at the mercy of Congress and this Court whenever a majority of this Court concludes, on the basis of any of the several judicially created "tests" now in vogue, that abridgment of these freedoms is more desirable than freedom itself. Only a few days ago, the application of this constitutional doctrine wiped out the rule forbidding prior censorship of movies in an opinion that leaves the door wide open, if indeed it does not actually invite, prior censorship of other means of publication. And the Blackstonian condemnation of prior censorship had long been thought, even by those whose idea of First Amendment liberties have been most restricted, to be the absolute minimum of the protection demanded by that Amendment.

I once more deny, as I have found it repeatedly necessary to do in other cases, that this Nation's ability to preserve itself depends upon suppression of the freedoms of religion, speech, press, assembly, and petition. But I do believe that the noble-sounding slogan of "self-preservation" rests upon a premise that can itself destroy any democratic nation by a slow process of eating away at the liberties that are indispensable to its healthy growth. The very foundation of a true democracy and the foundation upon which this Nation was built is the fact that government is responsive to the views of its citizens, and no nation can continue to exist on such a foundation unless its citizens are wholly free to speak out fearlessly for or against their officials and their laws. When it begins to send its dissenters, such as Barenblatt, Uphaus, Wilkinson, and now Braden, to jail, the liberties indispensable to its existence must be fast disappearing. If self-preservation is to be the issue that decides these cases, I firmly believe they must be decided the other way. Only by a dedicated preservation of the freedoms of the First Amendment can we hope to preserve our Nation and its traditional way of life.

It is already past the time when people who recognize and cherish the life-giving and life-preserving qualities of the freedoms protected by the Bill of Rights can afford to sit complacently by while those freedoms are being destroyed by sophistry and dialectics. For at least eleven years, since the decision of this Court in *American Communications Assn.* v. *Douds,* the forces of destruction have been hard at work. Much damage has already been done. If this dangerous trend is not stopped now, it may be an impossible task to stop it at all. The area set off for individual freedom by the Bill of Rights was marked by boundaries precisely defined. It is my belief that the area so set off provides an adequate minimum protection for the freedoms indispensable to individual liberty. Thus we have only to observe faithfully the boundaries already marked for us. For the present, however, the two cases decided by this Court today and the many others like them that have been decided in the past 11 years have all but obliterated those boundaries. There are now no limits to congressional encroachment in this field except such as a majority of this Court may choose to set by a value-weighing process on a case-by-case basis.

I cannot accept such a process. As I understand it, this Court's duty to guard constitutional liberties is to guard those liberties the Constitution defined, not those that may be defined from case to case on the basis of this Court's judgment as to the relative importance of individual liberty and governmental power. The majority's approach makes the First Amendment, not the rigid protection of liberty its language imports, but a poor flexible imitation. This weak substitute for the First Amendment is, to my mind, totally un-acceptable for I believe that Amendment forbids, among other things, any agency of the Federal Government—be it legislative, executive or judicial—to harass or punish people for their beliefs, or for their speech about, or public criticism of, laws and public officials. The Founders of this Nation were not then willing to trust the definition of First Amendment freedoms to Congress or this Court, nor am I now. History and the affairs of the present day show that the Founders were right. There are grim reminders all around this world that the distance between individual liberty and firing squads is not always as far as it seems. I would overrule *Barenblatt*, its forerunners and its progeny, and return to the language of the Bill of Rights. The new and different course the Court is following is too dangerous.

Konigsberg v. State Bar of California

366 U.S. 36

Decided April 24, 1961

Few of Justice Black's opinions could have been harder to write than his dissent in the 5-to-4 decision in the second case of Raphael Konigsberg v. State Bar of California and the Committee of Bar Examiners of the State of California. For in his majority opinion in the first Konigsberg Case (page 297), Justice Black found that there had been no evidence to show that Konigsberg was not of good moral character and that hence he was qualified finally for admission to the bar. The Supreme Court overturned the adverse judgment in California and remanded the case "for further proceedings not inconsistent" with its decision.

Justice Black found the further proceedings against Konigsberg's admission to the bar more than a little "inconsistent." The Bar Committee now said that Konigsberg's conduct obstructed its work. This second Konigsberg Case reached the Supreme Court some four years after the first. Justice Harlan wrote the majority opinion in second Konigsberg and was joined by Justices Frankfurter, Clark, Whittaker, and Stewart. Justice Black's strong dissent was joined by Chief Justice Warren and Justice Douglas. The Chief Justice also joined in a separate dissent by Justice Brennan, who relied primarily on the Speiser Decision.

How much the Speiser ruling (page 316) meant to Justice

Black was made clear when he expressed the view in his Konigsberg *dissent that the decision in second* Konigsberg *"cut the heart out of one of the very few liberty-protecting decisions that this Court has rendered in the last decade."*

MR. JUSTICE BLACK, *with whom* THE CHIEF JUSTICE *and* MR. JUSTICE DOUGLAS *concur, dissenting*

When this case was here before, we reversed a judgment of the California Supreme Court barring the petitioner Konigsberg from the practice of law in that State on the ground that he had failed to carry the burden of proving his good moral character and that he did not advocate forcible overthrow of the government. In doing so, we held that there was "no evidence in the record" which could rationally justify such a conclusion. Upon remand, the Supreme Court of California referred the matter back to the Committee of State Bar Examiners for further hearings, at which time Konigsberg presented even more evidence of his good character. The Committee produced no evidence whatever which tended in the slightest degree to reflect upon the good character and patriotism which we had already held Konigsberg to have established. The case is therefore now before us with the prior adjudication that Konigsberg possesses the requisite good character and patriotism for admission to the bar unimpaired.

What the Committee did do upon remand was to repeat the identical questions with regard to Konigsberg's suspected association with Communists twenty years ago that it had asked and he had refused to answer at the first series of hearings. Konigsberg again refused to answer these questions and the Committee again refused to certify him as fit for admission to the bar, this time on the ground that his refusal to answer had obstructed the required investigation into his qualifications, a ground subsequently adopted by a majority of the Supreme Court of that State. . . .

Konigsberg's objection to answering questions as to whether he is or was a member of the Communist Party has, from the very beginning, been based upon the contention that the guarantees of free speech and association of the First Amendment as made controlling upon the States by the Fourteenth Amendment preclude California from denying him admission to its bar for refusing to answer such questions. In this I think Konigsberg has been correct. California has apparently not even attempted to make actual present membership in the Communist Party a bar to the practice of law, and even if it had, I assume it would not be contended that such a law could be applied to conduct that took place before the law was passed. For such an application would, I think, not only be a clear violation of the *ex post facto* provision of the Federal Constitution, but would also constitute a bill of attainder squarely within this Court's holdings in *Cummings* v. *Missouri* and *Ex parte Garland*. And yet it seems to me that this record shows, beyond any shadow of a doubt, that the reason Konigsberg has been rejected is because the Committee suspects that he was at one time a member of the Communist Party. I agree with the implication of the majority opinion that this is not an adequate ground to reject Konigsberg and that it could not be constitutionally defended.

The majority avoids the otherwise unavoidable necessity of reversing the judgment below on that ground by simply refusing to look beyond the reason given by the Committee to justify Konigsberg's rejection. . . .

The recognition that California has subjected "speech and association to the deterrence of subsequent disclosure" is, under the First Amendment, sufficient in itself to render the action of the State unconstitutional unless one subscribes to the doctrine that permits constitutionally protected rights to be "balanced" away whenever a majority of this Court thinks that a State might have interest sufficient to justify abridgment of those freedoms. As I have indicated many times before, I do not subscribe to that doctrine for I believe that the First Amendment's unequivocal command that there shall be no abridgment of the rights of free speech and assembly shows that the men who drafted our Bill of Rights did all the "balancing" that was to be done in this field. The history of the First Amendment is too well known to require repeating here except to say that it certainly cannot be denied that the very object of adopting the First Amendment, as well as the other provisions of the Bill of Rights, was to put the freedoms protected there completely out of the area of any congressional control that may be attempted through the exercise of precisely those powers that are now being used to "balance" the Bill of Rights out of existence. . . .

The Court attempts to justify its refusal to apply the plain mandate of the First Amendment in part by reference to the so-called "clear and present danger test" forcefully used by Mr.

Justice Holmes and Mr. Justice Brandeis, not to narrow but to broaden the then prevailing interpretation of First Amendment freedoms. I think very little can be found in anything they ever said that would provide support for the "balancing test" presently in use. Indeed, the idea of "balancing" away First Amendment freedoms appears to me to be wholly inconsistent with the view, strongly espoused by Justices Holmes and Brandeis, that the best test of truth is the power of the thought to get itself accepted in the competition of the market. The "clear and present danger test" was urged as consistent with this view in that it protected speech in all cases except those in which danger was so imminent that there was no time for rational discussion. The "balancing test," on the other hand, rests upon the notion that some ideas are so dangerous that the government need not restrict itself to contrary arguments as a means of opposing them even where there is ample time to do so. Thus here, where there is not a semblance of a "clear and present danger," and where there is more than ample time in which to combat by discussion any idea which may be involved, the majority permits the State of California to adopt measures calculated to suppress the advocacy of views about governmental affairs.

I recognize, of course, that the "clear and present danger test," though itself a great advance toward individual liberty over some previous notions of the protections afforded by the First Amendment, does not go as far as my own views as to the protection that should be accorded these freedoms. I agree with Justices Holmes and Brandeis, however, that the primary purpose of the First Amendment was to insure that all ideas would be allowed to enter the "competition of the market." But I fear that the creation of "tests" by which speech is left unprotected under certain circumstances is a standing invitation to abridge it. This is nowhere more clearly indicated than by the sudden transformation of the "clear and present danger test" in *Dennis* v. *United States*. In that case, this Court accepted Judge Learned Hand's "restatement" of the "clear and present danger test": "In each case [courts] must ask whether the gravity of the 'evil,' discounted by its improbability, justifies such invasion of free speech as is necessary to avoid the danger." After the "clear and present danger test" was diluted and weakened by being recast in terms of this "balancing" formula, there seems to me to be much room to doubt that Justices Holmes and Brandeis would even have recognized their test. And the reliance upon that weakened "test" by the majority here, without even so much as an attempt to find either a "clear" or a "present" danger, is only another persuasive reason for rejecting all such "tests" and enforcing the First Amendment according to its terms. . . .

. . . The Court, by stating unequivocally that there are no "absolutes" under the First Amendment, necessarily takes the position that even speech that is admittedly protected by the First Amendment is subject to the "balancing test" and that therefore no kind of speech is to be protected if the Government can assert an interest of sufficient weight to induce this Court to uphold its abridgment. In my judgment, such a sweeping denial of the existence of any inalienable right to speak undermines the very foundation upon which the First Amendment, the Bill of Rights, and, indeed, our entire structure of government rests. The Founders of this Nation attempted to set up a limited government which left certain rights in the people—rights that could not be taken away without amendment of the basic charter of government. The majority's "balancing test" tells us that this is not so. It tells us that no right to think, speak, or publish exists in the people that cannot be taken away if the Government finds it sufficiently imperative or expedient to do so. Thus, the "balancing test" turns our "Government of the people, by the people and for the people" into a government over the people.

I cannot believe that this Court would adhere to the "balancing test" to the limit of its logic. Since that "test" denies that any speech, publication, or petition has an "absolute" right to protection under the First Amendment, strict adherence to it would necessarily mean that there would be only a conditional right, not a complete right, for any American to express his views to his neighbors—or for his neighbors to hear those views. In other words, not even a candidate for public office, high or low, would have an "absolute" right to speak in behalf of his candidacy, no newspaper would have an "absolute" right to print its opinion on public governmental affairs, and the American people would have no "absolute" right to hear such discussions. All of these rights would be dependent upon the accuracy of the scales upon which this Court weighs the respective interests of the Government and the people. It therefore seems to me that the Court's "absolute" statement that there are no "absolutes" under the First Amendment must be an exaggeration of its own views. . . .

The Court seeks to bring this case under the authority of the

street-regulation cases and defend its use of the "balancing test" on
the ground that California is attempting only to exercise its permissible power to regulate its Bar and that any effect its action
may have upon speech is purely "incidental." But I cannot agree
that the questions asked Konigsberg with regard to his suspected
membership in the Communist Party had nothing more than an
"incidental" effect upon his freedom of speech and association.
Why does the Committee of Bar Examiners ask a bar applicant
whether he is or has been a member of the Communist Party? The
avowed purpose of such questioning is to permit the Committee to
deny applicants admission to the bar if they "advocate" forcible
overthrow of the government. Indeed, that is precisely the ground
upon which the majority is here upholding the Committee's right
to ask Konigsberg these questions. I realize that there has been
considerable talk, even in the opinions of this Court, to the effect
that "advocacy" is not "speech." But with the highest respect for
those who believe that there is such a distinction, I cannot agree
with it. For this reason, I think the conclusion is inescapable that
this case presents the question of the constitutionality of action by
the State of California designed to control the content of speech.
As such, it is a "direct," and not an "incidental" abridgment of
speech. Indeed, if the characterization "incidental" were appropriate here, it would be difficult to imagine what would constitute a
"direct" abridgment of speech. The use of the "balancing test"
under these circumstances thus permits California directly to
abridge speech in explicit contradiction to the plain mandate of
the First Amendment.

But even if I thought the majority was correct in its view that
"balancing" is proper in this case, I could not agree with its decision. In the first place, I think that the decision here is unduly
restrictive upon individual liberty even under the penurious
"balancing test." The majority describes the State's interest which
is here to be "balanced" against the interest in protecting the
freedoms of speech and association as an interest in "having lawyers
who are devoted to the law in its broadest sense, including not only
its substantive provisions but also its procedures for orderly
change." But is that an accurate statement of the interest of the
State that is really at stake here? Konigsberg has stated unequivocally that he never has, does not now, and never will advocate the
overthrow of the government of this country by unconstitutional
means, and we held when the case was here before that his evi-

dence was sufficient to establish that fact. Since the Committee has introduced no evidence at any subsequent hearing that would lead to a contrary conclusion, the fact remains established. So the issue in this case is not, as the majority's statement of the State's interest would seem to indicate, whether a person who advocates the over- throw of existing government by force must be admitted to the practice of law. All we really have on the State's side of the scales is its desire to know whether Konigsberg was ever a member of the Communist Party.

The real lack of value of that information to the State is, to my mind, clearly shown by the fact that the State has not even attempted to make membership in the Communist Party a ground for disqualification from the bar. Indeed, if the State's only real interest was, as the majority maintains, in having good men for its bar, how could it have rejected Konigsberg, who, undeniably and as this Court has already held, has provided overwhelming evidence of his good character? Our former decision, which I still regard as resting on what is basically just good common sense, was that a man does not have to tell all about his previous beliefs and associa- tions in order to establish his good character and loyalty.

When the majority turns to the interest on the other side of the scale, it admits that its decision is likely to have "adverse effects upon free association caused by compulsory disclosures," but then goes on to say that those adverse effects will be "minimal" here, first, because bar admission interrogations are private and, secondly, because the decisions of bar admission committees are subject to judicial review. As to the first ground, the Court simply ignores the fact that California law does not require its Committee to treat information given it as confidential. And besides, it taxes credulity to suppose that questions asked an applicant and answers given by him in the highly emotional area of Communism would not rapidly leak out to the great injury of an applicant—regardless of what the facts of his particular case may happen to be. As to the second ground given, the Court fails to take into account the fact that judicial review widens the publicity of the questions and answers and thus tends further to undercut its first ground. At the same time, such review, as is demonstrated by this and the com- panion case decided today, provides small hope that an applicant will be afforded relief against stubborn efforts to destroy him arbitrarily by innuendoes that will subject him to lasting suspicions. But even if I thought the Court was correct in its beliefs that the interrogation of a bar applicant would be kept confidential and that judicial review is adequate to prevent arbitrary exclusions from the bar, I could not accept its conclusion that the First Amendment rights involved in this case are "minimal."

The interest in free association at stake here is not merely the personal interest of petitioner in being free from burdens that may be imposed upon him for his past beliefs and associations. It is the interest of all the people in having a society in which no one is intimidated with respect to his beliefs or associations. It seems plain to me that the inevitable effect of the majority's decision is to condone a practice that will have a substantial deterrent effect upon the associations entered into by anyone who may want to become a lawyer in California. If every person who wants to be a lawyer is to be required to account for his associations as a pre-requisite to admission into the practice of law, the only safe course for those desiring admission would seem to be scrupulously to avoid association with any organization that advocates anything at all somebody might possibly be against, including groups whose activities are constitutionally protected under even the most restricted notion of the First Amendment. And, in the currently prevailing atmosphere in this country, I can think of few organizations active in favor of civil liberties that are not highly controversial. In addition, it seems equally clear that anyone who had already associated himself with an organization active in favor of civil liberties before he developed an interest in the law, would, after this case, be discouraged from spending the large amounts of time and money necessary to obtain a legal education in the hope that he could practice law in California.

Thus, in my view, the majority has reached its decision here against the freedoms of the First Amendment by a fundamental misapplication of its own currently, but I hope only temporarily, prevailing "balancing" test. The interest of the Committee in satisfying its curiosity with respect to Konigsberg's "possible" membership in the Communist Party two decades ago has been inflated out of all proportion to its real value—the vast interest of the public in maintaining unabridged the basic freedoms of speech, press, and assembly has been paid little if anything more than lip service—and important constitutional rights have once again been "balanced" away. This, of course, is an ever-present danger of the "balancing test" for the application of such a test is necessarily tied to the emphasis particular judges give to competing societal values.

Judges, like everyone else, vary tremendously in their choice of values. This is perfectly natural and, indeed, unavoidable. But it is neither natural nor unavoidable in this country for the fundamental rights of the people to be dependent upon the different emphasis different judges put upon different values at different times. For those rights, particularly the First Amendment rights involved here, were unequivocally set out by the Founders in our Bill of Rights in the very plainest of language, and they should not be diluted by "tests" that obliterate them whenever particular judges think values they most highly cherish outweigh the values most highly cherished by the Founders.

Moreover, it seems to me that the "balancing test" is here being applied to cut the heart out of one of the very few liberty-protecting decisions that this Court has rendered in the last decade. *Speiser* v. *Randall* struck down, as a violation of the Federal Constitution, a state law which denied tax exemptions to veterans who refused to sign an oath that they did not advocate "the overthrow of the Government of the United States or of the State of California by force or violence or other unlawful means . . ." The case arose when certain veterans insisted upon their right to the exemptions without signing the oath. The California Supreme Court rejected the veterans' constitutional contention that the State law violated due process by placing the burden of proof upon the taxpayer to prove that he did not advocate violent overthrow of the Government. This Court reversed, with only one Justice dissenting, on the ground that the necessary effect of such an imposition of the burden of proof "can only result in a deterrence of speech which the Constitution makes free." Indeed, the majority opinion in the *Speiser Case* distinguished the very cases upon which the majority here is relying on the ground that "the oaths required in those cases performed a very different function from the declaration in issue here. In the earlier cases it appears that the loyalty oath, once signed, became conclusive evidence of the facts attested so far as the right to office was concerned. If the person took the oath he retained his position. The oath was not part of a device to shift to the officeholder the burden of proving his right to retain his position." But that is precisely what is happening here. For, even though Konigsberg has taken an oath that he does not advocate the violent overthrow of the Government, the Committee has persisted in the view that he has not as yet demonstrated his right to admission to the bar. If that does not amount to the sort of shifting of the burden of proof that is proscribed by *Speiser*, I do not know what would.

The situation in the present case is closely analogous to that condemned in the *Speiser Case* and, indeed, the major factual difference between the two cases tends to make this case an even stronger one. Here, as in *Speiser*, the State requires an oath that the person involved does not advocate violent overthrow of the Government. Here, as there, the taking of the oath is not conclusive of the rights of the person involved. And here, as there, contrary to the implications in the majority opinion, I think it clear that the State places upon each applicant for admission to the bar the burden of proving that he does not advocate the violent overthrow of the Government. There is one difference between the two cases, for here Konigsberg agreed to take the oath required and he refused to answer only when the State insisted upon more. Surely he cannot be penalized for his greater willingness to cooperate with the State. . . .

In my judgment this case must take its place in the ever-lengthening line of cases in which individual liberty to think, speak, write, associate, and petition is being abridged in a manner precisely contrary to the explicit commands of the First Amendment. And I believe the abridgment of liberty here, as in most of the other cases in that line, is based upon nothing more than a fear that the American people can be alienated from their allegiance to our form of government by the talk of zealots for a form of government that is hostile to everything for which this country now stands or ever has stood. I think this fear is groundless for I believe that the loyalty and patriotism of the American people toward our own free way of life are too deeply rooted to be shaken by mere talk or argument from people who are wedded to totalitarian forms of government. It was this kind of faith in the American people that brought about the adoption of the First Amendment, which was expressly designed to let people say what they wanted to about government—even against government if they were so inclined. The idea underlying this then revolutionary idea of freedom was that the Constitution had set up a government so favorable to individual liberty that arguments against that government would fall harmless at the feet of a satisfied and happy citizenship. Thomas Jefferson voiced this idea with simple eloquence on the occasion of his first inauguration as President of the United States:

If there be any among us who would wish to dissolve this Union or to change its republican form, let them stand undisturbed as monuments of the safety with which error of opinion may be tolerated where reason is left free to combat it.

In the main, this is the philosophy under which this country has lived and prospered since its creation. There have, however, been two notable exceptions, the first being the period of the short-lived and unlamented Alien and Sedition Laws of the late 1700's, and the other being the period since the beginning of the Cold War shortly after the close of World War II, in which there has been a widespread fear of an imagined overwhelming persuasiveness in Communist arguments. The most commonly offered justification for the liberty-stifling measures that have characterized this latter period is that the Communists do not themselves believe in the freedoms of speech, press, and assembly so they should not be allowed to take advantage of the freedoms our Constitution provides. But, as illustrated by this and many other cases, the effect of repressive laws and inquisitions of this kind cannot be and is not limited to Communists. Moreover, the fact that Communists practice repression of these freedoms is, in my judgment, the last reason in the world that we should do so. We do not have to imitate the Communists in order to survive. Our Bill of Rights placed our survival upon a firmer ground—that of freedom, not repression.

Nothing in this record shows that Konigsberg has ever been guilty of any conduct that threatens our safety. Quite the contrary, the record indicates that we are fortunate to have men like him in this country for it shows that Konigsberg is a man of firm convictions who has stood up and supported this country's freedom in peace and in war. The writings that the record shows he has published constitute vehement protests against the idea of over-throwing this Government by force. No witness could be found throughout the long years of this inquisition who could say, or even who would say, that Konigsberg has ever raised his voice or his hand against his country. He is, therefore, but another victim of the prevailing fashion of destroying men for the views it is suspected they might entertain.

In re Anastaplo

366 U.S. 82

Decided April 24, 1961

George Anastaplo was born in St. Louis and reared in Carterville, Illinois, by parents who emigrated from Greece. During World War II, at the age of eighteen, he interrupted his undergraduate studies to join the Air Force and flew as a navigator in all the major theaters of military operations. After an honorable discharge in 1947, he resumed his education at the University of Chicago, where he obtained a degree and studied law. In 1950 he passed the Illinois Bar examination and appeared before the State Bar Committee on Character and Fitness as a preliminary to admission to the bar.

When the Committee asked Anastaplo to summarize his understanding of the fundamental principles of the United States government, he included in his reply a reference to the historic right of the people, as enunciated in the Declaration of Independence, to alter or abolish a government which becomes destructive of the rights to "life, liberty and pursuit of happiness." That led to questioning about "the right of revolution" and also about his possible membership in any organization on the Attorney General's blacklist. Anastaplo asked about the legitimacy and pertinency of such inquiries, and the result of the interchange was the Committee's refusal to certify him for admission. Subsequent questioning also included a query on whether he believed in "a Supreme

Being," and one Committee member said that so far as his vote was concerned, a man's "belief in the Deity . . . has a substantial bearing upon his fitness to practice law."

The seven-judge Illinois Supreme Court divided 4 to 3 in upholding the Committee's refusal to certify Anastaplo for admission. In the United States Supreme Court the scales were also tipped by one Justice. The majority of five were Justice Harlan, who wrote the Court's decision, and Justices Frankfurter, Clark, Whittaker, and Stewart, who joined it. The dissenters were Justices Black, who wrote the minority opinion, and Chief Justice Warren and Justices Douglas and Brennan.

Justice Black concluded his moving opinion with the following extract. It is included because of his ringing defense of the right of revolution as a right of all peoples to be exercised when brought under the yoke of a tyrannical government and also for his stirring appeal to the members of the legal profession to resist the degrading trend toward orthodoxy in thought and action.

Mr. Justice Black, *with whom* The Chief Justice *and* Mr. Justice Douglas *and* Mr. Justice Brennan *concur, dissenting*

. . . The opinion of the majority already recognizes that there is not one scrap of evidence in the record before us "which could properly be considered as reflecting adversely upon his [Anastaplo's] character or reputation or on the sincerity of the beliefs he espoused before the Committee," and that the Committee had not received " 'any information from any outside source which would cast any doubt on applicant's loyalty or which would tend to connect him in any manner with any subversive group.' " The majority opinion even concedes that Anastaplo was correct in urging that the questions asked by the Committee impinged upon the freedoms of speech and association guaranteed by the First and Fourteenth Amendments. But, the opinion then goes on to hold that Anastaplo can nonetheless be excluded from the bar pursuant to "the State's interest in having lawyers who are devoted to the law in its broadest sense. . . ." I cannot regard that holding, as applied to a man like Anastaplo, as in any way justified. Consider it, for example, in the context of the following remarks of Anastaplo to the Committee—remarks the sincerity of which the majority does not deny:

I speak of a need to remind the bar of its traditions and to keep
alive the spirit of dignified but determined advocacy and opposition. This is not only for the good of the bar, of course, but also
because of what the bar means to American republican government. The bar when it exercises self-control is in a peculiar position to mediate between popular passions and informed and principled men, thereby upholding republican government. Unless
there is this mediation, intelligent and responsible government is
unlikely. The bar, furthermore, is in a peculiar position to apply
to our daily lives the constitutional principles which nourish for
this country its inner life. Unless there is this nourishment, a just
and humane people is impossible. The bar is, in short, in a position
to train and lead by precept and example the American people.

These are not the words of a man who lacks devotion to "the law
in its broadest sense."

The majority, apparently considering this fact irrelevant because the State might *possibly* have an interest in learning more
about its bar applicants, decides that Anastaplo can properly be
denied admission to the bar by purporting to "balance" the interest
of the State of Illinois in "having lawyers who are devoted to the
law in the broadest sense" against the interest of Anastaplo and the
public in protecting the freedoms of the First Amendment, con-
cluding, as it usually does when it engages in this process, that "on
balance" the interest of Illinois must prevail. If I had ever doubted
that the "balancing test" comes close to being a doctrine of governmental absolutism—that to "balance" an interest in individual
liberty means almost inevitably to destroy that liberty—those
doubts would have been dissipated by this case. For this so-called
"balancing test"—which, as applied to the First Amendment,
means that the freedoms of speech, press, assembly, religion, and
petition can be repressed whenever there is a sufficient governmental interest in doing so—here proves pitifully and pathetically
inadequate to cope with an invasion of individual liberty so plainly
unjustified that even the majority apparently feels compelled expressly to disclaim "any view upon the wisdom of the State's
action."

I, of course, wholeheartedly agree with the statement of the
majority that this Court should not, merely on the ground that
such action is unwise, interfere with governmental action that is
within the constitutional powers of that government. But I am no

less certain that this Court should not permit governmental action that plainly abridges constitutionally protected rights of the People merely because a majority believes that on "balance" it is better, or "wiser," to abridge those rights than to leave them free. The inherent vice of the "balancing test" is that it purports to do just that. In the context of its reliance upon the "balancing test," the Court's disclaimer of "any view upon the wisdom of the State's action" here thus seems to me to be wholly inconsistent with the only ground upon which it has decided this case.

Nor can the majority escape from this inconsistency on the ground that the "balancing test" deals only with the question of the importance of the existence of governmental power as a general matter without regard to the importance of its exercise in a particular case. For in *Barenblatt* v. *United States,* the same majority made it clear that the "balancing test" is to be applied to the facts of each particular case: "Where First Amendment rights are asserted to bar governmental interrogation resolution of the issue always involves a balancing by the courts of the competing private and public interests at stake *in the particular circumstances shown.*" (Emphasis supplied.) Thus, the Court not only "balances" the respective values of two competing policies as a general matter, but also "balances" the wisdom of those policies in "the particular circumstances shown." Thus, the Court has reserved to itself the power to permit or deny abridgment of First Amendment freedoms according to its own view of whether repression or freedom is the wiser governmental policy under the circumstances of each case.

The effect of the Court's "balancing" here is that any State may now reject an applicant for admission to the bar if he believes in the Declaration of Independence as strongly as Anastaplo and if he is willing to sacrifice his career and his means of livelihood in defense of the freedoms of the First Amendment. But the men who founded this country and wrote our Bill of Rights were strangers neither to a belief in the "right of revolution" nor to the urgency of the need to be free from the control of government with regard to political beliefs and associations. Thomas Jefferson was not disclaiming a belief in the "right of revolution" when he wrote the Declaration of Independence. And Patrick Henry was certainly not disclaiming such a belief when he declared in impassioned words that have come on down through the years: "Give me liberty or give me death." This country's freedom was won by men who, whether they believed in it or not, certainly practiced revolution in the Revolutionary War.

Since the beginning of history there have been governments that have engaged in practices against the people so bad, so cruel, so unjust, and so destructive of the individual dignity of men and women that the "right of revolution" was all the people had left to free themselves. As simple illustrations, one government almost two thousand years ago burned Christians upon fiery crosses and another government, during this very century, burned Jews in crematories. I venture the suggestion that there are countless multitudes in this country, and all over the world, who would join Anastaplo's belief in the right of the people to resist by force tyrannical governments like those.

In saying what I have, it is to be borne in mind that Anastaplo has not indicated, even remotely, a belief that this country is an oppressive one in which the "right of revolution" should be exercised. Quite the contrary, the entire course of his life, as disclosed by the record, has been one of devotion and service to his country—first, in his willingness to defend its security at the risk of his own life in time of war and, later, in his willingness to defend its freedoms at the risk of his professional career in time of peace. The one and only time in which he has come into conflict with the Government is when he refused to answer the questions put to him by the Committee about his beliefs and associations. And I think the record clearly shows that conflict resulted, not from any fear on Anastaplo's part to divulge his own political activities, but from a sincere, and in my judgment correct, conviction that the preservation of this country's freedom depends upon adherence to our Bill of Rights. The very most that can fairly be said against Anastaplo's position in this entire matter is that he took too much of the responsibility of preserving that freedom upon himself.

This case illustrates to me the serious consequences to the bar itself of not affording the full protections of the First Amendment to its applicants for admission. For this record shows that Anastaplo has many of the qualities that are needed in the American Bar. It shows, not only that Anastaplo has followed a high moral, ethical, and patriotic course in all of the activities of his life, but also that he combines these more common virtues with the uncommon virtue of courage to stand by his principles at any cost. It is such men as these who have most greatly honored the profession of the law—men like Malsherbes, who, at the cost of his own life and the lives of his family, sprang unafraid to the defense of Louis XVI against the fanatical leaders of the Revolutionary government of France—men like Charles Evans Hughes, Sr., later Mr. Chief Justice Hughes, who stood up for the constitutional rights of Socialists to be Socialists and public officials despite the threats and clamorous protests of self-proclaimed super patriots—men like Charles Evans Hughes, Jr., and John W. Davis, who, while against everything for which the Communists stood, strongly advised the Congress in 1948 that it would be unconstitutional to pass the law then proposed to outlaw the Communist Party—men like Lord Erskine, James Otis, Clarence Darrow, and the multitudes of others who have dared to speak in defense of causes and clients without regard to personal danger to themselves. The legal profession will lose much of its nobility and its glory if it is not constantly replenished with lawyers like these. To force the bar to become a group of thoroughly orthodox, time-serving, government-fearing individuals is to humiliate and degrade it.

But that is the present trend, not only in the legal profession but in almost every walk of life. Too many men are being driven to become government-fearing and time-serving because the government is being permitted to strike out at those who are fearless enough to think as they please and say what they think. This trend must be halted if we are to keep faith with the Founders of our Nation and pass on to future generations of Americans the great heritage of freedom which they sacrificed so much to leave to us. The choice is clear to me. If we are to pass on that great heritage of freedom, we must return to the original language of the Bill of Rights. We must not be afraid to be free.

This remarkable dissent by Justice Black helped inspire a similarly remarkable petition for rehearing from Anastaplo, who, although not admitted to the bar, argued his own case in the Supreme Court. Extracts from the Anastaplo petition show how one brave and independent man encourages another. Noting that the effect of the Illinois examining committee was to lead applicants "to give the answers best fitted to admission to the Bar without difficulty," Anastaplo petitioned the Supreme Court in part as follows:

On what can the Committee rely to counteract the damage it does? Or is the hazing applicants receive preparatory to initiation into the profession designed to rid them of any lingering attachment they might have to courage, self-respect, and justice?

The merit of petitioner's resistance to such bullying is that it forces eventual consideration of the kind of bar and even the kind of citizen America wants. So long as he refuses to capitulate, that long will this question remain a serious one, even though its ultimate resolution will probably come at a time when it is no longer of any practical relevance to petitioner's legal and academic careers. Nevertheless, a bar worthy of its vital role in American republican government cannot emerge until it is recognized that there are principles and standards to which even a career at the bar may be deliberately sacrificed. Only when the bar is again made up, at least among its leaders, of men who accept this truth, only then can the profession be restored to the integrity and standing proper to it. Indeed, petitioner cannot hope, at a time when submission and self-interest are exalted above principle and civic virtue, to be more truly a lawyer than by reconciling himself to permanent exclusion from what he had once thought would be his profession.

Perhaps it is true that petitioner "took too much of the responsibility of preserving [his country's] freedom upon himself." But he was young enough to hope that Americans who would not heed old precepts might yet learn from new examples. . . .

It is only by an ungenerous disregard of the record as it developed, of the kind of challenges petitioner alone faced and of the manner in which he met them, that the action of the Illinois authorities has been upheld. The record—both before the Committee and on appeal—that record of testimony and briefs remains as a guide to reforms that are needed in the education and character of the American bar.

Petitioner is satisfied he has acted as one ought. He is further satisfied that his action will continue to serve the best interests of the bar and of the country. The generous sentiments of the dissenting opinions in Chicago, in Springfield, and in Washington keep alive hopes for the success of efforts to make the institutions and laws of our people a reflection of decency and perhaps even of nobility.

Petitioner leaves in the hands of the profession—lawyers, law teachers and judges alike—the career he might have had. He trusts he will be forgiven if he retains for himself only the immortal lines of another exile (*Inferno*, XV, 121–124),

> Then he turned back, and seemed like one of those who run for the green cloth at Verona through the open fields; and of them seemed he who triumphs, not he who loses.

Respectfully submitted,

GEORGE ANASTAPLO, *Petitioner*
Counsel pro se

Chicago, Illinois
June 19, 1961

Communist Party v. Subversive Activities Control Board

367 U.S. 1

Decided June 5, 1961

The Subversive Activities Control Board ordered the Communist Party of the United States to register as a "Communist-action organization" under the registration requirement of the Subversive Activities Control Act of 1950. In prolonged litigation the order was affirmed by the United States Court of Appeals of the District of Columbia and upheld in the Supreme Court in a close decision. The case was Communist Party of the United States *v.* Subversive Activities Control Board.

Some idea of the struggle within the Supreme Court in disposing of the case can be gained from the fact that the arguments (October 11 and 12, 1960), deliberations, writing of opinions, and delivery of the decision ranged across virtually the whole of the 1960 term. Then, when the opinions were printed, they amounted in themselves to a fair-sized volume. Justice Frankfurter's majority opinion, joined by Justices Clark, Harlan, Whittaker, and Stewart, covered some 65 pages. Chief Justice Warren's dissent ran a dozen pages and Justice Black's more than 32 pages. Justice Douglas delivered a 13-page dissent and Justice Brennan a partial dissent, a half dozen pages long, which Chief Justice Warren joined. Altogether the case took up some 250 pages in the United States Reports.

As in so many cases, there is no substitute for going to the full opinions and reading all the contentions and counter-contentions pro and con. That is particularly true in this instance where evaluations differ so widely and some of the divergences are so very great. Only about half of Justice Black's dissent appears in these extracts. But they are sufficient to make it clear that here is one of his major works—not only a notably straightforward and telling legal opinion, but also a testimonial of his belief in the patriotism and trustworthy good judgment of the American people.

MR. JUSTICE BLACK, *dissenting*

I do not believe that it can be too often repeated that the freedoms of speech, press, petition, and assembly guaranteed by the First Amendment must be accorded to the ideas we hate or sooner or later they will be denied to the ideas we cherish. The first banning of an association because it advocates hated ideas— whether that association be called a political party or not—marks a fateful moment in the history of a free country. That moment seems to have arrived for this country.

The Subversive Activities Control Act of 1950 here involved defines "Communist action" organizations and requires them to register with the Attorney General giving much information of every kind with regard to their property, income, activities, and members. The Communist Party has been ordered to register under that Act by the Subversive Activities Control Board and has challenged the validity of that order on the ground, among others, that the Act is unconstitutional in that it amounts to a complete outlawry of the Communist Party. The contention is that this Act, considered as a whole and in its relation to existing laws which affect members of the Party, imposes such overhanging threats of disgrace, humiliation, fines, forfeitures, and lengthy imprisonments upon registered organizations and their members, most of which burdens become effective automatically upon registration, that it will be impossible for the Party to continue to function if the registration order is upheld.

The Court's opinion is devoted chiefly to the task of explaining why it will not decide any of the substantial issues raised by this attack upon the constitutionality of the Act as it is actually written and will actually operate and why it must decide the case just as though none of these other burdens existed and we were dealing with an Act that required nothing more than the registration of an organization. I cannot agree to decide the case on any such hypothetical basis. If registration were the only issue in the case, I would agree at once that Congress has power to require every "person" acting as an agent of a foreign principal to file registration statements comprehensively showing his agency activities as is required, for example, by the Foreign Agents Registration Act. That Act requires the registration of any "person"—including an individual, partnership, association, corporation, organization, or other combination of individuals—"who acts or agrees to act, within the United States, as . . . a public-relations counsel, publicity agent, information-service employee, servant, agent, representative, or attorney for a foreign principal. . . ." Referring to that Act, I said in *Viereck* v. *United States:*

> Resting on the fundamental constitutional principle that our people, adequately informed, may be trusted to distinguish between the true and the false, the bill is intended to label information of foreign origin so that hearers and readers may not be deceived by the belief that the information comes from a disinterested source. Such legislation implements rather than detracts from the prized freedoms guaranteed by the First Amendment.

The Act before us now, however, unlike the Foreign Agents Registration Act involved in the *Viereck Case,* is not based on the principle that "our people, adequately informed, may be trusted to distinguish between the true and the false." Instead, the present Act, like many other pieces of current legislation, is based on the precisely contrary principle that "our people [even when] adequately informed may [not] be trusted to distinguish between the true and the false." In this regard, the principle upon which Congress acted in passing the Subversive Activities Control Act is identical to that upon which it acted in making membership in the Communist Party a crime in the Smith Act, a provision under which the Court has today sustained the conviction and imprisonment for six years of a person for being a mere member of the Communist Party with knowledge of its purposes. Statutes based upon such a principle, which really amounts to nothing more than the idea that the Government must act as a paternal guardian to protect American voters from hearing public policies discussed, do not implement "the prized freedoms guaranteed by the First Amendment"—they are designed to and do directly detract from those freedoms. . . .

Having thus made it mandatory that Communist organizations

and individual Communists make a full disclosure of their identities and activities, the Act then proceeds to heap burden after burden upon those so exposed. Certain tax deductions allowed to others are denied to a registered organization. Mail matter must be stamped before the organization sends it out to show that it was disseminated by a "Communist action" organization, with all the treasonable connotations given that term by the recitals of "fact" in the Act. Members of a registered organization cannot hold certain jobs with the Government, or any jobs with private businesses engaged in doing certain work for the Government. Members cannot use or attempt to use a passport and cannot even make application for a passport without being subject to a penalty of five years in the penitentiary. The Act thus makes it extremely difficult for a member of the Communist Party to live in this country and, at the same time, makes it a crime for him to try to get a passport to get out. . . .

In the context of this case, I can find no justification for the Court's refusal to pass upon the serious constitutional questions raised. The Court of Appeals met its responsibility by deciding the questions. The Government has not asked that the Court refrain from giving a full decision on these important matters. Assuming that the Act is wholly valid aside from registration and that Congress does have power to outlaw groups advocating dangerous ideas, it seems to me unfair to Congress for this Court to refuse to decide whether its Act can be fully enforced. And assuming that the Act is not wholly valid because of some limitation upon that power, it seems to me that we should say so now. By refusing to do so, the Court in effect allows this serious question to be decided by default. For the Party can no more continue to function with all of these tremendous burdens of undetermined constitutional validity overhanging it and its members than it could if the burdens were considered and upheld. The only sense in which the Court has avoided a constitutional issue is by permitting the destruction of a group seeking to raise the issue of the constitutionality of its destruction.

This whole Act, with its pains and penalties, embarks this country, for the first time, on the dangerous adventure of outlawing groups that preach doctrines nearly all Americans detest. When the practice of outlawing parties and various public groups begins, no one can say where it will end. In most countries such a practice once begun ends with a one-party government. There is something of tragic irony in the fact that this Act, expressly designed to protect this Nation from becoming a "totalitarian dictatorship" with "a single political party," has adopted to achieve its laudable purpose the policy of outlawing a party—a policy indispensable to totalitarian dictatorships. I think we should meet and decide this whole question now in the administration of a sound judicial policy that carries out our responsibilities both to Congress and to the American people.

In my judgment, the Act here under consideration is unconstitutional on at least three grounds in addition to its direct conflict with the self-incrimination provisions of the Fifth Amendment. It is, in the first instance, a classical bill of attainder which our Constitution in two places prohibits, for it is a legislative act that inflicts pains, penalties, and punishments in a number of ways without a judicial trial. The legislative fact-findings as to Communist activities, which the Court—despite the constitutional command for trial of such facts by a court and jury—accepts as facts, supply practically all of the proof needed to bring the Communist Party within the proscriptions of the Act. The Act points unerringly to the members of that Party as guilty people who must be penalized as the Act provides. At the same time, these legislative fact-findings fall little short of being adequate in themselves to justify a finding of guilt against any person who can be identified, however faintly, by any informer, as ever having been a member of the Communist Party. Most of whatever is lacking in the legislative fact-findings is later supplied by administrative fact-findings of an agency which is not a court, which is not manned by independent judges, and which does not have to observe the constitutional right to trial by jury and other trial safeguards unequivocally commanded by the Bill of Rights. Yet, after this agency has made its findings and its conclusions, neither its findings of fact nor the findings of fact of the legislative body can subsequently be challenged in court by any individual who may later be brought up on a charge that he failed to register as required by the Act and the Board. The Act thus not only is a legislative bill of attainder but also violates due process by short-cutting practically all of the Bill of Rights, leaving no hope for anyone entangled in this legislative-administrative web except what has proved in this case to be one of the most truncated judicial reviews that the history of this Court can afford.

I think also that this outlawry of the Communist Party and imprisonment of its members violates the First Amendment. The question under that Amendment is whether Congress had power to outlaw an association, group, or party either on the ground that it advocates a policy of violent overthrow of the existing government at some time in the distant future or on the ground that it is ideologically subservient to some foreign country. In my judgment, neither of these factors justifies an invasion of rights protected by the First Amendment. Talk about the desirability of revolution has a long and honorable history, not only in other parts of the world, but in our own country. This kind of talk, like any other, can be used at the wrong time and for the wrong purpose. But, under our system of government, the remedy for this danger must be the same remedy that is applied to the danger that comes from any other erroneous talk—education and contrary argument. If that remedy is not sufficient, the only meaning of free speech must be that the revolutionary ideas will be allowed to prevail.

This conclusion is not affected by the fact that those advocating a policy of revolution are in sympathy with a foreign government. If there is one thing certain about the First Amendment it is that this Amendment was designed to guarantee the freest interchange of ideas about all public matters and that, of course, means the interchange of *all* ideas, however such ideas may be viewed in other countries and whatever change in the existing structure of government it may be hoped that these ideas will bring about. Now, when this country is trying to spread the high ideals of democracy all over the world—ideals that are revolutionary in many countries —seems to be a particularly inappropriate time to stifle First Amendment freedoms in this country. The same arguments that are used to justify the outlawry of Communist ideas here could be used to justify an outlawry of the ideas of democracy in other countries.

The freedom to advocate ideas about public matters through associations of the nature of political parties and societies was contemplated and protected by the First Amendment. The existence of such groups is now, and for centuries has been, a necessary part of any effective promulgation of beliefs about governmental policies. And the destruction of such groups is now and always has been one of the first steps totalitarian governments take. Within recent months we have learned of such practices in other countries. Only a few weeks ago an executive edict outlawing all parties, groups, and associations all the way down through Rotary Clubs was issued in a country where the government is largely in the hands of a single man. Indeed, our own ancestors were not unfamiliar with this practice. Men and women belonging to dissenting religious, political, or social groups in England before the colonization of this country were sometimes imprisoned, mutilated, degraded by humiliating pillories, exiled, and even killed for their views.

A typical example of the type of legislation under which this sort of persecution was carried on is provided by a statute enacted in 1593 to destroy dissenting religious sects and force all the people of England to become regular attendants at the established church. The basic premise upon which its commands rested was not at all unlike that upon which the Act here proceeds:

> For the better discovering and avoiding of such traiterous and most dangerous Conspiracies and Attempts, as are daily devised and practised against our most gracious Sovereign Lady the Queen's Majesty and the happy Estate of this common Weal, by sundry wicked and seditious Persons, who terming themselves Catholicks, and being indeed Spies and Intelligencers, not only for her Majesty's foreign Enemies, but also for rebellious and traiterous Subjects born within her Highness Realms and Dominions, and hiding their most detestable and devilish Purposes under a false Pretext of Religion and Conscience, do secretly wander and shift from Place to Place within this Realm, to corrupt and seduce her Majesty's Subjects, and to stir them to Sedition and Rebellion. . . .

These attainted Catholics were not permitted to go "above five Miles" from their homes. For violation of this command they could be sentenced to prison and have all their goods, lands and other possessions forfeited "to the Queen's Majesty." One has only to read this statute to see how thorough-going government can be in making life miserable for groups whose beliefs have fallen into disfavor. . . .

. . . One cannot help but wonder whether this Court, were it called upon to consider the constitutionality of a provision of that kind in this country, would pass it off as involving nothing more than potential impairments of religious freedoms and a right to travel which the attainted persons might never want to exercise.

There were many other statutes of this kind passed in England before our Revolutionary War. By no means all of them were aimed at the Catholics. Indeed, during the times when the Catholics were themselves in power, almost identical repressive measures were adopted in an attempt to curb the rise of Protestantism. And the persecution of Puritans in England, dramatized by some of the most famous writers of the time, is a story that is, I hope, familiar to most Americans. It is a matter of history that not one of these laws achieved its purpose. Many men died, suffered, and were driven from their country. And, in a sense, it might be said that our own country profited from these laws because it was largely founded by refugees from English oppression. But England itself gained little if any profit from its policies of repression. The outlawed groups were not destroyed. Many people have thought that these repressive measures were more effective to bring about revolutions than to stop them. Be that as it may, it cannot be denied that the most tranquil period of English history, from an internal standpoint, has been the period since England abandoned these practices of trying to inculcate belief by oaths and force. . . .

At the very time England was going through its era of terror about the "Jacobins," a heated political struggle involving many of the same issues was going on in this country between the two chief political parties. One of those parties, the Federalists, wanted to outlaw the party of Jefferson on the ground that they too were "Jacobins" and therefore a threat to our security. The Jeffersonians quite naturally opposed such outlawry and in fact opposed any measure which would restrict the freedoms of speech, press, petition, and assembly. The difference between the two parties was expressed by Jefferson in this way: "Both of our political parties, at least the honest part of them, agree conscientiously in the same object, the public good . . . One fears most the ignorance of the people; the other, the selfishness of rulers independent of them. Which is right, time and experience will prove." This conflict of ideals and policies was temporarily resolved in favor of the Federalist and the result was the infamous era of the Alien and Sedition Acts. These laws, passed over vigorous Jeffersonian opposition, declared that it was necessary in order to protect the security of the Nation to give the President the broadest of powers over aliens and to make substantial inroads upon the freedoms of speech, press, and assembly.

The enforcement of these statutes, particularly the Sedition Act, constitutes one of the greatest blots on our country's record of freedom. Publishers were sent to jail for writing their own views and for publishing the views of others. The slightest criticism of government or policies of government officials was enough to cause biased federal prosecutors to put the machinery of government to work to crush and imprison the critic. Rumors which filled the air pointed the finger of suspicion at good men and bad men alike, sometimes causing the social ostracism of people who loved their free country with a deathless devotion. Members of the Jeffersonian Party were picked out as special targets so that they could be illustrious examples of what could happen to people who failed to sing paeons of praise for current federal officials and their policies. Matthew Lyon, a Congressman of the Jeffersonian Party, was prosecuted, convicted, and forced to serve a prison sentence in a disreputable jailhouse because of criticisms he made of governmental officials and their activities. This was a particularly egregious example of the repressive nature of the Sedition Act, for Lyon's conviction could not possibly have been upheld under even the most niggardly interpretation of the First Amendment. Lyon was but one of many who had to go to jail, be fined, or otherwise be made to suffer for the expression of his public views. Carpenters, preachers, lawyers, and many others furnished grist for the prosecutor's biased political activities in the "administration of justice." Unfortunately, our federal courts did not emerge from this fever of hysteria with the kind of reputations that shed luster on the business of judging. Although the Founders had provided for federal judges to be appointed for life, thus intending to give them the independence necessary for the higher responsibility they had, some federal judges, even including members of the highest courts, presided over grand juries and trials in a way that is sad to be recalled even at this late date.

All the governmental activities set out above designed to suppress the freedom of American citizens to think their own views and speak their own thoughts and read their own selections, and even more, occurred under the 1798 Sedition Act. And all these things happened despite the fact that the promoters of that legislation were unable to make it as strong as their philosophical and political brethren in England had made their Act for the complete suppression of all kinds of societies. But even this comparatively less repressive law and its enforcement was too much of an infringement upon personal liberty to stand the test of public opinion among the plain, sturdy pioneers of America. In the very next election following its enactment, Jefferson was elected President on a platform which contained, as its principal plank, a promise to abandon the Sedition Act and the policy of repression behind it. Members of Congress and the Senate were elected to help him carry out his pledge. The pledge was carried out, and in order to try to make amends to those who had suffered under this obnoxious law, Congress was busy for many years indemnifying those who had been prosecuted under its provisions and even their descendants. The superior judgment of the people over that of their legislators who passed the Act in the first place was graphically illustrated when Matthew Lyon, who had been sent to jail for refusing to refrain from criticizing Federalist officeholders, was triumphantly re-elected by the people of Vermont while still in jail.

I regret, exceedingly regret, that I feel impelled to recount this history of the Federalist Sedition Act because, in all truth, it must be pointed out that this law—which has since been almost universally condemned as unconstitutional—did not go as far in suppressing the First Amendment freedoms of Americans as do the Smith Act and the Subversive Activities Control Act. All the fervor and all the eloquence and all the emotionalism and all the prejudice and all the parades of horrors about letting the people hear arguments for themselves were not sufficient in 1798 to persuade the members of Congress to pass a law which would directly and unequivocally outlaw the party of Jefferson, at which the law was undoubtedly aimed. The same arguments were made then about the "Jacobins," meaning the Jeffersonians, with regard to their alleged subservience to France, that are made today about the Communists with regard to their subservience to Russia. Even the language of the charges that were hurled was substantially the same as that used in the charges made today. The Jacobins were "trained, officered, regimented, and formed to subordination, in a manner that our militia have never yet equalled"; and "it is as certain as any future event can be, that they [the Jeffersonians] will take arms against the laws as soon as they dare . . ."

These charges expressed fears that were echoed time and time again during the congressional debate on the Alien and Sedition Acts. The very same fears are again being voiced today as a justification for curtailing the liberties of the people of America. Thus, Section 2(15) of the Subversive Activities Control Act under consideration says that "[t]he Communist movement in the United States is an organization numbering thousands of adherrents, rigidly and ruthlessly disciplined" only awaiting "a moment when . . . overthrow of the Government of the United States by force and violence may seem possible of achievement . . ."

This excuse for repression is, of course, not a distinctively

American creation. It is the same excuse that was used for the 1799 English Act described above. Thus, Charles Abbot, a member of Parliament, urged as one of the justifications for outlawing the societies named in that Act: "The malignancy of their character is distinguishable by the restless spirit which it infuses into the lowest orders of the people, encouraging them to take up arms, and teaching them that they have great and powerful partisans and leaders *who are secretly prepared to seize the favorable moment* for showing themselves openly at their head, when they can hope to do so with impunity." [Emphasis supplied.]

The truth is that this statutory outlawry of the Communist Party is not at all novel when considered in the perspective of history. Quite the contrary, it represents nothing more than the adoption by this country, in part at least, of one of the two conflicting views that have emerged from a long-standing and widespread dispute among political philosophers as to what kind of government will best serve the welfare of the people. That view is that governments should have almost unlimited powers. The other view is that governmental power should be very strictly limited. Both the Smith Act and the Subversive Activities Control Act are based upon the view that officials of the Government should have power to suppress and crush by force critics and criticisms of governmental officials and their policies. The contrary view, which Congress necessarily rejected in passing these laws, is that current public officials should never be granted power to use governmental force to keep people from hearing, speaking, or publishing such criticisms of government or from assembling together to petition their government to make changes in governmental policies, however basic the majority may deem these policies to be.

It is my belief that our Constitution with its Bill of Rights was expressly intended to make our government one of strictly limited powers. The Founders were intimately familiar with the restrictions upon liberty which inevitably flow from a government of unlimited powers. By and large, they had found this experience a painful one. Many of them were descended from families that had left England and had come to this country in order to escape laws that could send them to jail or penalize them in various ways for criticizing laws and policies which they thought bore too heavily and unfairly upon them. Others had personally felt the brunt of such repressive measures. Only after they won the Revolutionary War did these people have an opportunity to set up a government to their liking. To that end they finally settled upon the Constitution, which very clearly adopted the policy of limiting the powers of the Federal Government. Even then the people of this country were not completely satisfied. They demanded more precise and unequivocal limitations upon the powers of government and obtained the Bill of Rights, the central provisions of which were the First Amendment guarantees of complete religious and political freedom.

In the very face of the provisions of the First Amendment, however, the Court today upholds laws which ignore the wisdom of the Founders' decision to set up a limited government and adopt the policy of force to crush views about public matters entertained by a small minority in this country. This, to me, marks a major break in the wall designed by the First Amendment to keep this country free by leaving the people free to talk about any kind of change in basic governmental policies they desire to talk about. I see no possible way to escape the fateful consequences of a return to the era in which all governmental critics had to face the probability of being sent to jail except for this Court to abandon what I consider to be the dangerous constitutional doctrine of "balancing" to which the Court is at present adhering. That doctrine is not a new one. In fact, history shows that it has been the excuse for practically every repressive measure that government has ever seen fit to adopt. Mr. Pitt proved, in 1799, that he was a master of the concept and language of "balancing" in his speech urging the passage of laws to muzzle the press of England in order to prevent the dissemination of the "revolutionary" ideas that England should have parliamentary reform:

> We cannot too highly prize that sacred liberty [of the press] when we consider that it has been instrumental in bringing our Constitution to that envied perfection which it possesses. Yet it must also be admitted that when abused, the most fatal consequences have ever resulted from it. It has been the great principle of the Constitution that the liberty of the press should flourish, but it is also clear from the nature of the principle itself, and for the security of the press, that the author or publisher of every work should be amenable to the laws of his country.

And there certainly was no shortage of "balancers" in our own Congress when the Alien and Sedition Acts of 1798 were passed.

The "balancing test" of First Amendment freedoms is said to justify laws aimed at the advocacy of overthrow of the Government "as speedily as circumstances would permit." Thus, the "test" being used here is identical to the arguments used to justify the Alien and Sedition Acts of 1798 in this country and the 1799 Sedition Act in England. The unprecedented incorporation into our constitutional law of this time-worn justification for tyranny has been used to break down even the minimal protections of the First Amendment forged by Mr. Justice Holmes and Mr. Justice Brandeis which would bar prosecution for speech or writings in all cases except those in which the words used "so imminently threaten immediate interference with the lawful and pressing purposes of the law that an immediate check is required to save the country."

I realize that these laws are aimed only at the Communist Party. No one need console himself, however, that the policy of using governmental force to crush dissident groups upon which they are based can or will be stopped at that point. The weakening of constitutional safeguards in order to suppress one obnoxious group is a technique too easily available for the suppression of other obnoxious groups to expect its abandonment when the next generally hated group appears. Only eleven years ago, this Court upheld a governmental penalty directed at Communists on the ground that "only a relative handful" would be affected by the penalty involved in that case. Today, it upholds statutes which I think totally outlaw that party, claiming nonetheless that "[n]othing which we decide here remotely carries . . . [the] implication . . . [that] Congress may impose similar requirements upon any group which pursues unpopular political objectives or which expresses an unpopular political ideology." I am very much afraid that we will see the day when the very implication which the Court now denies is found.

I am ready to admit that strong arguments can be made for saying that governments in general should have power to suppress speech and press. These arguments are particularly strong in countries where the existing government does not represent the will of the people because history shows that people have a way of not being willing to bear oppressive grievances without protest. Such protests, when bottomed upon facts, lead almost inevitably to an irresistible popular demand for either a redress of those grievances or a change in the government. It is plain that there are governments in the world today that desperately need to suppress such protests for they probably could not survive a week or even a day if they were deprived of the power to use their informers to intimidate, their jails to imprison, and their firing squads to shoot their critics. In countries of that kind, repressive measures like the Smith Act and the Subversive Activities Control Act are absolutely necessary to protect the ruling tyrants from the spread of information about their misdeeds. But in a democracy like ours, such laws are not only unnecessary but also constitute a baseless insult to the patriotism of our people.

I believe with the Framers of the First Amendment that the internal security of a nation like ours does not and cannot be made to depend upon the use of force by government to make all the beliefs and opinions of the people fit into a common mold on any single subject. Such enforced conformity of thought would tend only to deprive our people of the bold spirit of adventure and progress which has brought this Nation to its present greatness. The creation of public opinion by groups, organizations, societies, clubs, and parties, has been and is a necessary part of our democratic society. Such groups, like the Sons of Liberty and the American Corresponding Societies, played a large part in creating sentiment in this country that led the people of the Colonies to want a nation of their own. The Father of the Constitution—James Madison— said, in speaking of the Sedition Act aimed at crushing the Jeffersonian Party, that had that law been in effect during the period before the Revolution, the United States might well have continued to be "miserable colonies, groaning under a foreign yoke."

In my judgment, this country's internal security can better be served by depending upon the affection of the people than by attempting to instill them with fear and dread of the power of government. The Communist Party has never been more than a small group in this country. And its numbers had been dwindling even before the Government began its campaign to destroy the Party by force of law. This was because a vast majority of the American people were against the Party's policies and overwhelmingly rejected its candidates year after year. That is the true American way of securing this Nation against dangerous ideas. Of course, that is not the way to protect the Nation against *actions* of violence and treason. The Founders drew a distinction in our Constitution which we would be wise to follow. They gave the Government the fullest power to prosecute overt actions in violation of valid laws but withheld any power to punish people for nothing more than advocacy of their views.

I am compelled to say in closing that I fear that all the arguments and urgings the Communists and their sympathizers can use in trying to convert Americans to an ideology wholly foreign to our habits and our instincts are far less dangerous to the security of this Nation than laws which embark us upon a policy of repression by the outlawry of minority parties because they advocate radical changes in the structure of government. This widespread program for punishing ideas on the ground that they might impair the internal security of the Nation not only sadly fails to protect that security but also diverts our energies and thoughts from the many far more important problems that face us as a Nation in this troubled world.

I would reverse this case and leave the Communists free to advocate their beliefs in proletarian dictatorship publicly and openly among the people of this country with full confidence that the people will remain loyal to any democratic government truly dedicated to freedom and justice—the kind of government which some of us still think of as being "the last best hope of earth."

Scales v. United States

367 U.S. 203

Decided June 5, 1961

The 1940 Smith Act made it a felony to be a member of any organization that advocates the overthrow of the Government by force or violence if the member knew the organization's purposes. Following the Dennis *Decision (page 223), the Government obtained in 1955 a conviction under the membership clause in a North Carolina Federal Court. As a result of further proceedings, the conviction was reversed and the case,* Junius Irving Scales v. United States, *moved about in the courts until it was finally settled by the Supreme Court in a 5-to-4 ruling, issued six years after the first conviction. The decision upheld Scales's conviction as constitutional.*

Justice Harlan delivered the majority opinion, joined by Justices Frankfurter, Clark, Whittaker, and Stewart. The dissenters were Chief Justice Warren, Justices Black, Douglas, and Brennan, all of whom except the Chief Justice wrote opinions. In a sense, Scales *was a companion to* Communist Party v. Subversive Activities Control Board *(page 416), the Communist registration case, decided the same day by the same 5-to-4 division within the Court.*

Justice Black found that Scales had been twice deprived of constitutional rights—not accorded due process and not guaranteed freedom of speech and assembly.

MR. JUSTICE BLACK, *dissenting*

Petitioner was convicted for violation of the Membership Clause of the Smith Act which imposes a penalty of up to twenty years' imprisonment together with a fine of $20,000 upon anyone who "becomes or is a member of, or affiliates with, any . . . society, group or assembly of persons [who teach, advocate, or encourage the overthrow of the existing government by force or violence], knowing the purposes thereof. . . ." Rejecting numerous contentions urged for reversal, the Court upholds a six-year sentence imposed upon petitioner under the authority of its prior decisions in *Dennis* v. *United States* and *Yates* v. *United States*. My reasons for dissenting from this decision are primarily those set out by Mr. Justice Brennan—that Section 4 (f) of the Subversive Activities Control Act bars prosecutions under the membership clause of the Smith Act—and Mr. Justice Douglas—that the First Amendment absolutely forbids Congress to outlaw membership in a political party or similar association merely because one of the philosophical tenets of that group is that the existing government should be overthrown by force at some distant time in the future when circumstances may permit. There are, however, two additional points that I think should also be mentioned.

In an attempt to bring the issue of the constitutionality of the membership clause of the Smith Act within the authority of the *Dennis* and *Yates Cases*, the Court has practically rewritten the statute under which petitioner stands convicted by treating the requirements of "activity" and "specific intent" as implicit in words that plainly do not include them. Petitioner's conviction is upheld just as though the Membership Clause had always contained these requirements. It seems clear to me that neither petitioner nor anyone else could ever have guessed that this law would be held to mean what this Court now holds it does mean. For that reason, it appears that petitioner has been convicted under a law that is, at best, unconstitutionally vague and, at worst, *ex post facto*. He has therefore been deprived of his right to be tried under a clearly defined, pre-existing "law of the land" as guaranteed by the Due Process Clause and I think his conviction should be reversed on that ground.

Secondly, I think it is important to point out the manner in which this case re-emphasizes the freedom-destroying nature of the "balancing test" presently in use by the Court to justify its refusal to apply specific constitutional protections of the Bill of Rights. In some of the recent cases in which it has "balanced" away the protections of the First Amendment, the Court has suggested that it was justified in the application of this "test" because no direct abridgment of First Amendment freedoms was involved, the abridgment in each of these cases being, in the Court's opinion, nothing more than "an incident of the informed exercise of a valid governmental function." A possible implication of that suggestion was that if the Court were confronted with what it would call a direct abridgment of speech, it would not apply the "balancing test" but would enforce the protections of the First Amendment according to its own terms. This case causes me to doubt that such an implication is justified. Petitioner is being sent to jail for the express reason that he has associated with people who have entertained unlawful ideas and said unlawful things, and that, of course, is a *direct* abridgment of his freedoms of speech and assembly— under any definition that has ever been used for that term. Nevertheless, even as to this admittedly direct abridgment, the Court relies upon its prior decisions to the effect that the Government has power to abridge speech and assembly if its interest in doing so is sufficient to outweigh the interest in protecting these First Amendment freedoms.

This, I think, demonstrates the unlimited breadth and danger of the "balancing test" as it is currently being applied by a majority of this Court. Under that "test," the question in every case in which a First Amendment right is asserted is not whether there has been an abridgment of that right, not whether the abridgment of that right was intentional on the part of the Government, and not whether there is any other way in which the Government could accomplish a lawful aim without an invasion of the constitutionally guaranteed rights of the people. It is, rather, simply whether the Government has an interest in abridging the right involved and, if so, whether that interest is of sufficient importance, in the opinion of a majority of this Court, to justify the Government's action in doing so. This doctrine, to say the very least, is capable of being used to justify almost any action Government may wish to take to suppress First Amendment freedoms.

Torcaso v. Watkins

367 U.S. 488

Decided June 19, 1961

*It was a strange inconsistency that Maryland, the "Free State,"
whose Colonial founder, Lord Baltimore, left England partly because he would not take a religious test oath, should have imposed
as a condition to holding public office "a declaration of belief in
the existence of God." Yet Maryland did make that imposition and
for a long time all of Maryland's public officials gave the declaration apparently without reservation. Then came a non-conformist
appointee of the Governor of Maryland to the office of Notary
Public. He refused to declare belief in God on the ground that
the requirement was in conflict with the First Amendment, under
which a citizen is just as free to disbelieve as to believe.*

*The challenger lost in the Maryland courts and appealed to the
Supreme Court, where the case arrived as* Roy R. Torcaso v.
Clayton K. Watkins, Clerk of the Circuit Court for Montgomery
County, Maryland. *In an era of many split decisions in Bill of
Rights cases, the nine Justices all agreed that the Maryland requirement was unconstitutional. Justice Black wrote the Court's opinion,
joined by Chief Justice Warren and Justices Douglas, Clark, Brennan, Whittaker, and Stewart. Justices Frankfurter and Harlan
concurred in the result.*

*Justice Black quoted from or referred to three earlier deci-
sions discussed previously: the* Everson *(page 147),* McCollum
(page 182) and Zorach *(page 250) Cases. The* Torcaso *ruling,
which was at once both praised and condemned, was one of the*

most significant to issue from the Supreme Court in Justice Black's long tenure.

MR. JUSTICE BLACK *delivered the opinion of the Court*

Article 37 of the Declaration of Rights of the Maryland Constitution provides:

> [N]o religious test ought ever to be required as a qualification for any office of profit or trust in this State, other than a declaration of belief in the existence of God . . .

The appellant Torcaso was appointed to the office of Notary Public by the Governor of Maryland but was refused a commission to serve because he would not declare his belief in God. He then brought this action in a Maryland Circuit Court to compel issuance of his commission, charging that the State's requirement that he declare this belief violated "the First and Fourteenth Amendments to the Constitution of the United States. . . ." The Circuit Court rejected these federal constitutional contentions, and the highest court of the State, the Court of Appeals, affirmed, holding that the state constitutional provision is self-executing and requires declaration of belief in God as a qualification for office without need for implementing legislation. The case is therefore properly here on appeal under 28 U.S.C. Section 1257 (2).

There is, and can be, no dispute about the purpose or effect of the Maryland Declaration of Rights requirement before us—it sets up a religious test which was designed to and, if valid, does bar every person who refuses to declare a belief in God from holding a public "office of profit or trust" in Maryland. The power and authority of the State of Maryland thus is put on the side of one particular sort of believers—those who are willing to say they believe in "the existence of God." It is true that there is much historical precedent for such laws. Indeed, it was largely to escape religious test oaths and declarations that a great many of the early colonists left Europe and came here hoping to worship in their own way. It soon developed, however, that many of those who had fled to escape religious test oaths turned out to be perfectly willing, when they had the power to do so, to force dissenters from their faith to take test oaths in conformity with that faith. This brought on a host of laws in the new Colonies imposing burdens and disabilities of various kinds upon varied beliefs depending largely upon what group happened to be politically strong enough to legislate in favor of its own beliefs. The effect of all this was the formal or practical "establishment" of particular religious faiths in most of the Colonies, with consequent burdens imposed on the free exercise of the faiths of nonfavored believers.

There were, however, wise and far-seeing men in the Colonies —too many to mention—who spoke out against test oaths and all the philosophy of intolerance behind them. One of these, it so happens, was George Calvert (the first Lord Baltimore), who took a most important part in the original establishment of the Colony of Maryland. He was a Catholic and had, for this reason, felt compelled by his conscience to refuse to take the Oath of Supremacy in England at the cost of resigning from high governmental office. He again refused to take that oath when it was demanded by the Council of the Colony of Virginia, and as a result he was denied settlement in that Colony. A recent historian of the early period of Maryland's life has said that it was Calvert's hope and purpose to establish in Maryland a colonial government free from the religious persecutions he had known—one "securely beyond the reach of oaths . . ."

When our Constitution was adopted, the desire to put the people "securely beyond the reach" of religious test oaths brought about the inclusion in Article VI of that document of a provision that "no religious Test shall ever be required as a Qualification to any Office or public Trust under the United States." Article VI supports the accuracy of our observation in *Girouard* v. *United States*, that "[t]he test oath is abhorrent to our tradition." Not satisfied, however, with Article VI and other guarantees in the original Constitution, the First Congress proposed and the States very shortly thereafter adopted our Bill of Rights, including the First Amendment. That Amendment broke new constitutional ground in the protection it sought to afford to freedom of religion, speech, press, petition, and assembly. Since prior cases in this Court have thoroughly explored and documented the history behind the First Amendment, the reasons for it, and the scope of the religious freedom it protects, we need not cover that ground again. What was said in our prior cases we think controls our decision here. . . .

While there were strong dissents in the *Everson Case*, they did not challenge the Court's interpretation of the First Amendment's coverage as being too broad, but thought the Court was applying that interpretation too narrowly to the facts of that case. Not long afterward, in *Illinois ex rel. McCollum* v. *Board of Education*, we were urged to repudiate as dicta the above-quoted *Everson* interpretation of the scope of the First Amendment's coverage. We declined to do this, but instead strongly reaffirmed what had been said in *Everson*, calling attention to the fact that both the majority and the minority in *Everson* had agreed on the principles declared in this part of the *Everson* opinion. And a concurring opinion in *McCollum*, written by Mr. Justice Frankfurter and joined by the other *Everson* dissenters, said this:

> We are all agreed that the First and Fourteenth Amendments have a secular reach far more penetrating in the conduct of Government than merely to forbid an "established church." . . . We renew our conviction that "we have staked the very existence of our country on the faith that complete separation between the State and religion is best for the State and best for religion."

The Maryland Court of Appeals thought, and it is argued here, that this Court's later holding and opinion in *Zorach* v. *Clauson* had in part repudiated the statement in the *Everson* opinion quoted above and previously reaffirmed in *McCollum*. But the Court's opinion in *Zorach* specifically stated: "We follow the *McCollum* case." Nothing decided or written in *Zorach* lends support to the idea that the Court there intended to open up the way for government, state or federal, to restore the historically and constitutionality discredited policy of probing religious beliefs by test oaths or limiting public offices to persons who have, or perhaps more properly, profess to have a belief in some particular kind of religious concept.

We repeat and again reaffirm that neither a State nor the Federal Government can constitutionally force a person "to profess a belief or disbelief in any religion." Neither can constitutionally pass laws nor impose requirements which aid all religions as against non-believers, and neither can aid those religions based on a belief in the existence of God as against those religions founded on different beliefs.

In upholding the State's religious test for public office the highest court of Maryland said:

> The petitioner is not compelled to believe or disbelieve, under threat of punishment or other compulsion. True, unless he makes the declaration of belief he cannot hold public office in Maryland, but he is not compelled to hold office.

The fact, however, that a person is not compelled to hold public office cannot possibly be an excuse for barring him from office by state-imposed criteria forbidden by the Constitution. This was settled by our holding in *Wieman* v. *Updegraff*. We there pointed out that whether or not "an abstract right to public employment exists," Congress could not pass a law providing " '. . . that no federal employee shall attend Mass or take any active part in missionary work.' "

This Maryland religious test for public office unconstitutionally invades the appellant's freedom of belief and religion and therefore cannot be enforced against him.

The judgment of the Supreme Court of Maryland is accordingly reversed and the cause is remanded for further proceedings not inconsistent with this opinion.

Reversed and remanded.

Poe v. Ullman

367 U.S. 497

Decided June 19, 1961

Justice Black has never written an opinion just because he wanted to get some words of his into the record. A Black opinion has meant that the Justice had something to say about the case. The nature of his participation in the Connecticut birth control controversy is a case in point. The three cases, merged as Paul Poe et al. v. Abraham Ullman, State's Attorney, Jane Doe *v.* Abraham Ullman, *and* C. Lee Buxton *v.* Abraham Ullman, *produced one of the most unusual 5-to-4 alignments of the highest tribunal in a decade.*

Acting under the State's anti-birth control statute, Connecticut authorities raided a clinic and seized a quantity of contraceptive devices, literature, and medical equipment and supplies. Police arrested a physician and a nurse working in the clinic and charged them with advising married women on the use of contraceptives. The litigation produced a case known in Connecticut as State v. Nelson, *which upheld the statute. In the record of the* Poe Case, *it was said that this was a "serious setback to the birth control movement" which "led to the closing of all the clinics in the State, just as they had previously been closed in the State of Massachusetts."*

Using assumed names, as the Connecticut procedure allows in such cases, two citizens closely interested in the issue brought suit. One was a married woman who had been advised by a physician that another pregnancy would endanger her life. Justice Frankfurter announced the judgment of the Supreme Court and was joined by Chief Justice Warren and Justices Clark and Whittaker. The essence of the Frankfurter opinion was that Connecticut's failure to press the enforcement of the statute removed "the immediacy which is an indispensable condition of constitutional adjudication." Justice Brennan, concurring, said it would be "time enough to decide the constitutional questions when, if ever, that real controversy flares up again."

Justices Black, Douglas, Harlan, and Stewart dissented. The Douglas and Harlan dissents were thorough, detailed, and well-documented. Describing as "transparent" the Frankfurter argument that there was nothing "justiciable" before the Court, Justice Douglas said: "If there is a case where the need for this remedy in the shadow of a criminal prosecution is shown, it is this one, as Mr. Justice Harlan demonstrates." In the light of the Court's judgment and the strong written dissents by two of his colleagues, the brief Black entry in the decision told much. It read:

MR. JUSTICE BLACK dissents because he believes that the constitutional questions should be reached and decided.

Mapp v. Ohio

367 U.S. 643

Decided June 19, 1961

For almost fifty years, beginning with the Supreme Court's decision in Weeks v. *United States in 1914, the Federal courts have barred the introduction of a defendant's papers and effects in evidence when they were obtained by "unreasonable searches and seizures" in violation of the Fourth Amendment. Then in 1949, in* Wolf v. *Colorado (page 200) the Court held that "in a prosecution in a state court for a state crime the Fourteenth Amendment does not forbid the admission of evidence obtained by an unreasonable search and seizure." The* Wolf *Case was followed by a series of decisions that added confusion to conflict. Notable among these were* United States v. *Rabinowitz in 1950 (page 206),* Rochin v. *California in 1952 (page 231), and* Irvine v. *California in 1954 (page 268). Pleas to overturn* Wolf *were raised term after term, and finally in* Dollree Mapp v. Ohio, *the Court in 1961 made a fresh start at bringing order out of near chaos.*

Miss Mapp, whose Cleveland flat was forcibly entered and searched without a warrant, was convicted under Ohio law of possessing "lewd and lascivious books, pictures and photographs." The Ohio Supreme Court, although it sustained the conviction, found that it was based primarily upon the introduction in evidence of books and pictures "unlawfully seized during an unlawful search of defendant's home." Justice Clark, speaking also for Chief Justice Warren and Justices Black, Douglas, and Brennan, reversed the conviction. Overturning Wolf, *the Court now said: "We hold that*

*all evidence obtained by searches and seizures in violation of the
Constitution is, by that same authority, inadmissible in a state
court." Justices Black and Douglas also wrote separate concurrences.*

*Justice Harlan, joined by Justices Frankfurter and Whittaker,
dissented. They contended that "the* Wolf *rule represents sounder
constitutional doctrine than the new rule which now replaces it."
Justice Stewart agreed in part with Justice Harlan's dissenting opinion, but favored reversal of the conviction because he found the
pertinent provision of Ohio law inconsistent with the Fourteenth
Amendment. Justice Black, after reviewing the* Boyd, Weeks,
Wolf, Rochin, *and* Irvine *Decisions as well as his own positions,
closed his concurring opinion with the following paragraph.*

Mr. Justice Black, *concurring*

Only one thing emerged with complete clarity from the *Irvine
Case*—that is that seven Justices rejected the "shock-the-conscience"
constitutional standard enunciated in the *Wolf* and *Rochin Cases*.
But even this did not lessen the confusion in this area of the law because the continued existence of mutually inconsistent precedents
together with the Court's inability to settle upon a majority opinion
in the *Irvine Case* left the situation at least as uncertain as it had
been before. Finally, today, we clear up that uncertainty. As I understand the Court's opinion in this case, we again reject the con-
fusing "shock-the-conscience" standard of the *Wolf* and *Rochin
Cases* and, instead, set aside this state conviction in reliance upon
the precise, intelligible and more predictable constitutional doctrine
enunciated in the *Boyd Case*. I fully agree with Mr. Justice Bradley's opinion that the two Amendments [Fourth and Fifth] upon
which the *Boyd* doctrine rests are of vital importance in our constitutional scheme of liberty and that both are entitled to a liberal
rather than a niggardly interpretation. The courts of the country
are entitled to know with as much certainty as possible what scope
they cover. The Court's opinion, in my judgment, dissipates the
doubt and uncertainty in this field of constitutional law and I am
persuaded, for this and other reasons stated, to depart from my
prior views, to accept the *Boyd* doctrine as controlling in this state
case and to join the Court's judgment and opinion which are in
accordance with that constitutional doctrine.

Hill v. United States

368 U.S. 424

Decided January 22, 1962

In James Francis Hill *v.* United States, *the question was whether a conviction was invalidated by the failure of a Federal judge in the Eastern District of Tennessee to ask the defendant if he wished to make a statement in his own behalf. A federal jury found Hill guilty of transporting in interstate commerce both a kidnapped person and a stolen automobile. When he appeared for sentencing, he was represented by court-appointed counsel. The judge did not advise the convicted man of his right to speak for himself and his counsel made no mention of it. Hill did not appeal but went to the penitentiary under consecutive twenty-year sentences in 1954.*

Some five years later he filed, from within prison, a motion to vacate the sentences on the ground that at the time of sentencing he had been "denied the right under Rule 32 (a) of the Federal Rules of Procedure, Title 18 U.S.C., to have the opportunity to make a statement in his own behalf and to present any information in mitigation of punishment." The District Court denied the motion and the denial was affirmed by the Federal Court of Appeals. The Supreme Court by a 5-to-4 division sustained the lower courts in an opinion by Justice Stewart, joined by Justices Frankfurter, Clark, Harlan, and Whittaker. Justice Black dissented with the concurrence of Chief Justice Warren and Justices Douglas and Brennan.

The Black opinion is particularly interesting in that it combines two major concerns of its author in the field of legal con-

troversies arising under the Bill of Rights—scrupulous regard for adequate protections for those accused of crime and the right of each individual to speak out for himself.

MR. JUSTICE BLACK, *with whom* THE CHIEF JUSTICE, MR. JUSTICE DOUGLAS, *and* MR. JUSTICE BRENNAN *concur, dissenting*

The petitioner James Hill brought this proceeding to vacate two sentences under which he is imprisoned in a federal penitentiary, alleging that the sentences are illegal because the trial judge who imposed them had not given him the opportunity required by Rule 32 (a) of the Federal Rules of Criminal Procedure "to make a statement in his own behalf and to present any information in mitigation of punishment." Conceding that the sentences thus challenged were imposed without according petitioner his right to speak, the Court nonetheless denies relief under Rule 35's provision for the correction of "illegal" sentences on the ground that the sentences, though imposed in flat violation of Rule 32 (a), were not "illegal" within the special meaning which the majority now ascribes to that word for the purposes of Rule 35. The basic explanation offered for this drastic contraction of the ordinary meaning of the word "illegal" is this single statement in the Court's opinion:

> The punishment meted out was not in excess of that prescribed by the relevant statutes, multiple terms were not imposed for the same offense, nor were the terms of the sentence itself legally or constitutionally invalid in any other respect.

That statement to me amounts to something less than an entirely satisfactory justification for such a begrudging interpretation of Rule 35.

The Court's holding certainly finds no support in the language of Rule 35. That Rule, although painstakingly drawn by lawyers and approved both by Judges and by the Congress, simply provides for the correction of an "illegal sentence" without regard to the reasons why that sentence is illegal and contains not a single word to support the Court's conclusion that only a sentence illegal by reason of the punishment it imposes is "illegal" within the meaning of the Rule. I would have thought that a sentence imposed in an illegal manner—whether the amount or form of the punishment meted out constitutes an additional violation of law or not—would be recognized as an "illegal sentence" under any normal reading of the English language. And precisely this sort of common-sense understanding of the language of Rule 35 has prevailed generally among the lower federal courts that deal with questions of the proper interpretation and application of these Rules as an everyday matter. Those courts have expressed their belief that, even where the punishment imposed upon a defendant is entirely within the limits prescribed for the crime of which he was convicted, a sentence imposed in a prohibited manner—as, for example, a sentence imposed upon an absent defendant in violation of the command of Rule 43 that a defendant be present at sentencing—is an "illegal sentence" subject to correction under Rule 35.

The Court's contrary decision today, however, was perhaps foreshadowed last Term by the narrow scope given to Rule 32 (a) when the issue of the meaning of that Rule came before us for the first time in *Green* v. *United States*. That case, like this one, involved an attempt to vacate a sentence as "illegal" under Rule 35 on the ground that the trial judge had failed to accord the defendant his right to make a statement before sentencing. The record there showed merely that the trial judge, in the presence of both the defendant and his counsel, had asked generally, "Did you want to say something?" and that, in response to this question, the attorney rather than the defendant had spoken. Recognizing that the right accorded by Rule 32 (a) is a personal right which must be extended to the defendant himself, the Court nonetheless denied relief, largely upon the view expressed by four members of the Court that: "A record, certainly this record, unlike a play, is unaccompanied with stage directions which may tell the significant cast of the eye or the nod of the head. It may well be that the defendant himself was recognized and sufficiently apprised of his right to speak and chose to exercise this right through his counsel." This conclusion was reached in spite of the fact that the Government's brief before this Court expressly conceded that Green had not been personally afforded an opportunity to speak.

But even in *Green*, not one member of the Court went so far as even to intimate—unless such an intimation was implicit in the concurring opinion of Mr. Justice Stewart—that a sentence undeniably imposed in disregard of the legal right of a defendant to speak for himself would not be an "illegal sentence." Four members of the Court—The Chief Justice, Mr. Justice Douglas, Mr. Justice

Brennan and I—expressly stated the view that such a sentence could be corrected under Rule 35's provision for the correction of "illegal" sentences. And four other members of the Court, in an opinion written by Mr. Justice Frankfurter, emphasized the importance of the right of the defendant to speak for himself, saying: "The most persuasive counsel may not be able to speak for a defendant as the defendant might, with halting eloquence, speak for himself." Although it is true that these latter four members of the Court joined in refusing to set aside the sentence in that case, their stated ground was: "The defendant has failed to meet his burden of showing that he was not accorded the personal right which Rule 32 (a) guarantees, and we therefore find that his sentence was not illegal." In the light of all these statements, it is not surprising that the Courts of Appeals for both the First and the Fifth Circuits have regarded the combined opinions in *Green* as requiring the correction of sentences as illegal when the defendant is able "to meet his burden of showing that he was not accorded the personal right which Rule 32 (a) guarantees."

I think that a due observance of the requirements of Rule 32 (a), resting as they do upon the anciently recognized right of a defendant to speak to the court before sentence is imposed, is important to the proper administration of justice in the federal courts. And it seems to me that the Court is mistaken in thinking that the importance of that right is not reflected in this very case, for I cannot agree with the Court's conclusion that "there is no claim that the defendant would have had anything at all to say if he had been formally invited to speak." According to the petitioner's brief, the denial of his right to speak was particularly injurious to him here because he had several previous convictions which presumably were known to the sentencing judge. In this connection, he says: "Petitioner has been and is presently seeking collateral relief from those judgments and, indeed, has already had one set aside. This mitigating evidence, if known to the sentencing court, might have a profound impact upon the sentence imposed."

More importantly, however, whether the right to speak before sentence would have been of value to petitioner in this particular case or not, the right is one recognized by a rule which has the force of law and a sentence imposed in violation of law is plainly "illegal." If the Court is unhappy with the wording of Rule 35— a wording adopted by the Court itself and submitted to Congress for approval as required by law—whatever change is necessary to bring the Rule into conformity with the Court's present preferences should be incorporated into the explicit language of the Rule and submitted to Congress for its approval. I would reverse this case and remand it to allow the District Court to resentence petitioner after granting him his right to speak under Rule 32 (a).

Carnley v. Cochran

369 U.S. 506

─────

Decided April 30, 1962

In this collection's first opinion, Johnson v. Zerbst *(page 51),
Justice Black spoke in 1938 for a majority of the Supreme Court in
defense of the Sixth Amendment's guarantee of the right to assistance of counsel. Nearly a quarter century later Justice Black
cited* Johnson v. Zerbst *in his concurring opinion in* Willard Carn-
ley v. H. G. Cochran, Jr., Director of the Division of Corrections,
State of Florida.

    *Standing trial without benefit of legal aid, Carnley was con-
victed in Florida of incestuous intercourse with his 13-year-old
daughter and sent to a state prison. While imprisoned, he obtained
a writ of* habeas corpus *on the ground that the failure to afford
him the assistance of counsel for his defense deprived him of a
right guaranteed by the Fourteenth Amendment. In granting
certiorari,* the Supreme Court appointed counsel to represent Carn-
ley before the highest bench. Without dissent, seven participating
Justices reversed the holding of the Florida Supreme Court.

    *Justice Brennan gave the majority opinion and was joined by
Chief Justice Warren and Justices Black, Douglas, Clark, and
Stewart. Justice Harlan concurred in the result. Justice Frankfurter, who was ill, and Justice Byron R. White, newly appointed
by President Kennedy, did not participate. The Black opinion
showed how persistent Bill of Rights issues are. It was noteworthy
also in that it called for outright reversal of* Betts v. Brady *(page*

93), *one of the most regrettable decisions written during Justice Black's tenure.*

MR. JUSTICE BLACK, *concurring*

I concur in the Court's judgment of reversal and agree, for the reasons stated in its opinion, that petitioner was, even under the constitutional doctrine announced in *Betts* v. *Brady*, entitled to be represented by counsel. That case, decided in 1942, held that an indigent defendant charged with crime in a state court did not have a right under the Federal Constitution to be provided with counsel unless this Court could say "by an appraisal of the totality of facts in a given case" that the refusal to provide counsel for the particular defendant constituted "a denial of fundamental fairness, shocking to the universal sense of justice. . . ." I dissented from the Court's denial of counsel and its announcement of what I considered to be such an impossibly vague and unpredictable standard. Among other grounds, I thought the defendant in that case entitled to counsel because of my belief that the Fourteenth Amendment makes applicable to the States the Sixth Amendment's guarantee that "In all criminal prosecutions, the accused shall . . . have the Assistance of Counsel for his defence." That is still my view.

Twenty years' experience in the state and federal courts with the *Betts* v. *Brady* rule has demonstrated its basic failure as a constitutional guide. Indeed, it has served not to guide but to confuse the courts as to when a person prosecuted by a State for crime is entitled to a lawyer. Little more could be expected, however, of a standard which imposes upon courts nothing more than the perplexing responsibility of appointing lawyers for an accused when a trial judge believes that a failure to do so would be "shocking to the universal sense of justice." To be sure, in recent years this Court has been fairly consistent in assuring indigent defendants the right to counsel. As the years have gone on, we have been compelled even under the *Betts* rule to reverse more and more state convictions either for new trial or for hearing to determine whether counsel had been erroneously denied—a result that in my judgment is due to a growing recognition of the fact that our Bill of Rights is correct in assuming that no layman should be compelled to defend himself in a criminal prosecution. But all defendants who have been convicted of crime without the benefit of counsel cannot possibly bring their cases to us. And one need only look at the records of the right to counsel cases since *Betts* v. *Brady* in both state and federal courts to understand the capriciousness with which the "shocking to the universal sense of justice" standard bestows its protection upon persons accused of crime. I think that now is the time to abandon this vague, fickle standard for determining the right to counsel of a person prosecuted for crime in a state court. We can do that by recognizing that defendants in state courts have by reason of the Fourteenth Amendment the same unequivocal right to counsel as defendants in federal courts have been held to have by virtue of the Sixth Amendment [*Johnson* v. *Zerbst*]. For these and many other reasons, including those set out in *McNeal* v. *Culver* by Mr. Justice Douglas and joined in by Mr. Justice Brennan, I would overrule *Betts* v. *Brady* in this case. In so doing we would simply return to the holding of this Court in *Powell* v. *Alabama*, where it was stated with reference to prosecution for crime in the state courts that the ". . . right to be heard would, in many cases, be of little avail if it did not comprehend the right to be heard by counsel." I am aware that this statement was made in a capital case, but the Fourteenth Amendment protects life, liberty, and property and I would hold that defendants prosecuted for crime are entitled to counsel whether it is their life, their liberty, or their property which is at stake in a criminal prosecution.

THE CHIEF JUSTICE *and* MR. JUSTICE DOUGLAS, *while joining the opinion of the Court, also join this opinion*

Engel v. Vitale

370 U.S. 421

―――――

Decided June 25, 1962

When the Supreme Court met for the final day of its 1961–62 term, Solicitor General Archibald Cox appeared and spoke as follows:

Mr. Chief Justice and may it please the Court: As the current Term closes, Mr. Justice Black will have completed 25 full Terms as an Associate Justice of this Court. This is a rare event in the Court's history. Although it would be inappropriate to speak at length, the members of the Bar would wish me to call attention to the event and to mention Mr. Justice Black's extraordinarily great contributions during those 25 Terms to the country, to the law, and to the Court. May I add two other things on behalf of the entire Bar: first, that we have always enjoyed, and will always value, the opportunity to appear before him and thus join in the common enterprise of administering justice for all; second, that we wish him health and good fortune to serve for many Terms to come.

Responding to this warm tribute to the senior member of the Court, Chief Justice Warren said with equal warmth:

Mr. Solicitor General:

This is, indeed, a significant event in the life of the Court, and it is highly appropriate that you, Mr. Solicitor General, as a leader of the Bar, should initiate its recordation in today's proceedings.

We share to the fullest extent your appreciation of the great service Mr. Justice Black has rendered to our Nation, and we join your felicitous words concerning his continued service and his future happiness.

Of the 97 Justices who have been appointed to this Court, only 16 have served as long as Mr. Justice Black and none with greater fidelity or singleness of purpose. His unflagging devotion has been to the Constitution of the United States.

The importance of any period of time depends always upon its relation to other things. Abstractly, a quarter of a century in history is little more than a grain of sand in the hourglass of time, but, measured in terms of the service of one man to the well-being of a young and dynamic country such as our own, it is a long and important period of time.

It is with such a measuring stick and with affectionate regard that we measure and record in our proceedings the 25 years of service of Mr. Justice Black to this Court and our Nation.

During this same session, a short time later, June 25, 1962, Justice Black read the most controversial opinion of all the hundreds delivered by him in his quarter century of highest judicial service. It also became at once one of the most violently criticized opinions in the Supreme Court's history. This was the 6-to-1 majority opinion in the New York State public school prayer case, Steven I. Engel et al. *v.* William J. Vitale, Jr., et al. *Five parents— two Jews, one Unitarian, one Ethical Culturist, and one agnostic —with children in the New Hyde Park, Long Island, public schools, challenged the purported non-sectarian prayer that had the approval of the New York State Board of Regents for daily use in the State's public schools. The objection of the parents was turned down, 5 to 2, by the New York Court of Appeals.*

In finding the state-sponsored public school prayer a violation of constitutional religious freedom, Justice Black was joined by Chief Justice Warren and Justices Clark, Harlan, and Brennan. Justice Douglas concurred in a separate opinion, calling in effect for the reversal of the Everson Decision *(page 147), the first of Justice Black's major opinions dealing with the separation of Church and State. On this Justice Douglas said:*

My problem today would be uncomplicated but for *Everson* v. *Board of Education*, which allowed taxpayers' money to be used to pay "the bus fares of parochial school pupils as part of a general program under which" the fares of pupils attending public and other schools were also paid. The *Everson Case* seems in retrospect to be out of line with the First Amendment. Its result is appealing, as it allows aid to be given to needy children. Yet by the same token, public funds could be used to satisfy other needs of children in parochial schools—lunches, books, and tuition being obvious examples.

Justice Stewart alone dissented. Citing what he called "countless examples" of religious activities under governmental auspices, he quoted as controlling an assertion in the Zorach Decision *(page 250): "We are a religious people whose institutions presuppose a Supreme Being." The dissenter concluded: "I cannot see how 'an official religion' is established by letting those who want to say a prayer say it." Justice Frankfurter who was ill took no part in the decision, but his abiding concern for the scrupulous separation of Church and State left little doubt about where he would have stood. The newest member, Justice White, did not participate in the case.*

A storm broke immediately, embracing Congress and the country at large. There were demands that the six Justices who joined the decision resign forthwith. When the jurists did not oblige, these demands were stepped up to calls for impeachment. Cardinals Spellman and Cushing, Roman Catholic archbishops in New York and Boston respectively, used such words as "shocked" and "frightened" to describe their reactions. But President Kennedy, the first Roman Catholic to become Chief Executive, called for public support of the decision. He described it to the Washington press corps as "a welcome reminder to every American family that we can pray a good deal more at home and attend our churches with a good deal more fidelity, and we can make the true meaning of prayer much more important in the lives of all of our children."

Episcopal Bishop James A. Pike and Bishop Fred Pierce Corson, president of the World Methodist Council, opposed the ruling, but religious leaders were not of one mind. The Methodist Christian Advocate *said editorially: "Far from being tragic, the Supreme Court decision may well be a step forward wherein God can finally climb off the coins, and into the hearts of the American people." The only losers, continued the Methodist magazine, "are those persons who prefer their religion on a bland diet, deceiving themselves or being deceived into thinking that 'In God We Trust' will somehow make us a Christian nation." Leo Pfeffer, general counsel for the American Jewish Congress, applauded the decision as did* The New York Times, Washington Post, Milwaukee Journal, St. Louis Post-Dispatch, *and many other leading newspapers. The essence of the Court's opinion, namely, that what was wrong was not the prayer but the place, was missed by many of the complainants. Justice Black, a lifelong Baptist who for many years taught adults in Sunday Schools in Birmingham and Washington, was flooded with letters that accused him of being "Godless," "atheistic," and "Communistic." More generous correspondents advised that they were praying for the Supreme Court and especially for him.*

In a matter of hours, constitutional amendments to override the decision were introduced in both branches of Congress and quickly the annual Conference of Governors, with only Nelson A. Rockefeller of New York protesting, indorsed the amendment proposal. Ex-President Hoover also urged that the decision be overridden by constitutional change. In some states officials and educators said the ruling would not be applied against prayer and Bible reading programs in their public schools, but the New York State Board of Regents said it would respect the decision. Here is the majority opinion in its entirety, save for the footnotes, which, as it happens, are rich with historical information.

MR. JUSTICE BLACK *delivered the opinion of the Court*

The respondent Board of Education of Union Free School District No. 9, New Hyde Park, New York, acting in its official capacity under State law, directed the School District's principal to cause the following prayer to be said aloud by each class in the presence of a teacher at the beginning of each school day:

> Almighty God, we acknowledge our dependence upon Thee, and we beg Thy blessings upon us, our parents, our teachers and our country.

This daily procedure was adopted on the recommendation of the State Board of Regents, a governmental agency created by the State Constitution to which the New York Legislature has granted broad supervisory, executive, and legislative powers over the State's public school system. These state officials composed the prayer which they recommended and published as a part of their "Statement on Moral and Spiritual Training in the Schools," saying: "We believe that this Statement will be subscribed to by all men and women of good will, and we call upon all of them to aid in giving life to our program."

Shortly after the practice of reciting the Regents' prayer was adopted by the School District, the parents of ten pupils brought this action in a New York State Court, insisting that use of this official prayer in the public schools was contrary to the beliefs, religions, or religious practices of both themselves and their children.

Among other things, these parents challenged the constitutionality of both the State law authorizing the School District to direct the use of prayer in public schools and the School District's regulation ordering the recitation of this particular prayer on the ground that these actions of official governmental agencies violate that part of the First Amendment of the Federal Constitution which commands that "Congress shall make no law respecting an establishment of religion"—a command which was "made applicable to the State of New York by the Fourteenth Amendment of the said Constitution." The New York Court of Appeals, over the dissents of Judges Dye and Fuld, sustained an order of the lower state courts which had upheld the power of New York to use the Regents' prayer as a part of the daily procedures of its public schools so long as the schools did not compel any pupil to join in the prayer over his or his parents' objection. We granted *certiorari* to review this important decision involving rights protected by the First and Fourteenth Amendments.

We think that by using its public school system to encourage recitation of the Regents' prayer, the State of New York has adopted a practice wholly inconsistent with the Establishment Clause. There can, of course, be no doubt that New York's program of daily classroom invocation of God's blessings as prescribed in the Regents' prayer is a religious activity. It is a solemn avowal of divine faith and supplication for the blessings of the Almighty. The nature of such a prayer has always been religious, none of the respondents has denied this and the trial court expressly so found:

> The religious nature of prayer was recognized by Jefferson and has been concurred in by theological writers, the United States Supreme Court and State courts and administrative officials, including New York's Commissioner of Education. A committee of the New York Legislature has agreed.
>
> The Board of Regents as *amicus curiae*, the respondents and intervenors all concede the religious nature of prayer, but seek to distinguish this prayer because it is based on our spiritual heritage. . . .

The petitioners contend among other things that the State laws requiring or permitting use of the Regents' prayer must be struck down as a violation of the Establishment Clause because that prayer was composed by governmental officials as a part of a governmental program to further religious beliefs. For this reason, petitioners argue, the State's use of the Regents' prayer in its public school system breaches the constitutional wall of separation between Church and State. We agree with that contention since we think that the constitutional prohibition against laws respecting an establishment of religion must at least mean that in this country it is no part of the business of government to compose official prayers for any group of the American people to recite as a part of a religious program carried on by government.

It is a matter of history that this very practice of establishing governmentally composed prayers for religious services was one of the reasons which caused many of our early colonists to leave England and seek religious freedom in America. The Book of Common Prayer, which was created under governmental direction and which was approved by Acts of Parliament in 1548 and 1549, set out in minute detail the accepted form and content of prayer and other religious ceremonies to be used in the established, tax-supported Church of England. The controversies over the Book and what should be its content repeatedly threatened to disrupt the peace of that country as the accepted forms of prayer in the established church changed with the views of the particular ruler that happened to be in control at the time. Powerful groups representing some of the varying religious views of the people struggled among themselves to impress their particular views upon the Government and obtain amendments of the Book more suitable to their respective notions of how religious services should be conducted in order that the official religious establishment would advance their particular religious beliefs. Other groups, lacking the necessary political power to influence the Government on the matter, decided to leave England and its established church and seek freedom in America from England's governmentally ordained and supported religion.

It is an unfortunate fact of history that when some of the very groups which had most strenuously opposed the established Church of England found themselves sufficiently in control of colonial governments in this country to write their own prayers into law, they passed laws making their own religion the official religion of their respective Colonies. Indeed, as late as the time of the Revolutionary War, there were established churches in at least eight of the thirteen former Colonies and established religions in at least four of the other five. But the successful Revolution against English political domination was shortly followed by intense opposition to the practice of establishing religion by law. This opposition crystallized rapidly into an effective political force in Virginia where the minority religious groups such as Presbyterians, Lutherans, Quakers, and Baptists had gained such strength that the adherents to the established Episcopal Church were actually a minority themselves. In 1785–1786, those opposed to the established Church, led by James Madison and Thomas Jefferson, who, though themselves not members of any of these dissenting religious groups, opposed all religious establishments by law on grounds of principle, obtained the enactment of the famous "Virginia Bill for Religious Liberty" by which all religious groups were placed on an equal footing so far as the State was concerned. Similar though less far-reaching legislation was being considered and passed in other States.

By the time of the adoption of the Constitution, our history shows that there was a widespread awareness among many Americans of the dangers of a union of Church and State. These people knew, some of them from bitter personal experience, that one of the greatest dangers to the freedom of the individual to worship in his own way lay in the Government's placing its official stamp of approval upon one particular kind of prayer or one particular form of religious services. They knew the anguish, hardship, and bitter strife that could come when zealous religious groups struggled with one another to obtain the Government's stamp of approval from each King, Queen, or Protector that came to temporary power. The Constitution was intended to avert a part of this danger by leaving the Government of this country in the hands of the people rather than in the hands of any monarch. But this safeguard was not enough. Our Founders were no more willing to let the content of their prayers and their privilege of praying whenever they pleased be influenced by the ballot box than they were to let these vital matters of personal conscience depend upon the succession of monarchs. The First Amendment was added to the Constitution to stand as a guarantee that neither the power nor the prestige of the Federal Government would be used to control, support, or influence the kinds of prayer the American people can say—that the people's religions must not be subjected to the pressures of government for change each time a new political administration is elected to office. Under that Amendment's prohibition against governmental establishment of religion, as reinforced by the provisions of the Fourteenth Amendment, government in this country, be it state or federal, is without power to prescribe by law any particular form of prayer which is to be used as an official prayer in carrying on any program of governmentally sponsored religious activity.

There can be no doubt that New York's state prayer program officially establishes the religious beliefs embodied in the Regents' prayer. The respondents' argument to the contrary, which is largely based upon the contention that the Regents' prayer is "non-denominational" and the fact that the program, as modified and approved by state courts, does not require all pupils to recite the prayer but permits those who wish to do so to remain silent or be excused from the room, ignores the essential nature of the program's constitutional defects. Neither the fact that the prayer may be denominationally neutral, nor the fact that its observance on the part of the students is voluntary can serve to free it from the limitations of the Establishment Clause, as it might from the Free Exercise Clause, of the First Amendment, both of which are operative against the States by virtue of the Fourteenth Amendment. Although these two clauses may in certain instances overlap, they forbid two quite different kinds of governmental encroachment upon religious freedom. The Establishment Clause, unlike the Free Exercise Clause, does not depend upon any showing of direct governmental compulsion and is violated by the enactment of laws which establish an official religion whether those laws operate directly to coerce non-observing individuals or not. This is not to say, of course, that laws officially prescribing a particular form of religious worship do not involve coercion of such individuals. When the power, prestige, and financial support of government is placed behind a particular religious belief, the indirect coercive pressure upon religious minorities to conform to the prevailing officially approved religion is plain. But the purposes underlying the Establishment Clause go much further than that. Its first and most immediate purpose rested on the belief that a union of government and religion tends to destroy government and to degrade religion. The history of governmentally established religion, both in England and in this country, showed that whenever government had allied itself with one particular form of religion, the inevitable result had been that it had incurred the hatred, disrespect and even contempt of those who held contrary beliefs. That same history showed that many people had lost their respect for any religion that had relied upon the support of government to spread its faith. The Establishment Clause thus stands as an expression of principle on the part of the Founders of our Constitution that religion is too personal, too sacred, too holy, to permit its "unhallowed perversion" by a civil magistrate. Another purpose of the Establishment Clause rested upon an awareness of the historical fact that governmentally established religions and religious persecutions go hand in hand. The Founders knew that only a few years after the Book of Common Prayer became the only accepted form of religious services in the established Church of England, an Act of Uniformity was passed to compel all Englishmen to attend those services and to make it a criminal offense to conduct or attend religious gatherings of any other kind—a law which was consistently flouted by dissenting religious groups in England and which contributed to widespread persecutions of people like John Bunyan who persisted in holding "unlawful [religious] meetings . . . to the great disturbance and distraction of the good subjects of this kingdom. . . ." And they knew that similar persecutions had received the sanction of law in several of the Colonies in this country soon after the establishment of official religions in those Colonies. It was in large part to get completely away from this sort of systematic religious persecution that the Founders brought into being our Nation, our Constitution, and our Bill of Rights with its prohibition against any governmental establishment of religion. The New York laws officially prescribing the Regents' prayer are inconsistent with both the purposes of the Establishment Clause and with the Establishment Clause itself.

It has been argued that to apply the Constitution in such a way as to prohibit state laws respecting an establishment of religious services in public schools is to indicate a hostility toward religion or toward prayer. Nothing, of course, could be more wrong. The history of man is inseparable from the history of religion. And perhaps it is not too much to say that since the beginning of that history many people have devoutly believed that "More things are wrought by prayer than this world dreams of." It was doubtless largely due to men who believed this that there grew up a sentiment that caused men to leave the cross-currents of officially established state religions and religious persecution in Europe and come to this country filled with the hope that they could find a place in which they could pray when they pleased to the God of their faith in the language they chose. And there were men of this same faith in the power of prayer who led the fight for adoption of our Constitution and also for our Bill of Rights with the very guarantees of religious freedom that forbid the sort of governmental activity which New York has attempted here. These men knew that the First Amendment, which tried to put an end to governmental control of religion and of prayer, was not written to destroy either. They knew rather that it was written to quiet well-justified fears which nearly all of them felt arising out of an awareness that governments of the past had shackled men's tongues to make them speak only the religious thoughts that government wanted them to speak and to pray only to the God that government wanted them to pray to. It is neither sacrilegious nor anti-religious to say that each separate government in this country should stay out of the business of writing or sanctioning official prayers and leave that purely religious function to the people themselves and to those the people choose to look to for religious guidance.[1]

It is true that New York's establishment of its Regents' prayer as an officially approved religious doctrine of that State does not amount to a total establishment of one particular religious sect to the exclusion of all others—that, indeed, the governmental endorsement of that prayer seems relatively insignificant when compared to the governmental encroachments upon religion which were commonplace two hundred years ago. To those who may subscribe to the view that because the Regents' official prayer is so brief and general there can be no danger to religious freedom in its governmental establishment, however, it may be appropriate to say in the words of James Madison, the author of the First Amendment:

> [I]t is proper to take alarm at the first experiment on our liberties.
> . . . Who does not see that the same authority which can establish
> Christianity, in exclusion of all other Religions, may establish with
> the same ease any particular sect of Christians, in exclusion of all
> other Sects? That the same authority which can force a citizen to
> contribute three pence only of his property for the support of any
> one establishment, may force him to conform to any other estab-
> lishment in all cases whatsoever?

[1] Editor's Note: At this point the opinion included the following footnote:

There is of course nothing in the decision reached here that is inconsistent with the fact that school children and others are officially encouraged to express love for our country by reciting historical documents such as the Declaration of Independence which contain references to the Deity or by singing officially espoused anthems which include the composer's professions of faith in a Supreme Being, or with the fact that there are many manifestations in our public life of belief in God. Such patriotic or ceremonial occasions bear no true resemblance to the unquestioned religious exercise that the State of New York has sponsored in this instance.

The judgment of the Court of Appeals of New York is reversed and the cause remanded for further proceedings not inconsistent with this opinion.

Reversed and remanded.

Meredith v. Fair

83 S. Ct. Rep. 10

Issued September 10, 1962

James H. Meredith was born on a farm near Kosciusko, Mississippi. He picked cotton there with his brothers and sisters, and attended segregated schools. After graduating from high school in St. Petersburg, Florida, where he lived for a year with an uncle, he volunteered for the Air Force in 1951, in the middle of the Korean War. He served in the United States and in Japan, and attained the rank of Staff Sergeant. After the war ended, he remained in the armed forces for seven years and was discharged in 1960. Then he decided to attend college.

Still a Mississippian, Meredith enrolled at Jackson State College, an all-Negro institution. In January 1961, he applied for transfer to the University of Mississippi to study political science with a view to entering political life. This application involved him in extensive legal proceedings. In anticipation of the academic year 1962–63, Meredith received a ruling from the United States Court of Appeals at New Orleans that called for his admission to "Ole Miss," a historic tax-supported university with a student body of 5,000 and a staff of about 400.

The mandate of the Court of Appeals, however, was stayed four times by one of its judges. As a consequence of this struggle within the Court of Appeals, the case of James H. Meredith, Movant, v. Charles Dickson Fair, et al., went before Justice Black, the Supreme Court member designated to give special attention to the Court of Appeals for the Fifth Circuit. On September 10, 1962, before the Supreme Court convened for its 1962 term, Justice Black issued the order printed here. Appreciating fully the importance of

Meredith's application and his order supporting it, Justice Black consulted with his colleagues about his course of action and found all the Justices in agreement with him.

With this order as the legal authority for his admission, Meredith went to the University of Mississippi to be registered and assigned to classes. He was met by Governor Ross Barnett, who personally refused the application. Meredith persisted in the exercise of his rights. And thus the worst constitutional crisis of this nation since the Civil War was precipitated. The campus and the town of Oxford—named for the Old World's great seat of learning—became the scene of violence and rioting, which resulted in widespread property damage, many injuries, and the fatal shooting of two men, one a French newspaper correspondent.

President Kennedy federalized the Mississippi National Guard, and made a memorable appeal for order on television and radio, September 30. Motor convoys and air lifts of troops were sent to the area, and a large force of federal marshals escorted Meredith back to the campus, where he was established in university quarters. On Monday, October 1, he was enrolled and attended his first class—in Colonial history. Former Major General Edwin A. Walker of Texas, who had commanded the federal troops at the previous desegregation disorders in Little Rock, Arkansas, appeared with students who rioted against the marshals and was arrested on charges of inciting an insurrection. He was flown away from the scene for safety and for psychiatric examination in a federal prison hospital. Four months later a grand jury in Mississippi declined to indict Walker and six other persons arrested during the riots.

Nothing that Oxford's leading citizen, the late William Faulkner, ever wrote as fiction about tragic Mississippi can compare with what actually happened in his home community in the autumn of 1962—the beginning of the centennial year of Lincoln's Emancipation Proclamation. Here is the text of the order issued by Justice Black, Alabaman and hence next-door neighbor to Mississippians.

Mr. Justice Black

This is a motion asking me to vacate orders of Judge Ben F. Cameron, a judge of the Court of Appeals for the Fifth Circuit, which purport to stay the execution and enforcement of mandates of that court. The Court of Appeals held that movant Meredith, a Negro, had been denied admission to the University of Mississippi solely because of his race. The court granted injunctive relief which has the effect of requiring the admission of Meredith to the University of Mississippi at the opening of its new academic year commencing in September 1962.

Judge Cameron, however, stayed the mandate of the Court of Appeals pending action by this Court on a petition for writ of *certiorari* by respondents in this motion. Later the Court of Appeals vacated the stay on the grounds (1) that Judge Cameron's action came too late, and (2) that his stay had been "improvidently granted." Judge Cameron nevertheless later issued three other stays, claiming that his first stay had rendered any further proceedings of the Court of Appeals "void and beyond the jurisdiction" of that court. The Court of Appeals has treated all of Judge Cameron's stays as ineffective and void.

The respondents, trustees, and officials of the University, who were enjoined by the Court of Appeals, have filed a petition for a writ of *certiorari,* and the movant Meredith has waived his right to file a brief in opposition to that petition. In this situation I am satisfied that the Court has jurisdiction and power under 28 U.S.C. Section 1651 to take such steps as are necessary to preserve the rights of the parties pending final determination of the cause and that 28 U.S.C. Section 2101 (f) and Rule 51 of the Rules of this Court give the same jurisdiction and power to me as a single Justice of this Court.

I agree with the Court of Appeals that the stays issued in this case can only work further delay and injury to movant, while immediate enforcement of the judgment can do no appreciable harm to the University or the other respondents. I further agree with the Court of Appeals that there is very little likelihood that this Court will grant *certiorari* to review the judgment of the Court of Appeals, which essentially involves only factual issues. I am therefore of the opinion that all the stays issued by Judge Cameron should be and they are hereby vacated, that the judgment and mandate of the Court of Appeals should be obeyed, and that pending final action by this Court on the petition for *certiorari* the respondents should be and they are hereby enjoined from taking any steps to prevent enforcement of the Court of Appeals' judgment and mandate.

Although convinced that I have the power to act alone in this matter, I have submitted it to each of my Brethren, and I am authorized to state that each of them agrees that the case is properly before this Court, that I have power to act, and that under the circumstances I should exercise that power as I have done here.

Stays vacated.

I V

Justice Black and the First Amendment "Absolutes"

A Public Interview

Justice Black and
the First Amendment "Absolutes":
A Public Interview

T HE BIENNIAL CONVENTION *of the American Jewish Congress culminated on April 14, 1962, with a banquet to honor Justice Black and to anticipate his completion of twenty-five years of service on the Supreme Court. Justice Black, who had consented to be interviewed at the banquet by Professor Edmond Cahn of the New York University Law School, expressly declined, in the interest of fair dealing with the public, to receive advance information of the nature or content of the questions. The following transcript presents the interview as it occurred, not revised in any way by Justice Black. It begins with Professor Cahn's preliminary remarks and continues with the questions and answers, as printed in the New York University Law Review, June 1962, pp. 549–63, from which it is reproduced with permission. Justice Black included the words of the First Amendment in a footnote, and it will not be amiss to repeat them here: "Congress shall make no law respecting an establishment of religion, or prohibiting the free exercise thereof; or abridging the freedom of speech, or of the press; or the right of the people peaceably to assemble and to petition the Government for a redress of grievances."*

THE INTRODUCTION

CAHN: I have the function of revealing the secret of the greatness of this great jurist and American, and that is the theme of the remarks I am about to give you. Probably no word in the English language has been cheapened so much by indiscriminate use as the word "great." For this reason, I usually dole it out with a caution approaching miserliness. When, therefore, I tell you unreservedly that Hugo Black is a great judge, you may be certain that I intend to employ a full superlative and am prepared to give particulars.

There are two respects in which he ranks clearly among the foremost and best in our judicial annals. I refer, on the one hand, to his sense of injustice and deep concern for the oppressed and, on the other hand, to his professional skill and technical acumen. In each of these he is not surpassed by anyone. But I do not think it is they that make him unique.

What does make Hugo Black one of the few authentically great judges in the history of the American bench? I believe I have found the answer. He is great because he belongs to a certain select company of heroes who, at various crises in the destiny of our land, have created, nurtured, and preserved the essence of the American ideal. It is interesting to look back on our history and see the same phenomenon appearing time and time again. As a crisis approaches, some man, who might otherwise remain relatively unimportant and obscure, discovers a word, a phrase, a sentence in a basic text that history and legal tradition have placed in his hands. He reads, kindles, ignites, and bursts into flames of zeal and resolution. The torch of his spirit leads first a few, then the vast majority of his countrymen—like a pillar of cloud by day and a pillar of fire by night—toward freedom, equality, and social justice.

This is what happened at the very birth of our country. Our Founding Fathers and Revolutionary heroes examined the charters that had been granted to the Colonies by the Crown of England. There they read the King's solemn promise that they were to possess and enjoy the "rights of free-born Englishmen." This became their fundamental text. Beginning in the 1760's, their insistence on this promise inflamed them to rebellion, revolution, and national independence.

It was the same kind of inspiration that later gave us our national Bill of Rights. As you know, the original Constitution, drafted at the Philadelphia Convention, contained no bill of rights. The Federalists contended that though bills of rights might be necessary against emperors and kings, they were needless in a republican form of government. They argued that the people ought to repose trust in popularly chosen representatives. But Thomas Jefferson indignantly referred them to the words of the Declaration of Independence which announced that governments derived their just powers from the consent of the governed: words to be taken literally, absolutely, and without exception. He declared, "A bill of rights is what the people are entitled to against every government on earth." His demand succeeded, and a Bill of Rights was added to the Constitution. The Bill of Rights protects us today because Jefferson stood firm on the inspired text.

Then there is the next momentous episode, the series of court decisions in which Chief Justice John Marshall held that Acts of legislation that violated the Constitution of the United States were null and void. What was the clause on which Marshall relied in asserting this awesome power for the Supreme Court? It was the provision, to which all Americans had pledged themselves, that the Constitution of the United States must be "the supreme law of the land."

President Lincoln also drew guidance and inspiration from a single basic text. He opposed the institution of slavery because, as he said, the country was dedicated to the proposition that "all men are created equal." Our own epoch has again demonstrated the explosive validity of that proposition.

What does one see happening in each of these historic instances? The majority of people, at least at the beginning, are wont to say that though the basic text may embody a fine ideal, it cannot work in practical application. They say it is utopian, visionary, unrealistic. They remark condescendingly that any experienced person would know better than to take it literally or absolutely. Accepting the words at face value would be naïve, if not simpleminded. In 1776, Worldly Wisemen of this kind said that, while the colonists might be entitled to the rights of Englishmen, they ought to put their trust in the King and Parliament and submit to a few convenient adjustments in the interest of imperial security. In 1788, they said that while a bill of rights might be desirable in theory, the people must learn to show confidence in their rulers. Why not leave it all to a majority, whether in Congress or in the Supreme Court? In every generation, the lesser minds, the half-hearted, the timorous, the trimmers talked this way, and so they always will. Ours would be a poor, undernourished, scorbutic freedom indeed if the great men of our history had not shown determination and valor, declaring: "Here are the words of our fundamental text. Here are the principles to which we are dedicated. Let us hold ourselves erect and walk in their light."

It is to this rare company of inspired leaders that Hugo Black belongs. He has been inflamed by the political and ethical ideals that Jefferson, Madison, and other libertarians of the Eighteenth Century prized the highest. Child of the Eighteenth Century Enlightenment and champion of the Twentieth Century Enlightenment (that is how I think of him), he draws his highest inspiration from the First Amendment in the Bill of Rights, which forbids the Government to abridge our freedom of speech, freedom of press, freedom of religion, and freedom of association. Since his appointment to the bench in 1937, he has incessantly called on the State and Federal Governments to respect these freedoms literally, completely, and without exception. They are, to him, the meaning and inner purpose of the American saga.

Justice Black's major premise and point of departure is the text of the Constitution, which he emphasizes in all his decisions. He believes that the main purpose of the Founders, in drafting and adopting a written constitution, was to preserve their civil liberties and keep them intact. On their own behalf and on ours, they were not satisfied with a fragment or fraction of the basic freedoms; they wanted us to have the whole of them.

Some people display a curious set of values. If government employees were to come into their homes and start slicing off parts of the chairs, the tables and the television set, they would have no doubt that what was happening was absolutely wrong. Not relatively or debatably, but absolutely wrong. But when the same Government slices their civil liberties, slashes their basic freedoms or saws away at their elementary rights, these people can only comment that the case is too complicated for a doctrinaire judgment, that much can be said on both sides of the matter, and that in times like these the experts on sedition, subversion, and national security know what they are doing. (Sometimes I wonder whether it is quite fair to assume that the experts know what they are doing; perhaps it would be more charitable to assume that they do not know.)

Justice Black's uncompromising zeal for freedom of speech, press, religion, and association might not have seemed so urgently necessary in previous periods of our history. In Lincoln's day, men naturally felt more excited about emancipation from slavery; in Franklin D. Roosevelt's day, more excited about food, employment, and social welfare. But today, when democracy stands here and on every continent presenting its case at the bar of destiny, our supreme need is to share Hugo Black's devotion to the First Amendment and his intrepid defense of the people's rights.

The American covenant was solemnly inscribed on the hearts of our ancestors and on the doorposts of our political history. It is a covenant of freedom, justice, and human dignity. Through keeping it in a quarter-century of judicial decisions, he has proved himself a great jurist. Through keeping it in all the transactions of our public life, we can prove ourselves a great and enlightened nation.

THE INTERVIEW

CAHN: Let me start by explaining the purpose of this interview. Two years ago, when you delivered your James Madison Lecture at New York University, you declared your basic attitude toward our Bill of Rights. This was the positive side of your constitutional philosophy. Tonight I propose we bring out the other side, that is, your answers to the people who disagree with and criticize your principles. The questions I will ask, most of them at least, will be based on the criticisms. As you know, I consider your answers so convincing that I want the public to have them.

Suppose we start with one of the key sentences in your James Madison Lecture where you said, "It is my belief that there *are* 'absolutes' in our Bill of Rights, and that they were put there on purpose by men who knew what words meant and meant their prohibitions to be 'absolutes.'" Will you please explain your reasons for this.

JUSTICE BLACK: My first reason is that I believe the words do mean what they say. I have no reason to challenge the intelligence, integrity, or honesty of the men who wrote the First Amendment. Among those I call the great men of the world are Thomas Jefferson, James Madison, and various others who participated in formulating the ideas behind the First Amendment for this country and in writing it.

I learned a long time ago that there are affirmative and negative words. The beginning of the First Amendment is that "Congress shall make no law." I understand that it is rather old-fashioned and

shows a slight naïveté to say that "no law" means no law. It is one
of the most amazing things about the ingeniousness of the times
that strong aguments are made, which *almost* convince me, that it
is very foolish of me to think "no law" means no law. But what it
says is "Congress shall make no law respecting an establishment of
religion," and so on.

I have to be honest about it. I confess not only that I think the
Amendment means what it says but also that I may be slightly influenced by the fact that I do not think Congress *should* make any
law with respect to these subjects. That has become a rather bad
confession to make in these days, the confession that one is actually
for something because he believes in it.

Then we move on, and it says "or prohibiting the free exercise
thereof." I have not always exercised myself in regard to religion
as much as I should, or perhaps as much as all of you have. Nevertheless, I want to be able to do it when I want to do it. I do not want
anybody who is my servant, who is my agent, elected by me and
others like me, to tell me that I can or cannot do it. Of course, some
will remark that that is too simple on my part. To them, all this discussion of mine is too simple, because I come back to saying that
these few plain words actually mean what they say, and I know of
no college professor or law school professor, outside of my friend,
Professor Cahn here, and a few others, who could not write one
hundred pages to show that the Amendment does not mean what
it says.

Then I move on to the words "abridging the freedom of speech
or of the press." It *says* Congress shall make no law doing that.
What it *means*—according to a current philosophy that I do not
share—is that Congress shall be able to make just such a law unless
we judges object too strongly. One of the statements of that philosophy is that if it shocks us too much, then they cannot do it. But
when I get down to the really basic reason why I believe that "no
law" means no law, I presume it could come to this, that I took an
obligation to support and defend the Constitution as I understand
it. And being a rather backward country fellow, I understand it to
mean what the words say. Gesticulations apart, I know of no way
in the world to communicate ideas except by words. And if I were
to talk at great length on the subject, I would still be saying—although I understand that some people say that I just say it and do
not believe it—that I believe when our Founding Fathers, with

their wisdom and patriotism, wrote this Amendment, they knew what they were talking about. They knew what history was behind them and they wanted to ordain in this country that Congress, elected by the people, should not tell the people what religion they should have or what they should believe or say or publish, and that is about it. It says "no law," and that is what I believe it means.

CAHN: Some of your colleagues would say that it is better to interpret the Bill of Rights so as to permit Congress to take what it considers reasonable steps to preserve the security of the nation even at some sacrifice of freedom of speech and association. Otherwise what will happen to the Nation and the Bill of Rights as well? What is your view of this?

JUSTICE BLACK: I fully agree with them that the country should protect itself. It should protect itself in peace and in war. It should do whatever is necessary to preserve itself. But the question is: preserve what? And how?

It is not very much trouble for a dictator to know how it is best to preserve his government. He wants to stay in power, and the best way to stay in power is to have plenty of force behind him. He cannot stay in power without force. He is afraid of too much talk; it is dangerous for him. And he should be afraid, because dictators do not have a way of contributing very greatly to the happiness, joy, contentment, and prosperity of the plain, everyday citizen. Their business is to protect themselves. Therefore, they need an army; they need to be able to stop people from talking; they need to have one religion, and that is the religion they promulgate. Frequently in the past it has been the worship of the dictator himself. To preserve a dictatorship, you must be able to stifle thought, imprison the human mind and intellect.

I want this Government to protect itself. If there is any man in the United States who owes a great deal to this Government, I am that man. Seventy years ago, when I was a boy, perhaps no one who knew me thought I would ever get beyond the confines of the small country county in which I was born. There was no reason for them to suspect that I would. But we had a free country and the way was open for me. The Government and the people of the United States have been good to me. Of course, I want this country to do what will preserve it. I want it to be preserved as the kind of government it was intended to be. I would not desire to live at any place where my thoughts were under the suspicion of government and where my words could be censored by government, and where worship, whatever it was or wasn't, had to be determined by an officer of the government. That is not the kind of government I want preserved.

I agree with those who wrote our Constitution, that too much power in the hands of officials is a dangerous thing. What was government created for except to serve the people? Why was a Constitution written for the first time in this country except to limit the power of government and those who were selected to exercise it at the moment?

My answer to the statement that this Government should preserve itself is yes. The method I would adopt is different, however, from that of some other people. I think it can be preserved only by leaving people with the utmost freedom to think and to hope and to talk and to dream if they want to dream. I do not think this Government must look to force, stifling the minds and aspirations of the people. Yes, I believe in self-preservation, but I would preserve it as the Founders said, by leaving people free. I think here, as in another time, it cannot live half slave and half free.

CAHN: I do not suppose that since the days of Socrates a questioner ever got answers that were so co-operative.

In order to preserve the guaranteed freedom of the press, are you willing to allow sensational newspaper reports about a crime and about police investigation of the crime to go so far that they prejudice and inflame a whole state and thus deprive the accused of his right to a fair jury?

JUSTICE BLACK: The question assumes in the first place that a whole state can be inflamed so that a fair trial is not possible. On most of these assumptions that are made with reference to the dangers of the spread of information, I perhaps diverge at a point from many of those who disagree with my views. I have again a kind of an old-fashioned trust in human beings. I learned it as a boy and have never wholly lost that faith.

I believe in trial by jury. Here again perhaps I am a literalist. I do not think that trial by jury is a perfect way of determining facts, of adjudicating guilt, or of adjudicating controversies. But I do not know of a better way. That is where I stand on that.

I do not think myself that any one can say that there can be enough publicity completely to destroy the ideas of fairness in the minds of people, including the judges. One of the great things about trials by jury in criminal cases that have developed in this country —I refer to criminal cases because there is where most of the persecutions are found in connection with bringing charges against unpopular people or people in unpopular causes—we should not forget that if the jury happens to go wrong, the judge has a solemn duty in a criminal case not to let an unfair verdict stand. Also, in this country, an appellate court can hear the case.

I realize that we do not have cases now like they had when William Penn was tried for preaching on the streets of London. The jury which was called in to send him off quickly to jail refused to do so, and suffered punishment from the judge because they would not convict a man for preaching on the streets. But that is a part of history, and it is but one of thousands of cases of the kind. Those people had publicity; that is why they would not convict William Penn. They knew, because the people had been talking, despite the fact that there was so much censorship then, that William Penn was being prosecuted largely because he was a dissenter from the orthodox views. So they stood up like men and would not convict. They lost their property, some of them their liberty. But they stood up like men.

I do not myself think that it is necessary to stifle the press in order to reach fair verdicts. Of course, we do not want juries to be influenced wrongfully. But with our system of education we should be in better condition than they were in those days in England, when they found that the jury was one of the greatest steps on their way to freedom. As a matter of fact, Madison placed trial by jury along with freedom of the press and freedom of conscience as the three most highly cherished liberties of the American people in his time.

I do not withdraw my loyalty to the First Amendment or say that the press should be censored on the theory that in order to preserve fair trials it is necessary to try the people of the press in summary contempt proceedings and send them to jail for what they have published. I want both fair trials and freedom of the press. I grant that you cannot get everything you want perfectly, and you never will. But you won't do any good in this country, which aspires to freedom, by saying just give the courts a little more power, just a little more power to suppress the people and the press and things will be all right. You just take a little chunk off here and little bit there. I would not take it off anywhere. I believe that they meant what they said about freedom of the press just as they meant what they said about establishment of religion, and I would answer this question as I have answered the other one.

CAHN: Do you make an exception in freedom of speech and press for the law of defamation? That is, are you willing to allow people to sue for damages when they are subjected to libel or slander?

JUSTICE BLACK: My view of the First Amendment, as originally ratified, is that it said Congress should pass none of these kinds of laws. As written at that time, the Amendment applied only to Congress. I have no doubt myself that the provision, as written and adopted, intended that there should be no libel or defamation law in the United States under the United States Government, just absolutely none so far as I am concerned.

That is, no federal law. At that time—I will have to state this in order to let you know what I think about libel and defamation—people were afraid of the new Federal Government. I hope that they have not wholly lost that fear up to this time because, while government is a wonderful and an essential thing in order to have any kind of liberty, order or peace, it has such power that people must always remember to check them here and balance them there and limit them here in order to see that you do not lose too much liberty in exchange for government. So I have no doubt about what the Amendment intended. As a matter of fact, shortly after the Constitution was written, a man named St. George Tucker, a great friend of Madison's, who served as one of the commissioners at the Annapolis convention of 1786 which first attempted to fill the need for a national constitution, put out a revised edition of Blackstone. In it he explained what our Constitution meant with reference to freedom of speech and press. He said there was no doubt in his mind, as one of the earliest participants in the development of the Constitution, that it was intended that there should be no libel under the laws of the United States. Lawyers might profit from consulting Tucker's edition of Blackstone on that subject.

As far as public libel is concerned, or seditious libel, I have been very much disturbed sometimes to see that there is present an idea that because we have had the practice of suing individuals for libel, seditious libel still remains for the use of government in this country. Seditious libel, as it has been put into practice throughout the centuries, is nothing in the world except the prosecution of people who are on the wrong side politically; they have said something and their group has lost and they are prosecuted. Those of you who read the newspaper see that this is happening all over the world now, every week somewhere. Somebody gets out, somebody else gets in, they call a military court or a special commission, and they try him. When he gets through sometimes he is not living.

My belief is that the First Amendment was made applicable to the states by the Fourteenth. I do not hesitate, so far as my own view is concerned, as to what should be and what I hope will sometime be the constitutional doctrine that just as it was not intended to authorize damage suits for mere words as distinguished from conduct as far as the Federal Government is concerned, the same rule should apply to the states.

I realize that sometimes you have a libel suit that accomplishes some good. I practiced law twenty years. I was a pretty active trial lawyer. The biggest judgment I ever got for a libel was $300. I never took a case for political libel because I found out that Alabama juries, at least, do not believe in political libel suits and they just do not give verdicts. I knew of one verdict given against a big newspaper down there for $25,000, and the Supreme Court of Alabama reversed it. So even that one did not pan out very well.

I believe with Jefferson that it is time enough for government to step in to regulate people when they *do* something, not when they *say* something, and I do not believe myself that there is *any* halfway ground if you enforce the protections of the First Amendment.

CAHN: Would it be constitutional to prosecute someone who falsely shouted "fire" in a theater?

JUSTICE BLACK: I went to a theater last night with you. I have an idea if you and I had gotten up and marched around that theater, whether we said anything or not, we would have been arrested. Nobody has ever said that the First Amendment gives people a right to go anywhere in the world they want to go or say anything in the world they want to say. Buying the theater tickets did not buy the opportunity to make a speech there. We have a system of property in this country which is also protected by the Constitution. We have a system of property, which means that a man does not have a right to do anything he wants anywhere he wants to do it. For instance, I would feel a little badly if somebody were to try to come into my house and tell me that he had a constitutional right to come in there because he wanted to make a speech against the Supreme Court. I realize the freedom of people to make a speech against the Supreme Court, but I do not want him to make it in my house.

That is a wonderful aphorism about shouting "fire" in a crowded theater. But you do not have to shout "fire" to get arrested. If a person creates a disorder in a theater, they would get him there not because of *what* he hollered but because he *hollered*. They would get him not because of any views he had but because they thought he did not have any views that they wanted to hear there. That is the way I would answer: not because of what he shouted but because he shouted.

CAHN: Is there any kind of obscene material, whether defined as hard-core pornography or otherwise, the distribution and sale of which can be constitutionally restricted in any manner whatever, in your opinion?

JUSTICE BLACK: I will say it can in this country, because the courts have held that it can.

CAHN: Yes, but you won't get off so easily. I want to know what you think.

JUSTICE BLACK: My view is, without deviation, without exception, without any ifs, buts, or whereases, that freedom of speech means that you shall not do something to people either for the views they have or the views they express or the words they speak or write.

There is strong argument for the position taken by a man whom I admire very greatly, Dr. Meiklejohn, that the First Amendment really was intended to protect *political* speech, and I do think that was the basic purpose; that plus the fact that they wanted to protect *religious* speech. Those were the two main things they had in mind.

It is the law that there can be an arrest made for obscenity. It was the law in Rome that they could arrest people for obscenity after Augustus became Caesar. Tacitus says that then it became obscene to criticize the Emperor. It is not any trouble to establish a classification so that whatever it is that you do not want said is within that classification. So far as I am concerned, I do not believe there is any halfway ground for protecting freedom of speech and press. If you say it is half free, you can rest assured that it will not remain as much as half free. Madison explained that in his great Remonstrance when he said in effect, "If you make laws to force people to speak the words of Christianity, it won't be long until the same power will narrow the sole religion to the most powerful sect in it." I realize that there are dangers in freedom of speech, but I do not believe there are any halfway marks.

CAHN: Do you subscribe to the idea involved in the clear and present danger rule?

JUSTICE BLACK: I do not.

CAHN: By way of conclusion, Justice Black, would you kindly summarize what you consider the judge's role in cases arising under the First Amendment and the Bill of Rights?

JUSTICE BLACK: The Bill of Rights to me constitutes the difference between this country and many others. I will not attempt to say most others or nearly all others or all others. But I will say it constitutes the difference to me between a free country and a country that is not free.

My idea of the whole thing is this: There has been a lot of trouble in the world between people and government. The people were afraid of government; they had a right to be afraid. All over the world men had been destroyed—and when I say "government" I mean the individuals who actually happened to be in control of it at the moment, whether they were elected, whether they were appointed, whether they got there with the sword, however they got there—the people always had a lot of trouble because power is a heady thing, a dangerous thing. There have been very few individuals in the history of the world who could be trusted with complete, unadulterated, omnipotent power over their fellowmen.

Millions of people have died throughout the world because of the evils of their governments. Those days had not wholly passed when the Pilgrims came over to this country. Many of them had suffered personally. Some of them had their ears cut off. Many of them had been mutilated. Many of their ancestors had. Some of your ancestors came here to get away from persecution. Certainly, mine did.

There had been struggles throughout the ages to curb the dangerous power of governors. Rome had a sound government at one time. Those who study it carefully will find that, except for the slave class, they had, so far as most of the people were concerned, a good form of government. But it turned, and then they had Augustus and the other Caesars, and the Neros and Caligulas and Tiberiuses.

One of the interesting things about Tiberius is that in all the history I have read he is about the only man of great prominence who ever defended informers. He made the statement that the informers were the guardians of Rome. Recently I have heard that said here once or twice.

When our ancestors came over here and started this country, they had some more persecutions of their own. It was not limited to any one religion. A lot of my Baptist brethren got into trouble; a lot of the Methodist brethren got in trouble; a lot of the Episcopal Church got in trouble, the Congregational Church—each of them in turn. A lot of the Catholics got in trouble. Whichever sect was in control in a state for a time, they would say that the others could not hold office, which is an easy way of getting rid of your adversaries if you can put it over. Even for half a century after the Constitution was adopted, some of the States barred the members of certain faiths from holding office.

Throughout all of this—as the Jewish people know as well as any people on earth—persecutions were abroad everywhere in the world. A man never knew, when he got home, whether his family would be there, and the family at home never knew whether the head of the family would get back. There was nothing strange about that when Hitler did it. It was simply a repetition of the course of history when people get too much power.

I like what the Jewish people did when they took what amounted to a written constitution. Some of the states did it before the time of the Federal Constitution; they adopted written constitutions. Why? Because they wanted to mark boundaries beyond which government could not go, stripping people of their liberty to think, to talk, to write, to work, to be happy.

So we have a written Constitution. What good is it? What good is it if, as some judges say, all it means is: "Government, you can still do this unless it is so bad that it shocks the conscience of the judges." It does not say that to me. We have certain provisions in the Constitution which say, "Thou shalt not." They do not say, "You can do this unless it offends the sense of decency of the English-speaking world." They do not say that. They do not say, "You can go ahead and do this unless it is offensive to the universal sense of decency." If they did, they would say virtually nothing. There would be no definite, binding place, no specific prohibition, if that were all it said.

I believe with Locke in the system of checks and balances. I do not think that the Constitution leaves any one department of government free without there being a check on it somewhere. Of course, things are different in England; they do have unchecked powers, and they also have a very impressive history. But it was *not* the kind of history that suited the people that formed our Constitution. Madison said that explicitly when he offered the Bill of Rights to the Congress. Jefferson repeated it time and time again. Why was it not? Because it left Parliament with power to pass such laws as it saw fit to pass. It was not the kind of government they wanted. So we have a Bill of Rights. It is intended to see that a man cannot be jerked by the back of the neck by any government official; he cannot have his home invaded; he cannot be picked up legally and carried away because his views are not satisfactory to the majority, even if they are terrible views, however bad they may be. Our system of justice is based on the assumption that men can best work out their own opinions, and that they are not under the control of government. Of course, this is particularly true in the field of religion, because a man's religion is between himself and his Creator, not between himself and his government.

I am not going to say any more except this: I was asked a question about preserving this country. I confess I am a complete chauvinist. I think it is the greatest country in the world. I think it is the greatest because it has a Bill of Rights. I think it could be the worst if it did not have one. It does not take a nation long to degenerate. We saw, only a short time ago, a neighboring country where people were walking the streets in reasonable peace one day and within a month we saw them marched to the back of a wall to meet a firing squad without a trial.

I am a chauvinist because this country offers the greatest opportunities of any country in the world to people of every kind, of every type, of every race, of every origin, of every religion—without regard to wealth, without regard to poverty. It offers an opportunity to the child born today to be reared among his people by his people, to worship his God, whatever his God may be, or to refuse to worship anybody's God if that is his wish. It is a free country; it will remain free only, however, if we recognize that the boundaries of freedom are not so flexible; they are not made of mush. They say, "Thou shalt not," and I think that is what they mean.

Now, I have read that every sophisticated person knows that you cannot have any absolute "thou shalt nots." But you know when I drive my car against a red light, I do not expect them to turn me loose if I can prove that though I was going across that red light, it was not offensive to the so-called "universal sense of decency." I have an idea there are some absolutes. I do not think I am far in that respect from the Holy Scriptures.

The Jewish people have had a glorious history. It is wonderful to think about the contributions that were made to the world from a small, remote area in the East. I have to admit that most of my ideas stem basically from there.

It is largely because of these same contributions that I am here tonight as a member of what I consider the greatest Court in the world. It is great because it is independent. If it were not independent, it would not be great. If all nine of those men came out each Monday morning like a phonograph speaking one voice, you could rest assured it would not be independent. But it does not come that way. I want to assure you that the fact that it does not come that way does not mean that there is not a good, sound, wholesome respect on the part of every Justice for every other Justice.

I do hope that this occasion may cause you to think a little more and study a little more about the Constitution, which is the source of your liberty; no, not the source—I will take that back—but a protection of your liberty. Yesterday a man sent me a copy of a recent speech entitled "Is the First Amendment Obsolete?" The conclusion of the writer, who is a distinguished law school dean, was that the Amendment no longer fits the times and that it needs to be modified to get away from its rigidity. The author contends that the thing to do is to take the term "due process of law" and measure everything by that standard, "due process of law" meaning that unless a law is so bad that it shocks the conscience of the Court, it cannot be unconstitutional. I do not wish to have to pass on the laws of this country according to the degree of shock I receive! Some people get shocked more readily than others at certain things. I get shocked pretty quickly, I confess, when I see—and this I say with trepidation because it is considered bad to admit it—but I do get shocked now and then when I see some gross injustice has been done, although I am solemnly informed that we do not sit to administer justice, we sit to administer law in the abstract.

I am for the First Amendment from the first word to the last. I believe it means what it says, and it says to me: "Government shall keep its hands off religion. Government shall not attempt to control the ideas a man has. Government shall not attempt to establish a religion of any kind. Government shall not abridge freedom

of the press or speech. It shall let anybody talk in this country."
I have never been shaken in the faith that the American people are
the kind of people and have the kind of loyalty to their government
that we need not fear the talk of Communists or of anybody else.
Let them talk! In the American way, we will answer them.

V

Some Books and Articles

V

Some Books and Articles

Books about Justice Black

Frank, John P.: *Mr. Justice Black. The Man and His Opinions*. New York: Alfred A. Knopf; 1949.

Williams, Charlotte: *Hugo L. Black. A Study in the Judicial Process*. Baltimore: The Johns Hopkins Press; 1950.

Books about the Supreme Court or Bill of Rights Issues in Justice Black's Tenure

Barth, Alan: *The Price of Liberty*. New York: Viking Press; 1961.

Berns, Walter: *Freedom, Virtue and the First Amendment*. Baton Rouge: Louisiana State University Press; 1957.

Black, Charles L., Jr.: *The People and the Court. Judicial Review in a Democracy*. New York: Macmillan; 1960.

Blanshard, Paul: *The Right to Read. The Battle Against Censorship*. Boston: Beacon Press; 1955.

Cahn, Edmond: *The Predicament of Democratic Man*. New York: Macmillan; 1961.

———: *Supreme Court and Supreme Law*. Bloomington: Indiana University Press; 1954.

Carr, Robert K.: *Federal Protection of Civil Rights. Quest for a Sword*. Ithaca: Cornell University Press; 1947.

Caughey, John W.: *In Clear and Present Danger. The Crucial State of Our Freedoms*. Chicago: The University of Chicago Press; 1958.

Chafee, Zechariah: *The Blessings of Liberty*. Philadelphia: J. B. Lippincott; 1954.

———: *Free Speech in the United States*. Cambridge: Harvard University Press; 1946.

Christman, Henry M.: *The Public Papers of Chief Justice Earl Warren.* New York: Simon and Schuster; 1959.

Commager, Henry Steele: *Freedom, Loyalty, Dissent.* New York: Oxford University Press; 1954.

Countryman, Vern: *Douglas of the Supreme Court. A Selection of His Opinions.* Garden City: Doubleday; 1959.

Curtis, Charles P.: *Law as Large as Life. A Natural Law for Today and the Supreme Court as Its Prophet.* New York: Simon and Schuster; 1959.

———: *Lions Under the Throne. A Study of the Supreme Court.* Boston: Houghton Mifflin; 1947.

Cushman, Robert E.: *Civil Liberties in the United States.* Ithaca: Cornell University Press; 1956.

Davis, Elmer: *But We Were Born Free.* Indianapolis: Bobbs-Merrill; 1954.

Dilliard, Irving, ed.: *The Spirit of Liberty. Papers and Addresses of Learned Hand.* Third edition, enlarged. New York: Alfred A. Knopf; 1960.

Douglas, William O.: *A Living Bill of Rights.* New York: Anti-Defamation League of B'nai B'rith and Doubleday; 1961.

———: *The Right of the People.* Garden City: Doubleday; 1958.

Downs, Robert B., ed.: *The First Freedom. Liberty and Justice in the World of Books and Reading.* Chicago: American Library Association; 1960.

Dumbauld, Edward: *The Bill of Rights and What It Means Today.* Norman: University of Oklahoma Press; 1957.

Emerson, Thomas I., and Haber, David: *Political and Civil Rights in the United States.* Buffalo: Dennis; 1952.

Fellman, David: *The Defendant's Rights.* New York: Rinehart; 1958.

Fraenkel, Osmond K.: *Our Civil Liberties.* New York: Viking Press; 1944.

Frank, John P.: *Marble Palace. The Supreme Court in American Life.* New York: Alfred A. Knopf; 1958.

Freund, Paul A.: *The Supreme Court of the United States. Its Business, Purposes and Performance.* Cleveland: World; 1961.

Gellhorn, Walter: *American Rights. The Constitution in Action.* New York: Macmillan; 1960.

Gordon, Rosalie M.: *Nine Men Against America. The Supreme Court and Its Attack on American Liberties.* New York: Devin-Adair; 1958.

Griswold, Erwin N.: *The Fifth Amendment Today.* Cambridge: Harvard University Press; 1955.

Hand, Learned: *The Bill of Rights.* Cambridge: Harvard University Press; 1958.

Jackson, Robert H.: *The Supreme Court in the American System of Government.* Cambridge: Harvard University Press; 1955.

Kauper, Paul G.: *Civil Liberties and the Constitution.* Ann Arbor: The University of Michigan Press; 1962.

Kelly, Alfred E., ed.: *Foundations of Freedom in the American Constitution.* New York: Harper and Brothers; 1958.

Konefsky, Samuel J.: *Chief Justice Stone and the Supreme Court.* New York: Macmillan; 1946.

———: *The Constitutional World of Mr. Justice Frankfurter.* New York: Macmillan; 1949.

Konefsky, Samuel J.: *The Legacy of Holmes and Brandeis. A Study in the Influence of Ideas.* New York: Macmillan; 1956.

Konvitz, Milton R.: *Bill of Rights Reader. Leading Constitutional Cases.* Ithaca: Cornell University Press; 1954.

———: *Fundamental Liberties of a Free People. Religion, Speech, Press, Assembly.* Ithaca: Cornell University Press; 1957.

Kurland, Philip B.: *Religion and the Law. Of Church and State and the Supreme Court.* Chicago: Aldine; 1962.

Lamont, Corliss: *Freedom Is as Freedom Does. Civil Liberties Today.* New York: Horizon Press; 1956.

Madison, Charles A.: *Leaders and Liberals in Twentieth Century America.* New York: Frederick Ungar; 1961.

Mason, Alpheus T.: *Harlan Fiske Stone. Pillar of the Law.* New York: Viking Press; 1956.

———: *The Supreme Court from Taft to Warren.* Baton Rouge: Louisiana State University Press; 1958.

McCloskey, Robert G.: *The American Supreme Court.* Chicago: The University of Chicago Press; 1960.

McCune, Wesley: *The Nine Young Men.* New York: Harper and Brothers; 1947.

Meiklejohn, Alexander: *Political Freedom. The Constitutional Powers of the People.* New York: Harper and Brothers; 1960.

Mendelson, Wallace: *Justices Black and Frankfurter. Conflict in the Court.* Chicago: The University of Chicago Press; 1961.

O'Brian, John Lord: *National Security and Individual Freedom.* Cambridge: Harvard University Press; 1955.

O'Neill, J. M.: *Religion and Education Under the Constitution.* New York: Harper and Brothers; 1949.

Pfeffer, Leo: *Church, State and Freedom.* Boston: Beacon Press; 1953.

President's Committee on Civil Rights, The: *To Secure These Rights.* Washington, D.C.: United States Government Printing Office; 1947.

Pritchett, C. Herman: *Civil Liberties and the Vinson Court.* Chicago: The University of Chicago Press; 1954.

———: *Congress versus the Supreme Court, 1957–1960.* Minneapolis: University of Minnesota Press; 1961.

———: *The Roosevelt Court. A Study in Judicial and Political Values, 1937–1947.* New York: Macmillan; 1948.

Pusey, Merlo J.: *Charles Evans Hughes.* Two Volumes. New York: Macmillan; 1951.

Rodell, Fred: *Nine Men. A Political History of the Supreme Court of the United States from 1790 to 1955.* New York: Random House; 1955.

Rogge, O. John: *The First and the Fifth.* New York: Thomas Nelson and Sons; 1960.

Schwartz, Bernard: *The Supreme Court. Constitutional Revolution in Retrospect.* New York: Ronald Press; 1957.

Spurlock, Clark: *Education and the Supreme Court.* Urbana: University of Illinois Press; 1955.

Stokes, Anson Phelps: *Church and State in the United States*. Three volumes. New York: Harper and Brothers; 1950.

Swisher, Carl Brent: *The Supreme Court in Modern Role*. New York: New York University Press; 1958.

Thomas, Helen Shirley: *Felix Frankfurter. Scholar on the Bench*. Baltimore: The Johns Hopkins Press; 1960.

Weinberger, Andrew D.: *Freedom and Protection. The Bill of Rights*. San Francisco: Chandler; 1962.

Law Reviews

The American University Law Review, Vol. X, No. 1 (January 1961). Issue dedicated to Justice Black on the occasion of his seventy-fifth birthday.[1]

The Yale Law Journal, Vol. LXV, No. 4 (February 1956). Issue dedicated to Justice Black on the occasion of his seventieth birthday.

Representative Articles

Armstrong, W. P.: "Mr. Justice Black." *Tennessee Law Review*, Vol. XX, No. 7 (April 1949), pp. 638–43.

Barnett, V. M., Jr.: "Mr. Justice Black and the Supreme Court." *University of Chicago Law Review*, Vol. VIII, No. 1 (December 1940), pp. 20–41.

Berman, Daniel M.: "Freedom and Mr. Justice Black. The Record After Twenty Years." *Missouri Law Review*, Vol. XXV, No. 2 (April 1960), pp. 155–74.

——: "Hugo L. Black. The Early Years." *Catholic University Law Review*, Vol. VIII, No. 2 (May 1959), pp. 103–16.

Black, Hugo L.: "The James Madison Lecture. The Bill of Rights." *New York University Law Review*, Vol. XXXV, No. 4 (April 1960), pp. 865–81.

——: "Justice Black and the First Amendment 'Absolutes.' A Public Interview." *New York University Law Review*, Vol. XXXVII, No. 4 (June 1962), pp. 549–63.

Dilliard, Irving: "A Supreme Court Majority?" *Harper's*, Vol. LXXIII, No. 1038 (November 1936), pp. 598–601.

——: "Truman Reshapes the Supreme Court." *Atlantic Monthly*, Vol. CLXXXIV, No. 6 (December 1949), pp. 30–33.

——: "Warren and the New Supreme Court." *Harper's*, Vol. CCXI, No. 1267 (December 1955), pp. 59–68.

Gordon, Murray A.: "Justice Hugo Black. First Amendment Fundamentalist." *Lawyers Guild Review*, Vol. XX, No. 1 (Spring 1960), pp. 1–5.

[1] Contains a list of all of Justice Black's opinions beginning with the 1937 term and running half way through the 1960 term, divided into three categories: majority opinions, concurrences, and dissents (pp. 100–15). It also includes an extensive list of speeches and articles by Justice Black (pp. 116–19).

Green, John Raeburn: "The Bill of Rights, the Fourteenth Amendment and the Supreme Court." *Michigan Law Review*, Vol. XLVI, No. 7 (May 1948), pp. 869–910.

Green, R. F.: "Mr. Justice Black versus the Supreme Court." *University of Newark Law Review*, Vol. IV, No. 2 (Winter 1939), pp. 113–48.

Hamilton, Walton: "Mr. Justice Black's First Year." *The New Republic*, Vol. LXXXXV, No. 1227 (June 8, 1938), pp. 118–22.

Havighurst, Harold C.: "Mr. Justice Black." *National Lawyers Guild*, Vol. I, No. 3 (June 1938), pp. 181–5.

Howe, Mark DeWolfe: "Justice in a Democracy." *Atlantic Monthly*, Vol. CLXXXIV, No. 6 (December 1949), pp. 34–6.

Lerner, Max: "Justice Black, Dissenting." *The Nation*, Vol. CXLVI, No. 10 (March 5, 1938), pp. 264–6.

Lewis, Anthony: "Historic Change in the Supreme Court." *The New York Times Magazine* (June 17, 1962), pp. 7, 36, 38–9.

Rodell, Fred: "New Look on the Supreme Court." *Frontier*, Vol. IX, No. 1 (November 1957), pp. 11–12.

Time, Vol. LXXX, No. 1 (July 6, 1962), pp. 7–9.

Weissman, David L.: "Mr. Justice Black at 70. The Man and His World." *Lawyers Guild Review*, Vol. XVI, No. 4 (Fall 1956), pp. 101–2.

VI

Tables of Cases

Table of Cases Cited

This is a list of cases that Justice Black refers to in his citations or footnotes. The asterisks mark the cases in which he wrote an opinion.

Table of Cases by Categories

A Note on the Type

———

THE TEXT of this book was set on the Linotype in JANSON, a recutting made direct from type cast from matrices long thought to have been made by the Dutchman Anton Janson, who was a practicing type founder in Leipzig during the years 1668–87. However, it has been conclusively demonstrated that these types are actually the work of Nicholas Kis (1650–1702), a Hungarian, who most probably learned his trade from the master Dutch type founder Dirk Voskens. The type is an excellent example of the influential and sturdy Dutch types that prevailed in England up to the time William Caslon developed his own incomparable designs from these Dutch faces.

Typography and binding design by
VINCENT TORRE

A Note about the Author

HUGO LAFAYETTE BLACK was born in Harlan, Alabama, on February 27, 1886. He was awarded the LL.B., University of Alabama, 1906, then went into practice in Ashland, Alabama, in 1906, and in Birmingham, Alabama, in 1907. He was Police Judge, 1910–11, and Prosecuting Attorney of Jefferson County, Alabama, 1915–17. After military service, 1917–18, he returned to his general practice in Birmingham, 1919–27. In 1926 he was elected United States Senator and was re-elected in 1932. He was President Franklin D. Roosevelt's first Supreme Court appointee in 1937 and has been Senior Justice since 1946. He is the author of *A Constitutional Faith* (Knopf, 1968). He was married in 1921 to Josephine Foster; they had two sons and a daughter. In 1957, five years after his first wife's death, he married Elizabeth Seay DeMeritte. They live in Alexandria, Virginia.

A NOTE ABOUT THE EDITOR

IRVING DILLIARD was born in Collinsville, Illinois, on November 27, 1904. He studied at the University of Illinois and Harvard, where he was one of the first Nieman Fellows. He started his career with the St. Louis *Post-Dispatch* in 1923 and worked on the staff until 1960. From 1949 to 1957 he was editorial page editor. In World War II he served on General Eisenhower's staff and later commanded a unit attached to General Patton's Third Army. He has received American, British, and French military decorations. Mr. Dilliard has contributed to magazines and to the *Dictionary of American Biography*, the *Dictionary of American History*, *Encyclopedia of the Social Sciences*, and *Encyclopaedia Britannica*. He edited *The Spirit of Liberty: Papers and Addresses of Learned Hand* (Knopf, 1952). He has awards from the Civil Liberties Union and the American Bar Association. Mr. Dilliard married Dorothy Dorris. They have two daughters and live in Collinsville, Illinois.

72
74
75
76
77
79
81
83
85
88